THE SEARCH FOR FRANK PINE

BY HIS GRANDSON – JOHN DANIELS

Published By
John Daniels
SM2 6HR

A Firs Book

The Search for Frank Pine

Spiderwize
Remus House
Coltsfoot Drive
Woodston
Peterborough
PE2 9BF

www.spiderwize.com

A CIP catalogue record for this book is available from the British Library.

DEDICATIONS

To my wife Carole
for her forbearance in my family history excercise.

To my children Louisa and Neil and grandchildren
Florence, Genevieve and Jane.
They may better know their grandparents than I did mine.

In the memory of Anil Adatia
with whom I was unable to share
the joys of our mutual grandchild, Jane.

**In the Memory of My
Mother Lena
Grandfather Frank Pine
Aunt Edna Pine
Aunt Phyllis Pine
Aunt Constance Pine
And Grandmother Lilian Pine (nee Beckingsale)**

CONTENTS

PHOTOGRAPH SETS AND MAPS

There are may more pictures embedded in the text – mostly my own collection

I think this picture is about 4 years earlier than the previous one – say 1912

SOME OPENING WORDS

BY 1932 FRANK HAROLD PINE (FHP)
was at the height of his powers.

An accountant with Spear Brothers & Clark,
he was Chairman of Monkton Combe (Combe Down) Council.
He was also President of the Bath Friendly Societies Council
and President of the Bath Branch of the Hearts of Oak Benefit Society,
as he had been for much of the past decade.

Perhaps most importantly he was Chairman of the Bath Hospital Box Scheme
in which, since 1923, he had played a crucial role in ensuring
the financial survival of the Royal United Hospital Bath,
so facilitating its removal to Combe Park
and its current role as a major regional hospital.
For 8 years he was a member of the RUH Management Board.

Most important for me is that he was the grandfather I never knew in person -
but I have come to know him and his many talents through my researches.

This is a family history that extends beyond FHP.
It concerns his wife's family the Beckingsales with whom he closely identified.
It also extends to the members of the Daniels family who, like FHP, migrated to
Combe Down and with whom he and his family closely associated.
This particularly includes Robert Daniels and his family
– Anne, Vi, Norah, Norman and Mabel.

So this is a story about my family - that starts with my parents.
It is a story about Combe Down, Bath, in the 1920s and 1930s
and its political activities focussing on the Parish Council;
also its social activities - especially those of the Combe Down Old Scholars.
Most importantly it is a story about the Bath RUH and the Hospital Box Scheme.

It is an ordinary people's history.
It is a story that deserves to be told.

JOHN DANIELS

THE SEARCH FOR FRANK PINE – AND THE INEVITABILITY OF JOHN & ROGER DANIELS

Preface: VJ Day!

On Saturday 10 August 1945 my father Herbert Daniels married my mother Lena Pine. Their wedding photo was on the front Page of Bath Daily Chronicle of the following Tuesday, which had the headline **'Japs Accept Capitulation'**.

How did they manage that – well the photo caption states **"HOSPITAL BOX PIONEERS DAUGHTER - Miss Lena Pine, youngest daughter of the late Mr FH Pine of Combe Down Bath, whose ardent pioneering work did so much to ensure the success of the Bath RUH Box Scheme was married on Saturday to Mr HF Daniels. Here they are leaving Holy Trinity, Combe Down."**

So who was Frank Pine and how inevitable was my parent's liaison?

In seeking to answer this question I have looked at the histories of the Pine and Daniels families on Combe Down, Bath (and links between the two families) through the public record and in the press - most especially the available newspaper record for Bath in the first half of the twentieth century. I have tried to obtain a broad picture of FHP's interests and activities and, as a key player, the range of people he associated with in the friendly societies movement, the local authorities and the hospitals. It is interesting to see those activities carried out against a background of social, economic, political and technological change. It has brought alive and in context the people who were but names in my parents and aunts' conversations.

There are limitations in using a press record of mainly Saturday or weekly editions of the Bath Chronicle but it has enabled me to provide what is mostly a diary of press articles with a minimum of comment. Despite those limitations I feel that a reasonably clear story can still be told with all the raw, and sometimes mundane, directness that can be found in the press reports.

Acknowledgements

First and foremost I must give great credit to the British Library for the huge exercise of scanning past editions of national and local newspapers to produce a fully searchable archive. I have in my possession over 390 press articles – all but a few of which I have downloaded. These articles are mainly from the Bath Weekly Chronicle & Herald (and one or two from the Western Daily Press) which is so far all that has been scanned and released by the British Library. I have used the search engine at www.britishnewspaperarchive.co.uk. I have reproduced some of the newspaper articles that are in my possession (mainly the daily Chronicle and Herald). However, since the British Library PDFs do not reproduce well, I have mainly quoted or referred to the articles that I have downloaded from the archive.

I must thank the British Library for granting permission to use the downloaded articles in this diary of my families' activities and for waiving any fees. I am pleased to credit the Library as the original source of these articles. I understand from the advice of the British Library that unsigned newspaper articles of 70 years ago or older are, in any event, out of copyright. As for other publications, I am grateful to the Combe Down Heritage Society for permission to reproduce an article from their Newsletter of September 2014 (entitled **Down Memory Lane**).

To supplement over 390 press reports on Frank Pine and his family, Robert Daniels and his family, the Beckingsale family and Monkton Combe Parish Council I have also engaged, with the support of a number of other people, in a genealogical exercise. In terms of births, marriages and deaths, census, probate and army data I have transcripts and copies of over 370 original documents (including 159 Pine, 88 Daniels and 122 Beckingsale).

For a great deal of the information on the Daniels family I am hugely indebted to the work and assistance of my Cousin Tony Daniels' wife Sue. Also I thank my Cousin Maureen's daughters, Julia Todd and Karen Haigh, for supplementing that information. For information on the Pine and Beckingsale families I am equally indebted to my Cousin John Taylor's wife Jill. My brother Roger Daniels, my daughter Louisa Bagshaw and my wife's cousins, Wendy Ellis and Gordon (David) Williams, have also given me helpful information, pictures and insights. I am also grateful for the assistance I had from four on-line contacts. Theresa Douglas tracked down FHP's military records and gave me the lead by which I found his birth certificate; Ken Powis and Kate Beckingsale helped clarify the initial branches of the Beckingsale family; and Malcolm Conroy helped identify the origins of Mabel Symons and the life of Fanny E Daniels.

Other friends have also been of assistance – Elizabeth Previtt (nee Baxter) and Philip Russell who gave me some background to a Hearts of Oak meeting (reported in the Bath Chronicle and Herald of 23 February 1911) at which his grandfather and others of his musical family performed. I am also pleased to have made acquaintance on-line with Bill Rothery (of Deer Creek, Saskatchewan in Canada), the grandson of my grandfather Frank Pine's army colleague of the late 1890s - Crossley Barstowe Rothery. He put me right on some of the matters dealt with in relation to a Bath Chronicle and Herald report dated 7 November 1925 on 'Linking Old Comrades - Bath paragraph penetrates to far off settlement', and provided some interesting photographs.

Apart from Bill Rothery's, most of the more than 100 photographs and illustrations are from my own personal collection and where I have reproduced material from other sources I have endeavoured to obtain permission to reproduce it. I am indebted to Bath in Time – Bath Central Library for certain photographs and the right to reproduce them namely the pictures of the Friendly Societies Council, Alderman Chivers and Lady Sarah Grand, the RUH in 1910 - and as built in the 1930s - and HC Lavington. I am also much obliged to Laurence Hooton (at 85 still living at Walnut Tree Farm, Milton Keynes) for 3 photos of Robert Daniels c1900 and of Vi Daniels c1955 and in 1969 (with her sister Norah, cousin Mabel in 1955 and brother-in-law George in 1969). I am also indebted to Ruth Lafford (nee Daniels) for photographs and material concerning her father Norman Daniels, grandfather Robert and their families.

This has not been an academic history littered with footnotes and diverse sources. I am aware of these limitations: there is scope for much more in terms of the newspaper record, church records and the minutes of the RUH Management Board. But within these limitations, it has been a great joy to tell the story of some fairly ordinary families that in many ways epitomise the changes that have occurred in the last 200 years. If this is to some extent a family scrapbook well at least it has informed me a bit about where I came from. To my mind the Pines, Daniels and Beckingsales were anything but ordinary families.

JOHN DANIELS

WHAT I HAVE LEARNED OF MY FAMILY IN THE SEARCH FOR FRANK PINE

Although this work is about the origins of my maternal Grandfather (F H Pine) and what he did in the 20th Century, it is also about my mother and her sisters and my Great Uncle Robert Daniels. Both families, the Pines and the Daniels lived on Combe Down in The Firs (originally known as Richardson Avenue) at numbers 17 and 8 respectively. My brother Roger and I therefore owe our existence to the number of social links between the 2 families. As her father had died over 3 years before, at her wedding my mother was given away by Mr A J Caudle (who owned the flower shop in Charles Street and was a friend of FH Pine).

I have some understanding of the links between the Pines and the Daniels and the story of FH Pine from recollecting what was said by my parents and aunts when I was growing up (including visits to Vi Daniels and Mabel Symons at 8 The Firs when we went to see my Aunts Phyllis and Edna Pine at 17 The Firs). But I now have a much fuller understanding from the opportunity to search the archives of the Weekly Bath Chronicle and Herald.

The Value of the Newspaper Record

As noted above (page 13), my search for Frank Pine (FHP) as he was, and what he made of himself, has been greatly assisted by the British Library exercise of scanning past editions of national and local newspapers to produce a fully searchable archive. I have been downloading articles mainly from the Bath *Weekly* Chronicle & Herald which is so far all that has been scanned and released by the British Library. Out of all the issues in the period 1900-1950, the search engine at *http://www.britishnewspaperarchive.co.uk* has identified over 300 entries relevant to the life of F H Pine, my mother and her sisters and Robert Daniels. I also have a very few cuttings from copies from the *daily* Bath Chronicle & Herald, which was published 6 days a week.

At Annex A I attach a list of newspaper articles that I have summarised and used in the following text that concern FH Pine and his activities. At Annex B are newspaper articles on Combe Down Old Scholars from 1927 to 1939 that report on some of their social activities and twice-yearly dramatic productions in which my mother and her sisters Phyllis and Connie took part, along with Robert Daniels niece, Mabel Symons, and his son Norman Daniels. At Annex C there are newspaper articles on Robert Daniels and his family. Annex D lists newspaper articles concerning the Monkton Combe Parish Council for the periods 1901-1919 and 1934-1949 when FHP was not on the council. Apart from logging who was on the council in these periods (see Appendix 7), I have not reported the matters considered.

If I took at face value (and without question) what I heard as a child then, certainly, I have a great many questions now – despite the prolific newspaper record I have so far accessed. However Frank Pine died in April 1942 - almost 5 years before I was born in February 1947 - and his wife Lilian died September 1947 (so I had only briefly been a babe in my maternal grandmother's arms). Anyone who knew them in Bath would be over 90 now. Even so it is fascinating to see, in many of the articles I have been able to download, his letters to the press and extracts of his speeches and various statements. So I feel I can hear him speaking in his very own, always well-chosen, words.

The Character of FHP

It is difficult now to assess the character of Frank Pine. However generous he was with his time, he was seemingly careful with his money - perhaps understandable given his difficult childhood. My cousin John Taylor has told me that his father, Albert Taylor, was constantly having cigarettes cadged off him by FHP, who never offered Albert one of his own. John says that his mother Connie met Albert at a dance hosted in Bath by the Mayor following a staff convention of the Royal Liver Insurance Company (for which Albert worked in Liverpool). Of course the Pine sisters, as daughters of FHP, were well in line for any invites to civic dances. Thereafter Albert spent every third weekend in Bath travelling 170 miles each way by motorbike, and sending his dress clothes on in advance.

Frank Pine refused to pay for Connie and Albert's wedding in 1938. John did not think this was because he thought Albert unworthy (as a Methodist or whatever) and FHP seems perfectly amicable in the wedding photos. According to John, his mother Connie had reached a point with her father of feeling that, whilst Phyllis could do no wrong, she could do no right. Of course Connie was a forthright and determined person like my mother Lena - they both had an outlook different from their unmarried sisters, Phyllis and Edna.

I should add that Aunts Phyllis and Edna doted on me and my brother in the 1950s and 1960s - often claiming to see elements of FHP in our make-up. We did our best to repay their attention when they entered into care at the end of their lives at Avonpark Care Home. In many ways they sought to emulate their father in their public lives. Phyllis worked for F I Tovey Ltd. Opticians in New Bond Street Bath for 47 years, retiring in April 1965, and had been a director of FI Tovey since 1959. She had been an active member of several organisations in Bath, having been a past President of the Bath Business and Professional Womens Club (1954-5 and 1960-61) and their representative on the Bath Council of Social Services. She had been a member of the British Empire Shakespeare Society since 1935. She also served for 8 years on the Tribunal of the

Ministry of Pensions, and 6 years as a committee member of the Bath Chamber of Commerce, as well as being a member of the Bath Youth Employment Committee.

Edna worked in her later years as office manager for Johnson's Central Newsagency and was also a member and President of Bath Business and Professional Women's Club (1965-66). Edna was also a member of Bath Choral Society (as was my cousin Maureen Daniels). The 1950s and early 1960s were probably the heydays of the Business and Professional Women's Clubs (at a time when only single women could pursue careers - even in the civil service women were expected to leave work on marriage) – the National Federation of Business and Professional Women's Clubs folded in 1969. Perhaps it was too much of a mirror of gentleman's clubs for a new era of married career women. So, like father like daughters, here is Phyllis in 1954 (with Mayor Ald. Gallop), in 1960 (With Mayor Cllr. Knight) and Edna in 1965 (with MP Edward Brown).

Frank Pine may well have enjoyed the gentleman's club atmosphere of the Hearts of Oak gatherings more than the female dominated ethos of his home life. His childhood relationship with the 'aunts' who brought him up was not easy. What was his relationship with his wife Lilian like? We can try to interpret the photographic evidence - in their 'wedding' photograph she looks sulky and he looks self-satisfied. In other photos he seems attentive and even joshing. In some photos Lillian can look even coquettish. That she looks most like Connie is an interesting thought. Certainly the photographic and press record indicates that she accompanied FHP to a number of his outside activities.

Perhaps FHP had the old fashioned notion that Phyllis should have married first, but the fact is that by 1938 even Lena, the youngest, was 28. Edna never had a serious boyfriend. However Phyllis had a fairly long standing friendship with a Mr (Herbert Hector) Jack Crees (they had been in the same year at school) but she declined his offer of marriage. In 1936 he took holy orders as a Catholic priest – however Phyllis always kept a photo of him as a priest on her bedroom dressing table.

Jack Crees was born in 1906 in Oldfield Park Bath before his family moved to the School House, Southstoke and died in 1974 aged 68. In a report about a Combe Down School Prize-giving in 1917 he and Phyllis were prize-winners and in the prize-giving of 1924 that FHP attended Jack Crees is mentioned as a Pupil Teacher who had passed the Preliminary examination with four distinctions. Some typed notes of Edna's indicate he was 21 on converting to Catholicism, and 30 on becoming a priest.

Those notes also record that Fr. Herbert Crees died in North Middlesex Hospital, after a stroke, aged 68. Before he retired to Edmonton, London, in 1966 he was Chaplain at Twyford Abbey, Middlesex, for six years. Previously he had been Rector of Westminster Cathedral Choir School (1945-53) and curate of St. Patrick's, Soho (1953-60). Fr. Crees was a schoolmaster until he became a Catholic in 1927. He was educated for the priesthood, at Campion House and St. Edmund's College, and was ordained in 1936. From then until 1945 he taught at St. Edmund's and at St. Hugh's Preparatory School. He had a stroke after taking 8 p.m. Mass on Easter Day and never regained consciousness. He died on Monday April 22nd 1974 (the year is not stated in Edna's note). A Requiem Mass was held at Edmonton April 30th; his burial was at Haycombe, Bath on May 1st.

In an on-line note about 'MEMORIES OF THE CHOIR SCHOOL 1946-49' it is stated: "Initially the School was run by Father Herbert Crees (Headmaster) and Father Ronald Shepherd who I think shared all or most of the teaching between them until two more priests, Father Kilcoyne and FatherWhitney, joined the staff."

Of course the renown of FHP may well have been a deterrent to any suitors for his daughters. My parents married after he died but knew each other well at least a year before Frank Pine died (they both attended Robert Daniels' wife's funeral). I believe my father Hebert Daniels found Frank Pine difficult to get on with. As a surgical appliance worker at the Orthopaedic Hospital in the 1930s and again in the 1950s (until he retired in the 1970s) I can well imagine that he might not have been comfortable with stories of FHP as a father-in-law who hob-knobbed with the hospital top brass!

To some extent Frank Pine's life may well have been a search for financial and social security. In the early 1900s, where our diary of press cuttings starts, the Friendly Societies offered something of a safety net to their contributors in terms of insurance against ill health and unemployment. The air of freemasonry infused the otherwise smoke-filled rooms of the meetings of the local branch of a friendly society - with members each calling the other 'Brother'. The brotherhood of man was an important notion for FHP and it was amongst his fellow members of the Hearts of Oak that we find men who were along-side him in the Bath Council of Friendly Societies and his hospital activities. Developing contacts as he moved through these activities also gave him a secure status in society.

I doubt that he ever achieved real financial security - he lived in a rented house all his life (as many did at the time). However it is an interesting thought that his income might well have excluded him from benefitting from the Hospital Box Scheme (with its limit of £6 a week at a time when the average wage was less than £4 a week) and that when the Paying Patients Scheme came in he was too old to benefit from it. If he was careful with his money he was seemingly altruistic with his time - although it did secure him a place at the top table on many occasions.

Frank Pine was unemployed for a period after he lost his job with Norton Dairies. Why did that happen - had his new employers, who had taken over the Bath and Somerset Dairies looked into his past, did they think he was not qualified for the job - or was it that they wanted him to give up all his public work with the council, the friendly societies and the hospital scheme? Did the newspaper article of 17 February 1923 on a 'Busy Combe Down Man' blot his copybook? How did he get work with Spear Brothers and Clark and what sort of job was it? It is interesting that he appeared on the same platform as Alderman Spear in February 1935 when the current successes of the Box Scheme were being lauded. Alderman Spear was clearly a strong supporter of the project.

A Self-Made Man helped by the Press

In many ways there are certain things FHP had in common with his successor as the Chairman of Combe Down Parish Council - Mr RW Cornish. Both were aspiring self-made men from working class origins. However Mr Cornish, as vice-chairman of Bath Independent Labour Party in the late 1920s and as a Labour candidate for council elections in Bath, before he moved to Combe Down, saw no shame in that heritage. One would imagine that he and FHP might not have seen eye to eye on hospital matters as Frank Pine was clearly an enthusiast for voluntary hospitals and spoke against the idea of municipal or state hospitals. On the other hand there was no great pressure for a state hospital scheme in the 1930s (only the disruptions of wartime made a case for that) and you can see a union like NALGO signing up for the Box Scheme.

It is certainly the case that for 3 years FHP and Mr Cornish worked together amicably as Chairman and Vice-Chairman of the Parish Council. The agenda changed towards the unemployed and council housing but FHP seems to have embraced it. There is no evidence that FH Pine and R Daniels left the council in 1934 in a huff. FHP was still a very active vice-chairman of the hospital scheme and he joined the Hospital

Management Board later that year. As for Mr Cornish, he became a JP in 1937 and continued on the parish council until 1948 when he also became vice-chairman of the Weston Bench of JPs.

Whatever FHP was like as a person - and my Aunts Phyllis and Edna delighted in seeing aspects of FHP in me - there is much to admire in his public record. A great deal more was published in the local press in those days - long lists of people attending weddings, funerals and meetings (even lists of apologies for absence). Very often FHP was near the top of the list or was the main feature of the article. In those days when a local 28 page paper could comprise 5 or 6 columns per page there was a lot of space to fill. What was said at a Council Meeting could be reported in its full and frank original glory (that would nowadays be actionable). That is a huge contrast to local papers nowadays: but in those days people could live their lives in the local press - it was the Facebook of its age (when there was no e-mail but letters delivery could be 3 or 4 times a day). Also FH Pine was no slouch at self-publicity, as may be gauged from his letters in the paper and his apparent good relationships with its editorial staff.

The Inevitability of John & Roger Daniels (Thanks to Robert Daniels)

A few doors down from 17 The Firs Combe Down at 8 The Firs lived Robert Daniels, brother of my paternal grandfather Worthy Daniels. Whilst living in the family village of Littleton Drew he was apprenticed in 1883 to William Bushel of the near-bye village of Burton as a blacksmith. In the 1890s he moved to Combe Down as the local blacksmith (and part-time policeman).

FHP and Robert Daniels both appear in a 1912 report on a Unionists meeting and Robert Daniels was also (between 1928 and 1934) a member with FHP of Monkton Combe Parish Council and helped with work on the Firs Field – he supplied the gates that stood until a few decades ago. He also helped with the Hospital Box Scheme. Robert Daniels' niece, Mabel Symons (who lived with him, his wife and his two daughters and a son Norman) was a great friend of my mother Lena. Mabel was the sixth child of his sister in law (see the chapter below on Robert Daniels).

For most of the 1930s my mother and her sisters Phyllis and Connie were members of the Combe Down Old Scholars Dramatic Group and, with Mabel, performed in their twice yearly productions (all pictured and reviewed in the local paper). Norman Daniels did the scenery and lighting (see the chapter below on the Combe Down Old Scholars).

When he was working in Bath at the Orthopaedic Hospital in the 1930s my father Herbert Daniels would have visited his uncle Robert Daniels quite often. So given the strong links between the Pines and the Daniels – the rest is history!

MORE THAN A FAMILY HISTORY:
A SOCIAL, POLITICAL AND ECONOMIC HISTORY OF THE FIRST HALF OF THE TWENTIETH CENTURY

Social Security

F H Pine's life reflected the evolution of the modern welfare state from the role of the Friendly Societies (that first offered some financial protection against unemployment and ill health). In 1900 joining a friendly society, if you could afford it, was the only way of securing some assurance against unemployment, the cost of treatment for ill health, funeral costs and other misfortunes. Workhouses under the Poor Law still existed, although (like St Martin's in Bath) these were slowly evolving into municipal hospitals for the less well off and for chronic cases. This sat alongside municipal provision for isolation hospitals for infectious diseases. Voluntary Hospitals, like the Royal United Hospital (RUH) in Bath, were also intended to help everyone - but were teaching hospitals focussing on acute cases. Unfortunately their funding from rich benefactors had been drying up as a result of death duties. In 1911 the RUH was already facing significant deficits, despite some benefits from an early working man's box scheme. There were also hospitals for paying patients (such as the Forbes Fraser - as the RUH Private Hospital came to be known).

On a spare-time basis (separate from his main employment as an accountant with the Bath and Somerset Dairy and, later, Spear Bros. and Clark) F H Pine was heavily involved in the Friendly Society movement. Firstly there was his involvement with the Hearts of Oak (of which he became their local auditor and President) and then as Chairman of Bath Friendly Societies Council. From 1923 (as Chairman and then Vice-Chairman of the Hospital Box Scheme) he was, to a fair extent, a key player in the survival of the RUH, in its re-location in 1932 to Combe Park, and in its subsequent development (not least of all as a member of the RUH Management Board from 1934 until his death). The Forbes Fraser Hospital also benefitted when the Hospital Box Scheme extended to the more affluent middle classes. These schemes also reflected the growing demand for health services given improved health treatments (e.g. the use of X-ray). Developing technology was felt in a number of ways (e.g. ambulance services, radios for hospital patients).

> In her book 'Discovering Friendly and Fraternal Societies: Their Badges and Regalia' (Shire 2005) Victoria Solt Dennis has an interesting opening chapter on the History of the Friendly and Fraternal Societies. She notes that the term 'friendly society' has been in existence since at least the middle of the seventeenth century with the specific meaning of a mutual savings society, all of whose members paid a subscription into a common fund from which they were entitled

to claim for sickness, burial costs, and so on (a practice which, she notes, goes back to urban trade groups in ancient Rome and Greece). Fraternal societies tended to have convivial monthly meetings and annual feasts - but in the seventeenth and eighteenth centuries this distinction had become blurred. Freemasonry was but one aspect of this broad movement - as was the trade union movement (e.g. the Tolpuddle Martyrs Agricultural Friendly Society). Governments of the time sought to limit the scope for secret meetings and unlawful oaths.

Mediaeval craft-based Guilds (with members calling each other 'brothers' and 'sisters') had both beneficent and social functions. Reflecting on the mutual benefit clubs of the seventeenth century in 1697 Daniel Defoe proposed that all working people be obliged to join a nationwide friendly society to make provision for sickness and unemployment - and so reduce the burden on parishes of Poor Law relief.

The role of Friendly Societies became acknowledged by the Government and membership was encouraged. An Act of 1875 called for a system of auditing and registration. People joined Friendly Societies in large numbers and they could be found in small villages and large towns alike; indeed by the late 1890's there was in the order of 27,000 registered Friendly Societies.

In 1908 state pensions for the over 70s relieved the friendly societies of the burden of funding some of the costs of the aging sick. The 1911 National Insurance Act gave the friendly societies a role in managing contributions and benefits under the Act. However it increased the numbers of members who were not interested in the social side of the society. **We can see in the press record for Frank Pine the big emphasis on the social side of the Hearts of Oak up to and during the First World War - but no mention of it afterwards.** As Victoria Solt Dennis suggests - the growth of popular entertainment in the inter-war years (radio, cinema, sport, amateur shows etc) also caused that social side to fall away.

After the Second World War National Insurance was considerably expanded to include the whole population and not just working men and single working women. Also it was administered through the state rather than through the Friendly Societies. The development of the National Health Service also removed the need for health cover through the friendly societies. The friendly societies shrank, amalgamated or entered into more conventional insurance and savings schemes.

The Friendly Societies and the principle of mutuality on which they were based took a further battering in the late 20th century when, under the Thatcher governments, privatisation became the trend and many mutuals, whether building societies or insurance undertakings sought a stock exchange floatation. **The Hearts of Oak Friendly Society (founded in 1843)** was formally taken over by the Reliance Mutual Insurance Society on 27 July 2007. It had been technically insolvent for 8 years. Hearts of Oak had faced a declining policy base, rising costs and reducing financial resources. Tax changes had reduced the benefits of being a friendly society. Hearts of Oak had been closed to new business since 1999 and

was one of the larger friendly societies in the UK, ranked 9th by size of funds with £320m of assets under management, its 66,000 policies included with-profits and unit linked endowments, whole life, pensions and annuities.

HC Lavington, who was instrumental in the creation of the Hospital Box Scheme, was a member of The Loyal Order of Ancient Shepherds Home Branch 955. **The Shepherds Friendly Society** still exists as a UK friendly society and is one of the oldest mutual insurers in the world. It is an incorporated society in the United Kingdom within the meaning of the Friendly Societies Act 1992. It has 66,000 members. Shepherds Friendly started life as a sickness and benefits society, Ashton Unity, which was formed in Ashton-under-Lyne, Lancashire on Christmas Day in 1826. It was later renamed as the Loyal Order of Ancient Shepherds, "loyal" referring to the Crown and "shepherds" to the Nativity of Jesus. Its objects were "to relieve the sick, bury the dead, and assist each other in all cases of unavoidable distress, so far as in our power lies, and for the promotion of peace and goodwill towards the human race". It later spread across the country, organised into local branches; like other friendly societies such as the Oddfellows. These were known as 'lodges', and officers wore regalia somewhat similar to those of freemasons. Shepherds Friendly Society has grown from a traditional insurance provider to a modern diversified financial services organisation. It offers a wide range of savings, protection and insurance plans for its members. However, it still retains its structure as a mutual, non-profit making organisation owned by and for its members rather than shareholders (Source: mainly Wikipedia).

Politics and Public Service

Also, in his spare time, Frank Pine was from 1920 (and probably before) a member, and from 1922 chairman, of Monkton Combe Parish Council (the lower tier local authority for Combe Down, below the Bathavon Rural District Council and Somerset County Council). Apart from about a year or so he was chairman until 1934. He joined a fairly apolitical system of local government - all too often the preserve of retired colonels and an old boy network (rather like the friendly societies). However the technology and politics of the evolving twentieth century increasingly impinged. He became involved in, amongst other things, the development of public lighting on Combe Down (first gas and then electric), the provision of telephone kiosks, and the promotion of Council Housing on Combe Down.

He clearly believed in public service, co-operative effort, and the brotherhood of man. F H Pine was clearly of a progressive mind and not sympathetic to a simple ratepayers' point of view (as put forward by Captain Daubeny of the Bathavon Rural District Council in the 1931 debate about extending Bath's boundaries to include Combe Down). He did not have the same strong links to the Conservative Party as Robert Daniels.

After losing his seat in 1931 when the Labour Party sought control of the council at Combe Down, Frank Pine was seconded back to the council, and as chair, by Mr R W Cornish (of the Labour Party). Mr Cornish, who was his vice-chairman, subsequently succeeded him as chair in 1934 when he (and Robert Daniels) left the council. Mr Cornish, who became a JP in 1937, remained on the council - 9 years of them as chairman - until 1948 when he left the council (a year later the clerk Mrs Page retired). Mr Cornish had somewhat broken the mould of the old apolitical parish council.

Many elements of the old Poor Law remained in place until its complete abolition in 1948. The creation of Poor Law Unions under the 1834 Poor Law Amendment Act took away the responsibility for the poor and sick that had long been placed upon individual parishes. The Poor Law Unions were abolished in 1930 under the 1929 Local Government Act which handed their responsibilities for public assistance to the county councils and county boroughs. By 1948 legislation had passed those responsibilities on to the National Assistance Board and the National Health Service. However in the 1920s and 1930s a parish-based sense of responsibility for the poor and sick can be seen in the deliberations of Monkton Combe Parish Council on the subjects of the unemployed and council housing and in the organisation of the Hospital Box Scheme on a parish and ward basis.

In summing up the ethos of politics and public service in the first half of the twentieth century one can see a world in which people were driven by a strong sense of self-less public duty and of obligations to help those less fortunate. This was an ethos that went right across the social and political spectrum. It was one in which individuals and their employers provided scope for social welfare initiatives. It was also, unlike our present times, an era in which the profit motive was not an everyday concern in the sphere of social provision or even in economic activities. The efficiency of state provision was questioned - but generally it was growing. Indeed it is interesting to note that electric lighting for Combe Down was originally provided by the electrical department of Bath Corporation.

Transport & Communications

Rail Travel revolutionised the movement of working class families in search of job opportunities in the nineteenth century. This is reflected the movements of the families in my narrative - as many of them moved from their rural origins to places like London, Bristol and Bath. The railways played a growing role in leisure activities in the twentieth century. Holidays or day trips to Bournemouth would involve a journey from Bath Green Park along the Somerset and Dorset Joint Railway. That railway travelled under the Firs Field and The Firs in the Combe Down Tunnel - at over a mile long it was the longest unventilated single track tunnel in the country. Climbing out of Bath long passenger trains often needed 3 steam engines - 2 at the front and a banker.

Even before the Holidays With Pay Act 1938 the Pine sisters had holidays on the south coast and Isle of Wight using lodges provided by the Girls Friendly Society (GFS). These holidays offered opportunities for mixing with women from other parts of the country and abroad (such as the Caribbean or Europe - for example my mother's pen friend Magda Koch from Austria). Before the First War day trips by horse and carriage might be arranged by a Friendly Society like The Hearts of Oak (there are examples of this in the press record for Frank Pine). After the war day trips by charabanc were often organised as works outings (there are a couple of examples involving FHP and one of my mother on a trip with colleagues from Boots the Chemist). For my mother and her friends the Combe Down Old Scholars arranged day trips.

Electric trams came to Bath in 1904 and an extensive network was built but the growth of motor transport and the increasing popularity of motor buses with sheltered upper decks (and the impact of trams in terms of congestion in the narrow streets of Bath) led to the scrapping of the Bath trams by May 1939. The line serving Combe Down went via the Bear Flat, Wellsway, Midford Road, Bradford Road and North Road, terminating just before Claverton Down Road. The frequency of service was a regular concern of Monkton Combe Parish Council.

Aviation assumed an increasing importance in the public imagination in the 1930s with Jack Cobham's air displays - with opportunities for ordinary people like my mother to experience short air trips or 'flips'. In the late 1930s Mrs Elliott at 18 The Firs flew to Paris to see her son, who was in the French Foreign Legion (see the sub-section below on The Firs). In 1941 my mother Lena Pine became a WAAF.

I must say I am rather intrigued by the photograph of Mrs Elliott's plane. If it is right, then Mrs Elliott flew with British Airways Ltd that was formed in 1935 (not to be confused with the British Airways that was created in 1974 from the merger of the state airlines BOAC and BEA). British Airways Ltd was merged with the rival state airline Imperial Airways in November 1939 to create BOAC.

In the late 1930s Imperial Airways were still using the big lumbering Handley Page biplanes of the mid 1920s on the Paris route. However in 1937 British Airways Ltd took delivery of 7 of the modern twin engine monoplane Lockheed 10 Electra with twin tails (in which Chamberlain flew to Cologne for his first Bad Godesburg meeting with Hitler). On 3 September 1938, the first of nine Lockheed 14s was delivered (in one of which Chamberlain flew to Munich for his last meeting with Hitler). The photograph looks like a Lockheed 14 - so Mrs Elliott may have flown to Paris in 1939.

Communications in the twenty-first century have increasingly focussed on the electronic - with TV and radio, e-mail, mobile phones and the internet (not least of all Facebook). In lacking the immediacy of these other channels - postal services and newspapers have declined somewhat. However before the First World War telegrams offered opportunities for rapid personal communication and in that era the Monkton Combe Council was much concerned about the retention of a telegraph office on Combe Down. In the 1920s the Council's concern shifted to the establishment and maintenance of a public telephone kiosk on Combe Down.

Another concern of the Council was the promptness and frequency of postal deliveries which could be as many as 3 a day. In the 1920s it was possible to respond to a letter received early morning and for the reply to be received later the same day. Local newspapers of 28 pages and 4-7 columns carried a lot of detail of council meetings (who attended and what was said) and events like funerals (who attended or sent flowers, biographical and service details) and weddings (details of the couple, what was worn, the service and reception). Who needed Facebook then?

TRAVEL AND LEISURE IN THE 1920S AND 1930S

A Boots staff outing to Cheddar and Wookey Hole

Lena Pine's First Flight 1936   Magda Koch Bournemouth 1937– and other GFS friends

Mrs Elliott's plane to Paris   **Mrs Elliott and young friends**

Economics

Economic trends are instructive. They can be seen in the doldrums that the Hospital Box Scheme faced in the late 1920s and the early 1930s in its struggle to maintain - let alone exceed - its original target of raising £5,000 a year for the Royal United Hospital. A key focus for the parish council after 1931, particularly after the Labour Party incursion, was help to the unemployed. However from 1935 one can see a huge surge in the growth of the Box Scheme whereby the original targets were exceeded by more than double. Economic trends undoubtedly had a part to play and Frank Pine was right to think in the early 1930s that better times were on their way - at least in the South West.

The original scheme had developed into a contributory scheme. If it was meeting more than a quarter of the hospital's costs by the late 1930s - then perhaps there was a need for it to do so. If the scheme was becoming a major source of income it was presumably also a growing source of patients, particularly with improved treatments and rising expectations. So the demands placed upon the hospital would have grown. A key factor, apart from some economic inflation, had to be growing affluence (not least with the Paying Patients Scheme catering for the better off).

One economic analysis notes that the 1930s economy was marked by the effects of the great depression. After experiencing a decade of economic stagnation in the 1920s, the UK economy was further hit by the sharp global economic downturn in 1930-31. This led to higher unemployment and widespread poverty. However, although the great depression caused significant levels of poverty and hardship (especially in the industrial heartlands), the second half of the 1930s was a period of quiet economic recovery. In parts of the UK (especially London and the South East) there was a mini economic boom with rising living standards and prosperity.

It is worth bearing in mind that statistics do not tell the full story. Unemployment rates in the 1930s were barely higher than the unemployment rates we have experienced in the 1980s and 2000s. However there is a big difference. In the 1930s unemployment benefit was minimal – to be unemployed left workers at the real risk of absolute poverty. In the current period unemployment benefits are relatively meagre, but they enable absolute poverty to be avoided. In that sense the depression of the 1930s created more economic poverty than the current recession. (Tejvan Pottinger - www.economicshelp.org/blog/7483/economics/the-uk-economy-in-the-1930s). The economic doldrums of 1930-32 were quickly followed by economic growth levels of over 3.5% for the rest of the decade.

Social and Health Trends - The Role of Women; Leisure and Longevity

It is possible to see several social trends in the period 1900-1940 from the narrative about Frank Pine's life in the press. A starting point is Frank Pine's involvement in the Hearts of Oak Friendly Society and its men's club-type meetings that, to all appearances, shaded very easily into freemasonry. The Bath Hospital Box Scheme emerged from those smoke-filled male bastions as something that served the health needs of many women and children.

As Chancellor, Lloyd George established a system of National Health Insurance. The National Insurance Act 1911 (with tripartite financing from worker, employer and taxpayer) gave the prospect of free health treatment (from a panel of GPs) and limited unemployment benefit to working men below a certain income level who were contributors to the scheme (and similarly to some single working women). Benefits did not extend to dependants and contributions were not graduated according to income but were paid at a flat rate – approximately half by the employee and half by the employer.

In return for their contributions, individuals received cash benefits for sickness, accident and disability. These were paid at a fixed rate, regardless of severity and were distributed through insurance companies and friendly societies. Contributors also had the right to free but limited care from a doctor on a local list or panel – yet were only entitled to hospital treatment when suffering from tuberculosis. As for doctors, they received a 'capitation fee' – a standard payment for each panel patient. Many doctors declined to join the panel.

Lloyd George's insurance service may have been Britain's largest pre-1948 health care system, yet it wasn't alone in providing medical assistance. The Poor Law offered relief to the most impoverished Britons, and workhouses provided their own infirmaries. The public health system in local government also provided a wide range of services, such as support for school meals and health education. By the 1930s, it had expanded its hospital provision, taking on Poor Law hospitals (such as St Martin's in Bath).

The other major hospital system offering care to patients before the advent of the NHS was that of the voluntary hospitals. The majority of these were initially supported by donations from subscribers who had the right to sponsor patients for admission. Yet, by the 1920s and 1930s, they found themselves in the midst of a financial crisis as death duties and the recession hit the estates of wealthy donors. Schemes were started like those in Kent and Canterbury, Bath and District and Cardiff and District to raise funds for a local hospital that gave some assurance of access to hospital care and health care for dependants – the families of working men. Hitherto many of these had no formal health cover and had to use self-medication or medicines bought over the counter from the local pharmacist. As a result an illness, or paying for medical attendance at a birth, could cause major financial problems for families across the country.

Of course these schemes increased demands upon the local hospitals. It remained that Britain's health care system, pre-1948, did not work well and the war, with servicemen and evacuees moving around the country and away from their home territories, made local-based solutions to health care and health funding impracticable. The wartime government's direction of the nation's hospitals pointed to something like the NHS being set up - although whether it should have entirely sacrificed local accountability is a moot point.

For married women and dependent children the National Insurance Act 1911 had little to offer. If they were not covered by a friendly society they were dependant on Poor Law hospitals or the charity of a voluntary hospital. It is not surprising that a newly enfranchised female population were strongly attracted to the Hospital Box Scheme and that they played a significant part amongst its 700 voluntary workers. Indeed by the end of the 1930s the Chairman of the RUH Management Board was a woman - Mrs Shaw Mellor (who had joined the Board as a Box Scheme representative and had been Vice-Chairman since 1932).

On the Monkton Combe Parish Council (following the death of the long-standing Clerk Mr Page) the Clerk's widow, Mrs Page, in due course succeeded him as Clerk (following a brief interregnum). That appointment was strongly endorsed by Frank Pine - an action that was much acclaimed by Mr Cornish, the Labour Councillor and Vice-Chairman of the Council. Of course the apparent takeover of the Council by the Labour Party in 1931 was also a key trend of the times.

One thing that is striking about the family stories in this tome are the changes in the life expectancy between the various generations. In the first part of the nineteenth century the likely death of children or of the death of women in childbirth led to large families and re-marriage. This is particularly illustrated in the lives of Thomas Beckingsale (1800-1850) and William Beckingsale (1835-1886) and their wives and children. For my great grandparent's generation in the mid to late nineteenth century a hard life could lead to the early death of the breadwinner with the surviving spouse - the wife - having to cope with a large family alone. Examples of this include the last wives of Thomas and William Beckingsale (Ruth and Anne) and Ellen Filer (nee Beckingsale). For that generation the railways facilitated greater labour mobility but it was very difficult to keep families together when jobs in service meant living on the job. All of this would have created health and stress issues.

My grandparent's generation born in the last part of the nineteenth century sought alternatives to domestic service - although the main alternatives tended to be shop work or manufacturing. With some improvements in public education such as the Board School attended by FH Pine, there was clearly an aspiration for better qualified work. Examples of this are Frank Pine, the accountant, Robert Daniels, the blacksmith and Worthy Daniels, the butcher. The achievements of this generation came, I think, at a significant cost in terms of health and longevity. The idea of having leisure activities on a regular weekly basis was, I am sure, not something that this generation readily expected. For this generation life expectancy meant theymight live until their mid 60s or the early 70s. An important factor in all this was the lack of comprehensive health care. Despite all that her husband had done to provide for affordable health care Lilian Pine died on the eve of the establishment of the NHS (which her husband might well have opposed) having recently expressed concern about the cost of doctors' appointments.

In the 1920s and 1930s my parent's generation had greater opportunities for leisure activities. To name but a few: circulating libraries, cinemas, theatre and music hall, concerts, radio, dances, whist drives, tennis and other sports, cycling, amateur dramatics, WEA courses and talks, and annual holidays by the sea (e.g., through the Girls Friendly Society). These all offered opportunities for rest and recreation that had mainly not been open to their parent's generation. The healthy benefits of a less stressful existence in their youthful years were compounded by full employment and the welfare state of the post 1947 years. So my parent's generation typically lived until their late 70s or early 80s.

The Firs Combe Down

The Firs, Combe Down, was named Richardson Avenue until the mid 1920s - allegedly it was originally named after the clergyman (a former vicar of All Saints) who owned the land. The Reverend Richardson turns up in the report on the unveiling of the Combe Down war memorial in May 1921. Built in 1901-2, The Firs was a classic Edwardian development for renting by the middle classes and artisans. As such it is very different from the estates of semi-detached houses that speculators built in suburban locations for sale to the younger generation of the middle classes and artisans two decades later - in the housing boom of the second half of the 1930s.

The Firs, Combe Down, provided solid middle class terrace houses and faced across the Firs Field that was entrusted to the parish council as a public space. I suspect that most of the houses in The Firs were rented. However that was common practice in those days - and Phyllis Pine only took out a mortgage to buy 17 The Firs in 1948, following the death of her mother. Her sale document shows it was first sold as new in February 1902.

Inside number 17 The Firs a passage linked the front door with the front reception room (and stairs to the upper floor) and past that to a second reception room, sometimes used for dining (and which led out to a glass conservatory). The passage continued to a third reception room (or parlour/kitchen) which had a largish window that faced out into the conservatory). Through that room one came to a kitchen/scullery with two large cupboards (one used for coal) and an outside toilet that was accessible from a back door at the side of the kitchen/scullery (next to the garden entrance to the conservatory). There was then a longish garden with a lane behind that led to a disused quarry. Upstairs in the late 20th century were 3 bedrooms above the 3 downstairs reception rooms - with a large bedroom in the front and a small bathroom in the middle (that was not an original installation), situated near the top of the stairs between the smallish middle and rear bedrooms.

At No 1 The Firs lived a Captain John Russell England – who served on Monkton Combe Council 1928-1931. I am sure he was the father of Stanley England, a leading light of Combe Down Old Scholars and the optician who worked with Phyllis Pine at Tovey's Opticians at New Bond Street in Bath until the late 1960s. Stanley and Phyllis joined Fl Toveys in 1914 and 1918, respectively, and they became fellow directors of Toveys in the late 1950s. Stanley was managing director following Irene Tovey's retirement in 1959 - but later Toveys was taken over by Dolland and Aitchison and the shop then moved to the Upper Borough Walls (originally established in 1750 Dolland and Aitcheson were, in turn, absorbed by Boots Opticians in 2009). The old shop became a branch of Laura Ashley.

At No 3 The Firs, according to the Bath Post Office Directory for 1932, lived a Miss Lucy E Long (presumably the friend of my mother's and her sister Connie who played the organ at their weddings). At No 4 there was a Miss Hardyman who featured on my mother's wedding present list. At No 7 The Firs lived a Mrs Pearce who was active in local social events (I am not sure if she was related to the Butcher Fred Pearce who died in 1940 - and who grazed animals in the Firs Field in the 1920s).

Robert Daniels lived with his family at 8 The Firs. He was the local blacksmith on Combe Down and attended the same Combe Down Unionist meeting as Frank Pine (and Fred Pearce) in 1912. A staunch conservative, he joined Monkton Combe Parish Council in 1928 but left with Frank Pine in 1934. He provided gates and fences for The Firs Field. He died in December 1949 but had given up his work as a blacksmith several years before (an occupation that is very much part of the past in the world of today).

At No 16 lived a Mr and Mrs Fisher (whom I also recollect) – Annie Fisher witnessed Lilian Pine's final will of 6 January 1947. In 1932, according to the Bath Post Office Directory, a William E Linscott lived at No 16.

If The Firs Combe Down was a place of the upwardly mobile it was also a place for those slipping down the ladder like the rather grand Mrs Elliot at No 18 whose son hastily left his bank job to join the French Foreign Legion. As noted above, she flew to Paris in the late 1930s to see her son on leave from the French Foreign Legion. Apart from his risky incognito visits to No 18 it was her last chance to see her son before the war! The 1932 Bath Post Office Directory lists Guy Elliot as the householder – I am not sure if this was her husband or her son.

At 21 The Firs lived a Miss Patch, Dressmaker – presumably of the same family as Harry Patch, the last serviving soldier of the First War, who lived on Combe Down (other relatives of the Patch family were involved in the Old Scholars and other activities on Combe Down, including the council). At 21a was WR Pearce, hairdresser.

The Firs about 1911 on a card Lilian sent to Aunt Jane and another from the same era posted 1946

The Firs Field, the War Memorial, the Church Army Hut and the Church Rooms

As these Combe Down locations feature in a number of ways in the following narrative I am grateful to the Combe Down Heritage Society for permission to reproduce the following article from their Newsletter of September 2014 (entitled **Down memory lane**).

The Ralph Allen Corner Stone is the latest of a number of Combe Down meeting places, other than public houses and schools, which have existed over the years. The first to be established in the mid-19th century were linked to the Church and Chapels where activities associated with their respective congregations could take place. The Nonconformist Union Chapel on Church Road had facilities for schooling and meetings while Holy Trinity Church used a small cottage on Tyning Road known as the Church

Rooms. This cottage, now demolished and replaced by the Old Church Court flats, was for many years the centre of Anglican church life and in the early 1900s also acted as a soup kitchen.

A much larger public building was built on the Avenue by a Captain Borland which opened in 1897 to celebrate Queen Victoria's 60th Jubilee. This was known as Avenue Hall and became the centre for non-religious functions such as concerts, meetings, auctions and even fancy-dress balls.

By the 1920s the Church Rooms in Tyning Road, as reported in the Bath Chronicle, "had become a disgrace to the parish" and the vicar, Revd. Watton, initially wanted to buy Avenue Hall as a replacement. The price was too high at that time so it was decided to build a new hall and for some years fund-raising took place at garden parties and the like for this cause. However, with a generous donation from the local Spear family and the sale of the Tyning Road cottage, Avenue Hall was eventually bought and re-opened in 1926 as the Church Rooms we know today. Since then the building has been used for much village activity, often not church-related.

An earlier incumbent of Holy Trinity, Revd Sweetapple, also provided for the community by organising a collection in 1917 to purchase Firs Field for the parish from the Misses Stennard for £750 and to keep in memory those who had laid down their lives in World War 1 with the establishment of a War Memorial.

Firs Field became the Combe Down village green and a fair used to be held there annually. It continues this public role, after a short interruption as the site of the mixing plant for mine stabilisation, as does the Scout Hut in its eastern corner, built in the 1960s to replace an earlier building known as the Church Army Hut and Social Centre.

A Concluding View

In the last weeks before his death in April 1942 Frank Pine could look back on a life that had experienced major social, political, economic and technological change. He died just prior to the Bath Blitz - which was a significant event in Bath, with a mass grave being used to bury many of its victims. His funeral may have been reported in the daily paper - but what was one funeral amongst so many?

The Baedeker raids were a series of attacks by the German air force on English cities chosen for their cultural or historical significance, rather than for any military value. They were in response to the devastating increase in the effectiveness of the RAF's bombing offensive, starting with the bombing of Lübeck in March 1942.

Britain had no longer been on its own in the war – following the attack on the Soviet Union in June 1941 and, after Pearl Harbor, with America entering the war in December 1941. There was room for hope, despite continuing reverses in North Africa, in the Soviet Union and in the Pacific. A turn in allied fortunes was not to begin until the push-back of Axis forces began in the winter of 1942-43 with El Alamein November 1942 (starting the push across North Africa – in which Albert Taylor was involved). Between August 1942 and February 1943 the battles for Stalingrad and Guadalcanal turned the tide in those theatres of war. Privately Frank Pine confided to his daughters his thoughts that the next war would be between America and Russia.

Yet, against this backcloth, the local press still devoted a considerable bulk of its rationed newsprint to local and domestic concerns - the normal activities of peacetime (including collections for the hospital box scheme) went on seemingly unabated. As reported in the press, wartime had blurred the distinction between municipal and voluntary hospitals - and the case was being firmly considered for a national approach to health care, with hospitals organised on a regional basis. The ending of the box scheme with the establishment of the NHS, and a comprehensive national approach to social security, was 5 years away. In the light of his past commitments to the friendly societies and the voluntary hospital approach I wonder how, in 1942, Frank Pine would have viewed the future?

He might well have seen the direction in which health and social security provision were pointing - in terms of a greater state role. He might also have come to endorse many of the proposals made by Beveridge but he might have been critical of the comprehensive state provision whereby Beveridge was implemented.

The Beveridge Report of December 1942 on *Social Insurance and Allied Services*, known commonly as the **Beveridge Report** was influential in the founding of the welfare state which included the expansion of National Insurance beyond the provisions of the 1911 Act and the creation of the National Health Service (taking over the voluntary and municipal hospitals). Labour leaders opposed Beveridge's idea of a

National Health Service run through local health centres and regional hospital administrations, preferring a state-run body.

In a Fabian Society article **'From welfare state to welfare society'** of 27 December 2012, Barry Knight points out that what is less commonly known is that the 1942 report was the first in a trilogy. Subsequent volumes were **'Full Employment in a Free Society'** (1944) and **'Voluntary Action'** (1948). *(http://www.fabians.org.uk/from-welfare-state-to-welfare-society)*

The later reports are important because Beveridge saw himself as laying the groundwork of a 'welfare society', not a 'welfare state'. Social advance depended on everyone, with business and civil society playing their part. Indeed, Beveridge was furious that the Labour government implemented his proposals through state agencies rather than through the friendly societies. In his 1948 report, he complained about the 'damage' that the welfare state was doing to what people might have done for themselves. He suggested that the government should "encourage voluntary action of all kinds" and "remove difficulties in the way of friendly societies and other forms of mutuality". The system, he felt, should be owned by the people and not the state.

However Beveridge could be seen as a liberal/conservative establishment figure trying to adapt existing structures so as to involve a fair amount of 'laissez faire' and personal choice. There were however many who felt that in the 1930s that choice and membership of friendly societies was not open to many who were poor. Furthermore, the division of the poor between the provident/deserving poor and the improvident/undeserving poor as determined by the rather arbitrary 'means test' was unjust. Indeed there was a growing feeling that a healthy life for working people could only be tackled by state intervention to tackle poverty and to create a state health system. The piecemeal system based on the Poor Law, voluntary hospitals and friendly societies was outmoded.

In her book "The People – The Rise and Fall of the Working Class" Selma Todd refers to an important report by Margery Spring Rice in 1939 on "Working Class Wives – Their Health and Conditions" in which the author's approach had changed from her earlier view that voluntary effort alone could provide for people's health and well-being. I have to say this change is not clear to me from my reading of this report. However, as Selma Todd points out, Margery Spring Rice does conclude that "Whatever social and economic changes the future may bring, the principle of democratic development of individual happiness and welfare through communal services offered to every citizen, will always be a part of wise government". Her report on the findings of the Women's Health Enquiry included the raising of wage levels (and therefore the health and welfare of working people) by the extension of the machinery of Trade Boards and collective bargaining by trades unions, a system of family allowances paid to the mother and the extension of the national insurance system to cover the wives and dependent children of insured men.

BATH, 1923-4.

"FRIENDLY SOCIETIES' COUNCIL."

ORGANIZERS OF THE PROPAGANDA SCHEME TO ASSIST THE FUNDS OF THE ROYAL UNITED HOSPITAL.

Back Row, standing, left to right—G. Haverfield, A. S. Gunstone, F. J. Strong, F. B. Knight, C. Crew, H. Lintern, T. H. Ricks, J. B. Jones, A. J. Courtney.
Standing alone—W. Horwood.
Sitting, left to right—E. Orchard, H. C. Lavington, W. A. King, F. H. Pine, G. S. Hodges, H. F. Fiddes, J. Pollard, W. F. Amesbury.
Sitting on ground, left to right—W. H. Chorley, C. W. Harding.

THE SEARCH FOR FRANK PINE: THE EARLY YEARS

1. A First Stab at FHP's Origins

It has not been easy to reach a definitive view on FHP's origins – most especially in obtaining his birth certificate. It is broadly understood that he was born in Bristol in 1876 – although even the year has been debateable. So an initial trawl of the records unearthed a birth certificate for a Francis Harold John Pine born on 12 January 1876 at Gunnislake, Calstock, in Cornwall, the son of a Robert Harvey Pine, a Brick Maker, and Mary Pine (nee Pyatt).

However none of this seemed to ring true with what we knew about FH Pine - and he was definitely not known as FHJ Pine (I am not sure where my name John came from but I do know my second name Francis came from FHP). However, as my daughter Louisa Bagshaw and my cousin John Taylor's wife Jill first pointed out to me - if you trace Francis Harold John Pine through the public record, one discovers he was married in Bristol in June 1904. Indeed the census of 1901 for Beaufort House, Arlington Road, Road, Bristol has a William G Pine 28 (born 1873) and Francis HJ Pine 25 (born 1876) both single and Brick Makers, living with their uncle Richard Pine (41 born 1860), a Brick Burner, and his wife Mary A Pine (34 born 1867) - and all were born in Calstock Cornwall. The census of 1901 clearly has our Frank Pine living in Bath with his wife Lilian.

2. FHP's Birth Date

As I have mentioned, there has been some question as to his date of birth. Firstly his gravestone at Monkton Combe Church says he died 24 April 1942 aged 65. Secondly two Bath Chronicle and Herald press reports from 26 October 1926 and 27 October 1928 pinpoint his birthday as being celebrated on 20 October. In the first report in the 'Bath and County Notes' the column records that he 'received many congratulations on Wednesday on the celebration of his 50th birthday'. The second item simply states that he was 52 on Saturday (i.e. the previous Saturday). This all points to the prospect of his being born on 20 October 1876.

However, Frank Pine's military records state that he attested in Feb 1897, aged 19 yrs 4 months (which fits in with an October birth) - but he would have reached the age of 20 in October 1897, so his putative birth year would have been 1877 by that reckoning. Frank was aged 5 in the census of 1881 (referred to in detail below), and might so be ascribed a birth year of 1876. However, if he had been born October 1876, he would not have been aged 5 until the autumn of 1881, several months after the census. Of course he was a nurse child (see next section), so perhaps his carers were not entirely sure of his exact age at the time of the census. In 1891, living with his relatives, he was aged 14. This would tie in with an October 1876 birth. In 1901 both Frank and his wife are 24 and this would be consistent with an October 1876 birth. In 1911 he was 35, as was his wife Lilian, so again, this is slightly inconsistent with an October 1876 birth.

3. **His First Census Mentions**

The census of 1881 has a Frank Pine, Nurse Child, aged 5, born in Bristol Gloucester living at 15 Wilson Street, Bristol St Paul with a William Williams, a 36 year old Wood Sawyer from London, his 34 year old wife Fanny from Gloucester and his 85 year old father-in-law David Mitchell, a Chelsea Pensioner from Somerset.

In the census of 1891 residing at 1, Gordon Terrace, Clifton, Bristol we have Frank Pine, a grandson aged 14 born in Bristol Gloucester and working as a photographer's assistant. He was living in a household with, as its head, his grandfather William Pine, widower and retired cutler *(clearly a miss-spelling of Butler)* who was aged 71 - born 1820 in Ilfracombe, Devon. In the same household were his two single daughters Mary Anne Pine aged 39 and Elizabeth Pine aged 37 both born in Clifton, Bristol (i.e. 1852 and 1854) and, in terms of their employment, they were both described as 'Nurse – Domestic'. According to my Aunt Edna Pine, FHP was brought up in Bristol and lived near the Hotwells area. Gordon Terrace no longer exists, but the neighbouring Belle Vue Terrace does and is in the right area.

That Frank Pine was described as "nurse child" in the 1881 census could be interpreted as child of the nurse. However, as he was staying with a wood sawyer & his family, who were unlikely to employ a nurse, it is more likely that he was 'farmed out' to this Williams family because his mother could not care for him in the house in which she was working. According to one web site, the definition of 'nurse child' is a child taken into the home of someone who cares for him/her as a result of circumstances that require the child's care away from his/her home.
(http://www.rootschat.com/forum/index.php/topic,55106.0.html).

In the 1891 census both Mary Ann & Elizabeth were nurse domestics (looking after the children in other people's families). As both Frank and the women are Pines and the women are described as unmarried and he and they are recorded as the grandson and daughters of William, there is a strong indication that Frank Pine was illegitimate and that one of the women was his mother.

My brother and I recollect our mother Lena saying that Frank Pine was brought up by two aunts who did not treat him kindly. It is possible that, if one of those aunts was his unmarried mother, they shared his up-bringing because the birth mother had to have him hidden away, for the sake of an affluent employer in whose household he was conceived. I will set out below some evidence for initially considering this hypothesis in relation to Elizabeth Pine.

I am indebted to my brother Roger, my wife's cousin Wendy Ellis, Jill the wife of my cousin John Taylor, my daughter Louisa Bagshaw and Theresa Douglas (whom I encountered through Genes Reunited) for a good deal of the original research and many of the comments in this section.

4. <u>The problems with the census records</u>

It is not easy tracing people in the nineteenth century – people moved around far more than in previous ages. People not at home on the census day could be missed from the record. The pressures of domestic service split up poor families. Butlers like the younger William Pine, or John Dalling Pine, lived in their master's houses. So husbands had to live apart from wives, and quite young children were farmed out to grandparents, uncles and aunts or complete strangers. That was quite a typical prospect for the impoverished servant class - like most of the Pines.

The spelling of names could vary from one census to the next (e.g. Simons or Symons). It is possible that name variations were deliberate and not accidental (as perhaps might be the case with Mary Ann Pine or Annie Pyne etc.). Searching computer records depends on accurate transcripts of the original record – but errors can occur so that for 1871 Tobias Pine is mis-transcribed as Falcus Pine (easily done when you see the writing). Even Lilian Pine is sometimes spelt Lillian! To add to the confusion many apparently unrelated Pine families (not referred to here but spotted in my trawl of census data) tended to use the same popular names (e.g. Susan, Mary Ann etc.). Also, as noted above, dates of birth could be a bit fluid. For Frank Pine's great grandfather William and his wife Mary there is some discrepancy between their ages in the 1841 census and those given in 1851 and 1861 (I understand ages could be rounded up or down to nearest 5 years in the 1841 census).

The somewhat forensic process of linking up the often far from perfect data contained in frequently incomplete records of censuses, birth, marriages and deaths can seem like deducing a jigsaw picture from a less than full set of poorly shaped pieces. The key issues in making such assumptions are the name of the person linked to their birthplace and date of birth (there is rarely more than one person of the same name born in the same small place in the same year).

5. Another stab at FHP's Origins

I am very much indebted to the aforementioned Theresa Douglas for pointing me in the direction of what does appear to be the definitive truth about FHP's origins. She noticed a birth record for Bristol in late 1876 for a Francis Harold Hampshire. Although it was a probable red herring I obtained the birth certificate and found the following record: Born on 20 October 1876 Francis Harold (Boy) at 4 Montague Street, Bristol; the father was given as Francis Spencer Hampshire (Shipping Agent); the Mother and Informant was shown as Annie Hampshire, formerly Pine, of 4 Montague Street, Bristol. The date of registration was 27 November 1876 (close to the end of the 42 day registration period). What is left of Montague Street these days is just a service road between the backs of offices and student housing near the bus station.

It is likely that Francis Spencer Hampshire did not know that his name was given as the father; and it is pretty certain that Annie Pine was never married to him (she was described as a spinster in her father's probate record of 1893). Clearly the registrar either did not seek, or was not given, proof of her marital status. Interestingly, as Mary Anne Pine, she did marry a shipping *clerk* in 1895, a William Urch. Francis Spencer Hampshire, bachelor and shipping merchant, did in fact marry an Annie Alice Pollitt on 21 June 1877 at Sefton, Lancashire. Fathers of both the bride and groom were shipping brokers. His father was substantially involved in trade with Brazil, principally through Liverpool. Francis Spencer Hampshire, born in 1849, died in 1924 leaving an estate of £68,316 (£3.7m in current terms). His heirs continued with the Brazilian trade well after the Second World War. I have no evidence that any money from the Hampshire's ever came FHP's way.

6. The Background of His Grandfather William Pine, His Aunts and the Pine family

In the 1841 census It would appear that Frank Pine's grandfather, William Pine was born in 1820 in Ilfracombe. In 1841, aged 20, he was living in Clarence Cottage, Ilfracombe with his father (also called William) and mother Mary (both aged 50 – and therefore born in c1791), with sister Elizabeth (15) and brothers John (15) and Charles (11) and a man the same age as William senior called William Marshall (presumably no connection to the Henry Marshall at Caledonia Place in Bristol to whom he was a servant in 1871).

One son of William Pine senior was Charles Pine (born c1829). So other cousins of Elizabeth and Mary Ann Pine are the off-spring of him and his wife Susan (born c1827) – notably (those mentioned in Elizabeth's will) Peter Eddy Pine (born c1861), Nellie Pine (born c1862), and Edith Dalling Sibbald (nee Pine and born c1864). Although Elizabeth Pine's will was drafted in 1908, only two people mentioned in her will (cousin Peter Eddy and Jane, wife of George Pine) pre-deceased her death in 1927. I will deal in detail with that will and the other branches of the family in the following sections.

In 1849 the younger William Pine (FHP's grandfather) married Mary Anne Simons at St Michael on the Mount in Bristol. **In 1850** their son William Masey Pine was born in Clifton, Bristol.

In 1851 the older William Pine (62 and a painter it appears) would seem to be still living at Clarence Cottage, Ilfracombe - with his wife Mary (64), daughter Eliza (28) and son Charles (22) (although none of the ages given matches the earlier record). It is interesting to note from the same census that in a nearby property in Ilfracombe High Street was a William Dalling, a shoemaker, with his wife and son. Curiously the name Dalling crops up as a second name in two of Charles Pine's children – Tobias John and Edith.

In the 1851 census, aged 31, the younger William Pine was a lodger working as a 'footman' at 41 Windsor Terrace, Clifton, Bristol. He was one of 3 servants in the household of Isaac Cooke, a solicitor. He is shown as being married. Meanwhile his wife Mary Ann Pine was living with their young son William M Pine (1) at 11 Princes Place, Clifton, Bristol. Mary Ann Pine's death sometime before the 1861 census clearly had a shattering impact on her family (daughters Mary and Elizabeth were born in 1852 and 1854).

In 1861 the younger William Pine was 41, and a widower, and living at Clayton Villa, Clifton Park (near St Vincent's Hill), Clifton, Bristol in the household of Mrs Anne M Knowlys (53, widow) with her 3 daughters and 4 other of her relatives. His occupation was recorded as Butler (birthplace Ilfracombe). In 1861, his daughter, FHP's 'aunt' Elizabeth Pine (born in Bristol, aged 7, appears to be living in Ilfracombe, at 106 High Street, with her grandparents, William (74, a painter) and Mary (72). Clearly Elizabeth (born 1854) was with grandparents in 1861 because her mother had recently died. However I cannot trace in the 1861 census record with whom it was that his daughter Mary Ann Pine was farmed out (she was then aged 9). William (Masey) Pine (aged 11) was recorded as living in 1861 in Frome Street, Clifton, Bristol with his uncle Edward Symonds and his wife and 5 children. I should add that I cannot find William M Pine in the 1871 census but he was recorded as dying in 1874 in Bedminster, Somerset – his name was then spelt William <u>Macey</u> Pine. **On 20 January 1863** William Pine senior died with effects to his widow of less than £100.

In 1871, the younger William Pine, a widower aged 51, was a butler at 28 Caledonia Place Clifton, for Henry Marshall, Physician and Surgeon. Elizabeth, aged 17 was an 'under nurse/domestic' at 29 Royal York Crescent, Clifton in the household of an army captain, William Brown. Meanwhile Mary Ann Pyne (19) – despite the spelling, I am sure it is the right person - was a servant (an under nurse domestic) to George F Atchley and his family at 27 Royal York Crescent, Clifton, Bristol.

In 1874, as noted above, William Macey Pine, brother to Mary Ann and Elizabeth Pine, died in Bedminster. Somerset.

In 1875 a William Amandus Urch married a Jane Merchant James (she was to die in 1894 – and in 1895 he married Mary Ann Pine: but more of that later).

In 1876 on 10 October Francis Harold Pine was born, according to the 'Hampshire' birth certificate. Also, **in 1876** on 5 December, Lilian Pine was born in Stratford on Avon to William Beckingsale (a Draper) and Anne Beckingsale (formerly Dash).

In 1881, FHP's grandfather the younger William Pine, aged 61, appears to be lodged with a Hannah Peck at 5 Waterloo Place, Clifton, Bristol and was described as a butler or domestic servant. In the 1881 census Elizabeth was a nurse domestic at 8, Albert Road, Clifton working for Edward Harley (aged 38), the joint registrar of Bristol County Court and a solicitor. In his household were his wife Jessie (32), daughter Mary (6), son Edward M Harley (5), and daughter Beatrice (3). Elizabeth Pine (26 - Nurse) heads a list of 4 servants - a cook (27), a parlour maid (20) and an Under Nurse (14).

Where was Mary Ann Pine? Well I think it is fair enough to suppose that she was the Annie Pyne (27 and born in Clifton, Bristol) who was one of 6 servants serving Edgar Chas Sumner Gibson and his family at St Andrew Street, Wells. He was recorded as being the Principal of the Theoligiene College, Wells (odd spelling!). As we have already established my grandfather, Frank Pine, was a Nurse Child, aged 5, (born in Bristol Gloucester) and was living at 15 Wilson Street, Bristol St Paul with a William Williams, a 36 year old Wood Sawyer from London, his 34 year old wife Fanny from Gloucester and his 85 year old father-in-law David Mitchell, a Chelsea Pensioner from Somerset.

Meantime William Urch (27) was living at Perry Street, Bristol with his wife Jane (28) and daughters Florence (4) and Edith (3).

Diverting into the family archive, we have some photographs of Frank Pine as a baby and as a schoolboy in which he does not look uncared for (the army records indicate he was vaccinated as a baby). A photograph from about 1885 shows him as a pupil of Clifton Church School (as the wording on the photo appears to say). Then there is a photograph of him as a choir boy (our mother may have said, perhaps erroneously, that he sang at St Mary Redcliffe, Bristol). Is the picture of him as a choir boy especially significant – pointing to a necessity for him to be christened and confirmed (as he was belatedly in 1889 - see below)? There is then another school photograph, perhaps from round about 1887 and similar to the previous one, except that the wording seems to be 'Clifton Industrial'. It is probably the same 'national' school.

The census and army records confirm what my mother told my brother and me - that Frank Pine was apprenticed as a photographer's assistant, from about 1890 until 1897. Apparently he retained an interest in photography and painting throughout his life. We have a pen and ink picture of York drawn by him and a few other pictures of his (see below). We have only one item that is clearly from his photographic output (of his daughter Phyllis as a baby) – although he may well have created the family photographs at the start of this book. There are a few photographs of him as a dapper young man in the 1890s mostly taken at the studios of Villiers and Quick in Park Street Bristol that (according to his army records) employed him until 1997. As to his army service, my mother and her sisters were also proud that FHP served in the Kings Royal Rifles in the late 1890s.

In 1889 a strong clue as to Frank Pine's mother was given in a Mormon Christening record (from Bristol Parish Registers 1538-1900). It shows Frank Pine as being christened on 3 October 1889 (at the age of almost 13) at Clifton Wood, St Peter, Gloucester. His mother's name was given as Mary Anne Pine.

By 1891 (as noted in section 3 above), the younger William Pine was a not so young widower of 71 - and was living with two grown-up daughters (the Nurse Domestics) Mary Anne (39) and Elizabeth (37) and his 14-year old grandson (and apprenticed photographer) Frank Pine at 1 Gordon Terrace, Clifton, Bristol. He was described as a retired cutler (or, as noted above, butler). So by 1891, as a retired man, he was at last able to live able to have some of his family under one roof. If so the experience would have been short-lived.

From 1893 an administration of goods record from the Bristol Record Office on-line catalogue shows a gift of Reverend FW Potto Hicks, Curate of St. James (city) on the administration of goods of William Pine, deceased of Clifton, retired butler. The date was 14 April 1893. According to Probate Records, William Pine died in Bristol 18 March 1893. His address was given as 1, Gordon Terrace Bristol and he was described as a retired butler. Administration was granted to Mary Ann Pine spinster. His effects were £323 5s. It is interesting that Elizabeth was still living at 1 Gordon Terrace in 1901. She lived there with her 77 year old widowed uncle and also a retired butler, John Dalling Pine, as head of household. JD Pine was to die in 1902.

Returning briefly to 1891 we find at 159 Stapleton Road, Bristol, William A Urch (37) was living at Perry Street, Bristol with his wife Jane M (38) and children Florence M (14) and Edith AA (13), William H (8), Lillian M (6) and Jenny AH (0). I am quite sure that this was the Jeannie Urch (20) living with Frank Pine and his family in 1911. **In 1894** Jane Merchant Urch died and **in 1895** William A Urch married Mary Ann Pine.

7. A New Era for FHP - 1897 onwards

For the period 1897-1899 we have Frank Pine's military record. He enlisted (attested) on 20 February 1897 aged 19 years 4 months (which would fit in with an October birth) so he would have been 20 in October 1897 - consequently his putative birth year would be 1877 by that reckoning. Initially he joined the Third Regiment of the Kings Own Royal Hussars but transferred to the Third Battalion of the Kings Royal Rifles on 6 May 1897 (regimental number 238). The Third Battalion were based in England from 1892-1898 *(according to the Kings Royal Rifles website http://www.krrcassociation.com).*

Frank Pine's attestation document says he had been a photographer apprenticed to Messrs Villiers and Quick of Bristol for 7 years and currently he had been serving in the militia – the Devon Artillery. His attestation and medical examination took place at Devonport. His height was 5 foot 6 inches and he was described as being of good physical development, weighing 131 lbs, with a fresh complexion, blue eyes and brown hair. Name and address of his next of kin was given as his mother Annie Pine of Stapleton Road, Bristol. He was re-vaccinated (having been vaccinated as a baby). His medical record shows him as having suffered tonsillitis, a sore throat (which involved hospitalisation) and some minor ailments at Aldershot in February, May and November 1897, at Waterford (Ireland) in September 1898 and Kilkenny in March 1899.

Curiously, if our researches are correct, his mother had been married to William Urch since 1895 – perhaps he did not easily recognise the fact (felt abandoned?). The fact is that Mary Ann Pine married William Amandus Urch at Easton St Gabriels. Stapleton Road runs through Easton. Carlyle Road where Mary Ann Urch lived in 1901 is not far from Stapleton Road, in the Lower Easton/Greenbank area. Mary Ann's probate of 1908 said that she was of Anworth, Stapleton - and widower William Urch still resided there in 1911. So I think Mary Ann fits very well with "Mother, Annie Pine, Stapleton Road, Bristol".

Frank Pine's military record shows him as having achieved certificates of education 3rd class in 23 May 1897 and 2nd class in 27 September 1897 - and having passed the professional examination to the rank of corporal 17 November 1898. He was promoted to corporal 2 March 1899 (backdated to 26 January 1899). He was discharged from the army on 12 May 1899 at his own request on the payment of £18. *(No small sum: equivalent to about £2,000 now – presumably Mary Ann or Elizabeth stumped up the money! Didn't my mother or aunts actually say an aunt bought him out of the army? Or was there someone else in the background? I have a feeling that at odd moments in the 1890s there might have been some extra financial support available to FHP.)*

Frank Pine arrived in Bath in 1899 to take up an administrative post with the Bath and Somerset Dairy where he served as a Cashier (accountant) for 26 years - and led the company for a year before being made redundant by the new owners, Norton Dairies, early in 1925 (possibly because of the amount of public work he had taken on?). He subsequently joined the pork pie makers Spear Brothers & Clark as a 'cashier' (accountant). Another interesting question is that if FHP joined the Bath and Somerset Dairy late in 1899 as a cashier – when did he train to be an accountant? Did he do it on the job – or did he do some studying first, perhaps even in the army? *Was his study of accountancy externally funded?*

In 1900 his life became more settled as he married Lilian Beckingsale on 16 April at St John the Baptist, Bathwick, Bath. They are both aged 23 (consistent with late 1876 birthdates). FHP was an accountant living at 4 Kingston Road and his father was given as 'William Pine, valet, deceased' (actually his grandfather – but a common device to cover illegitimacy). Lilian's address was shown  as 42 Fowler Road and her father was given as 'William Beckingsale, draper, deceased'. The wedding was witnessed by her brother Hubert Beckingsale and her sister Edith Annie Beckingsale. Their wedding cake card shows them living at 2 Pulteney Grove, Bath.

Twenty five years later a Bath Chronicle notice of 18 April 1925 read "Weddings – Silver Wedding Pine-Beckingsale – April 16th 1900 at St John Baptist Bathwick by the Rev Arthur Roberts, Frank Harold to Lillian, daughter of the Late W Beckingsale of Cheltenham." As discussed in a separate section below, branches of the Beckingsales had a haberdashery shop and shirt factory and other retail outlets for grocery and ironmongery in Cheltenham. Although stressing the Beckingsale line the newspaper notice almost pointedly makes no mention of Frank Pine's own ancestry.

In 1901 the census shows Francis Harold Pine (24), born in Bristol, Goucestershire, and cashier to a Dairy Co, married to Lillian Pine born in Stratford on Avon, Warwickshire, and living at 2 Pulteney Grove, Bath. Also at 2, Pulteney Grove were a family who were to become their long term friends - John Charles Pinhorn (30) Boots Warehouse Manager, born in Southampton, Hants and his wife Marian Jane (36) born in Walworth, Surrey, and their daughter, May Edith (11 months and born in Bath). In 1902 JC Pinhorn was a member of The Loyal Order of Ancient Shepherds (Home Lodge 955) and he was one of the auditors at their annual financial meeting.

I have this picture of May Pinhorn sent to Phyllis Pine Christmas 1925 and, as can be seen, she had thick wirey hair. My brother and I well remember her in the late 1950s. By 1911 the Pinhorns were living at 102 High Street, Watford and he was described as a Retail Boot Trade Manager. He died in Croydon in 1944 and an extract from the Croydon St Saviour's Church Magazine described him as one of their oldest sidesmen who, for some years, had assisted in the church accounts. May Pinhorn died in Croydon in 1967.

Also in 1901 we find, living at 1 Gordon Terrace, Clifton, Bristol, John D Pine (77 - a retired butler) with his niece Elizabeth Pine (46 - a Nurse Domestic). William Urch (still a Merchant Shippimg Clerk) and Mary (nee Pine) Urch, (both now 47), were living at 12 Carlyle Road, Easton, Bristol with his children Lillian M Urch (16) and Jenny A Urch (10).

In 1908 Mary Ann Urch died on 24 October. The Probate Date was 17 December 1908 and she died in Bristol. Probate Registry gives her address as Anworth Stapleton, Bristol. Administration was granted to her husband, William Amandus Urch, Merchant's Clerk, with her effects valued at £687 17s 7d. It may well have been her sister's death that prompted Elizabeth Pine to write her will in that year.

In 1911 the 2 April 1911 census shows us that Frank and Lilian Pine and their family were living, with a live-in maid (Jeannie Urch aged 20), at 19 Forester Avenue, Bathwick (accommodation with 6 rooms – the number of rooms would have included any kitchen but excluded any bathroom according to the rules of the 1911 census). Frank Pine (Cashier at Dairy Co) and Lilian were 35 (somewhat inconsistent with their being born in 1876) and the girls were Phyllis (6), Constance (4), Edna (2) and Lena (1). The family moved a couple of years later (minus Jeannie Urch, the maid) to Combe Down and 17 Richardson Avenue (later renamed The Firs) that faced the Firs Field.

Jeannie Urch was quite clearly FHP's late mother's step-daughter and may well have lodged with the family rather than being employed by them. Frank and Lilian Pine had 4 daughters – Phyllis (1905 – who worked, and became a partner, at Tovey's opticians), Connie (who married in 1938 and moved to Birkenhead), Edna (who ended up as office manager at Johnson's Central News Agency) and, in 1910, Lena (my mother).

Also in 1911 at 69 Jacobs Wells Road, Clifton we find Elizabeth Pine, spinster (56) living, apparently on her own in two rooms, as a retired Nurse Domestic. Also at 69 Jacob Wells Road in 1911, was a key beneficiary of her will – a single lady Charlotte Anne

Louisa Potter (41) working at home as a dressmaker and living in a separate household of 5 rooms with her parents James (85) and Anne (84).

Elsewhere in 1911 at Anworth Stapleton, Bristol we find William A Urch (58 - widower and still a Merchants Clerk) living with his single daughter Florence Mary Urch (34) in a 6 room dwelling.

8. The Bath & Somerset Dairy years 1899-1925

Frank Pine arrived in Bath in 1899 to take up an administrative post with the Bath and Somerset Dairy which he served as a Cashier (accountant) for 26 years. He led the company for a year before being made redundant by the new owners, Norton Dairies, early in 1925.

The newspaper record considered in following sections is of limited help in setting out his career with the dairy. The first newspaper entry on Frank Pine is in the Bath Chronicle of Thursday 25 July 1901. It reads **"On Friday Evening a pleasant ceremony at the Bath & Somerset Dairy** – the assistant secretary Mr Paull was presented with a marble timepiece on the occasion of his approaching marriage; on behalf of the staff Mr F H Pine Cashier made the presentation, in a few well chosen words, in the presence of a large number of staff."

On 14 December 1912 there is a report of **Bath and Somerset Dairy Presentations** relating to a Miss Fellows who was leaving to get married, after 10 years service with the company in a clerical role. She was presented with a dinner service, carver rests and an autograph album (inscribed) by the staff and the directors of the company gave her a cheque. In the absence of the general manager Mr Tucker, Mr Pine the Cashier made one of the presentations.

Until the 1950s many milk companies delivered milk, door to door, by horse drawn drays. During World War I, there were dire shortages of men, horses and vehicles when they were commandeered for the war effort. This hampered any business which was reliant on the timely distribution of its products, such as a dairy company.

I have seen press reports of the tribunal that considered exemptions for military service turning down requests from the Bath and Somerset Dairy for exemptions for its delivery men. Indeed such requests were generally turned down – the view being that if people wanted milk they could collect it from the dairy.

However I have two press cuttings from 1915 that have been handed down to me that show that Frank Pine, at 39, was exempted from full military service – subject to him joining the Special Volunteer Reserve (I believe he may have helped out with rifle training at some kind of camp on the Firs Field – which, as a former corporal in the Kings Royal Rifles he was equipped to do).

BATH AND SOMERSET DAIRY.

Mr. Bailis Tucker applied for Frank H. Pine, 39, married, 17, Richardson avenue, Combe Down, assistant manager, cashier, and accountant, of the Bath and Somerset Dairy Co. He said 41 men had entered the Army and munitions and close oversight of the women who had replaced the men was necessary. Mr. Pine inspected the 12 branch dairies and staffs.—Col. Clayton thought that Mr. Bailis Tucker, with female assistance, might do the work.—Certificate until January 31; section 4/2, to join the S.V.R.

A FURNITURE DEALER.

Mr Bailis Tucker Managing Director of the Bath and Somerset Dairy made the application for Frank H Pine, assistant manager, cashier and accountant of the company because 41 men had left for the army and munitions work and close oversight of the women who had

BATH AND SOMERSET DAIRY.

Mr. Bailis Tucker asked for further exemption for Frank H. Pine (39), 17, Richardson Avenue, Combe Down, assistant manager in the employment of the Bath and Somerset Dairy Co.; it was said of him "Mr. Pine steps into every breach to keep the work of distribution going on." Mr. Tucker added that Pine inspected the twelve branch dairies and generally supervised the Company's business as understudy to himself.

Certificate till January 31; no further appeal without leave, to join the Volunteers.

replaced the men was necessary. He said "Mr Pine steps into every breach to keep the work of distribution going on" He inspected the 12 branch dairies and generally supervised the company's business as understudy to himself.

United Dairies was formed in 1917 when Wiltshire United Dairies, Metropolitan and Great Western Dairies, and the Dairy Supply Company merged in an attempt to pool their resources and keep their companies operating until the end of the war. But so successful was the merger under Chairman Sir Reginald Butler that the company began to expand, buying other dairies and creameries across the United Kingdom.

I have a press article of 24 April 1920 which records that Wiltshire Farmers Limited who recently acquired the business of the Bath and Somerset Dairy Co had recently purchased a Weston-super-Mare dairy. *It is tempting to think that Wiltshire Farmers Limited and Wiltshire United Dairies were one and the same company and that a subsidiary that operated the Bath and Somerset Dairy was the Norton St Philip Dairy Co (Ltd.) of which Frank Pine was briefly Head Cashier. In the 1950s United Dairies still traded in Bath as Norton Dairies although my brother recollects some deliveries in vans marked 'Hornby Dairies'. However a newspaper report of 20 December 1924, referred to below, suggests that the Norton St Philip Dairy Co found its way under the United Dairies umbrella through Hornby Dairies.* By the early 1950s, United Dairies had become the UK's largest dairy products company. But the company had become inefficient, and needed to improve its operations. In 1959 it merged with its rival Cow & Gate to create Unigate. The dairying side of Unigate's business was sold in 2000 to Dairy Crest.

The Bath Chronicle of 26 June 1920 recorded that Mr H Bailis Tucker, for many years the manager of the Bath and Somerset Dairy Co was about to retire and his successor was to be a Mr CT Francis who had had several years experience in high class London dairy business.

On 14 July 1920 – Mr Bailis Tucker, who was presumably yet to retire, gave Frank Pine the reference which I have reproduced in the following pages.

As recorded below there was in the Chronicle of 17 June 1922 the report of a **Wilts & Somerset Farmers Staff Outing**. "A happy party, numbering over 90, were taken in three char-a-bancs of the Bath Electric Tramways on their annual staff outing to Cheddar and Weston Super Mare on Thursday morning......The chair was occupied by Mr Frank H Pine who was supported by Mr C T Francis and Mr H G Collett ....."*(They were all members of the Bath and Somerset Dairy that may well have sponsored the trip and it is curious that Mr CT Francis appears to have a supporting role.)*

As discussed below, in the Bath Chronicle of **17 February 1923 is a key article** headed **'Mr Frank H Pine - A Busy Combe Down Man and his Public Offices'** and reads "Mr Frank Harold Pine who has just been elected Chairman of the Bath Friendly Societies Council, is a gentleman well known in all parts of the city. He is a Bristolian but came to Bath in 1899 and had been with Bath & Somerset Dairies for 23 years until last year when he became Head Cashier of the Norton St Philip Dairy Co (Ltd.)."

On 20 December 1924 the Western Daily Press had an article **Milk Supply – Important Local Businesses change hands.** The report states that "the whole of the business of Messrs FW Gilbert Limited and the Norton St Philips Dairy Co Ltd. Bath have been acquired by Mr Herbert E Hornby of Keynsham Manor, near Bristol who, with his father, has been associated with some of the most important dairy concerns in the country". As discussed above, *I find this item difficult to reconcile with the one in the Bath Chronicle of 24 April 1920.*

Clearly the dairy industry was in a state of flux in the period after the Great War. It is difficult to understand who the owners of the Norton St Philip Dairy Co were in 1925 and what FH Pine's role was after the departure of Mr H Bailis Tucker and the arrival of Mr C T Francis. The reference obtained from Mr Tucker in 1920 suggests that Frank Pine saw his future with the company as uncertain. Certainly his departure was a far from happy event – as evidenced by his parting letter to the staff that was published in the both the daily and weekly editions of the Bath Chronicle!

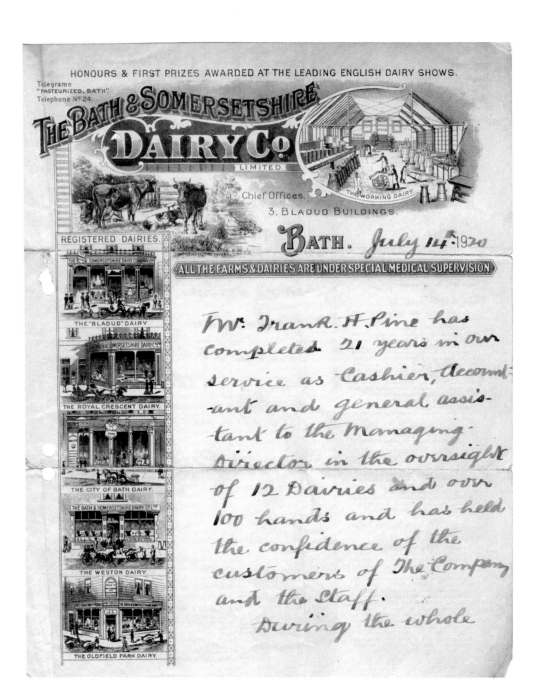

Telegrams
"PASTEURIZED, BATH"
Telephone Nº 24

The BATH & SOMERSETSHIRE DAIRY Co

LIMITED.

Chief Offices.

3. BLADUD BUILDINGS,

THE WORKING DAIRY.

BATH. July 14th 1920

ALL THE FARMS & DAIRIES ARE UNDER SPECIAL MEDICAL SUPERVISION.

REGISTERED DAIRIES.

THE "BLADUD" DAIRY.

THE ROYAL CRESCENT DAIRY.

THE CITY OF BATH DAIRY.

THE WESTON DAIRY.

THE OLDFIELD PARK DAIRY.

Mr. Frank. H. Pine has completed 21 years in our service as Cashier, Account-ant and general assis-tant to the Managing Director in the oversight of 12 Dairies and over 100 hands and has held the confidence of the customers of The Company and the Staff.

During the whole

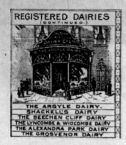

'The Times.'

Special Commissioner reporting in a lengthy article upon the methods adopted by The Company to safeguard the supply of dairy produce, wrote February 12th, 1900:

"The large population of Bath is now "in the enjoyment of a regular supply of "milk of faultless character."

'The Court Circular.'

Of February 17th, 1900, writing on the same subject, said

"Bath is fortunate in possessing one of the most "truly hygienic supplies of milk and dairy produce "in the kingdom, and may compare favourably "with London, New York, Paris or any other "leading city, in the far-seeing scope and enterprise "of The Bath and Somersetshire Dairy Company "Ltd., who have met and overcome the dreaded "evil of tuberculosis from cows by Pasteurizing "all milk and dairy goods they purvey and the "dangers of typhoid and scarlet fever, diphtheria, "and measles are thus eliminated, together with the "germs of all infectious diseases which have former-"ly been conveyed in milk and dairy produce. This "process of heating and chilling was first employed "by M. Pasteur in the destruction of germ life in "liquid food."

"The lacteal secretion of the cow, so precious "an article of diet for our children, the sick and "the strong, is by this means rendered SAFE."

"A "Times" commissioner has recently "written in that journal a full description of The "Pasteurizing Plant, showing why it was introduced "and what it does, to which we refer our readers "for detail. The well-known Pasteurised butter ""Our Own Churning"'a Registered brand, and "Pasteurised cream and Devonshire cream, is we "learn in great demand in the City, and large "quantities are daily despatched to London and the "provinces. Honours and First Prizes have been "repeatedly gained by these delicate articles."

'Bladud' The Bath Society Paper

In their issue of October 24th, 1900, stated

Dr. ODERY SYMES contributes to *The Bristol* "*Medico-Chirurgical Journal*, a quarterly Journal "of the Medical Sciences for the West of England "and South Wales, an interesting article on The "Pasteurization of Milk. In the course of his in-"vestigations he inspected The Pasteurizing Plant of "The Bath and Somersetshire Dairy Company, Ltd. " Comparing the process there adopted with that "at other dairies, he is careful to note that by the "system employed by The Bath and Somersetshire "Dairy Company, milk is kept in constant " circulation during the process of Pasteuri-"zation; hence no scum forms nor cream "rises during the process. He concludes his "article by declaring that "the process of Pas-"teurization affords a complete safeguard "against the risk of infectious diseases "being conveyed by milk."

period, his duties have been carried out to our entire satisfaction. He has prepared the Annual Accounts for the Auditors which were invariably balanced before they took the books in hand.

H. Bailis Tucker

Managing Director

THE DAIRIES OF THE COMPANY

Are thoroughly up-to-date, the Sanitary conditions being perfect. The supervision and control of the Farms, the Cattle, and the safety and quality of the Milk supply is entrusted by the Company to the following Gentlemen :

R J. H. SCOTT, F.R.C.S Ed.,
Medical Examiner of Farms.

J. W. GATEHOUSE, F.I.C., M.S.P A.,
Consultant Analyst

W. A. WELCH, M.R.C.V.S.,
Consultant Veterinary Surgeon.

H. BAILIS TUCKER,
Managing Director of the Company

An EMINENT BACTERIOLOGIST is also retained on behalf of The Company.

9. Elizabeth Pine's will 1927 and afterwards

In 1927 on 8 December Elizabeth Pine of 69 Jacobs Wells Road, Clifton, died. Her will was dated 15 July 1909 and her address was given as 6 Berkeley Vale Clifton which, as Gillian Taylor has noted from the probate record, is the same address as 69 Jacobs Wells Road where the 1911 census shows she was living alone (aged 56), in what was possibly a flat, as a retired nurse-domestic. The probate record shows that she was still living there at her death in 1927.

Elizabeth Pine's will appointed Edward Mortimer Harley of Small Street Bristol, solicitor, and Charlotte Potter of 6 Berkeley Vale Clifton, spinster, executor and executrix of her will. After a list of very specific bequests she bequeathed the residue and remainder of her estate and effects to Edward Mortimer Harley and Charlotte Potter or the survivor of them, subject to any list of memorandum left by her at her death. The will was witnessed by Edward Mortimer Harley and his clerk. This is an interesting, even dubious, range of roles for the solicitor. Edward Mortimer Harley was clearly the son of her employer in 1881 (he was roughly the same age as Frank Harold Pine).

What is even more intriguing are the specific bequests. "I give and bequeath the following pecuniary and specific bequests to my cousin Tobias John Dalling Pine my 250 pounds of five per cent preference stock in the Ilfracombe gas company. To my Cousin Peter Eddy Pine my 193 pounds of consolidated ordinary stock in the Ilfracombe gas company. To my Cousin Nellie Pine my 50 pounds of preference stock in the North British Railway Company. To my cousin Edith Dalling Sibbald the sum of £50.00. To my Cousin Susan Elizabeth Bevan the sum of £50.00. To Jane Pine the widow of my Cousin George Pine of 7 Albert Row Ilfracombe the sum of £20.00 and also my 45 pound shares in the Ilfracombe Sea Bathing Company Limited and if she shall predeceased me then I bequeath the said sum in shares equally between her four children. To Francis Harold Pine the sum of 200 pounds and my five 6 per cent £10.00 preference shares in the Bristol Steam Navigation Company Limited. To Mary Ann Bennett the sum of £20.00."

Elizabeth Pine was very specific about her relationship to her beneficiaries (as her cousins etc.) - apart from Edward Mortimer Harley, Charlotte Potter - *and Francis Harold Pine*. The probate record for 1928 (page 649) records that she died on 8 December 1927 (she would have been 72). Probate was granted to Edward Mortimer Harley and Charlotte Potter. Her estate was worth between £2,153 (effects) and £2,449 (resworn) - between £121,000 and £137,000 in current values. *Francis Harold Pine was left £250 (£14,000 in current values) - the joint largest specific bequest.*

Elizabeth left FHP a large bequest, but notably she omitted to spell out his relationship to her. Was it because it was still too embarrassing to admit he was her illegitimate nephew (or her illegitimate son, as I and others had initially thought)? Elizabeth was the last survivor of the 'nuclear' family of William Pine and Mary Ann Simmons. Brother William Macey/Masey Pine and sister Mary Ann Urch had both predeceased her, and FHP seems to have been the only issue of the three siblings, so he was her closest biological kin (unless there are any more skeletons in our family cupboard), and therefore her most natural blood heir. As noted above the death of her sister Mary Ann in 1908 may well have prompted Elizabeth to get around to writing her will. On the other hand it is surprising that in the 18 years since writing her will she did not seek to amend it even though at least two of her beneficiaries (Peter Eddy Pine and Jane Pine, widow of George) had passed on. Even so, her intention in spreading some financial help to her relatively impoverished family might be surmised.

How was it that a woman from such a poor background could have died so relatively comfortably off? She had worked as a 'nurse-domestic' but had been retired since at least 1911 (at the age of 56). Why did Edward Mortimer Harley have such a key role in her estate? Until I became certain that Mary Anne Pine was FHP's mother I had wondered if Elizabeth was his mother and that the birth of FHP might have been significant to the Harleys - such that Edward Mortimer might have regarded him as a half brother? But I am sure that is not the case. Yet I wonder how FHP would have reacted to her bequest in 1928? Had he kept in touch with her over the years?

So many questions remain that, at this distance in time, can only be answered by guesses. Also modern perspectives may not be appropriate now that the idea of 'owning' servants and having a deep shame about illegitimacy may seem alien.

All the evidence now clearly points to Mary Anne Pine/Urch as his mother. There is also FHP's link with Jenny Urch. So, on that basis, Elizabeth made FHP a key beneficiary because he was her sole blood line, whom she had played some part in raising, and perhaps may have helped financially at various stages (such as buying him out of the army). She was also doing her duty by her sister whose more modest inheritance passed to her husband, William Urch.

There are two more dates to put on record:

In 1942 Frances Harold Pine died on 17 April at Combe Down, Bath. He was 65 and his occupation was given on his death certificate as 'accountant'. He was certified as dying from coronary thrombosis, as certified by Dr Charles Hagenbach. Phyllis O Pine, daughter, was the informant.

In 1947 Lilian Pine died on 26 September at Combe Down, Bath. She was 70 and her occupation was given on her death certificate as 'widow of Frances Harold Pine accountant'. She was certified as dying from 'hemiplegia and aretino sclerosis', as certified by R Lane Walmeley. P O Pine, daughter, was the informant.

10. William Pine Senior's siblings: John Dalling, Elizabeth and Charles

As noted above in section 6, in the **1841 census** it would appear that Frank Pine's grandfather, William Pine, was born in 1820 in Ilfracombe. In 1841, aged 20, he was living in Clarence Cottage, Ilfracombe with his father (also called William) and mother Mary (both aged 50 – and therefore born in c1791), with sister Elizabeth (15) and brothers John (15) and Charles (11). Currently I have no information about Elizabeth and I will deal in the next section with Charles – so I first turn to John (Dalling) Pine.

In 1851 John Dalling Pine (30) was a servant in Dyffryn House, Aberdare, Glamorgan, in the household of a Mr Henry Austin Bruce (mis-transcribed as Brice or Brenes) a stipendiary magistrate, although his wife, Anabella Bruce, was given as the head of the household – the magistrate being away from home. The other members of the household were her daughters Margaret, Rachel and Jessie with Amelia Willicomb the nurse, Mary Lewis the cook, Mary Ann Kirkpatrick the housemaid, Louisa Griffiths the under-maid, Mary Evans the kitchen maid and John Dalling (Dollie) Pine, the footman.

In 1870 John Dalling married a Phillis Potter (that's the spelling given) but there were no children. **In 1871** (47 and 35) they were living in 1 Clarence Cottages, Ilfracombe where he was a hotel plate cleaner. **In 1881** (57 and 43) they were still in Ilfracombe, living at 10 Chichester Place, and he was now a Butler. **In 1891** (67 and 54) they were living at 10 Springfield Road, Ilfracombe, and he (transcribed as John Walling Pine) was described as a Retired Butler.

Phillis died **15 June 1892** and administration of her estate was granted to her husband, now a lodging house keeper. Her address was given as Aberdare Cottage, Springfield Road, Ilfracombe and her estate amounted to £268.10s 11d. **In 1901** John D Pine was living (aged 77 and a Retired Butler) at 1 Gordon Terrace, Bristol, with Elizabeth Pine.

In 1902 (13 January) John Dalling Pine died. The Probate Date was 20 February 1902 and he died in Bristol. – the Probate Record lists him as a 'gentleman' living at 1 Gordon Terrace, Lower Belle-View, Clifton Bristol. The administration of his estate was granted to Elizabeth Pine, spinster, with his effects valued at £563.13s 4d (about £62,000 now).

11. Other branches of the Pine family mentioned in Elizabeth's Will: Charles Pine and his off-spring

In 1851, as noted above in section 9, Charles Pine (22) was still living at home with his father the older William Pine (62 and a painter it seems) at Clarence Cottages, Ilfracombe with his mother Mary (64), and sister Eliza (28).

In 1852 Charles Pine married Susan Edye (elsewhere spelt Eddy or Eddye) in Plymouth – she came from Cornwall. **In 1861** Charles Pine, a House Painter (32), and Susan Pine (34) were living at 7 Andrew Street, Bromley, Middlesex, with their sons Frederick (7 - born in 1854 in Plymouth), Tobias (4 - born in 1857) and Peter Eddy (1 - born in 1860). Charles Pine died, aged 36, in **1866**.

In 1871 we find in Cobden Street, Bromley St Leonard, London, the widow of Charles, Susan Pine (44), heading a household comprising Tobias (mis-transcribed as Falcus Pine - 13), Peter Pine (10), Nellie Pine (9), Edith Pine (7) and Susannah Pine (4).

In 1881 Susan Pine, a dress maker (aged 54 - having moved to Railway Street, Bromley, London), was heading a household comprising Tobias Pine, a sail maker (23), Peter Pine, a house painter (20), and Nellie Pine (19). There is in the records I have found for 1881 no sign of Susannah Pine (or Susan Elizabeth), Charles and Susan's daughter, who would have been 14. **In 1884** Peter Pine married Bridget McCarthy in Poplar. **In 1886** Susan Elizabeth Pine (19) got married to George Thomas Bevan (32) in the parish of St Leonard St Mary, Bromley, in the Borough of Tower Hamlets.

In 1891 Susan (24) and George (36) were living at 17 Perry Street, Northfleet, Gravesend. He was a cement labourer and their children were George (13), Walter (11) and Nellie (3). Also in 1891 we find Peter Pine (30 and a painter) and his wife Bridget (29) living at 35 Barchester Street, Bromley (parish of Bromley St Leonards, Bromley and Bow constituency) with their children Peter J (3) and Mary D (1) and with a lodger Fred Price. On 18 February 1891 Edith Dalling Pine married William Sibbald, a seaman (both aged 26) in the parish church of Bromley St Leonard. Nellie Pine and Tobias John Dalling Pine were witnesses. Later, in the 1891 census, we find Nellie Pine (29 – a milliners' assistant) and newlywed Edith D Sibbald visiting Southend in the household of a Thomas Whitton, a railway guard. In December **1896 in Poplar** Tobias John Dalling Pine (39) of 31 Railway Street, married Ann Maria Ashley (42), a widow (born Downey).

In 1901 living at 139 Brunswick Road, Bromley, (Poplar Tower Hamlets constituency), London, was Tobias Pine (43), a painter still, with his wife Ann (46). His mother Susan Pine was a widow of 74, dependant on her family, and living at 142 St Leonards Road, Bromley (Poplar - Tower Hamlets constituency). Also in 1901 we have Peter Pine (40 and still a painter) and his wife Bridget (39) living at 37 Southill Street, Poplar (parish of St Saviours, Poplar and Tower Hamlets constituency) with their children Peter (13), Mary (11), John (8), Nellie (4) and Frederick (2) with a cousin Kate McCarthy (24 – a laundry maid). William and Edith Dalling Sibbald (both 36) were living at 70 Evensleigh Road, East Ham, London with their children, Eric Stanley (9) and Hilda (0). Finally Nellie Pine (39 and a trained nurse) could be found at 39 Vicarage Lane, West Ham, in the household of an Elias White, a Licensed Victualler, for whom she was a nurse (although others of the household served as bar staff).

In 1911 still living at 139 Brunswick Road, Poplar, London (in a dwelling of 3 rooms) was Tobias John Dalling Pine (53 - and a Painter and Decorator in the shipping industry) with his wife Ann Maria Pine (58), they had been married 14 years but were childless. In the same year, living in a dwelling of 6 rooms, at 20 Perry Street, Northfleet , were Susan (44) and George Bevan (56) with a whole new family of 6 – Charles (19), Frederick (16), Victor (14), Edith (12), Marjorie (10), Dorothy (4),and John (0). George was still a fitter's labourer in cement, the 2 elder sons were grocer's assistants and Victor was a house boy (domestic).

Also in 1911 Peter Pine (50 - and a described as a ship painter) was still living in 5 rooms at 37 Southill Street, Poplar; curiously his wife's name was given as Sarah not Bridget (but in either case the age of 49 is the same). Of their children, Peter (23) and Mary (21) seem to have flown the nest, but their other children were with them: John (18 and also described as a ship painter), Nellie (14) and Frederick (12) and there was a further child William (9). In 1911 the elder Nellie Pine (49, single and a trained nurse) was living at 49 Edith Road, East Ham with her sister Edith Sibbald (46), Edith's husband for 20 years William (47 – a Master Mariner) and their son Eric Stanley (16). It is possible their daughter Hilda had died.

At present I am not able to add to their story save to say that Peter Pine died on **28 January 1924** (aged 63) at 37 Southill Street, Poplar. Administration of his effects (valued at £203 19s. 4d.) was granted to his widow, Bridget. Tobias J Pine died in **1934** (aged 76). Edith Dalling Pine (daughter of Charles) married to William Sibbald, a master mariner in 1891, had two children, Eric Stanley and Hilda. Gill Taylor advises me that Eric Stanley was one of the first 'chemical soldiers' and was killed in 1916, buried at Vlamertinghe. Edith Dalling Sibbald (widow, living at Eric Cot, Manor Road, Laindon) died **8 August 1945** and administration of her effects (of £2,086 2s. 8d.) was granted to her sister Susan Elizabeth Bevan (widow) and Susan's son, Frederick Pine (ships painter).

Nellie Eddy Pine of St James Hospital, Trafalgar Road, Gravesend, Kent, **died 22 October 1953** with effects of £1,159 Administration was granted to Susan Elizabeth Bevan, widow. She would have been about 89. Susan Elizabeth Bevan of 47 Perry Street,

Northfleet, **died 31 August 1956**. She would have been 91. Her effects (despite her inheritances from Elizabeth, Edith and Nellie) were valued at £1,214 17s. 5d. Administration was granted to John Bevan, cost accountant – presumably her youngest son, then aged 45.

It is clear that the off-spring of Charles Pine represented a fairly close-knit family. With at least 18 grand-children it is likely that a number of his great-great grandchildren are alive as my contemporaries today. Some 5 of his grandchildren were beneficiaries under Elizabeth Pine's will.

12. <u>Other branches of the Pine family mentioned in Elizabeth's Will: George Pine Senior and his off-spring</u>

In 1841 there was another family of Pines living at Walters Court, Ilfracombe. At its head was a George Pine who was married to a Sarah – both were 45 years of age (so born in c1796). I suspect that he was the brother of the elder William Pine. His children were Thomas (15), Charles (10), Mary (8), Sarah (6), John (4) and George (1 – so born 1840). These appear to be the cousins of Elizabeth Pine (albeit first removed). George, who 30 years later was married to a Jane and had a daughter Bessie was, with his wife Jane, mentioned in Elizabeth Pine's will (discussed in section 8 above).

In 1851 in Ilfracombe, at Parlement Court, was the man I have assumed to be William Pine Senior's brother – George Pine (60 in this case, so born c1791). He was a block maker and his household included his wife Sarah (57 in this case, so born c1794) and daughter Jane (45 – on Parish Relief), son James (22), daughter Sarah (16) and son George (11). The latter, as I have mentioned above, later married Jane and so was mentioned in Elizabeth's will. I will continue with his story in this section.

In 1861 George Pine senior (born 1791 or 1796) must have died as the census shows Sarah Pine (57? - Block Maker) was a widow and living at Water Street, Ilfracombe with her son James (30 – a hotel worker), Daughter Sarah Lock Pine (25 – a seaman's wife) and son George (21 – a seaman). However in **1871** at Fore Street, Albert Court, Ilfracombe we find George Pine (31), his wife Jane (30) and daughter Bessie Jane. There is then a gap in the records I have been able to trace.

In 1901 in Ilfracombe, at 7 Albert Street (not Court - nor Fore Street as in the transcription), we find the younger George Pine (61), a mariner, with his wife Jane (60), son James (23) a house painter, and daughter Francis T Pine (22) a domestic servant. Clearly George died subsequently because in **1911** in Ilfracombe, at 7 Albert Court, Jane Pine (71 and an old age pensioner and a widow) headed a household living in 4 rooms with her daughter Bessie Jane Pine (40 and single), son George Pine (36 - married and a night watchman) and son James Henry Hallet Pine (33 - single and a painter). **In 1915** Jane Pine died. She was 75 and had been listed as a beneficiary under Elizabeth Pine's will of 1908.

13. Conclusions on the Public Record

Thanks to my cousin Tony Daniels and especially his wife Sue, I have a family tree of the Daniels' family going back to the late 17th Century. I have seen also extensive family trees of the Beckingsales. However, the origins of my maternal grandfather, Frank Harold Pine (FHP), still retain an element of mystery. It is clear that he was brought up in a household with his grandfather and the grandfather's two daughters. The clear evidence is that FHP was the son of Mary Ann Pine who eventually obtained respectability from her marriage to William Urch. Yet questions remain – not least in terms of how Elizabeth came by her modest fortune.

The Hampshire link has offered significant opportunities for further research and, thanks to Theresa Douglas, I have a fair amount of material on Francis Spencer Hampshire, his parents, children and grandchildren that I have not reproduced here. It is interesting, but ultimately unproductive, to look at the faces of his grandchildren in Brazilian Immigration records of the 1940s to try and spot likenesses. Of course there is an issue of genetic inheritance and the debate about nature or nurture. In practice the family had no impact on FHP's story. To my mind FHP overcame the limitations of both nature and nurture. Indeed his story underlines the spur of ambition that can result from an unstable home background if linked to a desire to seek security in education, a stable family life and the approbation of a wider society. I have in mind also my capable and ambitious paternal grandmother Lucy (nee Mortimer) Daniels.

I am so very well aware that, when all is said and done, FHP's mother and her sister never intended that anybody would ever know what may now have been uncovered. I am sure that FHP knew the truth, but obviously he would not have wished anyone else to know. Being tight-lipped about his past, and concerned about the good names of his daughters, may also account from a tetchy temperament that my Aunt Connie experienced. Yet, all in all, FHP was a man whom his off-spring could be proud of and inspired by, a self-made man in the real sense of the word. He was a man who came from nothing and became a significant person in the local community and who did much good. He was an extraordinary man for his time.

14. <u>Postcript: Ann Pine</u>

Just when I thought I had gone as far as I could with Ann Pine a suitcase of family treasures sprang a surprise. It contained some materials passed to me by my Aunt Edna Pine. In 2001 at her final home – Waterhouse, Monkton Combe – I went through some pictures, with Edna, putting names to them. On the back of a rather elabourate frame I wrote 'Ann Pine, Mum's grandmother' without, at the time, really reflecting on who she was. Clearly Edna knew who she was in dictating what to put on the back of the frame! Also I am quite sure it is not Anne Beckingsale (she looked differently and was never a Pine), so here we have a picture of Ann Pine, Frank Pine's mother – probably at the age of about 45 in 1895 at the time she married William Urch. A keepsake she may have given her son not long before he joined the army. It is not difficult to see her in him in his later years. Subsequently I have discovered two more photographs that I am sure are also of her – perhaps in 1880 and 1890?

ANN PINE – c.1895?

ELIZABETH PINE's HOME: JACOB'S WELLS ROAD (SECOND RIGHT)

POSSIBLE PICTURES OF ANN PINE – c.1880 and c.1890?

M GUTTENBERG, PHOTO   BRISTOL.

W.H. MIDWINTER. Photographer.   BRISTOL.

THE ARTISTIC TALENTS OF FRANK PINE

THE GEORGE NORTON ST PHILIP

YORK MINSTER 1936

FHP had two flutes - a full sized one, and the one-key flute below that we still possess.

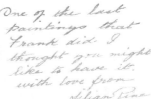

One of the last paintings that Frank did. I thought you might like to have it. with love from Lilian Pine

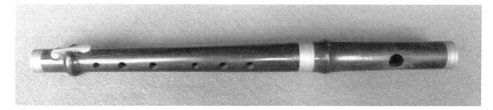

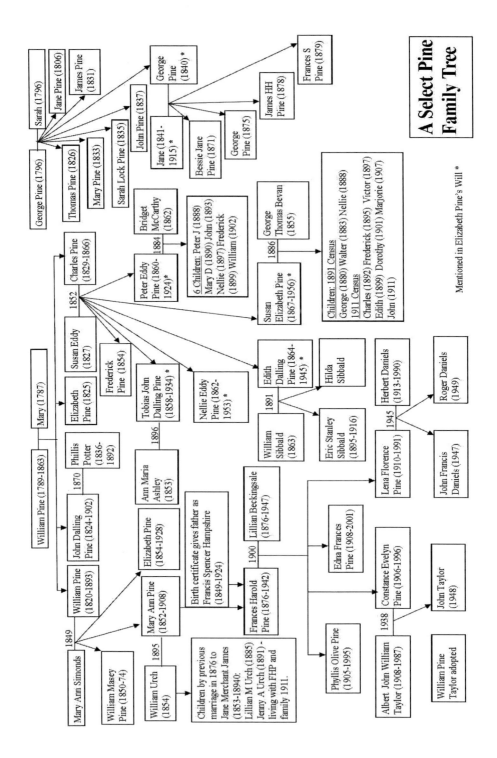

A Select Pine Family Tree

George Pine (1796)
Sarah (1796)
Jane Pine (1806)
James Pine (1831)
Thomas Pine (1826)
Mary Pine (1833)
Sarah Lock Pine (1835)
John Pine (1837)
George Pine (1840) *
Jane (1841-1915) *
Bessie Jane Pine (1871)
George Pine (1875)
James HH Pine (1878)
Frances S Pine (1879)

Mary (1787)
William Pine (1789-1863)
Charles Pine (1829-1866)
Elizabeth Pine (1825)
Susan Eddy (1827)
Frederick Pine (1854)

1852

Peter Eddy Pine (1860-1924)*
Bridget McCarthy (1862)
1884
6 Children: Peter J (1888) Mary D (1890) John (1893) Nellie (1897) Frederick (1899) William (1902)
Susan Elizabeth Pine (1867-1956) *
George Thomas Bevan (1855)
1886
Children: 1891 Census
George (1880) Walter (1883) Nellie (1888)
1911 Census
Charles (1892) Frederick (1895) Victor (1897) Edith (1899) Dorothy (1901) Marjorie (1907) John (1911)

Tobias John Dalling Pine (1858-1934) *
Nellie Eddy Pine (1862-1953) *
Edith Dalling Pine (1864-1945) *
William Sibbald (1863)
1891
Hilda Sibbald
Eric Stanley Sibbald (1895-1916)
Herbert Daniels (1913-1990)
Lena Florence Pine (1910-1991)
1945
Roger Daniels (1949)
John Francis Daniels (1947)

Phillis Potter (1836-1892)
John Dalling Pine (1824-1902)
1870
William Pine (1820-1893)
Elizabeth Pine (1854-1928)
Ann Maria Ashley (1853)
1896

Birth certificate gives father as Francis Spencer Hampshire (1849-1924)

Mary Ann Simonds
William Masey Pine (1850-74)
1849
Mary Ann Pine (1852-1908)
William Urch (1854)
1895

Children by previous marriage in 1876 to Jane Merchant James (1853-1894):
Lillian M Urch (1885)
Jenny A Urch (1891) - living with FHP and family 1911.

Frances Harold Pine (1876-1942)
Lillian Beckingsale (1876-1947)
1900
Edna Frances Pine (1908-2001)
Constance Evelyn Pine (1906-1996)
Albert John William Taylor (1908-1987)
1938
John Taylor (1948)
William Pine Taylor adopted
Phyllis Olive Pine (1905-1995)

Mentioned in Elizabeth Pine's Will *

DOCUMENTED RECORD OF THE PINE FAMILY

Year	Address	Name	Situation	Age	Where Born
1841	Clarence Cottage	William Pine	Head	50	Ilfracombe
	Ilfracombe	Mary Pine	Wife	50	Ilfracombe
	Devon	William Pine	Son	20	Ilfracombe
		Elizabeth Pine	Daughter	15	Ilfracombe
		John Pine	Son	15	Ilfracombe
		Charles Pine	Son	11	Ilfracombe
		William Marshall		50	Ilfracombe
1841	Walters Court	George Pine	Head	45	Devon
	Ilfracombe	Sarah Pine	Wife	45	Devon
	Devon	Thomas Pine	Son	15	Devon
		Charles Pine	Son	10	Devon
		Mary Pine	Daugher	8	Devon
		Sarah Pine	Daugher	6	Devon
		John Pine	Son	4	Devon
		George Pine	Son	1	Devon
1849	St Michael the Angel	William Pine	Marriage		
	on the Mount Bristol	Mary Ann Simmons	Marriage		
1850	Clifton Bristol	William Masey Pine	Birth		
1851	Clarence Cottage,	William Pine	Head/Painter	62	Berrynabor
	High Street	Mary Pine	Wife	64	Ilfracombe
	Ilfracombe Devon	Eliza Pine	Daughter	28	Ilfracombe
		Charles Pine	Son/Painter	22	Ilfracombe
1851	41 Windsor Terrace	Cooke Isaac A	Head/Solicitor	44	
	Clifton	Cooke Marjorie	Wife		
	Bristol	Cooke Agnes	Daughter		
		Cooke Geogina	Daughter		
		Elizabeth B	Servant		
		Sarah B	Servant		
		PINE, William (Footman)	Lodger/Married	31	Ilfracombe
1851	11 Princes Place	PINE Mary A	Married	26	Norfolk
	Clifton Bristol	PINE William M	Son	>1	Bristol Clifton
1851	Parlement Court	George Pine	Head/Block Maker	60	Berrynarbor
	Ilfracombe	Sarah Pine	Wife	57	Ilfracombe
	N Devon	Jane Pine	Daughter/Parish Relief	45	
		James Pine	Son/Servant	22	
		Sarah Pine	Daughter	16	Ilfracombe
		George Pine	Son	11	Ilfracombe
		Mary Jane Rees	visitor	15	Ilfracombe

Year	Address	Name	Situation	Age	Where Born
1851	Dyffryn House Aberdare Merthyr	Anabella Bruce 3 daughters, 6 servants incl	Head	30	
		John Dalling Pine	Footman	28	Ilfracombe
1852	Plymouth Devon	Charles Pine Susan Edye	Marriage Marriage		
1860	Poplar London	Peter Eddy Pine	Birth		
1861	Clifton Villa Clifton Park Clifton Bristol	Anne M Knowlys 3 daughters 4 other relatives	Head	53	
		William Pine	Widower/Butler	41	Ilfracombe
1861	Frome Street Clifton Bristol	Edward Symonds	Head/Porter	36	Yarmouth
		Fanny Symonds	Wife	34	Somerset
		Mary Ann Symonds	Daughter	13	Bristol
		Edward Symonds	Son	10	Bristol
		Fanny Symonds	Daughter	8	Bristol
		Samuel Symonds	Son	6	Bristol
		Rosina Symonds	Daughter	4	Bristol
		Eliza Symonds	Daughter	2	Bristol
		William Pine	Nephew	11	Bistol
1861	106 High Street Ilfracombe Devon	William Pine	Head/Painter	74	Berrynarbour
		Mary Pine	Wife	72	Ilfracombe
		Elizabeth Pine	Grand-daughter	7	Bristol
1861	Water Street Ilfracombe Devon	Sarah Pine	Widow/Block Maker	57	Ilfracombe
		James Pine	Son/Hotel Worker	30	Ilfracombe
		Sarah Lock Pine	Daughter/Seamans Wife	25	Ilfracombe
		George Pine	Son/Seaman	21	Ilfracombe
1861	7 Andrew Street Bromley London	Charles Pine	Head/House painter	32	Ilfracombe
		Susan Pine	Wife	34	Pymouth
		Frederick Pine	Son	7	Poplar
		Tobias JD Pine	Son	4	Poplar
		Peter Eddy Pine	Son	1	Poplar
1863	Ilfracombe Devon	William Pine	Death		
1866	Chelsea London	Charles Pine	Death		
1870	Barnstable Devon	John Dalling Pine Philis Potter	Marriage Marriage		
1871	28 Caledonia Place Clifton Bristol	Henry Marshall PINE, William	Physiciam & Surgeon Servant/Widower	51	Ilfracombe

Year	Address	Name	Situation	Age	Where Born
1871	27 Royal York Crescent Clifton Bristol	William W Brown	Head/Capt N Glos Militia	33	Bristol Glos
		Sarah Brown	Wife	28	Bristol Glos
		William H Brown	Son	5	Bistol Clifton
		Chrales W Brown	Son	4	Bistol Clifton
		Louis W Brown	Son	3	Bistol Clifton
		Ethel C W Brown	Daughter	1	Bistol Clifton
		Elsie M W Brown	Daughter	3m	Bistol Clifton
		Francis Chadney	Head Nurse Domestic	27	Hertfordshire
		PINE, Elizabeth	**Under Nurse Domestic**	**17**	**Bristol Clifton**
1871	8 Cotham Side, St James & St Paul Clifton Bristol	George F Atchley	Head	35	Gloucester
		Georgeana Atchley	Wife	22	Cornwall
		Edward GCF Aitcley			
			Son	2	Gloucester
		Shirley C Atchley	Daughter	0	Gloucester
		Caroline Laekey	Servant	19	Somerset
		Mary Ann Pyne	**Servant**	**19**	**Gloucester**
1871	Cobden St, Bromley St Leonard London	**Susan Pine**	**Head**	**44**	**Cornwall**
		Falcus Pine	**Son**	**13**	**Middlesex**
		Peter Pine	**Son**	**10**	**Middlesex**
		Nellie Pine	**Daughter**	**9**	**Middlesex**
		Edith Pine	**Daughter**	**7**	**Middlesex**
		Susannah Pine	**Daughter**	**4**	**Middlesex**
1871	Fore St, Albert Court Ilfracombe Devon	**George Pine**	**Head**	**31**	**Devon**
		Jane Pine	**Wife**	**30**	**Devon**
		Bessie Jane Pine	**Daughter**	**0**	**Devon**
1871	1 Clarence Cottages Ilfracombe Devon	**John Pine**	**Head/Hotel Plate Cleaner**	**47**	**Ilfracombe**
		Phillis Pine	**Wife**	**35**	**Middlesex**
1874	Bedminster, Somerset	**William Macey Pine**	**Death**		
1875		**William Amandus Urch**	**Marriage**		
		Jane Merchant James	**Marriage**		
1876	4 Montague St St James Bristol	**Francis Harold Hampshire**	**Birth**		
1876		**Lillian Beckingsale**	**Birth**		
1881	5 Waterloo Place Clifton Bristol	Hannah Peck	Refresment House Keeper		
		William Pine	**Lodger/Widower/Butler**	**61**	**Ilfracombe**

Year	Address	Name	Situation	Age	Where Born
1881	St Andrew St Wells	Edgar Chas Sumner Gibson	Head/Principal Colllege	33	
		Mary Grace Gibson	Wife	28	Somerset
		William Sumner Gibson	Son	4	Somerset
		Kenneth Sumner Gigson	Son	1	Yorkshire
		5 other servants plus:			
		Annie Pyne	**Nurse Domestic Servant**	29	**Bristol**
1881	8 Albert Road Clifton Bristol	Edward A Harley	Registrar Court, Solicitor	38	**Bristol**
		Jessie Harley	Wife	32	
		Mary Harley	Daughter	6	Bristol
		Edward M Harley	Son	5	Bristol
		Beatrice Harley	Daughter	3	Bristol
		Elizabeth Pine	**Servant/Nurse**	26	**Bristol**
		Charity A Belmont	Servant/Cook	27	
		Sarah Baker	Servant/Parlourmaid	20	
		Harriet Hill	Servant/Under Nurse	14	
1881	15 Wilson Street St Paul Bristol	William Williams	Head/Wood Sawyer	36	London
		Fanny L Williams	Wife	34	Gloucester
		Daniel Mitchell	Father in Law/Chelsea Pens	85	Somerset
		PINE, Frank	**Nurse Child**	**5**	**Bristol**
1881	Perry Street Bristol	**William A Urch**	**Head/Commercial Clerk**	**27**	**Bristol**
		Jane M Urch	**Wife**	**28**	**Bristol**
		Florence M Urch	**Daughter**	**4**	**Bristol**
		Edith A A Urch	**Daughter**	**3**	**Bristol**
1881	Railway Street Bromley London	**Susan Pine**	**Head**	**54**	**Cornwall**
		Tobias Pine	**Son/Sailmaker**	**23**	**Middlesex**
		Peter Pine	**Son/Painter (House)**	**20**	**Middlesex**
		Nellie Pine	**Daughter/House Maid**	**19**	**Middlesex**
1881	10 Chichester Place Ilfracombe Devon	**John Pine**	**Head/**	**57**	**Ilfracombe**
		Phillis Pine	**Wife**	**43**	**Middlesex**
1884	Poplar London	**Peter Eddy Pine**	**Marriage**		
		Bridget McCarthy	**Marriage**		
1886	St Leonard St Mary Bromley London	**George Thomas Bevan**	**Marriage**		
		Susan Elizabeth Pine	**Marriage**		
		Nellie Pine	Witness		
		Tobias John Dalling Pine	Witness		
1891	1, Gordon Terrace Clifton Bristol	**William Pine**	**Head/Wid/ Retired Butler**	**71**	**Ilfracombe**
		Mary Ann Pine	**Daughter/Nurse Domestic**	**39**	**Bristol**
		Elizabeth Pine	**Daughter/Nurse Domestic**	**37**	**Bristol**
		Frank Pine	**Grandson/Photo Assistant**	**14**	**Bristol**

Year	Address	Name	Situation	Age	Where Born
1891	159 Stapleton Road St Philip Bristol	William A Urch	Head/Merchants Clerk	37	Bristol
		Jane M Urch	Wife	38	Bristol
		Florence M Urch	Daughter	14	Bristol
		Edith A A Urch	Daughter	13	Bristol
		William H Urch	Son	8	Bristol
		Lillian M Urch	Daughter	6	Bristol
		Jenny A H Urch	Daughter	0	Bristol
1891	10 Springfield Road Ilfracombe Devon	John (Walling) Pine	Head	67	Ilfracombe
		Phillis (spelt Phyllis) Pine	Wife	54	Middlesex
1891	54 Park Street Southend	James Whitton	Railway Guard		
		Wife, niece & 2 railwayman boarders			
		Edith D Sibbald		26	London, Bromley
		Nellie Pine	Milliners Assistant	29	London, Bromley
1891	36 Barchester St Bromley London	Peter Pine	Head/Painter	30	London, Bromley
		Bridget Pine	Wife	29	Poplar
		Peter J Pine	Son	3	Poplar
		Mary D Pine	Daughter	1	Poplar
		Fred Price	Lodger	54	
1891	20 Perry Street Northfleet Gravesend	George Bevan	Head/Cement Labourer	36	Gravesend
		Susan Bevan	Wife/Laundress	24	Poplar
		George Bevan	Son	11	Kent, Northfleet
		Walter Bevan	Son	9	Kent, Northfleet
		Nellie Bevan	Daughter	3	Kent, Northfleet
1891	St Leonard St Mary Bromley London	William Sibbald	Marriage	26	
		Edith Dalling Pine	Marriage	26	
1893	Barton Regis Bristol	William Pine	Death		
1894	Barton Regis Bristol	Jane Merchant Urch	Death		
1895	Barton Regis Bristol	Mary Ann Pine	Marriage		
		William A Urch	Marriage		
1896	Poplar London	Tobias John Dalling Pine	Marriage/Painter		
		Ann Maria Ashley	Marriage		
		John Fenton	Witness		
		Edith J Sibbald	Witness		

Year	Address	Name	Situation	Age	Where Born
1897		Francis Harold Pine	Military Record		
1900	St John the Baptist Bathwick Bath	Francis Harold Pine	Marriage/Cashier Dairy Co		
		Lillian Beckingsale	Marriage (Certificate)		

Year	Address	Name	Situation	Age	Where Born
1901	2 Pulteney Grove Bathwick Bath	Francis Harold Pine	Head/Cashier to Dairy Co	24	Bristol
		Lillian Pine	Wife	24	Stratford on Avon
		John Charles Pinhorn	Head/Warehouse manager	30	Southampton
		Maria Jane Pinhorn	Wife	36	London
		May Edith Pinhorn	Daughter	11 m	Bath
1901	1 Gordon Terrace Clifton Bristol	John D Pine	Head/Wid/Retired Butler	77	Ilfracombe
		Elizabeth Pine	Niece/Nurse Domestic	46	Bristol Clifton
1901	Carlyle Road Easton Bristol	William A Urch	Head/Merch Shipping Clerk	47	Bristol
		Mary A Urch	Wife	47	Bristol
		Lillian M Urch	Daughter	16	Bristol
		Jenny A Urch	Daughter	10	Bristol
1901	139 Brunswick Road Bromley London	Tobias Pine	Head/Painter	43	Bromley
		Ann Pine	Wife	46	Bromley
1901	70 Evensleigh Road East Ham London	William Sibbald	Head/Mariner 1st Mate	36	Liverpool
		Edith Dalling Pine	Wife	36	Bromley
		Eric S Pine	Son	9	Bromley
		Hilda Pine	Daughter	0	East Ham
1901	39 Vicarage Lane West Ham London	Elias White	Head/ Licensed Victualler		
		Eleanor White	Wife		
		4 lodgers - bar staff			
		Nellie Pine	Nurse/Trained Nurse	39	
1901	37 Southill Street Poplar London	Peter Pine	Head/Painter	40	Poplar
		Bridget Pine	Wife	39	
		Peter Pine	Son	13	
		Mary Pine	Daughter	11	
		John Pine	Son	8	
		Nellie Pine	Daughter	4	
		Frederick Pine	Son	2	
		Kate McCarthy	Cousin/Laundry Maid	24	

Year	Address	Name	Situation	Age	Where Born
1901	142 St Leonards Road Bromley London	Susan Pine	Hd/Wid/Depend on Family	74	
1902	1 Gordon Terrace, Lower Belle-view Clifton Bristol	John Dalling Pine	Death		
1908	Bristol	Mary Ann Urch	Death		
1911	19 Forester Avenue Bath Somerset	Francis Harold Pine	Head/Cashier to Dairy Co	35	Bristol
		Lillian Pine	Wife	35	Stratford on Avon
		Phyllis Pine	Daughter	6	Bath
		Constance Pine	Daughter	4	Bath
		Edna Pine	Daughter	2	Bath
		Lena Pine	Daughter	1	Bath
		Jeannie Urch	General Servant Domestic	20	Bristol
1911	69 Jacobs Wells Road Clifton Bristol	Elizabeth Pine	Retired Nurse Domestic	56	Single
1911	69 Jacobs Wells Road Clifton Bristol	James Edwin Potter	Head/Brickmaker rtd OAP	85	Bristol St Phillips
		Ann Stokes Potter	Wife	84	Bradford on Avon
		Charlotte Anne Louisa Potter	Daughter/Dressmaker	41	
1911	Anworth Stapleton Bristol	William A Urch	Head/Widower/ Merchants Clerk	58	Bristol
		Florence Mary Urch	Daughter	34	Bristol
1911	139 Brunswick Road Bromley Poplar	Tobias J Dalling Pine	Head/Painter Decorator	53	Bromley
		Ann Maria Pine	Wife	58	Bromley
1911	7 Albert Court Ilfracombe Devon	Jane Pine	Head/Old Age Pensioner	71	Ilfracombe
		Bessie Jane Pine	Daughter	40	Ilfracombe
		George Pine	Son/Night Watchman	36	Ilfracombe
		James Henry Hallet Pine	Son/House Painter	33	Ilfracombe
1911	70 Evensleigh Road East Ham London	William Sibbald	Head/Master Mariner	47	Liverpool
		Edith Dalling Pine	Wife	46	Bromley
		Eric Stanley Sibbald	Son	16	Bromley
		Nellie Eddy Pine	Sister in law/Trained Nurse	49	Bromley

Year	Address	Name	Situation	Age	Where Born
1911	37 Southill Street Poplar London	Peter Pine	Head/Ship Painter	50	Poplar
		Bridget (Sarah) Pine	Wife	49	Poplar
		John Pine	Son/Ship Painter	18	Poplar
		Nellie Pine	Daughter	14	Poplar
		Frederick Pine	Son	12	Poplar
		William Pine	Son	9	Poplar
1915	Barnstaple Devon	Jane Pine	Death	75	
1924	37 Southill Street Poplar London	Peter Eddy Pine	Death	63	
1927	Bristol Gloucester	Elizabeth Pine	Death	74	Bristol
1934	Poplar London	Tobias J Pine	Death	76	
1943	17 The Firs, Combe Down Bath	Francis Harold Pine	Death	65	Bristol
1945	Eric Cot, Manor Road Laindon Essex	Edith Dalling Sibbald	Death	81	
1947	17 The Firs, Combe Down Bath	Lillian Pine	Death	70	Stratford on Avon
1953	St James Hospital, Trafalgar Rd Gravesend Kent	Nellie Eddy Pine	Death	89	
1956	47 Perry Street Northfleet Gravesend	Susan Elizabeth Bevan	Death	91	

THE YOUNG FRANK PINE (Dates are rough guesses)

c.1877   c.1879   c.1885

c.1885 Clifton Church School   c.1889 St Mary Redcliffe?

c.1898 The Kings Royal Rifles

THE YOUTHFULL FRANK PINE & MARRIAGE

Some pictures from the late 1890s - and after marriage 1900

With Phyllis and Connie and newly wed

NEWSPAPER ARTICLES ON FRANK HAROLD PINE (FHP) – AN OVERVIEW

The British Library Exercise

As noted above (pages 13 and 16), the British Library exercise of scanning past editions of national and local newspapers to produce a fully searchable archive is a massive exercise. I have been downloading articles mainly from the Bath *Weekly* Chronicle & Herald (which is so far all that has been scanned and released by the British Library) for the period 1900-1950.

Out of over 1,000 copies of the Bath Weekly Chronicle & Herald for the period 1922-1942 there are almost 300 entries relating to FHP. When (and if) the daily Chronicle & Herald comes on-line there could be much more than double this number of references. Key records of a street photo of FHP in the late 30s with Fred Cook (a member of the Chronicle's staff) and of the weddings of Connie Pine to Albert Taylor and Lena Pine to Herbert Daniels, of which we have separate copies, were only in the *daily* Chronicle & Herald – as doubtless were the births of sisters Connie, Edna and Lena Pine (only Phyllis' birth is recorded in the weekly paper).

In looking at these articles and reporting on them I have been disposed to record not only Frank Pine's views and roles in relation to various activities but also the range of people with whom he interacted and their views and roles. From all this emerges an interesting social history of a variety of evolving religious, philosophical, social and political attitudes against the background of rapidly changing society in terms of technology, the role of women, social security and medical needs - and much else. So I have taken advantage of the scope for diversions!

The Prominence of FH Pine

If there was almost a one in three chance of encountering FHP in the Weekly there were some issues in which he appeared in as many as 3 or 4 separate articles. Of course local papers then were nothing like their pale imitations these days (sadly the Bath Chronicle is now only a weekly) – every local event was chronicled in detail with many lists of names: as mentioned above, local papers were the Facebook of their time.

I have long been aware that FHP achieved a certain prominence in civic life – firstly as an auditor of the Bath Branch of the Hearts of Oak Friendly Society (and by 1926 he was its Chairman), then as Chairman of the Council of the Bath Friendly Societies from which he went on to be Chairman of the Bath Hospital Box Scheme, the aim of which was to rescue the main voluntary hospital, the Royal United Hospital, from the substantial debts it faced in the early 1920s and also to provide low income households with the assurance of free hospital and medical treatment. He was also a member of the RUH Management Board from 1934 until his death.

The Bath Hospital Box Scheme facilitated the removal of the RUH to a new site in Combe Park, Bath in 1931. In promoting the scheme (that depended on an army of local volunteers) FHP was tireless in attending meetings in Bath wards and in places around Bath, North Somerset and Wiltshire (e.g. Colerne, Castle Combe, Trowbridge and Bradford on Avon). Subsequently a scheme was developed for the more affluent middle classes based on treatment at the Forbes Fraser Hospital. Of course in this time the role of Poor Law/Municipal Hospitals (like St Martin's, Bath) was also developing.

As set out in a Chronicle article of 8 September 1923 the aim of the Hospital Box Scheme was to raise £5,000 annually *(about £250,000 in current terms)* to meet an RUH deficit of £5,000 per annum. Boxes would be placed in 12,000 households to collect two pence a week (c £1 a week now) and emptied quarterly. It was a Friendly Society scheme independent, but in close connection with, the Hospital Managing Board. It had a Central Executive comprising Frank Pine as Chairman of the Council and 5 others including the Chairman of the Hospital Management Board. There were District Committees and area stewards.

The Mayor, Alderman Cedric Chivers was to take an active interest in scheme through meetings with ward Councillors. Each ward would have a Chairman, Secretary, Treasurer and a dozen stewards. When the NHS began in June 1948 the distinction between Municipal Hospitals (like St Martin's) and Voluntary Hospitals (like the RUH) had been blunted by wartime requirements. However in September 1947, with the Box Scheme due to end the next June, the total amount collected in the previous quarter was £7,058 or £28,000 in a year. Even so the RUH debt was £52,401 (about £1.9m in current terms) – due mainly to the war: escalating pharmaceutical costs and extra patients.

From the early 20s until the mid 30s, at the same time as he was involved in the Hospital Box Scheme, FHP was almost continuously the Chairman of the lower tier local authority for Combe Down (under the Bath Rural District Council) – the Monkton Combe Parish Council. He was also involved in church affairs and was a school governor, and chaired fund-raising whist drives. In whatever he did he seemed to gravitate to a leading role. In 1922 in a report on a Wilts & Somerset Farmers Staff Charabanc outing to Cheddar and Weston-Super-Mare it is stated that "F H Pine was in the chair supported by C T Francis & H G Collett".

As Chairman of the Combe Down Council he was involved in a range of issues – lighting and sewerage for Combe Down, the amenities of the Firs Field, maintenance of the war memorial, help to the unemployed and to those affected by the Somerset Floods of the early 30s, and the need to build council houses.

In 1927, given the burden of the Hospital Box Scheme, FHP resigned the chairmanship of the local council but remained as vice-chairman. A newspaper article stated he "has rendered very useful service to the 'Down' where he has resided for some years, and in many ways benefited the inhabitants by his tenure in office, for he had all the work at his finger-ends, and displayed a vision which is not commonly found on the lesser local government bodies."

In 1931 the issue of Combe Down joining Bath was proposed by the city. As (once again) Chairman of the Council, FHP sought to be non-committal - but Captain Daubeny, the Combe Down representative on the RDC, came with an unannounced petition and a motion favouring a Combe Down ratepayers view of not joining Bath (with a seconder already arranged). I suspect FHP was not best pleased to be ambushed in this way. After the vote in favour of the motion he said "that whatever happened now or in ten years time, the day would come when Combe Down would be absorbed in Bath, They might resist that as they would, but it was his private opinion." Combe Down did not join Bath until the mid 1950s.

Although he attended a Conservative and Unionist gathering in 1912 I do not see FHP as being a party political person. In 1931 the Labour Party on Combe Down got 4 councillors (including Mr Cornish and Mr Miller) onto the council and FHP was ousted in the elections. Mr Cornish was not elected to the Chair, and with Mr Cornish's support FHP was seconded to the Council to resume as Chair, with Mr Cornish as his deputy, until he left the council in 1934.

At the end of 1931 Mr Miller died, and in January 1932 Vice-Chairman Mr Cornish proposed FHP as a full member - as someone who had been nominated and put before the ratepayers. He said "quite irrespective that, quite recently they were placed in a peculiar position, and Mr Pine acted resourcefully, courageously and promptly. He thought it would be an act of grace and justice on the part of the Council definitely to co-opt him as a member of the council. He felt personally that it would come better from him than anyone else to make the proposition, as Mr Miller and he had as much to do with Mr Pine's defeat as anyone". Recognising the way that Mr Pine had dealt with one or two matters, not only the matter connected with the Clerk, but one or two others, he moved that Mr Pine be seconded as a member. A Mr Millett (not Miller!) seconded and the motion was carried unanimously.

Mr Pine thanked them and said he was pleased he had won the confidence of the gentlemen who, to put it bluntly, had 'kicked him out' the last time. Since those who had turned him out had worked with him it had been a happy experience and totally different from what he had expected. They had worked very harmoniously and Mr Cornish had stood by him most loyally.

There are many other stories that can be read from these articles. As they report, FHP attended a great many funerals of the great and the good of Bath. He attended the re-opening of the Assembly rooms in 1938. The development of the Hospital Scheme and the many issues Combe Down Council addressed - including the growing pressures for council housing (he was in favour) - can be followed. In 1932 FHP resigned as Chairman of the Hospital Box Scheme but remained as Vice-Chairman until his death in 1942. He remained a very active Vice-Chairman. In 1934 he stood down from Combe Down Council and Mr RW Cornish became Chairman.

To some extent two key press cuttings *that are reproduced on the next page* give an overview from 17 February 1923 (A Busy Combe Down Man) to 25 April 1942 (his obituary that was published on the eve of the Bath Blitz which gutted the Assembly Rooms). FHP's life reflected the evolution of the modern welfare state from the role of the Friendly Societies (that first offered some assurance against unemployment and ill health).

MR. FRANK H. PINE.

A Busy Combe Down Man and His Public Offices.

Mr. Frank Harold Pine, who has just been elected chairman of the Bath Friendly Society Council, is a gentleman well known in every part of this city. He is a Bristolian, but came to Bath in 1899, and had been with the Bath and Somerset Dairy Company for 23 years until last year, when he became head cashier to Norton St. Philip Dairy Co. (Ltd.). Mr. Pine lives at Combe Down, where he takes a keen interest in the amenities of the place. He is Chairman of the Monkton Combe Parish Council, of which he has been a member for some years. In addition to this office he is an overseer of the parish, and a sidesman at Holy Trinity, Combe Down. For 24 years he has been a member of the Hearts

of Oak Society and has acted as President of the Bath branch, besides being a county member of the Federation for many years. Mr. Pine, who, among his numerous offices, is an active member of the committee of the local horticultural society, holds the opinion that young men do not take up public work as they should, and believes that the community would be better for it if they did. As he is now only 47 years of age the above record of his work will show that he has not been idle in regard to these matters so far as his own life is concerned.

BATH HOSPITAL SCHEME PIONEER

DEATH OF MR. FRANK PINE

A pioneer of the Bath Region Hospital Contributory Scheme, and a well-known figure in the business life of the city, Mr. Frank Harold Pine passed away at his home, 17, The Firs, Combe Down, on Friday, at the age of 65.

His death, which will be deplored by a wide circle of friends, follows a lengthy illness.

Mr. Pine was one of a small band of enthusiasts who, 20 years ago, under Friendly Society auspices, launched the Hospital

The late Mr F. H. Pine

"Box Scheme," of which he later became the chairman. He resigned this position in 1932, since when he had been vice-chairman.

He was also a member of the Management Board of the Bath Royal United Hospital.

Combe Down Council Chairman.

Among Mr. Pine's other public work was membership of Monkton Combe (Combe Down) Parish Council, of which he was chairman for two or three years.

In the days of the old Bath and Somerset Dairies, he was assistant manager, under Mr. Baylis Tucker, and afterwards was for a time manager of the Norton Dairies.

Subsequently he joined the administrative staff of Spear Bros. and Clark, Ltd., at Bath.

He was an amateur artist of considerable talent, and an enthusiastic photographer.

He is survived by a widow and four daughters

THE NEWSPAPER RECORD 1901-1919

The *Bath Journal* was first published in 1743, and was later renamed *Boddely's Bath Journal*. It was subsequently renamed *Keene's Bath Journal* in January 1822, and was eventually taken over by the *Bath Herald* in March 1916. The newspaper also originated from the *Bath Chronicle and Universal Register* taking over from the *Bath Advertiser* which was published from 1755. By 1919 it had changed its name to the *Bath and Wilts Chronicle* as a result of a merger with another paper. The *Bath Herald* was merged with the *Bath Chronicle* in 1925 to become the *Bath Chronicle and Herald*, and that then was also the title of the weekly edition of the paper (until amended in 1936 to *Bath Weekly Chronicle and Herald*). The *Somerset Guardian* and the *Wiltshire News* were to continue as separate titles.

In an article from April 1925 (mentioned in the next paragraph) it was noted that the Chronicle and the Herald had their origins in the 18th century but the publication of daily editions had only begun in the last 50 years. For the sake of the narrative about Frank Pine it is worth recording that the Board of the newspaper company as constituted in April 1925 was primarily from the old Chronicle board with the addition of Col. Egbert Lewis and his son Capt. Alfred Lewis (presumably both from the Herald) with Sir Harry T Hatt as Chairman. (Col. Egbert Lewis was RUH chairman for over 20 years; both he and Sir Harry T Hatt had a long association with the RUH and the box scheme into the 1930s.)

The early 1960s (after the ending of the weeky edition) was a time for another minor name change of the daily paper to *Bath and Wilts Evening Chronicle.* In October 2007, the *Bath Chronicle* switched from daily to weekly publication, every Thursday. The paper celebrated its 250th anniversary in October 2010, publishing a special supplement to mark the occasion *(Source: Wikipedia and an article in the daily and weekly first editions of the Bath Chronicle and Herald of 14 and 18 April 1925 respectively).*

Most of the early entries below are from the Bath Chronicle dated Thursday. As is now the case, Thursday was a popular date for the publication of a weekly journal. Later, from 1912 onwards, the publication date was a Saturday. I have used underlinings for headings, dates and to highlight key issues, bold for **key speeches or comments**, and italics for *committee members*.

1900-1919: The Dairy, The Hearts of Oak Era, Early Family mentions and a military wedding (16 Articles)

The first newspaper entry on Frank Pine is in the Bath Chronicle of Thursday 25 July 1901. It reads **"On Friday Evening a pleasant ceremony at the Bath & Somerset Dairy** – the assistant secretary Mr Paull was presented with a marble timepiece on the occasion of his approaching marriage; on behalf of the staff Mr F H Pine Cashier made the presentation, in a few well chosen words, in the presence of a large number of staff."

Before moving on to the next newspaper entries involving FHP it is worth recording that in the Bath Chronicle of Thursday 6 February 1902 (Page 5) there is an article on **The Loyal Order of Ancient Shepherds** *and their annual financial meeting. Amongst those present at the Home Lodge 955 was* **JC Pinhorn** *(one of the auditors) who was a Pine family friend: he, and his wife and daughter May, lived in the same house as the newly-wed Frank and Lillian Pine in 1900. I remember his daughter,* **May Pinhorn** *as a good friend of my mother and her sisters. Also present was* **HC Lavington** *(one of the secretaries) who was instrumental in the creation of the Hospital Box Scheme.*

The next 3 articles show Frank Pine similarly involved in the semi-social activities of the Hearts of Oak. In the Bath Chronicle of Thursday **22 February 1903** it's the **Hearts of Oak Benefit Society Second Annual Dinner**. There were some 240 or so in Assembly Rooms, with the Mayor presiding, and FHP is listed 'amongst those present' in a list of about 60. Mr HC Lavington responded to a toast.

In the following year the Chronicle of **Thursday 3 March 1904** reports on the **3rd annual dinner of Bath Branch of the Hearts of Oak** at the Assembly Rooms: around 150 were present with **FH Pine and H Beckingsale** listed as members of the local committee - H Beckingsale is reported as proposing a toast. Also present were **HC Lavington, AC Wills and HF Fiddes** (whose names turn up in later times with the Box Scheme).

The next year the Chronicle of Thursday **9 February 1905** notes that 80 were at the Bath Branch Annual Dinner at Fortt's Restaurant including **H Beckingsale Hon. Secretary of the Bath Branch and FH Pine**. Matters mentioned included payments for Sick Pay and Funerals, those in distress and mortgages. Mr Wills, Mr Fiddes and Mr Beckingsale proposed toasts. The evening concluded with some musical entertainment.

Next are some more personal items. On the front advertisements page of the Bath Chronicle (established 1767 and 'Advertiser for Somerset, Gloucester, Wilts, Dorset, Devon, Cornwall and South Wales') for **Thursday 9 March 1905** is a simple family announcement **"Pine: On March 2nd at 19 Forester Avenue, the wife of Frank H Pine, a daughter"** to record the *birth of Phyllis*.

I have the following photograph which is my only documented record of Frank Pine's photographic work, although I am sure the family groups at the begining of this book are by him. On the back of the photograph in FHP's handwriting is "Phyllis Olive, 24th July 1905 Age 4 months 3 weeks, Taken by "Daddy".

There is then a gap in the press reports until Thursday **9 February 1911** when a report on **Bathwick Sunday School lists Connie Pine** as an infant (NB the Pines had not moved to Combe Down yet - see also the census record referred to above in the chapter on FHP's early years).

So we are back to reports on the Bath Branch of the **Hearts of Oak Friendly Society**. On Thursday **23 February 1911** is a report of the Bath Branch Annual Dinner at Fortt's Restaurant. Those present included the Mayor TB Silcock, Alderman Knight and several councillors including AW Wills. **FH Pine is listed as one of the hon. auditors and HF Fiddes is assistant hon. secretary.** Mr Beckingsale sent a telegram regretting his absence. The Mayor spoke of plans on coronation day for a happy day for the children (with parties etc). Mr FH Pine toasted the visitors. For the concluding entertainment Mr J Russell (accompanied by Miss Daisy Russell) played solos on the trumpet and post horn.

My friend Philip Russell was pleased to see this reference to his great grandfather and the musical family that were his great-grandfather's offspring. The J. Russell referred to in connection with the Hearts of Oak meeting is Philip's great grandfather Joseph Russell and Daisy was his eldest child. It is interesting that our respective families crossed paths early on, even if only tangentially. Daisy was a member of the Pump Room Orchestra, as were Joseph and Philip's grandfather Reg (whose biography Philip has written) and possibly some of the other Russells.

Bathonians as State Trumpeters

The State trumpeters waiting to sound a fanfare on the arrival of the judges at the Bristol Assize Courts last week. On the right is Mr. Joseph Russell, who has for 30 years performed this duty. On this occasion he was assisted by his son, Mr. Reg. Russell.

All of them obviously picked up work wherever they could, like this 'gig', and they could all play several instruments, as the occasion demanded. Daisy married the RPO's clarinettist Walter Lear and they subsequently moved to London, where Walter became perhaps the foremost British classical clarinettist and saxophone player of his generation, playing as principal soloist with the Royal Philharmonic Orchestra, the BBC Symphony Orchestra and the orchestra of the Royal Opera House, among others. He was also an influential teacher and was for many years Professor of Saxophone at Trinity College of Music, London. Sadly, none of the Russells ever achieved anything like his fame. I have above a picture from the Bath Chronicle of 5 July 1924 of Joseph and Reg Russell.

The Bath Chronicle of **Saturday 2 March 1912** has two interesting reports on the same page. Firstly there is the **Hearts of Oak Bath AGM** where HL Fiddes read the Annual Report and referred to a mass meeting in the Guildhall in November 1911 on the subject of National Insurance and to the annual outing - this time to Castle Combe. The penultimate paragraph records that FHP was elected auditor of Hearts of Oak Bath Branch. In conclusion members were encouraged to join the government scheme under the **1911 National Insurance Act** through the Hearts of Oak in preference to other societies. The other article concerns the **'Combe Down Unionists - Annual Supper and Smoking Concert'** at the Victoria Rooms, Hadley Arms, Combe Down. Amongst the people listed are the following names familiar to me: F Pearce, FG Frankling, **R Daniels**, F Appleby, H Ings, **Pine** *(no initials)* and W Dallimore *(whose son or grandson produced the booklet listed in my bibliography)*. Captain Daubeny sent apologies for his absence.

Returning to the Hearts of Oak theme we have in the Saturday **18 July 1912** Chronicle a report on the **Hearts of Oak Annual Outing** by charabanc and taxi cabs to Downside Abbey with 70 people on the trip of which almost 60 are listed including FH Pine, H F Fiddes, W J Scudamore (Senior & Junior) and AC Burrell. *The adjoining article is interesting as it discusses the extent to which the 1911 National Insurance Act covered women (answer: compared with 11-12 million working men contracted to an employer only 3 million women similarly employed were covered - as married working women were not covered).*

On **14 December 1912** there is a report of **Bath and Somerset Dairy Presentations** relating to a Miss Fellows who was leaving to get married, after 10 years service with the company in a clerical role. She was presented with a dinner service, carver rests and an autograph album (inscribed) by the staff and the directors of the company gave her a cheque. In the absence of the general manager Mr Tucker, **Mr Pine** the Cashier made one of the presentations.

In the seven column page 5 of the (presumably broadsheet) Bath Chronicle of Saturday **18 November 1913** the sixth column is headed **'Local Intelligence'** and item 15 reports on a **Committee Meeting of the Hearts of Oak Bath Branch** (at which FHP was present). The meeting concluded there should be no income limit to medical benefits under the 1911 National Insurance Act. On a more light-hearted note The Bath Chronicle of **Saturday 23 August 1913** records a **Hearts of Oak Benefit Society annual trip** (Page 6, Column 4), There were 60 in 4 horse brakes on a trip to Edington, Wilts via Hilperton and thence to the Monastery Garden and lake. The return journey begun at 7.30pm was via Westbury, Trowbridge and Bradford on Avon - returning to Bath at 11.00pm. FHP, H and B Beckingsale *(Lillian Pine's brothers)*, WJ Scudamore (junior and senior) and HF Fiddes were in the party.

We next move to 1915 and **Saturday 13 March 1915** where, on page 5 column 4 (the second column under the heading **'Local Intelligence'**) item 4 reports that at the **Hearts of Oak AGM** FHP was again appointed auditor. There was reference to the death of a Mr Piggott of Harringay, London, born in 1818, who had joined Hearts of Oak in 1843 (the year of its foundation) - so he had been a member for over 72 years!

The Bath Chronicle of Saturday **20 November 1915** page 5 has in the third column of **'Local News of the Week'** an item entitled **'Military Wedding at Claverton'** reporting that on Sunday November 14th an ex Bath Rugby Club and Sapper George Johnson had married the daughter of an RSM Royal Field Artillery. The bridegroom was on 3 days leave before returning to active service in France. **Frank Pine** (Late Corporal 3rd Kings Royal Rifles) was Best Man.

The last entry for this decade is from **22 March 1917**. In **'Local News'** (column 2 item5) **The Annual Meeting of the Bath Branch of the Hearts of Oak Benefit Society** at the Foresters Hall is reported. **FHP is now Hearts of Oak Vice President as well as auditor.** *Officers elected were: President, Mr W J Scudamore; Vice President, Mr F H Pine; Treasurer, Mr A W Wills; Secretaries, Messrs F Hamblin and H F Fiddes; Auditors, Messrs F H Pine and G Haverfield; Friendly Societies Council, Messrs F H Pine, G Haversfield, G Morris, W Davey, F Hamblin and H Fiddes etc.*

THE NEWSPAPER RECORD 1920-1925

1920-1925: A Challenging Time for a Busy Combe Down Man (57 Articles)

There are gaps in the newspaper records that could undoubtedly be filled to some extent if all the local newspaper editions could be accessed. So we now move into the 1920s and the first reference to FH Pine as a member of Monkton Combe Parish Council. He was clearly making a major contribution from the start.

1920: The Parish Council

As noted above, the Firs Field was purchased in 1917 by public subsctiption (with a view to it being a public common with a war memorial) and entrusted to the local council. However it posed many problems for the council to solve. The Bath Chronicle of **19 June 1920** is headlined **"Combe Down Affairs - Letting of Firs Field - Disposal of fire appliances".** *This meeting of Monkton Combe Parish Council had Mr Miles in the Chair, with FH Pine, W Williams, F C Appleby and the Clerk Mr Page.* The key issue was the use of the Firs Field as a recreation ground that had been used for grazing. "The Chairman said that that the first question was to determine the rent for the Firs Field. Prior to the erection of the Church Army Hut, Mr Pearce had paid £10 a year for the use of it, and had a right to mow it, and to keep people off it. Now it was a recreation ground and they must be cautious how they dealt with it. Mr Williams said he understood when the field was handed over to the Parish Council no fence was to be put up there. Those were the terms on which the council took it over, The Clerk (Mr Page) observed that it would be difficult to carry on a tennis court without a fence of some sort."

"Mr Pine asked if Mr Pearce had made any offer for the field. The Chairman said he had mentioned £3 or £4 and he had told him such a sum could not be considered. Mr Pine: If he is only going to pay a small sum the field had better be kept vacant; £3 or £4 is not worth considering. Mr Appleby asked if they could not let it for a short period for sheep to eat the grass off. Mr Williams said they should let it by the month, and thus be left free to take it for their own purposes when desired. The Clerk said it was rateable: £6 being assessed to the Parish Council, and £4 to the Church Army. It was a recreation ground, not agricultural land and the rates would come to about £2 10s a year." It was decided to go for monthly rentals of 10s for sheep grazing. The disposal of unwanted fire appliances (mainly 170 feet of hose) was also considered. Mr Pine proposed that £15 15s be asked for them.

The Firs Field would be a continuing preoccupation of the parish council and on Saturday **28 August 1920**, the next report on Combe Down Affairs was subtitled **'Misuse of Recreation Ground - Member Resigns in Protest'** *This was a report from the previous*

Tuesday's meeting of Monkton Combe Parish Council with Mr Miles in the Chair, supported by FJ Brown, FH Pine, EA Russell & W Williams. Mr FC Appleby had resigned to protest at vandalism of the Firs Field. FHP proposed his resignation should not be accepted and that he be asked to complete his term in office. FHP also proposed that games might be played on Firs Field by children under 16. Increased allotment rents and restored winter gas public lighting was also discussed - with the Bath Gas Company to be asked to tender for 21 lamps. It was reported that Bathford Parish Council did not want the discarded fire appliances.

For the third and last report I have from 1920 (of what may have been as many as 12 council meetings that year) we go to the Bath Chronicle of Saturday **20 November 1920** with a report entitled **'Combe Down Affairs - New Housing Sites Proposed - Firs Field Fences in Disrepair'.** *At this meeting of Monkton Combe Parish Council Mr Miles was in the Chair, supported by E Dudley, FH Pine, EA Russell, J & W Williams, FC Appleby (back in harness) and Mr Page (Clerk).* Dilapidation of the Firs Field Fences had been reported by the tenant to whom the field had been let at £6 per annum for sheep grazing. Mr Williams proposed delaying restoration until bylaws had been obtained and the Firs Field Recreation Committee had considered the matter. An application for additional North Road lighting was refused as an unnecessary expense. Mr E Dudley of the Rural District Council attended the meeting and raised the need for sites for a new local housing scheme, Mr Pearce's field at the top of the Carriage Drive, as proposed by Mr Dudley was discounted, and the cricket field was proposed. Four houses were being built in Monkton Combe.

1921: The War Memorial Unveiled and The Parish Council

War Memorial, Combe Down.

Let's move on to what reports we have from 1921. Firstly, on Saturday **23 May 1921** there is an article with 4 headings **'Reason of the War - God's Plan to Punish the World – Remarkable Address by the Rev D McLean - Unveiling of Combe Down's War Memorial'** (The war memorial was, and is, in the Firs Field and, according to this report was "built of the best Combe Down oolite, which has splendid wearing quality" - a statement soon to be tested!). The procession to the Memorial included members of the Parish Council Mr Miles (Chairman), Mr FH Pine, Mr W Williams and Mr E P Page (Clerk) and, amongst others, the Rev. A Richardson a former Vicar of the parish (and who gave his name to the road that was eventually re-named 'The Firs').

Mrs Cannon gave an address that, for the sake of the 50 Combe Down people who fell, looked to turning away from the old ways to a future of peace and love - a world federation, a league of nations. This was a *rather more inspiring address than the one that followed from the Rev. D McLean.*

The Rev. D McLean spoke of those who blamed God for allowing the war. But, he said, the Bible saw war as Gods punishment: he referred to Austria who had persecuted messengers of the cross, Serbia which had shared in the selfishness and greed that had marked the end of the Balkan war. Russia had ruled its people with a barbaric tyranny and persecuted God's people, the Jews - and France had given herself over to atheism and immorality. Belgium under King Leopold had massacred black people in the Congo, and Germany had succumbed to the gospel of brute force. Japan had become puffed up with conceit from a newly found importance, and Turkey was guilty of the murder of thousands of innocent Armenians. Britain's sins included greed and the grinding of the poor.

So for light relief we continue to the report of **27 August 1921** with 4 headings **'Combe Down Affairs - Lighting not to be increased - Stones thrown at the War Memorial - Warning to Neglectful Allotment Owners'.** *This meeting of Monkton Combe Parish Council had Mr Miles in the Chair, supported by FH Pine, EA Russell & Mr E P Page (Clerk).* On the basis of a Gas Company quotation it was decided to stick with 22 street lights because going to 42 lights would be too costly a burden on the rates. Mr Pine agreed with not doubling the number of lights unless they were clearly needed. Action against neglectful allotment holders was proposed as Mr Pine said they were unfair to the others. A local blacksmith **(presumably Robert Daniels)** was to give an estimate for new gate to access the Firs Field from The Avenue. With regard to boys throwing stones at the war memorial, Mr Pine said he believed there were a few marks on the memorial. The stone throwers were not local boys, but boys who came there in connection with the Fresh Air Fund or something of the sort.

1922: Chairing the Parish Council, Death of Mrs W Beckingsale, two dairy-oriented activities

In 1922 Frank Pine was elected Chairman of Monkton Combe Parish Council as we discover in the entry for 22 April - and he was acting as chairman for the meeting (had he already effectively taken over from Mr Miles?). However we first we begin with the death of his mother-in-law, Anne Beckingsale, who lived with them at 17 The Firs. Perhaps with 6 women in his household he had been glad to get out a bit!

A report dated Saturday **18 March 1922** on **'The late Mrs W Beckingsale'** states "The funeral took place on Wednesday afternoon *(15/3/22)* at Monkton Combe Cemetery of **Mrs W Beckingsale of 17 Richardson Avenue *(later The Firs)*** Combe Down, whose death took place on Saturday *(11/3/22)*.

The deceased was the widow of Mr William Beckingsale, of Cheltenham, and was in her 84th year. Prior to the interment, a service was held in Monkton Combe parish church at which the Rev GE Watton (Vicar of Combe Down) officiated. The mourners were Mr Horace Beckingsale (son), Mr Hubert Beckingsale (son), Mrs F Fullman (daughter), Mr & Mrs FH Pine (son in law and daughter) Mr S Beckingsale (stepson), Mr G Wiltshire, Frome (cousin), Mr Frank Wiltshire (cousin).

Those unable to attend through illness were Mr E Beckingsale, Cheltenham (brother-in-law), Mr WR Armstrong, Wootton Bassett (cousin), and Mr A Humphries, Wootton Bassett (cousin). Floral tributes were sent from Mr & Mrs Horace Beckingsale (London), Mr and Mrs F Fullman (London), Mrs Filer and family (Bristol), grandchildren, Mr and Mrs F Wiltshire, Mr and Mrs EH Wherrett, Mr & Mrs FH Pine, Mr Hubert Beckingsale and Mr S Beckingsale. The undertaker was Mr EH Wherrett." Anne Beckingsale (nee Dash) is pictured here at the back of 17 The Firs, probably late 1921.

In a report dated **22 April 1922 'Monkton Combe Council'** it was stated that "Mr FH Pine presided at the annual meeting of the Monkton Combe Parish Council held at the Church Rooms on Tuesday evening. *There were also present Messrs W Miles, FR Munday, FJ Brown, T Sansum, F Miller, J Williams, H Robinson and EP Page (Clerk).* Mr FJ Brown moved that Mr FH Pine be elected chairman for the ensuing year. Mr Munday seconded. Mr J Williams thought that Mr Miles should be re-appointed and embodied this in an amendment which did not find a seconder. The resolution was then carried by 5 votes to 2.

"Mr Pine responded and moved a vote of thanks to Mr Miles for his faithful service in the past. Mr H Robinson was elected Vice-Chairman. The retiring overseers - Messrs F Pine and Mr FGV Frankling were re-appointed with the council's thanks for their previous services. Upon the motion of Mr T Sansum, Messrs H Robinson and FJ Brown were appointed managers for the Combe Down and Monkton Combe Schools respectively. Messrs FH Pine, H Robinson and W Miles were elected trustees for the W Russell Bequest." Mr Page went through the annual accounts. Tenders were to be invited to repair the footpath between 11 and 12 Richardson Avenue.

Next we have a fairly brief item of **13 May 1922** on the **Monkton Combe Council** *attended by FH Pine in the Chair supported by Messrs FJ Brown, F Miller, H Robinson, EA Russell, T Sansum, J Williams, and EP Page (Clerk)*. "Extracts from the agreement conveying the Firs Field to the parish were read, and a discussion took place concerning the clauses prohibiting cricket and football. There being a right of way through the field, cricket with the regulation hard leather ball was considered dangerous, especially within the narrow limits of the field. The clerk was instructed to write to the donors for their views on the matter.....The Chairman hoped that the Prior Park authorities would consent to their band playing again in the Firs during the season."

Now another funeral and the first recorded attendance of Frank Pine at the commemoration of one of Bath's great and good. The Chronicle of **3 June 1922** records the **funeral of Mr G Weaver** aged 76 and, the article claimed, the inventor of the Penny-In-The Slot Weighing machine. He was a member of Weaver & Sons Bond Street and lived at Lansdown House for 42 years. Mr H Baylis Tucker and Mr FH Pine represented the old Bath & Somerset Dairy Company. *It may be noted that in the Chronicle obituary of Frank Pine it is stated "In the days of the old Bath and Somerset Dairies he was Assistant Manager under Mr Baylis Tucker and for a time manager of the Norton Dairies."*

Although I have a photo of Frank and Lillian Pine seemingly in charge of a Spear Brothers & Clark Charabanc Outing in 1928 - here is a report from **17 June 1922** of a **Wilts & Somerset Farmers Staff Outing**. "A happy party, numbering over 90, were taken in three char-a-bancs of the Bath Electric Tramways on their annual staff outing to Cheddar and Weston Super Mare on Thursday morning......The chair was occupied by Mr Frank H Pine who was supported by Mr C T Francis and Mr H G Collett ....."*(Members of the Bath and Somerset Dairy that may well have sponsored the trip.)*

So back to the parish council and a report dated **19 August 1922 'Combe Down Affairs - Parish Council Meeting - Objection to a Decision respecting the Firs Field - The War Memorial Maintenace'** The report extends to 1½ columns! At this meeting of Monkton Combe Parish Council *FH Pine is in the Chair, supported by FJ Brown, W Miles, F Miller, FR Munday, T Sansum & J Williams.* There was a tribute to the late Mr W H Clark, Chairman of the Bath Rural District Council. A letter was read from Capt. Daubeny saying that, as a result of an amendment by the parish council regarding the playing of games on the Firs Field, he therefore asked the council to accept his resignation as one of the representatives of the 3 donors of the Firs Field because he didn't want football or cricket played there, in accordance with the deed. Mr Appleby of the Combe Down Cricket Club read a letter from the Town Clerk of Bath noting that Combe Down already had a recreation ground for football and cricket at Holley's Corner presented to Bath Corporation by the late Mr Russell. Concern was expressed about the lack of an ambulance on Combe Down. An addition to the war memorial names was proposed and its maintenance was discussed. Moderately improved street lighting for Combe Down was discussed.

1923: A Busy Combe Down Man: The pace of life increases on at least 2 fronts

In the Bath Chronicle of **17 February 1923 (page 9) is a key article** with a rather young photograph of FHP for 1923 - it is headed **'Mr Frank H Pine - A Busy Combe Down Man and his Public Offices'** and reads " Mr Frank Harold Pine who has just been elected Chairman of the Bath Friendly Societies Council, is a gentleman well known in all parts of the city. He is a Bristolian but came to Bath in 1899 and had been with Bath & Somerset Dairies for 23 years until last year when he became Head Cashier of the Norton St Philip Dairy Co (Ltd.). Mr Pine lives at Combe Down where he takes a keen interest in the amenities of the place. He is Chairman of Monkton Combe Parish Council where he has been a member of some years.

"In addition to this office he is an overseer of the parish and a sides-man of Holy Trinity Church Combe Down. For 24 years he has been a member of the Hearts of Oak Society and has acted as President of its Bath branch, besides being a county member of the Federation for many years. Mr Pine who, among his many offices, is an active member of the committee of the local horticultural society, holds the opinion that young men do not take up public work as they should, and believes the community would be better for it if they did. As he is now only 47 years of age, the above record of his work will show that he has not been idle in those matters so far as his own life is concerned,"

Returning to the same issue of the Bath Chronicle of **17 February 1923** (page 16) we have an article entitled **'Combe Down Water - Company unable to Reduce Charges - Ministry of Health to be Approached - Phone facilities on the Down'**, This reported the Tuesday evening meeting of the Monkton Combe Parish Council at which *FH Pine presided with Messrs FJ Brown, W Miles, F Miller, FR Munday, H Robinson, EA Russell and T Sansum*. The Combe Down Water Company had responded by letter to a parish council resolution of 12 December to advise that water charges could not be reduced. A resolution was passed for the Ministry of Health to be approached on the matter. Mr Miles reported 60-70 donated trees had been planted in Firs Field. The need for a telephone kiosk on Combe Down was to be raised with the authorities in Bristol.

Two months later on **21 April 1923** there is a report on **Monkton Combe Council** focusing on the War Memorial and on the annual elections. The meeting had the same cast list as February (but without Miles and Robinson). *Attendance in the past year was recorded as follows: FJ Brown (8), W Miles (10), F Miller (13), FH Pine (13), H Robinson (7), EA Russell (11), T Sansum (11), J Williams (11) and FR Munday (4) because of protracted periods of illness.* **Mr FH Pine was re-elected as Chairman with H Robinson as Vice-Chairman** with FH Pine and FG Franklin re-appointed as Parish Overseers. The upkeep of the War Memorial was discussed.

A month later the report of **12 May 1923** on the **Monkton Combe Council** meeting (with *Pine, Robinson, Miller, Russell*, Brown and Miles) noted that the GPO had no plans for a Combe Down Phone Box and the Water Company's directors had affirmed that they would not reduce their charges. Mr Robinson expressed thanks to the Chairman (FHP) for his efforts to secure that Weston All Saints Band would play in the Firs Field. And so to the month of July and the report of **14 July 1923** entitled **Combe Downs Darkness** *(those present were Pine, Miller, Munday, Sansum, Robinson, Williams, Miles and Page - the Clerk)*, This related to the Parish Council's "bold policy" to seek extra lighting for Combe Down from the gas company (a few more lamps and a slightly longer winter period of illumination - it was noted the entrance to Prior Park was to have electric lighting).

Now in break from parish council matters, <u>the big issue of 1923</u>: the growing deficit of the Royal United Hospital as a voluntary hospital and Frank Pine's role, as Chairman of the Bath Friendly Societies' Council, in trying to bridge that gap. The Bath Chronicle's article of **8 September 1923** said it all in its headings: **'Aid for the Hospital - Bath Friendly Societies' Big Scheme - Efforts to raise £5,000 annually - Boxes for 12,000 householders - Suggested Sunday Morning Twopences'.** This article provides a good description of the scheme: the aim to raise £5,000 annually *(about £250,000 in current terms)* from boxes in 12,000 households at two pence a week *(c £0.40 a week now).*

This was to be a Friendly Society scheme independent but in close connection with the Hospital Managing Board. The friendly societies' council was to report quarterly to the Hospital Management and pay over the amounts raised. *The scheme would have a Central Executive comprising Mr Frank H Pine (Chairman of the Council), Mr F H Wayne (hon. secretary), Mr Walter Rawlinson, National Provincial and Union Bank of England, Old Bank Branch (hon. treasurer), Col. Egbert Lewis (Chairman of the Hospital Management Board), Messrs W A King, G S Hodges, A S Gunstone, and H C Lavington. Messrs Ham, Dennehy and Co., Chartered Accountants, Old Bank Chambers were the auditors. Mr Thomas Wills had been appointed as the Organising Secretary with central offices at 9 Bladud Buildings.*

There were to be District Committees and area stewards organised by ward. Households would have collecting boxes into which they would put 2d. per week. Stewards would be responsible for the registration of boxes for a specific group of households and the collection of monies from those boxes on a quarterly basis (the first weeks of March, June, September and December). It was hoped the first contributions could be collected and paid over by the end of the year. **Mayor Alderman Cedric Chivers** was to take an active interest in scheme by chairing a public meeting to give it a good send off.

After this initial announcement Frank Pine had a meeting of **Monkton Combe Council** to preside over. The report of **15 September 1923** noted that the meeting was attended by *Messrs Miles, Russell, Robinson, Brown, Miller, Munday and Page (Clerk)*. With no takers for the fire appliances from either Bath or Bathford, it was decided to retain them. There was a vote of thanks for the Weston Band playing in the Firs Field on alternate Thursdays in summer.

And now for something completely different that harked back to his time in the army - a report of **15 September 1923** entitled **'Kings Royal Rifle Corps'**. The Band of the 2nd Battalion of the Kings Royal Rifle Corps, then stationed in Cologne, had visited Wellow the previous Sunday as part of fortnight's engagement in Bath. Under a sub-heading 'The Company' it is stated that among the guests was the MP for Bath, Capt Foxcroft... "Among the visitors was Mr FH Pine, the Chairman of Monkton Combe Parish Council, who is an ex-Corporal of the Kings Royal Rifles 3rd Battalion. During the afternoon Mr

Oliphant secured a snapshot of five members of various battalions of the famous regiment. In addition to Mr Pine, this little band of veterans comprised Messrs D Hartley (1st Battalion), WJ Hanney (3rd Battalion), CE Penny and D Padfield." In going through some old photos I found one marked on the back "Wellow Sep 9 1923 taken by L Oliphant CMG" – so I am grateful for this press report in helping to identify what it was about – with FHP in the centre.

So on to **22 September 1923** - with a concern about **'Combe Downs Gas supply'** - we are in the Church Rooms, Combe Down at a Parish meeting to consider street lighting. *With FH Pine in the Chair, there was also present Messrs W Miles, F Miller, HR Ings, H*

Robinson, J Ross, EJ Shelford, S Rivington, J Williams, E A Russell, W Warren, F Maggs, and E P Page (Clerk). Mr Ings proposed that the number of gas lights be increased from 22 to 26 for six months to March 31 and a 4½d rate to cover lighting was proposed. Under any other business Mr Ings proposed that the Bath Gas Company should reduce Combe Down charges to those of Bath. Poor gas supply on Sundays was noted - with a consequent difficulty in cooking Sunday Dinner! **Mr Ings had the provisions store in The Avenue well into the 1960s.**

In a report of **6 October 1923** on **'Helping Bath Hospitals'** it was noted that "Definite progress has now been made with the propaganda scheme of the Bath and District Friendly Societies' scheme to assist the funds of the Royal United Hospital. A committee has now been formed in the furtherance of the scheme with the Mayor of Bath as chairman. *The other officers are Chairman of the Council, Mr FH Pine (Chairman, Monkton Combe Parish Council); hon secretary, Mr FH Wayne; organising secretary Mr T Wills; hon. treasurer, Mr Walter Rawlinson, (Manager, National Provincial and Union Bank of England)....The Executive Committee consists of the Chairman of the Friendly Societies' Council (i.e. F H Pine), Chairman of the Hospital Management Board (i.e. Col Egbert Lewis), the Hon Secretary, the Hon Treasurer and Messrs AS Gunstone, GS Hodges, WA King and HC Lavington (my italics)....* An appeal has been issued in the form of a pamphlet setting out the scheme. During the past few days, definite progress has been made in establishing the local committees in Twerton and Westmoreland wards of the city. For one portion of the Twerton East Ward the Chairman is Councillor FW Kitley and the secretary Mr CJ Welch of Livingstone Road. For the other portion of the ward the Chairman is Councillor G Lanning with Mr Wiliams (Englishcombe Park) as the secretary. In the Westmoreland ward Mr J Harding is the Chairman and Messrs Day and Charles are the joint secretaries."

"The Mayor (Alderman Chivers) has shown his practical interest in committee formation by attending two of the four meetings which have been held to date. The Mayoress (Madame Sarah Grand) has also expressed her willingness to cooperate with the scheme." Three more ward meetings were planned for that week. Towards the end of the month the Mayor was to chair a mass meeting in the Guildhall at which the Chairman of the Canterbury scheme would be present – Canterbury had raised £5,000 for their hospitals, despite being smaller than Bath.

The Bath Chronicle of **13 October 1923** had on Page 22 under **Bath & County Notes** (in column 2 item5) an item that reads "Mr F H Pine, chairman of Monkton Combe Parish Council, who takes a keen interest in the Bath Hospital scheme, has convened a meeting of members of Friendly Societies and others interested at Combe Down on October 16ᵗʰ when the question of supporting the movement will be discussed."

The same issue of **13 October** had on page 5 an article **'Reduced Rates at Combe Down - Protest at Gas Charges'**. *Once again FH Pine presided at meeting of Monkton Combe Council with Messrs T Sansum, W Miles, F Miller and EP Page (Clerk).* Mr FGV Frankling (overseer) said that the local Combe Down rate would be 7d in £ less than the previous year. On a separate point the Gas Company had refused to reduce charges to Combe Down and claimed that poor gas pressure was a matter for individual dwellings. Mr Miller was asked to put the claims of 150 residents about poor gas pressure on Sundays to the company.

The next 3 items concern the hospital box scheme. On **27 October 1923** is an article headed **'The Hospitals Need - Scheme in which all must help - Bath Friendly Societies Excellent plan'.** The first Meeting of the Council of Friendly Societies following the launch of the scheme was held. *FHP was in the chair, with FH Wayne (hon. secretary), Thomas Wills (Organising Secretary), Mr Walter Rawlinson (hon. treasurer) with 17 representatives of friendly societies (Shepherds, Hearts of Oak, Rationals, United Patriots and Foresters) including Brothers Arthur S Gunstone, HC Lavington and HF Fiddes.* Mr Pine said it was the first meeting since the ship had been launched, but time had been fully occupied, and the scheme had had a great welcome in all districts, every member of the friendly societies would have to shoulder some responsibility as the people of Bath were looking to the societies to see if they were capable of what they were talking about. Mr Wills noted that canvassing in the country districts would seem in some cases to trespass on the cottage hospitals, but these institutions would benefit as some sharing scheme would eventually be arrived at; the council were out to help them as well. The RUH would still be a free hospital, and the friendly societies would not interfere in its administration, and contributions towards treatment would still be solicited.

On **3 November 1923** the article **'Our Hospital'** covers 2 columns. A packed mass meeting at the Guildhall, Banqueting Hall was presided over by *Mayor Chivers, President of the Propaganda Committee, a long list of those supporting him included the Mayoress (Madame Sarah Grand), Major H G James (Chairman of the Kent and Canterbury Hospital Propaganda Scheme), Canon TG Gardiner, Lt-Col Egbert Lewis (Chairman of the Hospital Management Committee), Messrs Forbes Fraser, C Curd, WP Edwards, WH Smith, WA King, A Salter, HH Sprouting, B John, FG Wardle (Hospital Committee), Sir Harry Hatt, Messrs FH Pine*

Alderman Chivers and Lady Sarah Grand

(Chairman of the Council), W Rawlinson (hon treasurer), AS Gunstone, GS Hodges and HC Lavington (executive committee), Thomas Wills (organising secretary) .....(plus another 30 names). It was noted that at the end of 1922 the RUH had an annual deficit of nearly £4,000 making a total deficiency of £10,313. Raising £5,000 per annum would enable the hospital to pay its way by putting boxes in 12,000 homes - the Mayor noted 2,500 boxes were already in use.

Lt-Col Egbert Lewis noted that the hospital had received £8,000 to build a new hospital at Combe Park from the Red Cross and St John's funds left over from the war which could not be used for existing running costs. Since 1921 the hospital had asked patients to contribute towards their maintenance costs according to their means. Stothert & Pitt and other employers had been arranging for workers contributions of 1d a week for a flat rate of 15s a week hospitalisation costs for the worker and his dependants. Without those voluntary contributions of £3,179 in the previous year the hospital would have had to close its doors. Putting the hospital on the rates would have meant a 10p local rate, although costs of publicly managed institutions tended to rise. There was also the question of the apportionment of costs to those outside Bath.

Dr Forbes Fraser mentioned how well used the hospital was - it needed another 100 beds but there was insufficient space in the present location. Some still cherished the hope of the great scheme of removing the hospital to Combe Park. Major James related the financial difficulties of the Kent and Canterbury Hospital and the popularity of Canterbury scheme. Fund-raising in the area covered by the hospital, and encouraging everyone involved to consider it as 'our hospital', had now guaranteed the solvency of the hospital. Canon Gardiner said that everyone in the Bath area should think of the RUH as 'our hospital'. FHP, President of the Council, said of the friendly societies that if they believed in anything it was in the Brotherhood of Man. So it came about that, when they saw that unless the hospital received more support it would have to close its doors, they put their heads together and said 'this shall not be' - and so they came before them as citizens to appeal to them to keep 'Our Hospital' open.... He proposed a resolution "That this meeting of the citizens of Bath heartily approves the scheme of the Bath and District Friendly Societies Council for augmenting the funds of 'Our Hospital' and pledges itself to use its best endeavours to make it a success (applause)". Mr WA King, in seconding, made a plea for more workers for the scheme,

On **1 December 1923** in **Bath and County Notes** (Column 3 Item3) there is a report that "Considerable progress has now been made with the Bath Friendly Societies' scheme for assisting the Bath Royal United hospital. Mr T Wills, the organising Secretary tells me that no fewer than 5,750 collecting boxes are now in the hands of the stewards. Every district of Bath, with the exception of St Michaels ward and a portion of Lyncombe, has now been covered by the organisers operations. It is intended to make a serious start with the campaign in the rural districts early in the new year. Mr FH Pine presided at the meeting held at Upper Weston on Monday evening when Mr J Milburn was appointed Chairman of the district committee and Mrs Slee the Hon Secretary. A request was made for the enrolment of 11 stewards – 16 members of the audience responded."

There are two reports of interest in the same **22 December 1923** paper - On page 17 there is a report on the **funeral of the late Mr F J Hobbs** of Isabella House, Combe Down, a well known businessman and sidesman at Church. The report says that Mr FH Pine was unavoidably absent. Earlier on page 6 is a report of Monkton Combe Council in which Frank Pine led a tribute to Mr Hobbs *(with Russell, Brown and Sansum present)*.

1924: Ambassador for the Box Scheme, continuing council work - and a prize giving

In a report of **26 February 1924** Frank Pine's involvement with the **Hearts of Oak Benefit Society** resurfaces. "A well attended meeting in connection with the *Bath Branch of the Hearts of Oak Benefit Society, Mr FH Pine presiding. Others present included Mr HF Fiddes (delegate), Messrs JB Jones, FG Owens, H Pickett, J Morris, H Bees, GL Wetmore, G Cambridge, F England, G Haverfield, and JT Franks*. **FH Pine was elected chairman and delegate to the Friendly Societies Council** along with Messrs Fiddes, Jones, Haverfield and Wetmore. The chairman reported on the work of the Friendly Societies Council to assist the hospital. The society was to pay dental charges of up to £3 for insured members. Mr Fiddes was nominated as local delegate for 1924-7.

An item of **29 March 1924 'Batheaston & The Hospital'** (column 2 item3) notes that "a Committee was formed at Batheaston on Thursday evening to carry out locally the Friendly Societies' scheme to aid the Royal United Hospital. Mr FH Pine, Chairman of the Executive Committee, and Mr T Wills, organising secretary, fully explained the scheme."

In the same issue of **29 March 1924** (page 6) we see **'Combe Down Affairs - Electric Lighting Foreshadowed - Mr Pine to resign as Chairman and Overseer'** At the Tuesday evening monthly meeting of the Monkton Combe Parish Council – FHP presiding announces his intention to relinquish his Chairmanship, owing to the pressure of other public work. *Members present were Mr EP Page (clerk), H Robinson, T Sansum, FJ Brown, W Miles, F Miller and EA Russell.*

Concern was expressed at damage to the War Memorial by dogs. The extension of Electric Lighting on Combe Down was proposed. In a discussion about a deficit of expenditure over the rates collected, Frank Pine referred to the difficulties an Overseer experienced in assessing property and said he thought it was about time an independent man came to assess the place. The Clerk pointed out that an independent valuer would require his professional costs. Mr Robinson said that as a former Overseer he sympathised with Mr Pine, and he thought the council should agitate for the re-evaluation of the whole Monkton Combe parish. Some of the present assessments were most unfair.

Mr Pine stated, at the conclusion of the meeting, that the Council must be prepared to find another Chairman and Overseer very shortly. Most of them would be aware that he had undertaken the big task of raising £5,000 for the RUH in connection with the Friendly Societies' Scheme. Mr Robinson said he hoped that Mr Pine would stay in office until the next March, for they all recognised he had done his level best for the parish (applause). Mr Pine: We shall see what happens. If you find another Chairman, I shall support him.

However, in a report of **19 April 1924** we return to **'Monkton Combe Parish Council - Mr FH Pine asked to resume chair'.** "Mr H Robinson presided at annual meeting of Monkton Combe Parish Council held at the Church Rooms on Tuesday evening. *Others present were Messrs FJ Brown, W Miles, F Miller, EA Russell, T Sansum and J Williams.* It was decided that Mr F H Pine, who had intimated his intention of resigning, should be asked to resume the position of chairman during the ensuing year. Mr Robinson explained that Mr Pine had definitely stated that he wished to be relieved of the duties of overseer. He understood that Mr FG Frankling was willing to serve again in that capacity and Mr HR Ings was appointed as his colleague. Mr Robinson was re-elected as vice-chairman" Plans to renovate the inscriptions on the war memorial were deferred.

On **14 June 1924** an article **'Hospital Aid Scheme - Colerne Committee formed'** reported that "on Thursday a committee for Colerne in connection with the Bath Friendly Societies' Hospital Aid Scheme was established with marked enthusiasm by local residents" with a Chairman, Mr Shanks of Thickwood, and Secretary Mrs Shute of Hall Farm being appointed. Addresses were given by Messrs FH Pine, GS Hodges, WA King and A Salter.

We return on **5 July 1924** to the vexed issue of **the 'Combe Down War Memorial - Council Consider Adding Brass Name Plates'**. At a Monkton Combe Parish Council meeting *FH Pine is once again presiding with the support of Messrs EH Russell, T Sansum, F Miller, W Miles, J Williams & EP Page (Clerk).* They discussed the repair of the water fountain and the War Memorial with new bronze name plates where it had been weathered by exposure to the north winds (rather than just blacking in the names). An estimate was also to be sought from the Gas Company to have 28 street lights from the second week in September to the second week in April.

Now there is one heart warming piece from **2 August 1924** – '**Combe Down Senior School Prize giving'** with a large assembly of managers, parents and friends including FH Pine as Chairman of Monkton Combe Parish Council and managers of the 3 junior schools present. The headmaster Mr H Collins especially mentioned the teacher Miss Tanner, as the Chief Assistant. "**Mr FH Pine told an amusing story**, the moral of which was that boys and girls should learn at school that it is the giving of real practical help rather than advice which made people really useful members of society." Form Prizes included: **Form VII Lena Pine (form prize).** How proud my mother Lena would have been!

Back to earth with the item of **16 August 1924** on '**Combe Down Affairs - Electric Lighting'**. We return to Monkton Combe Parish Council with *FH Pine presiding with Messrs W Miles, F Miller, FR Munday, EH Russell, T Sansum, J Williams and FR Brown - the RDC Councillor Capt. CW Daubeny, Mr J Lipscombe (Bath Rural District Council) and Mr FW Kelway who attended this meeting with reference to the new sewerage scheme.* Under a 1911 deal whereby Combe Down was excluded from the city boundary extension, Combe Down had had to stop sewage draining into disused wells. A scheme started in 1914 was stopped in 1916 due to the war. The RDC was to lay new sewage mains but home owners would have to connect with the drains. Consideration was given to the installation of electric rather than gas lighting - but further consideration was postponed to next meeting. Concern was expressed about the improper use of the Tram Shelter at the Hadley Arms. The RDC was to start work on a Tyning Road improvement. Concern was also raised about quarrying under a highway (and the effect of blasting).

The story continues on **20 September 1924** with '**Combe Down Affairs - The New Memorial Tablet'** with the next meeting of Monkton Combe Parish Council and with *FH Pine presiding, supported by Messrs W Miles, H Robinson, EH Russell, T Sansum, J Williams & EP Page (clerk).* The Gas Company's estimate for lighting was accepted. Tenders for the erection of tablets on the war memorial were considered. FHP mentioned that the Ministry of Health had been contacted as they needed to approve an application for the council to meet the costs involved. The meeting authorised Mr Pine to interview a firm of Metal Workers when he visited London in the next week – he also undertook to call at the offices of the Ministry of Health to explain the exact position.

So we go to **18 October 1924** and '**Combe Down Affairs - War Memorial Improvement - Complaints about the Gas - Parish Councillors Uncooked Dinner'** and the next meeting of the Monkton Combe Parish Council. *FH Pine was presiding with Messrs FR Brown, W Miles, FR Munday, H Robinson, EH Russell, J Williams, F Miller, & EP Page (clerk).* The Ministry of Health had sanctioned expenditure of £30 for bronze name tablets to replace the names carved in the stone, which were becoming obliterated through weathering. Mr Miller said a certain person was not from Combe Down and should come off. FHP responded that "Nothing there is coming off. I can say that without hesitation (hear hear). A voice: let the lad rest." In a letter from Mr FJ Appleby concern was expressed about the state of the road at Bank Corner as it had been left by a cable laying company. The RDC was to be asked to consider this and also the frequency of rubbish collection. FHP said "a fortnight is a rather long time" to wait for refuse collection. One member had waited 3 weeks. Concern was expressed about the quality of some gas public lighting. Mr Miller mentioned being unable to cook Sunday lunch due to the quality of the gas supply, and that they had not got a satisfactory response from the Gas Company. Mr Pine remarked that Mr Miller's complaint was a personal matter. The Council had to concern itself with public lighting.

Finally a personal press cutting from the daily Chronicle of **Wednesday 31 December 1924** in which the Day By Day Column by Sul headlines **'To-day's Personality—Mr. F. H. Pine'** and reads "When the Friendly Societies' Hospital scheme has just handed £4,900 to the Royal United, it is appropriate that reference should be made to the part which Mr. Frank H. Pine, the chairman of the Friendly Societies' Council, has played in that wonderful effort. From the first he seized the idea with admirable enthusiasm, helped to work it with quite statesmanlike ability, and was imbued with an optimism which has proved absolutely well placed. Mr. Pine has devoted himself unsparingly to the task; every minute of his leisure is given up to it, and has shown what a man can do if he centres his energies upon one object. As a chairman, Mr. Pine is business-like and practical and has earned the regard of all who have the honour to serve under him."

COMBE DOWN SCHOOL c1915 & c1920

I cannot find a school photo for the date of the 2 August 1924 Prize Giving press report but if I am right in spotting my mother in them they date from about 1915 (above - second row back first right) and 1920 (below - third row back third right).
The headmaster is Mr Collins and the female teacher may be Miss Tanner.

1925: A Challenging Year - Unemployed but Public Work Continues - A Silver Wedding & Mr Rothery an old comrade

Having been in charge at Bath for Norton Dairies, following their take-over of the Bath and Somerset Dairies, in March Frank Pine was made redundant at the age of 48. In June there is a rather curious job advertisement. It is not clear when he joined Spear Brothers and Clark in an administrative role but I have a picture of him at the Bath and Somerset Show in 1926 in a tent displaying Spears pies. Why he left Norton Dairies is unclear but it may be that the company felt that he had too many extra-curricular demands.

So on **7 March 1925** in a small un-headed item on page 25 (bottom of column 3) presumably relating to the previous Saturday 1 March we read "Mr FH Pine, who for 26 years has been associated with the Bath and Somerset Dairy Co and its successor on Saturday severed that association. Mr Pine is Chairman of Monkton Combe Parish Council and has taken a leading part in the Bath Hospital Aid Scheme under the auspices of the Friendly Societies' Council."

That this was a bitter parting from an employment that had brought him to Bath in 1899 is reflected in the following item from **21 March 1925**. It is headed **'Parting Gift to Mr FH Pine - Recipient Thanks his Former Colleagues'**. The article says 'The following is a letter that Mr Frank H Pine has addressed to the staff of the Norton St Philip Dairy Co., Bath, to thank them for the presentation of a gold watch which was made to him privately last week.

"To the staff of the Norton St Philip Dairy Co., Bath. My Friends it is with mixed feelings I ask you all to accept my grateful thanks for your kind and generous expression of goodwill. After over a quarter of a century's associations with a large number of you it was a staggering blow to be so suddenly and compulsorily severed from you. At all times I have had the loyal support of the staff, and I take this opportunity of thanking the branch manageresses and heads of departments for many acts of kindness which helped to smooth the difficulties of our business life. I would wish to thank the outdoor and delivery staff for their assistance in the carrying out of my duties under adverse circumstances. Now the parting has come! May good health and happiness attend you one and all. Your handsome and useful gift will always be a reminder of our long and happy association.
Yours Fraternally Frank H Pine, 17 The Firs, Combe Down, Bath. March 15, 1925"

Does every dark cloud have a silver lining? Frank Pine had many friends who might have helped him and who might have been supportive of his extra-curricular activities. Anyway there was a silver lining of sorts as, on **18 April 1925** in what is now the *Bath*

Chronicle and Herald, there are two reports of his and Lillian's Silver Wedding. In the **Bath and County Notes** column (page 7 bottom of column 4 headed **'Silver Wedding'** is the following "Congratulations to Mr & Mrs FH Pine who this week celebrated their silver wedding. Mr and Mrs Pine were married at St John the Baptist's Bathwick on April 16th 1900. Mr Pine is the president of the Bath and District Friendly Societies Council, which has done so much to assist the Bath Hospital. He succeeded the late Mr C Stickland as Chairman of Monkton Combe Parish Council." *(Actually W Miles was Chairman for two years after Stickland and before FHP.)* Then on page 20 under **'Weddings – Silver Wedding'** is the family announcement "Pine-Beckingsale – April 16th 1900 at St John Baptist Bathwick by the Rev Arthur Roberts, Frank Harold to Lillian, daughter of the Late W Beckingsale of Cheltenham. *(No mention of his origins!)*

In a front page lead article of the **9 May 1925** edition of the Bath Chronicle and Herald is an article **'Keeping the Doors Open - Friendly Societies raise £4,900 in a year - Record Contribution for past quarter'** Reporting on the success of the Friendly Societies' scheme and its quarterly meeting at the RUH it is said "There was a capital attendance at Thursday's meeting, the Board Room at the hospital being filled. *The President (the Mayor) was unable to be present, and Mr Frank H Pine (the Chairman of the Council) presided. Others present included Messrs Walter Rawlinson (hon. treasurer), T Wills (organising secretary), GS Hodges, WA King and HC Lavington (members of the Executive Committee), JB Jones, W H Chorley, G Wetmore, W Horwood, F Orchard, C Crewe, J Pollard, Councillor B Knight, Perkins, T Ricks, Ponfield, F Harding (members of the Friendly Societies Council)."* There is a long list of those representing the many districts of the scheme. With £4,900 handed over to it, the hospital was able to show its first credit balance for a great many years. The cost of working the scheme was £269 14s (a little over 5%). On December 31 1924 some 13,330 boxes had been issued.

Speaking as Chairman, moving the adoption of the annual report, Frank Pine said "their simple scheme had been accepted by many, many thousands of the inhabitants residing in the area served by the hospital, and it was a matter of great satisfaction to them all that the campaign against debt and indifference had succeeded. It was no idle boast, or in any egotistical spirit, that they said that their hospital had been saved from financial disaster (applause). He said that there was one omission in the annual report, in that there was no expression of appreciation of Mr Thomas Wills (applause). He was the man who had pulled them through that stupendous undertaking (applause).

Mr Walter Rawlinson (treasurer) noted that payments had also been made to the Victoria Hospital, Frome and Freshford Nursing Home *(where I, John Daniels, was born).* Since the New Year Committees had been set up in the parishes of Hinton Charterhouse, Hemington and Faulkland, Englishcombe, Nettleton and Burton, West

Kington, Castle Combe, Freshford, Limpley Stoke, Shoscombe, Westwood, South Wraxall, Atworth, Monkton Farleigh and Holt.

Another Page 1 lead from **16 May 1925** is headed **'80 Patients Waiting - Scheme to relieve pressure on RUH - A Generous Offer'**. It reads "The Pump Room suite housed a very large company on Thursday evening, when the Mayor (Alderman Cedric Chivers JP) and the Mayoress (Madame Sarah Grand) held a reception, the occasion being the second annual gathering of the workers of the Friendly Societies' scheme for 'Our Hospital', otherwise the Royal United Hospital. No fewer than 850 invitations were sent, and it was estimated that some 700 were able to be present. A quarterly cheque for £1,330 was handed over to the Chairman of the RUH Board.

"The Mayor presided and with him on the special platform were the ex-Mayor Sir Percy Stothert (Chairman of the Hospital Board of Management) and Lady Stothert, Mr FH Pine (Chairman of the Executive Committee of the propaganda scheme), Mr Walter Rawlinson (treasurer), Mr WA King (executive committee), and Mr T Wills (organising secretary). Others present included the ex-Mayoress (Miss Foxcroft), Lieut-Col Egbert Lewis (ex chairman), and other members of the Royal United Hospital Board of Management; Mr SR Marsh (secretary of the Cardiff and District Friendly Societies' Hospital Propaganda Scheme and Mrs Marsh"

"Mr Pine, on behalf of the Friendly Societies Council thanked everyone for the earnest effort and hard work they had put into the scheme, and for the glorious success that had been achieved, and appealed for a continuation and extension of that help. Mr Rawlinson asked the Mayor to accept a cheque for £1,350 for the first three months of 1925, which the Mayor immediately presented to Sir Percy Stothert."

The Mayor said that more needed doing – there was a waiting list of 80: it was possible that the Forbes Fraser Hospital could help. He talked of a great scheme ahead that one day the RUH would be located to Combe Park. The evening concluded with an excellent programme of music in the concert room.

Despite his place at the centre of the top table on hospital matters, Frank Pine was still **in search of paying employment** as reflected in this personal advertisement in the paper on **4 June 1925**: "FRANK H PINE, Combe Down, seeks APPOINTMENT as Secretary-Cashier or similar responsibility: 26 years Experience preparing Accounts, Drawing Trial Balance for Audit, and Commercial Routine." *There is no address or contact details - this is clearly addressed to his contacts in the business community, especially those who might support his public activities like perhaps Alderman Spear - implicitly 'you know where to contact me'!*

Anyway FHP carried on with his public work undaunted as indicated in a report of **13 June 1925** on **'Combe Down's Needs - Development of the Recreation Ground Bowling Green Suggestion - Ban on Children Who March with the Band'** This was another meeting of Monkton Combe Parish Council with *Frank H Pine presiding. Others present were Messrs Oliver Hopkins and AC Milsom, Lieut-Col A J Pilcher, Mr H Robinson and the Clerk, Mr Page.* They considered the development of Firs Field as a Recreation Ground - and the option of developing a Bowling Green was to be pursued. Tennis Courts and Putting Greens were also suggested. The Chair mentioned that he had spent 3 years trying to get the support of the local band. Mr Robinson expressed concern about the conduct of children following the band in the streets. Mr Hopkins spoke about rats at a rubbish tip (he had only seen 2 during a visit there) - he felt that a press statement that a 'Pied Piper' was wanted on Combe Down was a bad advertisement!

And so to another funeral - and on **27 June 1925** there is an article **'Employees Tribute - Staff Follow at Funeral of Late Mr WJ Cook'.** He was Chairman of W & R Cook of Twerton and the funeral was at Combe Down Church, the previous Monday afternoon. The staff walked in procession from his house at Combe Ridge. After four paragraphs of family and company mourners and representatives of Bath Chambers of Commerce and Lansdown Golf Club there is a list of others present. This included the Mayor (Cedric Chivers), Mr F Maddox *(Bath Theatre impresario?)***,** Mr FH Pine (Chairman of Combe Down Church Council – *perhaps should have read 'Parish Council'*) with Messrs Ing and Page *(also listed as from the church council).* The internment afterwards was at the family vault at Clevedon Old Church Cemetery.

On **Saturday 1 August 1925** the Chronicle and Herald contained a report **'Bath Hospital – continued success of Friendly Societies' Scheme – Cheque for £1,300'.** "To my mind, this is an example of the triumph of the voluntary system" said the Mayoress (Madame Sarah Grand) in formally handing to Lieut-Col Egbert Lewis, the vice-Chairman of the Bath Royal United Hospital Committee, a cheque for £1,300, the result of the collections of the Bath Registered Friendly Societies' Council during the quarter which ended June 30th. This ceremony took place at the Guildhall on the previous Wednesday evening. Mr FH Pine presided. *Others present were Mr JM Sheppard (Secretary of the Royal United Hospital), Mr W Rawlinson (hon. treasurer of the Friendly Societies' scheme), Mrs Egbert Lewis, Councillor FB Knight, Messrs. HC Lavington, A Salter, HF Fiddes and W Withers.*

The article noted that the Mayor Cedric Chivers and the Mayoress had hosted members of the British Medical Association conference in Bath the previous week. The money received by the scheme in the quarter amounted to £1,403. A working arrangement had been reached with the Chippenham Cottage Hospital and cheques had been sent to them, and to Freshford Nursing Home and the Victoria Hospital, Frome, in relation to amounts collected in their areas.

Mr Pine remarked that he had been greatly impressed some time previously by reading a sentence of a report on the Hospital stating that: "Unless further financial support is forthcoming, the time must come when the Hospital must close its doors". He felt that it was due to the contributions of the public under the Friendly Societies' scheme that the Hospital had been enabled to keep open.' Mr Rawlinson noted that the scheme had already collected £2,600 that year. Madame Sarah Grand made a speech praising the scheme and speaking out against bureaucratic government involvement. In the absence of Sir Percy Stothert, Col Lewis received the cheque and said that he would be very sorry to see hospitals turned into state or municipally controlled undertakings. He did not think the German example of a state medical service should be imitated. He noted the progress of the scheme in the country areas and the kindness of Lord and Lady Methuen in convening a meeting at Corsham Court in support of the matter.

We return to the hospital scheme with a **5 September 1925** report **'Royal United Hospital - Marshfield Supporters'.** It records that a party of box holders and others interested in the Friendly Societies' scheme at Marshfield visited the Hospital on Sunday afternoon. Afterwards Mr FH Pine addressed the party on the progress of the scheme. Mr Bezer moved a vote of thanks for the opportunity of inspecting the Hospital and expressed himself, on behalf of the Marshfield people, as bring pleased with all they had seen.... Mr Salter replied and impressed on the visitors how necessary it was that the country districts in the hospital area should support the Hospital.

'Combe Down's Troubles' was the title of a piece on page 16 of the **19 September 1925** paper about the Monkton Combe Parish Council. *FH Pine presided along with Messrs Russell, Sansum, Brown, Milsom and Mr Robinson.* Mr Robinson was concerned that Combe Down had been obliged to put up with county postal arrangements - with no delivery from 11am Saturday until Monday morning. The need for improved winter gas lighting was also considered. Mr Pearce was to graze the Firs Field from Michaelmas until Lady Day. In the same issue of the 19 September paper (page 12) is a report from the same meeting headed **'Perfect Pests - Young Motorcyclists'** Mr Robinson expressed concern about youths on motor cycles with very inefficient silencers. FHP said 'something must be done' by the police.

In the the first of 2 reports of interest in the issue of **7 November 1925** is an article **'Our Hospital – Friendly Societies' Great Effort – Another Big Cheque'.** With Mayor Cedric Chivers and Mayoress Madame Sarah Grand present, the Chair was occupied by **Mr FH Pine**, *who was supported by Sir Percy Stothert (Chairman of the Hospital), Col. Egbert Lewis (Vice-Chairman of the Hospital), Councillor FB Knight, Councillor T Vezey, Messrs.*

HC Lavington, AS Gunstone, GH Hodges, A Salter, HF Fiddes, Mr W Rawlinson (vice-chairman and hon. treasurer of the Friendly Societies' scheme), Mr T Wills (organising secretary), and Mr JM Sheppard (Secretary of the Royal United Hospital) with stewards, secretaries, chairmen and scheme box holders.

The report for the quarter showed £1,344 collected, of which £1,200 was to go to the RUH, with other sums going to other hospitals. The amounts collected were: in Bath, £841, in Somerset £273 and in Wiltshire £229. The total handed over to the RUH to date was £8,750. The Chairman said he wanted to make it clear that the money paid to Bristol, to the Paulton Memorial Hospital, the Victoria Hospital, Frome and the Bradford on Avon Nursing Association was only the money raised in those areas. With Corsham in the scheme he looked to Chippenham joining shortly and Trowbridge in due course. The Mayor stressed the importance of moving the hospital to sunnier Combe Park.

I believe that Frank Pine once considered emigrating to Canada, as a friend of his had done. As a child, on a visit to my aunts at 17 The Firs, Combe Down, I always looked out for the latest copy, mailed from Canada by the Rothery family, of 'McLeans Magazine' with its cartoons of Jasper the Bear. My mother also had stories of the son of a Mr Rothery visiting Bath as a member of the Canadian armed services during the war - and his marvelling at all the chimney pots on the houses. There is an explanation. It lies in an article of the Bath Chronicle and Herald dated 7 November 1925 **'Linking Old Comrades - Bath paragraph penetrates to far off settlement'.**

It reads "A paragraph that appeared in our columns 12 Months ago has just been the means of bringing Mr Frank H Pine (Chairman of the Bath Friendly Societies Council) into touch with an old friend from whom he had not heard for many years. In the paragraph in question we recounted how Mr Pine, while on a holiday in London, visited the Royal Mint and saw silver half roubles and koepecks being made there. He had been told that no fewer than sixty-five million koepecks, with a large number of half roubles, were being made.

"One can never judge what unsuspected sources of romance will be touched by a simple item in a newspaper, or how far reaching its effects may be. Like a broadcast radio message it goes all over the world, and penetrates to the most remote parts of the Empire. In this particular instance the Bath Chronicle paragraph was reproduced far and wide. Among other places it was reprinted in Canada and a year later, in the far off settlement of Frenchman's Butte in Saskahewan, it caught the eye of a settler called Rothery, who was passing an idle hour scanning the back copies of various newspapers. When the reference to Frank H Pine caught his eye he began to 'sit up and take notice' for that was the name of an old comrade with whom he had served in the Kings Royal

Rifles before the Boer War. Could the gentleman who visited the Mint be the one and same man? He would write to Bath and see.

"Hence, a few days ago, Mr Pine received a letter from Canada, enclosing a cutting of the article referred to, inquiring if he were still alive, and indicating that, if the answer was in the affirmative, his old chum CB Rothery would be delighted to hear from him. Mr Pine responded to the request post-haste and we have just received a line from him recounting the above circumstances and adding 'Thank you for linking old comrades.' "

There is a sad footnote to this letter as on 29 December 1936 Edward J (Ted) Rothery sent a two page typed letter to 'Dear Mr Pyne' from Deer Creek, Saskatchewan to say that his father, to whom FHP had written, had passed away on 1 July 1936. He left 4 sons – himself, Edward ('who you may remember at Winchester'), Joe in the mounted Police and 2 younger ones – Don (14) and Phil (12). Edward refers to a daughter Eva, named after an aunt in Cheltenham ('my wife's father remembers a business there that must have been owned by Mrs. Pyne's uncle'). There is a comment 'We were very glad to hear from Walter Lever that you were again among the employed' (presumably old news). There is much in the letter about farming but he does mention that his father was buried in an Anglican Church built of stone two year's previously using a German stone-mason – and was unusual in North Saskatchewan where most houses were of wood.

From some biographical notes that I found on Wikitree (that his grandson Bill Rothery has since expanded upon for me) it is clear that CB (Crossley Barstowe) Rothery had an interesting life. According to these notes he was born in Salterhebble in Yorkshire 27 December 1877 and died 7 November 1936 (not July - I believe this was due to the stonemason recording on his gravestone that he died on the seventh day of the eleventh month rather than the first day of the seventh month).

He returned to England in 1902 after service in the Boer War and was later stationed in Ireland where he met his wife Rosina Alner (1883-1966) whom he married in Cork in 1904. He was posted to Bermuda where Edward James (Ted) Rothery was born 10 September 1906. Crossley was then posted to Crete (1908), Malta (where Joseph Alner Rothery was born 24 April 1910) and India (1910). When the Great War broke out ill health forced him into clerical work and he retired from the army after the war. The family immigrated to Canada in 1919 to a small log cabin with a sod roof to operate the post office at Monnery from 1921 to 1929, which moved to Frenchman Butte SK when the railroad came through.

Of Crossley's four Sons, Edward (Ted) died in 1977 and was buried in Deer Creek cemetery; Joseph Alner Rothery died 23 May 1995 and was buried at the RCMP cemetery Regina Saskatchewan. The two who were born in the log cabin were Frank Donald (Don) born 1 March 1922 who died 6 March 1994 and who was buried in the Deer Creek cemetery - and Philip born 8 May 1924 who died 2 December 2000 and who was buried in Saskatoon Saskatchewan.

I am sure it was CB's son Don (born in 1922) who visited Bath during the war – the name rings a clear bell. Bill Rothery recently told me that Don might have visited Bath at some time between 1942 and 1945, as he was enlisted in the RCAF and stationed in England. His only other visit to England was in 1987 when he may have met my Aunts Phyllis and Edna. I can now also recollect mention of one of the Rothery's being a Mountie. One cannot help endorsing the Chronicle item of 1925 which remarked: "One can never judge what unsuspected sources of romance will be touched by a simple item in a newspaper, or how far reaching its effects may be."

Towards the end of the year in the Chronicle of 12 December 1925 is a letter dated 8 December from Frank Pine entitled **'Opening the Hospital boxes'** - it reads:

"Sir, Once again our hundreds of voluntary stewards and stewardesses are about to collect the Decembers offerings of box holders under the Friendly Societies' Scheme for 'OUR' Hospital and I seek the publicity of your columns to ask for the assistance of our contributors during the collection by kindly allowing our workers inside their houses to open the boxes, as it is very difficult during the dark nights to count the contents of the boxes by the door. A large number of our collectors give up their leisure after a busy day, and many forfeit their weekly half-holiday, in the carrying out of this huge effort, and every consideration for their comfort would be much appreciated. And while I am writing I must seize the opportunity to call attention to our second appeal and re-canvas every district that has been, up to now, covered by the scheme. We are endeavouring to induce many thousands more who have not yet accepted our collecting boxes to do so and join with over 15,000 in doing a little each week to keep the doors of 'OUR' Hospital open. FRANK H PINE (Chairman) Friendly Societies Hospital Scheme. 17, The Firs, Combe Down. December 8th 1925".

Crossley Barstowe Rothery

1. At about the time of the Boer War

2. With his son Ted

3. The Old Homestead where he first settled in Canada

3. The church at Deer Creek where they are both buried

FRANK PINE - THE MIDDLE YEARS

c.1916?

c.1921 with Mrs Beckingsale

With Spear Brothers:
In 1926 at the Bath &
West Show.
In 1928 - a charabanc
outing

THE NEWSPAPER RECORD 1926-1930

1926-1930 - A Period of Conflicting Demands (56 Articles)

1926: Local Box Scheme Meetings, A Whist Drive and Parish Council Meetings

Although there are fewer reports in this year it may just be that events were recorded in the daily but not the weekly edition of the Chronicle and Herald.

In the Bath Chronicle of **6 February 1926** (page 6 end of column 4), in an article entitled **'Combe Down Whist Drive'**, we have Frank Pine as the MC at a whist drive and dance the preceding Monday in the new Church Rooms, attended by over 100 people (24 tables). The success of the evening was due to the capable arrangements made by Mrs Ponting, Mrs Maggs and the lady helpers. Mrs Daubeny presented the prizes.

In the same issue on the front page (end of column 3) we see **'Bath Hospital Scheme - Campaign in the Chippenham area'**. It reports on a meeting Thursday 4 February at Kingston St Mchael - Mr F Pine (supported by Messrs WA King and A Salter) explained the scheme. The same article was repeated in the 13 February issue.

In the issue of **13 February 1926** there is an article **'Monkton Combe Council - Efficiency of Fire Fighting Equipment.** We have FH Pine presiding over the council in their new quarters at the Avenue Hall supported by EA Russell, T Sansum, H Robinson, FJ Brown, Col Pilcher and A Page (clerk). The Chairman asked if all the fire hydrants were working as the roads had been recently re-tarred. Col Pilcher remarked that the hydrant had worked well at the recent school fire.

In the issue of **24 April 1926** (p23, col 2), in the item **'Monkton Combe Parish Council - Clerk's salary increased'**, *we have Frank H Pine presiding (and being re-elected as Chairman). He is supported by Messrs FJ Brown, O Hopkins, FR Munday, Col AJ Pilcher, Messrs H Robinson, EA Russell, and T Sansum. The following appointments were made: FG Frankling and HR Ings (reappointed Overseers) and H Robinson (Vice-Chair); EA Russell and O Hopkins (the Allotment & Firs Field Committee); H Robinson & Col Pilcher (the Finance Committee); and H Robinson & O Hopkins (the Lighting Committee). It was unanimously agreed to increase the clerk's salary to £25.*

Finally we next have 2 items from October - firstly on Saturday **23 October 1926** in **'Bath & County Notes'** (Col 2, 4th item), following an item about fund raising in Weston for the Box Scheme, there is a piece "**Mr Frank Pine** of Combe Down, chairman of the Monkton Combe Parish Council and of the Bath Friendly Societies' Hospital Aid Scheme, for which he has done so much good and self-sacrificing work, received many congratulations on Wednesday on the **celebration of his fiftieth birthday**."

On **30 October 1926** a short item at the end of column 4 announces "Mr Frank H Pine, chairman of the Bath and District Friendly Societies' Hospital Aid Scheme, and Mr Thomas Wills, the Organising Secretary, **will visit Trowbridge** on November 5th to address a meeting at the Town Hall, at which the beneficent work of the societies for the Bath Royal United Hospital and local hospitals in Wiltshire will be explained, with a view to linking Trowbridge with the scheme. Mr H Blair JP Chairman of Trowbridge Urban District Council has agreed to preside and he will be supported by Rev H Sanders JP, Mr H Dyer Chairman of the Wilts Working Men's Society, and Mr Frank Beer of the Pioneer Society. The meeting will commence at 7.30 pm."

1927: First period of Chairmanship of the Parish Council ends

Another period follows when it would have been nice to have unearthed more newspaper reports. FH Pine is no longer Chairman of the Parish Council after April (although, as a report of 12 November indicates, he may have remained a council member). He was back in the chair in April 1928.

So we start with a report of **12 March 1927 'Combe Downs Water - The Company's Provisional Order'** with a meeting of Monkton Combe Parish Council with *FHP presiding, supported by AC Milsom, EA Russell, O Hopkins and H Robinson.* The council debated a request by the water company to be awarded statutory powers for water supply by a resolution of the Council on a draft Provisional order. The matter was left on the table because, despite the chairman interviewing the water company's lawyers, the advantage to the council of acceding to the water company's request was unclear. It is interesting to see the following item in this paper about Combe Hay resisting the water company's supplies because of their adequate spring water.

Now two interesting items from the same edition of the paper dated **23 April 1927**. In **'Bath County Notes'** (3rd item col 3 of Page 4) this gossip column article, in referring to FHP 'retiring' from parish council, says he **"has rendered very useful service to the 'Down' where he has resided for some years, and in many ways benefited the inhabitants by his tenure in office, for he had all the work at his finger-ends, and displayed a vision which is not commonly found on the lesser local government bodies."** However on page 6 (end of column 3) under **'A Parish Council Chairmanship'** is a letter from Frank Pine disputing that he did retire as Chair of Parish Council – quite simply he was not elected. He thanks the paper for its publicity for the Box Scheme.

This is rather curious because another report in the same edition seemed to imply that he was stepping down - on page 17 columns 3 and 4 is the heading: **'Combe Down Lighting - Electricity to be Installed - The New Water Charges'** we read that at the annual meeting of the Monkton Combe Parish Council there were present *Mr FH Pine (Chairman), Col AJ Pilcher, Capt, Daubeny, Messrs AA Milsom, H Robinson, FR Munday, FJ Brown, T Sansum, O Hopkins, EA Russell, with the clerk (Mr EP Page).*

The chairman, before vacating the chair thanked the members for their attendance and support. "Mr Milsom proposed that Mr Robinson be asked to succeed Mr Pine as chairman of the Council. It was perhaps difficult to suggest any successor. Mr Pine had conducted their affairs for a long time past in a very able way. He felt that, after all these years, Mr Pine would be glad to be relieved of some of the duties. Mr Robinson had always taken a very active interest in parish affairs and, as a banker, naturally had business knowledge and plenty of spare time (laughter)." Mr Robinson was elected chairman and Col. Pilcher vice-chairman. Capt Daubeny explained how the Rural District Council had secured a 20% reduction of the proposed water Company rate. **Mr Pine proposed the re-appointment of Mr Page as secretary** *(or rather clerk)* **at £20 a year** - noting that in the old days Mr Page had been very much underpaid. Capt. Daubeny, speaking for the RDC, supported the motion; Mr Page had served the parish for 35 years. *This is a little odd because a year earlier on 24 April 1926 it had been proposed to raise Mr Page's salary to £25!*

It was moved by Mr Hopkins that a Bath Electric Lighting estimate be accepted. The chairman noted that it was about the same price as gas. The proposal for electric lighting was agreed.

On **18 June 1927** we find a long article **'Combe Down's Kindness - Generous Gift to a Rate Collector - Token of Esteem from Parishioners'**. It concerns a **presentation to Mr Page**, former assistant overseer (rate collector) of the parish organised by the former chairman (and still a member) of the Parish Council Mr F H Pine. Mr Pine was regrettably not present as he was in Chippenham addressing a meeting in aid of funds for the Royal United Hospital. However he had sent a very complimentary and apologetic letter in which he stated how faithfully and loyally the parish had been served by Mr Page. The article notes that in the previous year Mr Pine had secured an increased pay and pension for Mr Page. There was a good attendance at the presentation including Capt Daubeney of the RDC and Rev GE Watton (vicar) and members of the parish council. Mr Robinson, presiding, said how highly the parish council had thought of Mr Page for many years.

Capt Daubeney noted how Mr Page had served the parish for 35 years. In former times the profession of collector of the rates was by no means an agreeable one..... He spoke of the corrupt state of affairs 150 years ago, when political and indeed official honesty was indeed a very rare virtue. But in these days, whilst they were sometimes staggered at the size of their rates, they knew that the money in its entirety went to the purpose for which the rates were levied. It was entirely due to the courtesy and probity of men like Mr Page that the profession which he, until recently, had so much adorned had been raised to the honourable position it had latterly occupied. Mr Page was given a wallet of £32 from 116 subscribers. Mr Page responded that it was very odd that a man who had been at their pockets for 35 years should receive such a generous donation. The address to him, signed by H Robinson, Frank H Pine and HR Ings, noted his service as assistant overseer for 35 years.

On **30 July 1927** a short item at the end of column 4 **'A Sunday visit'** reports that a party of Box holders and others from Lansdown and St James visited the RUH accompanied by Messrs FH Pine, H Lavington and AS Gunstone. Mr Pine gave an address on the work of the hospital and its needs.

Once again, on **6 August 1927**, we are at **'Combe Down School - Annual Prize Distribution'**. FH Pine was listed 'among those present'. Delight was expressed by Capt Daubeny, as an old public schoolboy, at the **formation of The Old Scholars Association**. Mrs Daubeny presented the prizes. (*See the separate section below on the Old Scholars.*)

On the Chronicle front page, second item, second column, on **3 September 1927** is **'The Hospital - How to Render a Simple but Very Effective Service'**. This heads a letter from Frank Pine seeking fresh volunteers for the scheme to add to the 1200 stewards who did the quarterly collections from 25-30 houses each (currently some were doing 100 houses which was rather more than could be maintained). Lastly On **12 November 1927** there is a brief note **'Combe Down Council'** (end col 1) to record the taking place of a routine meeting of Monkton Combe Parish Council *chaired by H Robinson with Col Pilcher, Mr EA Russell, and Mr FH Pine.*

On **17 September 1927** is a report **'Our Hospital – Large Gathering at the Pump Room – Mayoral Reception'**. This records the fourth annual gathering of the workers of the friendly societies' scheme hosted by the Mayor Cedric Chivers and the Mayoress Madame Sarah Grand for which 1,400 invitations had been sent out. The Old Red House served refreshments at 4 or 5 buffets throughout the building, to a musical accompaniment as the mayor greeted the guests, and the Roman Baths were opened for inspection. The speeches began at 8 pm.

The Mayor presided and others on the platform were the Mayoress, the Lord Mayor of Bristol, the Mayor and Mayoress of Chippenham (DR and Mrs Nixon), the Mayor and

Mayoress of Calne (Mr and Mrs JF Bodinnar), Miss Foxcroft, Ald. FW Spear, Mr B John (Chairman of the Hospital Management Committee), **Mr FH Pine** (Chairman of the Hospital Scheme), Mr W Rawlinson (vice-chairman and hon. treasurer of the Friendly Societies' scheme), and Mr T Wills (organising secretary).

The Mayor said the committee of the hospital had been afraid to take the public into its confidence about its parlous finances. It needed vivifying. The people who subscribed 61 per cent of the income of the hospital ought to have a larger voice in its management (applause). The Mayor of Chippenham noted how much that medical men in the area owed to the RUH and paid tribute to a great Bath surgeon, Mr Forbes Fraser. Alderman Spear noted how £15,000 had been raised in 3 years. When he was mayor 12 years previously the hospitals income was only £5,000; now it had got up to £18,000. In the last few years £50,000 had been spent in taking the first steps to carry out the dream of moving the whole hospital to Combe Park.

Mr John noted the enormous area the RUH served – with over 200,000 inhabitants: everyone in that area should be encouraged to support the Friendly Societies' scheme. The mayor of Calne noted that four towns were represented by mayors in this charitable cause. The Lord Mayor of Bristol said there was something to learn from Bath about fund raising. **Mr Pine** moved a vote of thanks to the Mayor for a gathering that he said showed strength and unity. The event was followed by a concert from 9.15 until 10.40 pm in the Concert Room and at the same time there was dancing to the Billy Isaacs Orchestra until 11 o'clock once the Pump Room had been cleared after the meeting.

1928: Robert Daniels joins the Parish Council and Frank Pine Vice-Chairman

So we begin with **21 April 1928 'Monkton Combe Affairs - Annual Meeting of Parish Council'** H Robinson, in the chair, welcomed 2 new members - Mr WD Longman and Mr R Daniels. The other councillors present were Messrs FH Pine (vice-Chairman), FJ Brown, FR Munday, EA Russell, and Col AJ Pilcher. Some £20 was voted for Council's general expenses for the half year. Committee responsibilities were elected as follows: Firs Field - Russell and Daniels; Allotments (Combe Down) - Pine and Russell; Finance - Robinson and Pilcher; School Managers - Pine (Combe Down) and Brown (Monkton Combe).

On **9 June 1928** spread over more than 3 columns is a major article **'Over £21,000 - Work of the Bath Hospital Box Scheme - Greater Possibilities Yet'.** This concerns a meeting of Bath and District Hospital Box Scheme at the Royal United Hospital the preceding Monday with the *Chairman Mr Frank H Pine presiding, and the others present included Mr W Rawlinson (Vice-Chairman and Treasurer), Mr Benjamin John (Chairman of the RUH) Thomas Wills (Organising Secretary of the scheme), HC Lavington, GS*

Hodges and AS Gunstone with practically every area represented. The 1927 annual report recorded that during the year that £6,563 had been collected (compared with £5,985 in the previous year) with £4,800 paid over to the RUH and £1,031 to the cottage hospitals and other institutions. **Since 1924 £21,670 had been collected: with £19,900 given to the RUH and £1,770 to the cottage hospitals.** The scheme had done well, despite the impact of unemployment, particularly in the mining areas. Some falling off in Bath and Somerset was more than off-set in Wiltshire. Trowbridge & Chippenham were now part of the scheme.

The Chairman regretted that, through serious ill health, **Mr GS Hodges** had had to give up his role as Secretary of the Friendly Societies Council and presented him with a framed illuminated address to him (as Bro. Hodges) as a testament to his **services to the Council since its formation in 1905 and as its secretary for 11 years**. It was signed by Frank H Pine (Chairman), William Allen King (Vice-Chairman), William HJ Chorley (Secretary) and Henry F Fiddes (Treasurer).

The Hospital Box Scheme now had 6 representatives on the RUH Board following its decision in January to admit them (2 from Bath, 2 from Wilts, 1 from Somerset and 1 from the Friendly Societies Council). Mrs Gordon Smith and Cllr FB Knight were to represent Bath and Hon Mrs Shaw Mellor (Chippenham) and Mr A Blake (Trowbridge) were to represent Wiltshire; Mr J Milburne was to represent Somerset and MR HC Lavington the Friendly Societies. As amended the scheme now provided that for 3d a week contributions, a contributor and dependants could be admitted as an in-patient for free treatment without enquiry as to their means (although this was not currently applying to Chippenham, Trowbridge and Melksham Cottage Hospitals). There was a deficiency for the scheme in the Frome area. Details of the collections by area are set out in this article.

At a separate meeting on the next day (Tuesday), at Corsham, Lady Methuen handed over £1,100 to the Mayoress of Bath (Madame Sarah Grand) representing the Mayor who was unable to attend. *Also present were Lord Methuen, Mr B John (RUH Board Chairman), Mr WH Smith (of the Managing Board), Mr W Rawlinson (treasurer), Mrs Gordon Smith and Mrs Whittington (members of the Managing Board), Mr FH Pine (Chairman of the Friendly Societies Council), Mr T Wills (Organising Secretary), Mr AS Gunstone (Executive Committee), the Rev RC Hunt (Vicar of Corsham), Mr H Hunt (Chairman of the Parish Council), Mr G Harris (local secretary), Mrs T Wills, Mrs FH Pine, Mr RH Whittington (Bath) and Dr Martin (Box).*

Lord Methuen noted that the RUH had been £10,000 in debt in 1924. However a new location was needed compared with its gloomy situation in the centre of Bath. The Mayoress and Mr John expressed optimism, as a result of the success of the Friendly

Societies' Scheme, that funds could be raised for plans to relocate the RUH at the Pensions Hospital site at Combe Park. Mr John also mentioned a pension scheme for nurses.

I have set out a lot of the material from the preceding article because it contains some interesting insights into the founding of the Friendly Societies Council, the challenge of two consecutive major evening meetings - the names of people that keep cropping up - and the fact that Lillian Pine went along to one of them.

From the accessible newspaper record we move on 3 months to **22 September 1928** and another quarterly payment. The multiple headings for another massive 3 column article are **'Cheque for £1,100 - Handed Over for Bath Hospital - Bradford on Avon's Record - Danger of State Aided Hospitals'**. At Bradford on Avon a cheque for £1,100 was presented to Benjamin John, Chairman of the Hospital Management Board who said that "if our hospitals are to be voluntarily supported they must be adequately supported. They must have all the money they need to carry on their work, otherwise, I am convinced, we shall have rate-supported hospitals - but not if we can imbue every district with the spirit and generosity of Bradford on Avon".

Mr Baker, Chairman of Bradford UDC presided at the packed meeting on the Thursday evening. Also present were Mr JF Goodall JP, Col Egbert Lewis, Mr Tom Wills, Mr A Salter, Mr AF Gunstone, Mr Watts (Bradford Scheme Chairman), Mr G Denley (Bradford Secretary) and Mr W Bailey. Mr Baker did not see it necessary for Bradford to have its own hospital given the excellence of the cottage hospital at Trowbridge and the RUH. The Bradford Carnival had regularly supported the hospitals. He noted there were critics who said that hospitals should be state supported – but what was run by the state was not too efficient and did not get the enthusiasm and love for the job of a voluntary institution. It was regretted that, due to illness the Mayor of Bath could not attend, Mr Watts, local Chair of the Box Scheme read a letter from FH Pine regretting he could not be present. The evening concluded with a musical entertainment.

Under a separate heading **'Chippenham Campaign - Interest in the Box Scheme maintained'** is a report on the quarterly meeting at the RUH on the Box Scheme. The amended scheme had been accepted by the Chippenham Cottage Hospital and there would now be a big campaign in the Chippenham area.

> The adjoining article is rather interesting – entitled **'Poor Law reform - Bath Guardians write to Local MPs - Capt. Foxcroft Non-Committal - Mr Geoffrey Peto Favours the Proposals'**. The Bath Poor Law Guardians had written to, respectively, the MPs for Bath and Frome. Mr Peto of Frome clearly supported the reform and referred to the Denison House Public Assistance Committee

support for the government's plans for Local Government Reform. Mr Peto noted that most government critics thought that the county (even with the assistance of its local sub-committees) was too large to take the responsibility for the Poor Law. Denison took the opposite view - and whereas the government would make 62 county councils and 82 county boroughs the responsible authorities in England and Wales, Denison would reduce these 144 authorities to 11 in all. Mr Peto did not favour Denison where Somerset would be part of an area from Gloucestershire to Cornwall.

On Saturday **27 October 1928** is a small item at the end of column 4 that says **"Mr Frank H Pine Chairman of the Friendly Societies Hospital Scheme was 52 on Saturday"** (i.e. the previous Saturday). In the **10 November 1928** issue, in the section **'This Week in Bath - Notes and Jottings from All Quarters',** we find, at the end of column 2 **'Hospital scheme'** and a report on a meeting in Kingston St Michael on the Monday night with the visitors from Bath, Mr Frank H Pine and Mr A S Gunstone addressing a meeting on the scheme and answering questions.

On **17 November 1928** (end of column 5) we are back at the Church Rooms Combe Down for a meeting of **'Monkton Combe Council'.** *In Mr Robinson's absence Frank Pine took the chair. Also present were Messrs FJ Brown, R Daniels, JR England, WHD Longman, FR Munday and Col AJ Pilcher (Mr Robinson and Mr Russell were ill).* Footpath repairs and new lamps for Shaft Road were discussed.

On **1 December 1928** is an item **'New Hospital Scheme - Explained and Adopted at Castle Combe'** In a well attended meeting in the Village Hall, Castle Combe, on November 22 Mr Frank H Pine and Mr AS Gunstone explained and secured the adoption of the Box Scheme locally – to be serviced by the RUH and Chippenham Cottage Hospital.

1929: Despite offers to resign Frank Pine still in demand as Chairman of Friendly Societies and Council

On 16 February 1929 we find **'No Swapping Horses - Bath Friendly Societies Council Retains Tried Officials'.** Although offering to stand down, Frank Pine was re-elected as Chairman of the Bath Friendly Societies Council. There was a minutes silence for the death of Mayor Chivers. *Vice Chairman (Bro WA King), Treasurer (Bro HF Fiddes) and Secretary (Bro WH Chorley) were re-elected. Bro HC Lavington was re-elected as the council's representative on the RUH Board.* (I would note on the same page, the general election results - in 1923 Bath had a Liberal MP but in 1924, perhaps due to Labour intervention the *late* Capt Foxcroft got in).

At present I cannot find a newspaper article for the April general meeting of the parish council - although at the June and September meeting FH Pine was still in the chair. As we see in the report of **15 June 1929 'Monkton Combe Council - Cricket in the Firs Field'.** *With FH Pine presiding, supported by Col Pilcher, H Robinson, R Daniels EA Russell, FJ Brown* the council discussed the GPO terms for a central phone kiosk and agreed them. The issue of boys over 14 playing cricket in Firs Field with a hard ball was discussed and alternative locations for this were to be considered.

So to a report covering 6 columns, most of the page, in the same issue of **15 June 1929** on **'A Great Work - Friendly Societies aid to the Royal United Hospital - The Combe Park Scheme - Mayors Hope of 'Very Good News' before long'.** At this annual meeting of chairmen of all districts in the Guildhall *the Mayor (Cllr Aubrey Bateman, ex-officio President of the RUH) presided over a very good attendance which included Lt-Col Egbert Lewis (Vice-Chairman of the Hospital Board), Mr Frank H Pine (Chairman of the Friendly Societies Scheme) and Mr Walter Rawlinson (hon. Treasurer and vice-chairman) with apologies from Mr B John (Chairman of the Hospital).*

The 3p a week scheme whereby contributors were relieved of questions as to means, was growing. £5,786 (net) had been raised in 1928. There was disappointment that Frome was still outside the scheme. The executive said that there was a need to keep up voluntary contributions – state or municipal controls were the alternatives. Mayor Bateman was keen to support the dream of the late Mayor Chivers on the removal of the RUH to Combe Park. He said that the sums raised by the Friendly Societies and working men's contributions were creditable, but an appeal needed to be made to the better off. The report set out the sums raised in Bath, Wilts & Somerset and paid to 7 hospitals. The Bath Eye Infirmary and Bath Ear Nose and Throat Hospital were in the scheme for qualified box holders. 68 vouchers had been issued for free RUH treatment. The scheme had representation on Boards of the RUH and Chippenham Cottage Hospital. More stewards were needed in Trowbridge. Full Accounts and the terms of voucher scheme are set out in the press report. In the past year £5,821 had been collected (£2,345 from Bath, £709 from Somerset and £2,731 from Wiltshire) and £4,300 had gone to the RUH and £979 to the Cottage Hospitals.

On **22 June 1929** we have a report on **'A Brilliant Affair - Success of the Mayoral Garden Party - 800 Guests'.** The Mayor Audrey Bateman hosted this event in the Royal Victoria Park on Freedom Day - all the best-known local people were present (peers, an admiral, generals, judges, churchmen, magistrates etc). The police handled parking for over 300 cars. A long list of guests (headed by the Duke and Duchess of Somerset, the Mayors and Mayoresses of Chippenham, Swindon, Marlborough and Salisbury) includes a Mr & Mrs Daniels (probably not Robert and Annie) and Mr & Mrs F H Pine.

In the paper of **14 September 1929** we have two entries. Firstly on page 4 a small item in column 2 **'Bath Friendly Societies'** is about an annual Bath Friendly Societies Council meeting at which *Mr FH Pine presided* at the Foresters' Hall with *W King, Vice-Chairman, HF Fiddes, Treasurer, W Chorley, Secretary, and J Coles, FC Bishop, Haverfield and W Howood.* Mr Fiddes reported on the Hearts of Oak conference and the annual accounts were accepted. On page 16 of the same edition is a report on **'Combe Down Affairs'** and a Monkton Combe Parish Council meeting with *Frank H Pine presiding with R Daniels, FR Munday, EA Russell and Col. Pilcher with apologies from JR England.* The meeting considered that a precept of £35 was needed to meet a deficit on the lighting bill. It is interesting to note another article on the same page – the opening of Trowbridge Hospital.

On 21 September 1929 the Chronicle had an article headed **'£1,100 for hospital – Gratifying Result of Box Scheme'.** At the Church Hall, Combe Down, the Mayor (Mr Aubrey Bateman) handed over the cheque to Mr B John (Chairman of the Hospital). Major M Clark presided and he was supported also by Lieut-Col. Egbert Lewis, the Hon Mrs Shaw Mellor and Mr FH Pine. **Mr Pine** spoke about the working of the scheme saying that the only alternative was state-controlled hospitals that would lose human sympathy and the human touch. The cost of maintaining each in-patient was £2.16s a week, and the cost of the institution was close to £20,000 a year. Towards that sum the Friendly Societies' scheme had contributed 22½% in the last year. Mr Pine denied emphatically critics who said there was waste at the hospital. The Mayor noted the formation of a Hospitals' Council for Bath. He congratulated Combe Down for raising £559 under the scheme. In accepting the cheque Mr John congratulated Mr Bateman on being designated Mayor for a further year. The meeting was followed by a programme given by the Beechen Cliff Male Voice Choir.

In the quarterly report the total collected was £1,244 (£555 from Bath, £168 from Somerset and £520 from Wiltshire). Apart from £1,110 to the RUH, Chippenham Cottage Hospital received £85 16s 8d, Melksham Cottage Hospital £16 5s 2d, Freshford Nursing Association £5 16s 5d, the Westminster Hospital London £4 7s 10d, The Bristol Royal Infirmary £2 3s 11d, the Bath Ear Nose and Throat Hospital £1 16s 8d and the Paulton Memorial Hospital £1 11s 6d. The Westminster payment was made in accordance with the amended scheme. Calne had now come into the amended scheme but difficulties were being experienced with the Victoria Hospital, Frome (which presumably wanted more of the monies collected in the Frome area despite the indebtedness of Frome residents to the RUH).

Oh the limitations of local democracy! On **28 September 1929** a report on a planned parish meeting is entitled **'Where were they - Combe Down meeting - but no parishioners'.** Monkton Combe Parish Councillors turned up on Friday week for a parish meeting (*Frank H Pine presiding with R Daniels, H Robinson, Col Pilcher and JR England*), but no parishioners turned up in order to approve an increased rate with the Lighting Budget raised to £150, as the previous year's budget was insufficient. "The whole parish turned up last night" said Mr Pine, referring to the meeting when the Mayor handed over the hospital cheque "one cannot expect them to do so two nights following" The report concluded that it was equally likely the good people of Combe Down were at home, discussing and mentally digesting the Mayor's excellent speech on hospital administration as reported in that evening's Chronicle and Herald.

On **30 November 1929** there is a report **'Bath Friendly Societies - Whist Drive at the Red House'**. At this Thursday evening whist drive there had been 33 tables at the Red House: <u>Mrs</u> **Frank H Pine** awarded the prizes.

So to another big 3 column article on **7 December 1929: 'Mayors Appeal for Bath Hospital - Another £1,000 from Friendly Societies' Box Scheme Collections - The New Situation at Trowbridge - Frome's Unrecognised Indebtedness to the Institution'** The Quarterly cheque presentation to the RUH was at the Holy Trinity Hall, Bath. *Cllr Edward White presided and those present were the Mayor (Aubrey Bateman), Lt Col Egbert Lewis, Rev CS Cockbill (rector), Mr FH Pine (chairman of the fund), Mr W Rawlinson (treasurer), the Rev G White, Mr C Sealy, Cllr EJ Tiley, Mr WE Bailey, Mr T Wills (organising secretary), and several of the sisters and nurses from the hospital.*

Aubrey Bateman paid tribute to his predecessor as Mayor, Alderman Chivers, as 'probably the greatest Bathonian in living memory' and pledged to carry forward his scheme for a new hospital at Combe Park. He noted that since 1923 the Friendly Societies had kept the doors of the RUH open by raising, mostly from weekly wage earners, £27,300 for the RUH and £3,327 for the cottage hospitals. The agreement between the executive committee and the local committee at Trowbridge was due to end in March - the local committee wanted to give primacy to the new Trowbridge Hospital but it was hoped the RUH would not lose out. A meeting on 6 December was to inform Frome of their continuing net indebtedness of the scheme and similar concerns applied to Shepton Mallet as expressed in a meeting with Shepton Mallet Cottage Hospital.

On **14 December 1929 'Monkton Combe Parish Council'** we read of a small meeting with FH Pine presiding. The WL Russell Bequest in the form of coal for the poor was in the process of being distributed. 'Danger' notices had been placed near the Elementary Schools, Combe Down.

1930: Somerset Floods - Fund Raising for new RUH - The Scheme Expands - Friendly Societies and Parish Councils

Although 2013-2014 will go down in living memory as the year of the Somerset Floods, the level of precipitation and flooding in 1929-1930 on the Somerset Levels was far worse in terms of all records. So we find in the Chronicle and Herald of 4 January 1930 a small item **'Somerset Floods - Combe Down to join relief effort'**. At a meeting of Monkton Combe Parish Council Frank Pine, presiding, read out an appeal from Lord Bath. It was decided a parish meeting would be called to issue a circular in support of Lord Bath's appeal for the relief of the sufferers of the Somerset Floods. Consequently on 11 January 1930 a meeting was convened in the Avenue Hall, Combe Down, *and Chaired by Mr Frank H Pine (Chairman of Monkton Combe Parish Council) with Lieut-Col Arthur Pilcher, Major TH Clark, Father M O'Sullivan, Mr FJ Cox, Mr Pratt, Mr Miles, Mr Warren and Mr Daniels.* Responsibilities for raising funds were allocated.

On **25 January 1930** under **'Hospital Box Scheme'** in column 2 is a report of the annual meeting of officials and stewards of the Odd Down area of the Bath Friendly Societies' Scheme. In the year £50 had been collected, which was £12 more than in the previous year. Mr FH Pine was present and gave a very interesting discourse of the scheme's activity and thanked the officers and stewards for their active interest in the work of the hospital. Mr Billet (Chair) and Mr Noad (Hon sec) were re-elected. Mr Pine was heartily thanked for coming, and for his interesting talk.

The issue of **1 February 1930** had a <u>Full page article with picture of Lord Moyniham of Leeds</u> (President of the Royal College of Surgeons) entitled **'Scheme for a New Royal United Hospital at Combe Park – Launched at Great Guildhall Meeting – Brilliant Advocacy of Voluntary Hospitals by Lord Moyniham'** <u>The Lord Mayors appeal for £100,000 RUH at Combe Park had been inaugurated on the previous Thursday evening</u>. This was deliberately held on the anniversary of Mayor Chivers death. Lord Moyniham denied the Voluntary Hospital system was moribund.

Among those on the platform (apart from the Mayor and Lord Moyniham) were the Marquis of Bath, the Bishop of Bath & Wells (Dr Wilson), the Deputy Mayor (Ald. Sir Harry Hatt), the Archdeacon of Bath (Ven. SA Boyd), Dr Cave, Cllr Hon HS Davey, Mr FG Hamilton (Chairman of the Hospital), Mr FD Wardle, Mr W Rawlinson and Mr FH Pine (Chairman of the Friendly Society Scheme). A long list is given of other important persons present or who sent apologies for absence. At the back of the platform was a huge diagram showing that the Hospital served 693 square miles of which 305 were in Somerset, 332 in Wiltshire and 56 in Gloucestershire.

The article heading the Mayor's speech was '**According to needs not Circumstances**'. The Mayor said "We cannot withhold respect and admiration as we realise, in their various forms, the altruistic efforts of doctors, nurses and sympathetic laymen so that no suffering man or woman shall lack medical aid" He was seeking to implement the objective of the late Mayor Chivers ('Baths greatest Citizen within living memory'). The Bath Chronicle & Herald was praised for its advocacy of the new hospital. Lord Moyniham said that 'Both in matters of spirit and in matters of sheer business efficiency it (*voluntary hospitals*) is the incomparable English way of doing things. *Material on this continues on the next page.*

The paper had two interesting reports in its issue of **8 February 1930**, Firstly on page 1 column 2 is '**Somerset Flood Fund - Ready Response to Lord Bath's Appeal at Combe Down**'. House to house collections on Combe Down had hoped to raise £25-£30 but in the event £62 was raised before costs thanks to the efforts of Col Pilcher, Major TH Clark, Father M O'Sullivan, Messrs Charter, Cox, Daniels, Maggs, McIndoe, Page, Pratt and Tiley. Mr Frank H Pine (Chairman of the Parish Council said that all who had contributed were to be congratulated on such a good result. Donations of much lesser amounts (£1 - £19) from other Bath parishes are listed.

In the same paper of **8 February 1930** page 9 the Main Article is '**Cheque for £10,000 - Paid in to the Mayor of Bath's Hospital Fund**' by Mr Stanley Wills (*of the tobacco company*). It was planned that Bath Corporation would purchase the existing Hospital building for £30,000. The report contains a list of donations. Under a heading '**The Mayor and His Doubting Critics**' it is reported that, in connection with the Bath Friendly Societies' scheme, the Mayor (Cllr Aubrey Bateman) had made the first of a series of visits to districts by going to the Widcombe Institute on Tuesday. The meeting was chaired by the Rev, Lovegrove-Herman, supported by Mr FH Pine Chairman of the committee of the Box Scheme, Mr WA Sheppard and Mr Thomas Wills (secretary of the Box Scheme).

The next week on **15 February 1930** is a heading '**Combe Down Affairs - Hockey on to be allowed on the Firs Field**'. This was one of 3 issues before Monkton Combe Parish Council on Tuesday at which *FH Pine presided with R Daniels, H Robinson, EA Russell, FJ Brown, JR England*. Permission for hockey to be played on the Firs Field every other Saturday was granted by the Parish Council in response to a request from Mr. H Robinson on behalf of the team. The charge was to be 5s per game. A New phone kiosk had been erected on Combe Down but the GPO was to be asked about it having no light at night. FHP advised that the Somerset Floods Appeal had raised £60 5s 10d net.

Now two reports from **1 March 1930**; firstly on the funeral of '**Mr JM Sheppard**' (page 17 column 4). He was Secretary of the Royal United Hospital for nearly 32 years. At the

Church were FG Hamilton (RUH Chairman representing Mayor of Bath and President of the RUH), Col Egbert Lewis and other representatives of the RUH Board. In the following article about the Abbey Memorial Service at which the Mayor was present, it is recorded that FHP sent his apologies. Next (on page 26 bottom of column 2) we have **'Our New hospital - Friendly Societies' Whist Drive at Bath'** which refers to a Thursday whist drive of 37 tables at the Red House: HF Fiddes was MC and FH Pine spoke about 'Our New Hospital'.

Two more interesting entries in one day arise on **22 March 1930**. Firstly there is **'Combe Down Council - Response to Somerset Flood Fund'**. This is a report of Monkton Combe Parish Council with *FH Pine presiding with Lt-Col Pilcher, R Daniels, H Robinson, FR Munday, S Plummer and EP Page (Clerk).* The cost of lighting the phone kiosk was to be met. <u>At the annual parish meeting FHP was re-elected to the Chair</u>. Accounts of the Flood appeal were presented by its Treasurer, Mr Robinson, who remarked that best thanks were due to Mr Pine for having the balance sheet done out so splendidly, though he did not think it right Mr Pine should have borne this expense personally.

Next in the same 22 March issue we have **'Officers Appreciated - Work on Behalf of the New Bath Hospital Scheme'** <u>FH Pine is re-elected as chairman of Bath Friendly Societies Council</u> at its annual meeting. *Also re-elected were Mr WA King (Vice-chairman), Mr W Chorley (secretary), and Mr FD Fiddes (treasurer) - tributes were paid to Bro Gunstone (Rationals) for his dedication to the hospital scheme.* Bro King (Foresters) proposed that friendly societies operating under the Holloway system be invited to join the council, it being recognised that the older societies now operated this system.

> *The first "Holloway" friendly society was established in Stroud in 1875, and was called the Stroud and Mid Gloucester Working Man's Conservative Association's Sick Benefit Society. It was based on a scheme devised by George Holloway, M.P. for Stroud and represented a new kind of friendly society which aimed to provide its members not only with a sum of money during sickness, temporary disablement or for relatives at death, but also to provide a lump sum payable at retirement age. After three years the society had taken off dramatically and the membership had risen to 1,000, this was seen as an incredible achievement. The Stroud society became a model for similar benefit societies, many of which were established in the West Country, and by the end of 1924 there were 42 'Holloway' Societies in existence.*

> *According to a current FSA definition, Holloway products, sold by around a dozen friendly societies to mainly less well-off consumers, combine income protection insurance and an investment element which allows policyholders to share in the society's surplus.(For a time I subscribed to a small accident policy with The Original Holloway Friendly Society - JD.)*

Now on **12 April 1930** we have **'Lamps Damaged - Complaints at Combe Down'** and a report of the annual meeting of Monkton Combe Parish Council. *FH Pine presided with Col Pilcher (Vice-Chairman), R Daniels, H Robinson, FJ Brown and Nelson Plummer.* FH Pine was re-elected Chairman. **Mr JW Spark, Bath City Electrical Engineer** had written to the council about wilful damage to 2 of the relatively new electric lamps. Complaints were discussed about the behaviour of youths on the Downs when there were now only 2 policemen on the beat rather than 3, as previously. The Rural District Council was to be asked for refuse carts to be covered so that refuse would not blow off them.

Now for two articles entitled **'The New Bath Hospital'**. On **10 May 1930** it was noted that the Mayor's appeal for the building of the RUH at Combe Park was within sight of half its £100,000 target (Note a donation was marked "Channel Islands" per Mr Pine!). On 31 May 1930 it was recorded that the Mayor's Appeal Fund had £51,603, but £48,396 was still needed (NB also a donation marked "Grateful Patient" per FH Pine Esq.).

In the issue of **12 July 1930** on **'Combe Down Affairs'** we have Monkton Combe Parish Council with *FH Pine presiding with Lt-Col Pilcher, R Daniels, H Robinson.* A Bill from Bath Corporation's Electricity Department was passed for payment. Fencing around the Church Army hut and pit had been removed – this posed a risk to children so the Church Army was to be asked to repair it.

Church Army Hut c1930

Next we have two reports in the paper of **30 August 1930**. Firstly on page 12 there were 3 columns on the **'Bath Friendly Societies Fine Work'**. At the RUH, on the Monday Evening, a meeting in connection with the Friendly Societies Hospital Propaganda Scheme had been held. *FH Pine, as chairman of the Executive, had presided. Also present were Mr FG Hamilton (Chairman of the RUH Board), Lt-Col Lewis, Mr L Mears (Secretary of the RUH), and representatives of a large number of districts in the scheme.* Frome district (and its Victoria Hospital) was now to be in the scheme and a local organisation established. X-rays and massage for qualified box-holders and their dependants were to come within scheme, subject to the usual production of vouchers from a local secretary. Bath City and Wilts County Council were to pay for children of qualified box holders, referred by the local education authority, to have tonsil and adenoid operations. Fund raising from a fair in Shepton Mallet would be shared between the local hospital (which was in desperate need of assistance) and the RUH.

Mr Mears referred to the Doncaster scheme of stamped cards for two pence a week to raise funds for a new hospital.

Next in the same paper of **30 August 1930** , taking over all of page 23 (apart from a piece on a 93 year old widow seeking a new husband) we have **'County Campaign for Bath's Hospital - Cheque for £1,000 handed over at Corsham - Stirring Speeches by Lord Methuen, Mayor of Bath and Mrs Shaw Mellor'**. It recounts that on Wednesday at a meeting at the Town Hall, Corsham, Lord Methuen presided, supported by Lady Methuen, Mayor of Bath (Aubrey Bateman), the Hon Mrs Shaw Mellor, Mr FG Hamilton (Chairman of the RUH Board), Mr FH Pine (Chairman of the Box Scheme), Mr W Rawlinson (Treasurer of the Box Scheme) and another 8 persons are listed. There is a big list of notables in the audience.

Lord Methuen spoke as former Chairman of Kings College Hospital, London about its removal to Denmark Hill. He noted that Mr Wills had given £10,000 to the new Hospital and had promised another £10,000 if they could get another £30,000 for the hospital due to be finished September 1931 *(This was Mr Wills was of WD & HO Wills the cigarette manufacturers)*. The Mayor praised the chairmen, secretaries and collectors of the Friendly Societies. He spoke of the need to improve the health of the working population from that of a C3 nation at the start of the War.

So on to a small piece of **13 September 1930: 'Timber for Nothing - Monkton Combe Council's Offer and No Takers!'** This concerned a meeting of the Parish Council where an elm tree in Firs Field had blown down in the winter storms – and there were no takers to take it away for free. *F H Pine presided with Messrs Robert Daniels, H Robinson, FJ Brown and FR Munday.* The council agreed to guarantee the GPO £4 per annum for the lighting and maintenance of the telephone kiosk.

On **27 September 1930** we have **'Declined with Thanks - Baths Invitation to the Wilts Working Mens Society'** At a meeting of the Bath Friendly Societies Council a reply was read to the Council's invitation to the Wilts Working Mens Society. They declined to join the Bath & District Friendly Societies Council under the Holloway system for the present. Mr H Fiddes presided due to the absence of the President FH Pine through illness.

Now with **4 October 1930** and **'Lighting Matters'** we are at a meeting of Monkton Combe Parish Council with *FHP presiding with Lt-Col Pilcher, R Daniels, H Robinson and Mr Warren.* A precept for electric lighting was agreed. Mr England of 1, The Firs had requested a lamp on the corner of The Firs. Mr Robinson thought a lamp on such a narrow corner would be dangerous, which was why a previous lamp had been removed – tree clipping was proposed to improve lighting from the existing lights.

Finally on **26 October 1930** is a brief un-headed item (end col. 4) to say that FHP was to speak in Trowbridge on the Hospital scheme.

THE NEWSPAPER RECORD 1931

1931: Changing Times on the Council - A new RUH

1931: Labour and Housing, Bath's Boundaries, New Hospital, New Parish Clerk (37 Newspaper Items)

We start 1931 with a heart-warming item of **3 January 1931 'Gifts from Christmas tree - Children's Joyous Time at the Royal United Hospital'.** It is reported that "On Boxing Night, there was a good attendance of visitors, including many of the ladies and gentlemen of the committee, to witness the stripping of the Christmas Tree in the children's ward and the subsequent concert of the nurses in the Victoria Ward. Dr McKeag was Father Christmas, and the tree presented a delightful spectacle, laden with presents. Upon these the little patients fixed their eyes eagerly, and the joy in their faces as the presents were taken from the tree and handed to them by the nurses was a sight that it did one good to see. Among visitors were Lt Col Egbert Lewis, Mr A Salter and Mr FH Pine (Chairman of the Friendly Societies' Fund). The Mayor (Ald. T Sturge Cotterell had paid his visit on the previous day, as he had many other Boxing Day engagements."

> *Frank Pine was no slouch at celebrating Christmas at home - and my mother recalled how the visit of Father Christmas one snowy Christmas had been recorded by boot marks on the glass roof of the conservatory.*

Next we have two items of **14 February 1931**. Firstly a modest item on page 7 **'Monkton Combe Affairs - Question of War Memorial Upkeep'** and a meeting of Monkton Combe Parish Council. *FH Pine presided with Lt-Col Pilcher, R Daniels, H Robinson, W Miles and EA Russell, but EP Page (Clerk) was unable to attend due to Influenza.* An issue as to whether the council was empowered to maintain the War Memorial was raised and Mr Pine said he was definitely in favour of it. An account of the Bath Electric Light Department was passed for payment and the RDC was to be pressed to repair a pot-holed footpath near Monkton Combe Junior School.

The second item of **14 February** on page 9 reflected a significant change in the parish council with **'Election of Parish Councillors - A Surprise at Combe Down - Chairman of the Council Loses his Seat - Labour "Invasion"** '. It reads "Figuratively speaking, a bombshell broke at the Church Room, Combe Down, on Monday, when the new Parish Council was elected. There were nine candidates for the six vacancies on the Council. Cpt. Daubeny presided and gave the meeting ten minutes in which to propose that the election should be by ballot, but there was no proposition, and the voting was done by a show of hands.

"The result was that the Chairman (Mr FH Pine) lost his seat, and two other members Mr H Robinson and Col Pilcher, also failed to gain sufficient votes. Capt. JR England did not seek re-election. The four new candidates were at the top of the poll. The only members of the old council remaining were Mr EA Russell and Mr R Daniels who came at the bottom of the poll. *The councillors elected and the votes they received were: Mr F Miller (25); Mr AE Clease (23); Mr RW Cornish (21); Mr CG Millet (21); Mr EA Russell (12); and Mr R Daniels (9).* Mr Cornish is the chairman and Mr Miller the Treasurer of the newly-formed Combe Down Branch of the Frome Division Labour Party. A vote of thanks to Capt. Daubeny was proposed by Mr FH Pine (the former chairman) and seconded by Mr Cornish."

Oh well - hospital affairs continued to claim attention and in the issue of **11 April 1931** column 5 is heded **'Well Done Odd Down - £328 for Hospital in Seven Years'**. "The annual meeting of the Odd Down branch of the Friendly Societies' Hospital Box Scheme was held at St Phillip's Institute, on Monday evening, Mr FH Pine was in the chair.... Mr ET Billett was again elected District Chairman and Mr HT Parker, hon secretary in place of Mr WE Noad."

But what is this - two articles on **18 April 1931** on Combe Down Affairs - firstly on page 5 we have **'Mr FH Pine'** - a key article with a photo used in his obituary 11 years later. It reads **"The re-election of Mr FH Pine as Chairman of Monkton Combe Parish Council has rather puzzled some people, having regard to the fact that he was defeated as a candidate at the recent election, but everything is in order, the Act of Parliament providing for such an appointment. Mr Pine has for a considerable time been chairman of the parish council and, except for one year's break, has continuously served in this capacity. His re-election is recognition of his ability."**

"He took a very active part in inaugurating and - as Chairman continues the valuable work - in carrying on the Friendly Societies Scheme for assisting the Royal United Hospital - a scheme that has enabled this institution to keep its doors open, to the inestimable benefit of the working class community in the city, and of others."
So FHP displayed his working class credentials!

In the same issue of **18 April** page 26 we have **'Combe Down Affairs - Chairman re-elected at Parish Council Meeting'** that offers a fuller report of above item. "At the first meeting of the reconstituted Monkton Combe Parish Council at Combe Down on Wednesday evening Mr Frank H Pine was re-elected to the chair. A motion to the effect that Mr R W Cornish, a newcomer to the council be elected Chairman was defeated by five votes to four. Mr Cornish was unanimously elected vice-chairman. The Chairman and Mr Brown were elected school managers for Combe Down and Monkton Combe respectively." The council then addressed mundane concerns about waste scavenging, the closure of the infants' school playground during the dinner hour, and a concealed entrance opposite the Firs Field.

On **25 April 1931** we have **'Combe Down Aids Noble Cause - Whist Drive for Orthopaedic Hospital'** where it is reported that a survey of the work of the Children's Orthopaedic Hospital, Combe Park, was given to a large company at a whist drive in aid of the hospital at the Church Rooms, Combe Down by Mrs Lock deputising for Mr Francis Mallett, the Chairman of the Hospital. Mr G Frankling was the MC and proposed a vote of thanks to Mrs Lock, seconded by Mr FH Pine.

Next on **16 May 1931** we have **'Combe Down Incident and The Sequel - Precocious Youth and New Councillor'.** This involved one of the new councillors, Mr Millett, speaking to some youths over the age of 14 playing football contrary to deeds of covenant of the Firs Field which seemed to have been amicably resolved. There was a full attendance of the Council viz, *Messrs, FH Pine (chairman), FR Munday, SL Plummer, FJ Brown, RW Cornish, AG Cleaves, CG Millett, R Daniels, F Miller, EA Russell and the clerk (Mr EP Page).*

In the **31 May** paper and headed **'The New Bath Hospital - Twenty-second List of Donations - £48,396 Still Wanted'** (for the Mayors Hospital Appeal Fund) and we have an entry 'grateful patient' per FH Pine.

Moving on to **6 June 1931** we have, in a report exceeding 4 columns, **'Hospital Scheme - £33,999 Raised by Box Collections in 7 years - Free Treatment for Members'**. These were the headline points made by Mr Frank H Pine at a meeting at the RUH on the Tuesday. Of the £33,999 raised £32,100 went to the RUH and £3,958 to neighbouring institutions for the treatment of box holders. In the last year £5,028 had been collected - of which £2,213 was from Bath, £2,132 from Wiltshire and £682 in Somerset. Working expenses of the scheme were 8%. It was regretted that arrangements with the local committee at Trowbridge had come to an end. Regret was expressed at the death of Mr Benjamin John, former chairman of the RUH Board. Frome was now part of the scheme but there was a lack of local enthusiasm.

Now we find three reports from **13 June 1931**. Firstly on page 7 under **'Armchair Musings'** and **'Not 1 per cent'** it is noted that, in February the box scheme had invited 450 local employers to take part in a contributory plan for employees free treatment - but only 3 had responded. The article concluded "But enthusiasts who run this excellent organisation, <u>under the inspiring influence of Mr Frank Pine, the Chairman, and the shrewd guidance of Mr Thomas Willis, the Organising Secretary</u> will not be daunted by their disappointment. They have in other ways achieved big results." (***My underlining***)

Secondly on page 12 in the same issue of **13 June** there is an article **'Bath Hospital receives cheque for £1,000 - Friendly Societies Scheme Again Achieves Excellent Results - Sir Guy Nugent "Amazed" - Much Needed Generousity Saves Closing of Wards.'** The Church Rooms Upper Weston was the venue for handing over the quarterly cheque. Mr Milburn, chairman of the local committee presided with Sir Guy Nugent, Mr FG Hamilton (Chairman of the Board of Management of the RUH), Mr J Lawrence Mears (Secretary-Superintendant RUH), Mr FH Pine (Chairman of the Scheme) etc. Mr Pine paid tribute to the late Alderman Vezey who had been chairman of one of their wards in Bath. The Chairman of the Hospital Board Aubrey Bateman sent his wishes. FH Pine referred to 8 years before, coming out on a wintry foggy night with Mr Wills and one or two others to first organise the Weston branch. The Friendly Societies had set out to raise £5,000 a year and they had done it for the first two or three years but now it had dropped to £4,000 - they had now to get it back to £5,000.

Thirdly on **13 June 1931** we have **'Combe Down Affairs - Housing Problem Discussed in Private'**. Combe Down Council accepted an offer from Mr Hicks of Springfield Farm to mow the Firs Field in exchange for the hay. A letter was read from Capt Daubeny RDC about danger signs. Mr Cornish raised the need for more houses for working men - the Parish Council discussed the matter in committee. *It is clear that the need for new council houses was a key item on the Labour Party agenda - but FHP seems to have fully supported it.*

Frank Pine does not feature in the front page lead of **27 June 1931 'Greater Bath - Boundaries Adjustment Scheme - City's Population would be increased by 3,500 - Strong opposition expected'.** However it relates to talks between Somerset County Council, Bath City Council and Bath Rural District Council in Taunton. Combe Down and Weston Districts would be mainly affected. Upper Weston currently extended to Lansdown and the principal landowner was Mr RW Blathwayt. In 1911 proposals for Bath had included parts of Combe Down, Bathanpton, Batheaston and Bathford but the latter three were now not included. *See Frank Pine's position on 3 November in relation to 'Combe Down Clings to Independence'.*

On **4 July 1931** an article is headed **'Bath Friendly Societies - Suggested Deputation to Mineral Water Hospital'**. Here we have a meeting of the Bath Friendly Societies Council that suggests asking the Governors of the Mineral Water Hospital if they could send a deputation to look over the hospital. A long discussion took place on the subject of State Insurance (approved societies) under the 1911 Act. *Those attending were FH Pine (Chairman) with Messrs Knight, Gunstone, King, Chorley, Fiddes, Coles, Horwood, Haverfield and Amesbury.*

On **10 July 1931** in **'Not Fit for Pigs - Combe Down Slum Dwellings Criticised'** we return to the new Labour Party agenda for new council houses. "There are houses here that are unfit for pigs to live in!" exclaimed a member of Combe Down Parish Council at the Parish Rooms meeting chaired by Mr FH Pine. Mr Cornish asked the Councillors to move in the matter of pressing the RDC to build houses on Combe Down at rents that working people could afford to pay. It was decided to write to the RDC and ask for at least 36 new houses to be built.

On **15 August 1931** are two relevant articles in the same edition of the paper. Firstly thre is **'Hospital Box Scheme - Organisation Meeting at Peasedown'**. The local vicar Rev BC Carson had presided at a meeting on the Wednesday evening. Addresses were given by Mr FH Pine (Chairman of the Friendly Societies' Council) and Mr FG Hamilton (Chairman of the RUH Management Board). Also present were AS Gunstone, J Lawrence Mears (Secretary and Superintendent RUH) Tom Wills (Secretary of the Box Scheme). The Council agreed to an invitation to hold next quarterly cheque donating meeting at Wellow.

The same **15 August** edition reported on a new saga that continued through the year with **'Clerk who hates flattery - Retires after 37 Years at Combe Down - Illness the Cause'**. "There was a full attendance of members at the meeting of Monkton Combe Parish Council on Tuesday Evening, but no Clerk. The temporary duties of clerk were therefore discharged by Mr Cornish, the vice-chairman. A letter was read from Mrs Page, wife of the clerk, Mr Edward Palling Page, stating that her husband was very seriously ill and would not be able to continue with his occupation." Mrs Page offered to do what work she could (and to see the accounts were all up to date to the end of the September quarter). Chairman FH Pine said the letter was not unexpected as Mr Page had been in failing health for 3 or 4 years. He had been a devoted parish clerk for 37 years. *A sub-Committee to appoint a new clerk was formed of FHP, Mr Cornish and Mr R Daniels.*

The council considered a letter from Capt Daubeny in which the RDC sought information on the proposed site for new housing and the types of housing to be provided - parlour or non-parlour. Capt. Daubeny also suggested a parish meeting be convened on the extension of Bath boundaries. FW Kelway (RDC surveyor and inspector) and Capt. Dubeny now entered the meeting to discuss tipping places for household refuse. *Members present were FH Pine (Chair), RW Cornish (Vice-Chair), AG Cleaves, R Daniels, F Miller, DG Millett, ER Russell, FJ Brown and S Plummer.*

In the **29 August 1931** edition of the paper, under **'Situations Vacant'** we find (column 1 - 10th item): **Applications Invited** - an advert for a new Monkton Combe Clerk, Applications to 17 The Firs, Combe Down.

We are back to the hospital theme on **5 September 1931** with a 3 column spread on **'Bath & District Collections for Hospitals - RUH gets another £1,000 - Wilts contributes £482 and Bath gives £583 - Box Offerings Compared with Sweeps.'** This reports that there was a large gathering in the RUH Board Room on Tuesday for a meeting of Friendly Societies' Council on the quarterly report ending June. *Those present were FH Pine (Chair), HC Lavington, FG Hamilton, W Rawlinson, A Salter (Executive Committee) and many others.* A report on the quarterly meeting in June at the Church Room Upper High St, Weston noted that 'Miss Daniels had kindly undertaken the post as Secretary of the amalgamated districts of Dunkerton and Tunley'. Sir Guy Tunley presiding at that meeting had raised the question of a sweepstake. Mr Hamilton felt that sweepstakes for the hospital could be useful but they would not bring in regular amounts like the box scheme.

Now we may note four items in the same Chronicle and Herald of **12 September 1931**. Firstly on Page 20 **'TOC H at RUH - Sunday Afternoon Tour of Inspection'** records that on the preceding Sunday Afternoon there was a tour of inspection of the hospital by Toc H under the guidance of Mr A Salter of the Board of Management and Messrs FH Pine and AS Gunstone of the Friendly Societies' Council. Mr FG Hamilton Chairman of the RUH Board felt sure scope could be found for Toc H to support the hospital.

The second hospital item on **12 September**, back on Page 8, is **'Friendly Societies give £1,000 to Hospital'** reporting that the Chairman of the RUH Board received a £1,000 cheque at Wellow. So far the scheme had given £34,200 to the RUH and £4,359 other institutions. The meeting was hosted by Mr Oxley the local chairman with FH Pine, FG Hamilton (RUH Board) and many others. FH Pine made a lengthy speech remembering the first night he had come to Wellow about the scheme. The aim was to get each district to raise a sufficient sum of money under the scheme to pay for its own patients with a bit over because there had to be a margin for people who could not pay anything at all. To bolster his conclusion that pence makes pounds he noted that the finest and grandest palace built was but an assembly of marble and stone, a painting was thousands of touches of an artist's brush, a battleship an assembly of metal with rivets.

Now from the same paper of **12 September 1931** Page 6 is a report that at a meeting on Tuesday of **'Combe Down Council'** the only item for discussion was a letter from Mr Page, the former clerk, thanking the council for the appreciation shown to him. Some 30 applications had been received for his job. All members were present except Mr EA Russell who was ill, namely *FH Pine, RW Cornish, AG Cleaves, F Miller, CG Millett, FI Brown, S Plummer and FR Munday*. In the same issue, on page 23 there is an item **'Monkton Combe Housing'** briefly reporting that, at the request of the RDC, Monkton Combe Council was asked to supply list of 30 people desiring housing.

Two more items of note occur in the same paper of **19 October 1931.** Firstly, in **'Bath Friendly Societies - Visit to Mineral Water Hospital',** we see that the request reported on 4 July was granted - as a deputation of the Friendly Societies Council led by Frank Pine visited the Mineral Water Hospital, and saw the baths and X-ray department and the chapel. Those in the delegation were: from the Ancient Order of Foresters, Bros WF Amesbury and W Chorley; from Hearts of Oak, Bros FH Pine and HF Fiddes; from the Rational Friendly Society, Bros W Horwood and I Pollard; and from the Ancient Shepherds, Bros I Coles, I Orchard and WR Perkins.

The second small item of **19 September 'Monkton Combe Council - Mr AW Little appointed to Clerkship'** reports that Mr AW Little was appointed clerk to Monkton Combe Parish Council. For over 10 years he had been associated with Limpley Stoke Parish Council, firstly as clerk and later as chairman. For some time he had represented Limpley Stoke on the Bradford on Avon RDC.

Now we have four items from **3 October 1931.** Firstly a rather sad **'Parish Clerks Farewell - Mr EP Page's Tribute to Monkton Combe Parish Council - "Work a Pleasure".'** FH Pine read Mr Page's farewell letter to the Council thanking them for their kindness. "Will you kindly convey to the present council, thanking them for their not ungenerous fixing of salary and Messrs Millett, Daniels and Cornish for certain little courtesies performed by them recently." The question of an extra lamp at Shaft Road and management of the rubbish tip was also discussed. *Mr Pine presided, and the others present were RW Cornish, F Miller, AG Cleaves, FJ Brown and CG Millett.*

There is a following article on the RUH with 93 outpatients treated and 63 in patients admitted - 281 received massage, electrical or artificial sunlight treatment!

The third item from **3 October 1931** is **'Bath Butcher's Funeral - Mr James Baker of Widcombe'.** Messrs Spear Bros and Clark were represented by Mr FH Pine, Mr F Wooley, Mr Stacey, Mr Lincoln, Senior and Mr Lincoln, Jnr.

Now, fourthly, the most significant item from **3 October 1931** is **'Combe Down Clings to Independence - Wants Nothing from Bath! - Declares it is a village not a suburb'.** This is a report of the Parish Council meeting at the Church Rooms - presumably the one that Captain Daubeny had encouraged them to set up (as reported on 15 August). Mr FH Pine was in the chair, and Captain Daubeny of Bath RDC was present. The discussion concerned the proposed revision of Bath's boundaries, **"The Chairman said he wanted the discussion to be 'free, frank and open'. Many opinions had been expressed; he did not wish to say anything to guide them, but he really did not know whether what he said was going to help matters. What would happen was in the lap of the gods.**

"A very few steps divided them from the City of Bath. At one part of Combe Down Bath was just on the other side of the road. It had been pointed out to him that among people who had been born and bred in Combe Down, there was a strong local feeling that it should continue as a separate locality. Up to now he thought Combe Down had done remarkably well. There were others who had come to the Down, and had no local associations. They, too, had their opinions."

Captain Daubeny said that he had sent round a petition, which was signed by 209 ratepayers and property owners, and it was against any extension of Bath through boundaries in their direction. He had expected a larger attendance at the meeting on that most important question. There was a popular but erroneous idea that Combe Down was a populous suburb of Bath. It was not. It consisted of a few scattered houses amongst fir trees. After the period in which Ralph Allen built De Montalt Place for his quarrymen quarrying had remained the principal industry for nearly 150 years. It had not been a mushroom group of workmen's dwellings, but a self-contained and more or less isolated village.

He referred to the traditions of the Down, one being the 'Mayor-making' ceremony held at the 'Wiliam IV'; and also the burning of anyone in effigy. Anyone burned in effigy did not stay around much longer; the last this had occurred had been about 40 or 50 years previously. The Down possessed excellent shops, licensed houses, and church rooms second to none. It had also a football team, which had won 27 matches and drawn 2 out of 29 (applause). All that proved that it was a self contained place and wanted nothing from Bath.

Captain Daubeny noted he and his father had been heavy ratepayers for Combe Down and 4 times they had been elected to the RDC. The present boundaries between Bath and Combe Down had been set almost 100 years previously. In 1911 there was an attempt by Bath Corporation to enlarge their boundaries - after arbitration it was resisted, but on condition Combe Down should adopt a sewerage system instead of the old habit of discharging it into disused quarries. Since 1922 they had been paying a very heavy rate for sewage loans and disposal.

As part of Bath, Combe Down would be paying a 17s rate instead of 10s 6d. Incidentally, he said, the senior school at Combe Down, on which a further expenditure of £2,000 was in contemplation, would be absorbed into the Bath system of education. If they looked at Beechen Cliff they saw a monument of municipal enterprise in the shape of a school which had cost Bath over £100,000. It was Bath's wish to be a spa and health resort; the shopkeepers and hotel keepers would do best out of that; but they wanted Combe Down to share in the payment.

The question of assessment was afterwards discussed. It was stated that a house in Combe Down assessed at £70 or £80 would be raised to £100 as a part of Bath, Capt Daubeny admitted that he had not consulted the parish council, but had circulated his petition on his own responsibility.

The chairman *(FHP)* said that whatever happened now or in ten years time, the day would come when Combe Down would be absorbed in Bath, They might resist that as they would, but it was his private opinion.

Mr Robinson suggested that no resolution be put that night. The meeting was not fully representative, and they wanted more information. Capt Daubeny said he came with a resolution and he had obtained a seconder. The resolution was passed, namely "that this parish meeting of ratepayers and property owners in Combe Down ward of the civil parish of Monkton Combe most emphatically protests against the proposal of the Bath City Council to include the above ward within the boundaries of the city; and being of the opinion that such inclusion would be entirely prejudicial to our interests we respectfully invite the Somerset County Council to further our wishes in this matter." Major Clark seconded, and the resolution was carried with only 2 or 3 dissentients.

On **31 October 1931** (bottom of column 5 page 17) we have a letter from F H Pine and Thomas Willis entitled **'The Hospital Box Scheme - Reassuring Notice to Contributors'.** In response to a 'Wilts Doctor' letter in the 19 October issue of the daily Chronicle he wrote to explain that there was no hitch in the box scheme, as had been suggested, and that contributors in Chippenham would continue to receive free treatments under the scheme and that the executive committee would deal with any proposals from Chippenham Cottage Hospital.

Moving on to **21 November 1931** we find a two column article **'Baths New Hospital to Start Free of Bank Debt - £15,000 Owing Will be Wiped Out from City's £30,000 Payment - Col Davey's Statement - Hope that Finances Will Be Squared in a Year or Two - Friendly Societies £1,000.** At a meeting of the Friendly Societies Scheme at the RUH on the Thursday, an important statement was made by RUH Treasurer Col. Davey - having regard to the proposed move to Combe Park from the existing town centre premises which the council were purchasing for £30,000. He paid a warm tribute to the Friendly Societies whose £1,000 cheque had been presented at Bradford on Avon on the Wednesday. He also paid tribute to Aubrey Bateman and his appeals committee that had raised funds for the new hospital now being built at Combe Park. Mr FH Pine gave a long speech about support for the box scheme, noting that Trowbridge was not with them and that Melksham was only to a small extent - while the Frome area had still to be developed.

We now enter the valley of the shadow of death. Firstly on **28 November 1931** we have the whole of Page 10 on **'Death of Bath's Clerk of the Peace - The passing of Mr Arthur E Withy - Distinguished Old Edwardian'.** He was a lawyer and the holder of a range of public offices. In the Abbey FH Pine represented the Bath Friendly Societies.

In the same issue (on page 23) is **'Parish Clerk's death - Mr EP Page, of Combe Down'** - an event that was perhaps not unexpected. The report recounts that Mr Edward Palling Page (76), native of Swindon, died on the Wednesday. He came to Combe Down in 1885, and took up the position as a collector of rates and Clerk to Monkton Combe PC in 1894 until September of the current year (1931). He was vicar's warden of the parish church for 25 years. The Funeral was that day *(the Saturday of publication)* at 2.15pm Combe Down Parish Church. There is a further report on **5 December 1931 'Vicars Warden 25 years - Combe Down Mourns Passing of Mr EP Page'** which is a detailed report on his funeral – the Parish Council representatives included FH Pine and R Daniels.

On **12 December 1931** is a report **'Monkton Combe Council - Members Morn Losses by Death'.** Votes of condolence with the relatives of the late Mr Miles and Mr Page were passed. There was full attendance apart from R Daniels (unwell) to pay tribute to Mr Page. An offer by the butcher Mr Pearce to graze cattle on the Firs Field was declined. *I assume the death was of Mr W Miles, chairman of the parish council before FHP. Mr Pearce's butchers shop was a feature in Combe Down village well into the 1970s.*

We conclude the year with two items in the Chronicle and Herald of Christmas Eve **24 December 1931.** Firstly there was a letter from Mr FH Pine on **'Music for Hospital patients'** in which he comments favourably on the United Choirs of Bath and their benevolence in seeking to bring "the untold comfort of the wireless to inpatients in their beds of pain....I hope the general public will help in making this first effort of the combined choirs a success."

Rounding off the year nicely we have in the same issue **'Monkton Combe Council - Mr A W Little resigns the Clerkship'.** This is a report on a Special Meeting on 14 December at which Mr Little (Clerk) was present at which Chairman FH Pine read his resignation letter (not reported in detail). *The Chairman and the Vice-chairman Mr RW Cornish undertook to carry on the clerical work for the time being. Also present were F Miller, EA Russell, FJ Brown, R Daniels, AJ Cleaves, CJ Millett and S Plummer.*

THE NEWSPAPER RECORD 1932

1932: Changing Times - A new scheme chair

1932: New Housing, New Hospital Scheme Chair, New Clerk? New Hospital Opens (39 articles)

We start the year with a couple of deaths. Firstly on **2 January 1932** we have a piece on page 8 on **'The late Hon Mrs Davey - Funeral in Bath Abbey'**. FH Pine, in his Friendly Societies Hospital Scheme role is at the end of a long list of **Friends** headed by the Mayor Herbert Chivers.

In the same issue of **2 January** on page 9 we pick up on the last item of 1931 and the report on **'Death of Mr Miller Combe Down Parish Councillor'**. Mr Frank Miller was 65, an antique dealer by trade. "During War he served in 4th Somerset Light Infantry with his 4 sons, one of whom died. A Liberal until recently when, as there was no Liberal Club on Combe Down, he inclined towards the Labour Party. He served on the Council on two occasions and was a very earnest and active member." The following issue of 9 January is a report **'Combe Down Councillor - Funeral of Mr F Miller at St James Cemetery'** A service at the parish church preceded the interment which was attended by RW Cornish, EA Russell, R Daniels and CG Millett (parish councillors) - Mr Frank H Pine (Chairman of the Parish Council) was unable to be present. *(I would also note an adjoining article on the completion of the first stage of the building of the new City of Bath Statutory Isolation Hospital at Claverton Down begun in June 1930. Since legislation in the late 19th century, Isolation Hospitals had been a charge to the local authority)*

So we come to a rather fascinating episode that links back to Frank Pine's co-option back onto the Parish Council the previous April. Dated **16 January 1932** on **'Combe Down Losses - Mr Pine Co-opted to Fill Council Vacancy - The Clerkship'** it concerns a meeting of the Parish Council the previous Tuesday evening which is worth reproducing in part. "Before commencing the business, however, the chairman (Mr FH Pine) referred to the great loss they had sustained through the death of Mr Frank Miller, whom he described as a respected member, fearless in his opinions (hear, hear). The chairman also referred with regret to the death of Mrs Lloyd the wife of Archdeacon Lloyd (the Vicar of Combe Down). He thought it was appropriate that the council, representing as it did all classes, creeds and shades of opinion, should tender their sympathy to the Archdeacon who had won the hearts of all (hear, hear). A Vote of Sympathy with Mr AG Cleaves, who has undergone an operation for an injury to his eye was also passed."

"On the question of the co-option of a member to replace Mr Miller the Vice-Chairman (Mr RW Cornish) said that the usual practice was to co-opt someone who had been nominated and before the ratepayers, and was next on the list of voters. He believed their present Chairman was in that position. He proposed FHP as someone who had been nominated and put before the ratepayers. Irrespective of that, quite recently they were placed in a peculiar position, and Mr Pine acted resourcefully, courageously and promptly. He thought it would be an act of grace and justice on the part of the Council definitely to co-opt him as a member of the council. After the election they had co-opted Mr Pine as chairman. He felt personally that it would come better from him than anyone else to make the proposition, as Mr Miller and he had as much to do with Mr Pine's defeat as anyone. Recognising the way that Mr Pine had dealt with one or two matters, not only the matter connected with the Clerk, but one or two others, he moved that Mr Pine be seconded as a member. Mr Millett seconded and the motion was carried unanimously."

"Mr Pine thanked them and said he was pleased he had won the confidence of the gentlemen who, to put it bluntly, had 'kicked him out' the last time. Since those who had turned him out had worked with him it had been a happy experience and totally different from what he had expected. They had worked very harmoniously and Mr Cornish had stood by him most loyally. Mr Millett was elected to serve on the Firs Field, the Allotments and the Russell Bequest Committees in place of Mr Miller."

"The Chairman stated that, in their recent difficulty concerning a clerk, Mrs Page, with her knowledge of the work for nearly 40 years, kindly came forward to help them. In consultation with Mr Cornish he had arranged that she should carry on the work for this quarter up to March, by which time Mrs Page would know if she was going to stay in Combe Down or not. If she decided to stay, they could not be better served. They did not want any more experiments. He proposed the Council confirm the action in appointing Mrs Page clerk pro tem, at a salary rate of £16 per annum. Mr Daniels seconded and the motion was carried unanimously." On housing the Parish Council supported applications from 50 Combe Down residents for the Rural District Council to provide them with housing. Concern was expressed about late letter deliveries on Combe Down. Mr EA Russell of the Parish Council was to pursue this matter. *Those present at the meeting were Messrs FH Pine (chairman), RW Cornish (Vice-Chairman), R Daniels FJ Brown, CS Millett, EA Russell, and S Plummer. Mr Munday was stated to be indisposed.*

As the pressure builds up on what will prove to be a busy year we have 4 items from the Chronicle and Herald from the **6 February 1932**. Firstly (on page 4) **'Pioneer of Bath Hospital Scheme - Mr Frank Pine Resigns Chairmanship - Other Obligations'** heads the publication of a letter sent by Mr Frank Pine (Chairman of the Bath and District Friendly

Societies Box Scheme dated 1 Feb 1932 to the Scheme's secretary. **"Dear Mr Wills, now that our Hospital Scheme appears to be fairly well established, I have definitely decided to take a rest from the strenuous responsibility that has fallen on me as Chairman since 1923. I shall cease my official connection with the Bath Friendly Societies at our annual meeting, to be held soon.**

"Demands are being made on me in connection with Combe Down which absorbs much attention. Also, as you are aware, Mrs Pine is still a sufferer from rheumatism, so I am compelled to relax outside calls on my spare time, and devote it to my home, wife and parish. I feel that what we set out to do has been accomplished, i.e. to raise a substantial sum for the Royal United Hospital each year, and I shall ever remember with thankfulness the very devoted loyalty of the Executive, and everyone connected with the scheme (both past and present) on whom has fallen a tremendous call for self-denial and sacrifice during the past eight years.
Your faithfully Frank H Pine"

> *In the event Frank Pine carried on as Vice-Chairman of the Box Scheme and with Mr Hamilton in the dual role of Chairman of the Box Scheme and Chairman of the Hospital Management Board there was much for a vice-chairman to do. Indeed by March 1934 Frank Pine was one of the Friendly Societies' representatives on the RUH Management Board. He remained in these roles until his death in 1942. Mr Hamilton would step down from Chairman to Vice-Chairman of the Management Board by June 1933.*

On page 7 of the same issue of **6 February** Bellman's gossip column **Armchair Musings** has an item at the end of its first column headed **'Good Work Well Done'** It says

> "By the retirement of Mr Pine from the chairmanship of the Bath Friendly Societies Box Collecting Scheme that admirable movement has lost the active service of a most zealous supporter, who was one of its promoters. Mr Pine, a man of many interests, including the affairs of Monkton Combe - he is chairman of the Parish Council - has discovered that even in behalf of so fine a work as the Hospital Box collections he cannot 'go on forever'. Hence his decision to hand the responsibility of the chairmanship to a successor, whoever he might be. The good scheme will not lapse in consequence of Mr Pine's retirement, but from it will be withdrawn a strong directing mind. What might have happened to the Royal United Hospital if these box collections had not been instituted, and maintained, one does not bear to contemplate. For some years the hospital has been thereby enriched by over four thousand pounds per annum. A splendid achievement!"

Again in the same issue of **6 February** (page 16) is **'Whist at Combe Down - Old Scholars Association'**. This was the Combe Down Old Scholars Whist Drive at the Church Rooms on the Wednesday evening. With some 16 tables in play, Mr Richards was the MC and Mr Frank H Pine presented the prizes.

The fourth item in the **6 February** paper (page 8) may have re-opened a major sore for FHP. It is entitled **'Workmates as bearers - Funeral of Mr G Slade at Bath'**. Mr Slade (63) was with Bath & Somerset Dairy Co and Norton Dairies until illness forced him to relinquish his post. 6 workmates acted as his bearers. The Dairy Foreman Mr HG Collett headed a number of outdoor staff of the Norton Dairies. Mr FH Pine (representing Somerset Dairies) attended. *(He and Mr Collett had been on the Wilts and Somerset Farmers outing reported in the paper on 17 June 1922.)*

As the article published in the next week's paper confirms (see my next paragraph), Frank Pine also attended the funeral that was reported in the preceding item **'Death of Mr W Speed - 36 Years on the staff of Spear Bros and Clark, Ltd'** which briefly notes that a large number of directors and staff of the company attended the funeral. *(The main article on this page is interesting - the new City of Bath Boy's School was opened on Thursday on Beechen Cliff a quarter of a century after its old premises in the Municipal Buildings had been condemned by the Board of Education. The school had cost £50,000 - not £100,000 as stated by Capt Daubeney in the item of 3 October 1931 when he urged Combe Down not to give up its independence).*

Now we find three items from **13 February 1932**. Firstly on page 7 we see: **'Bath Works Manager - Colleagues Tribute at Funeral of Mr W Speed'**. The majority of mourners were employees of Spear Bros & Clark Ltd with which he was associated for 36 years, mainly as works manager. After a list of the family "There were amongst those present Alderman FW Spear and Mrs EA Spear (directors), Mr GL Cass (general manager), Mr J Griffin (Chippenham Manager), Mr FH Pine (Cashier, Bath)". The Members of Staff included a list of about 50 persons followed by a list of over 30 other representatives.

Secondly from **13 February** Page 17 is a report **'Combe Down Housing - Applicants canvassed by Rural District Council'** on another Parish Council meeting with *FH Pine in the chair with RW Cornish (Vice-chairman), R Daniels, EA Russell and CG Millett.* It was reported that Mr Kelway RDC Surveyor and his assistant had been checking on the bona fides of prospective council house tenants on the Parish Council list. There was a question as to whether the rents would be 8s, 9s or 12s. Mr Cornish was concerned that people had been asked if they would want their application to go forward if the rent was 12s - which he thought was an unfair request. Concern was expressed at the lateness of the morning post delivery (9 am rather than 7.30 am). Also there was concern about the excessive RDC lopping of trees in The Firs, a private road.

Thirdly from **13 February** on the same page 17 at the bottom of column 5 we find **'Hospital Box Scheme - Combe Down District Stewards'** and a report on their meeting at Combe Lodge on Tuesday Evening. Major TH Clark JP presided and others present included Mrs H Noad, **Miss E Pine,** Messrs E Tyley, W Warren, FC Hill and F Maggs (hon sec) who was resigning (to be replaced by Mr FC Hill). The thanks of the Executive Committee were accorded to Mr Maggs later in the evening by Mr FH Pine (Chairman). Since commencement of the scheme in October 1923 Combe Down had raised £765. *It is interesting to see that Edna had become involved in the Box scheme - whilst her sisters were involved in the Combe Down Old Scholars productions!*

Now we come to two items in the Bath paper for **27 February 1932**. Firstly on page 7 **'Mr W A King Bereaved - Chairman of Bath Insurance Committee mourns wife'.** At the funeral service at Holy Trinity Church, Bath Friendly Societies were represented by Messrs FH Pine and GS Hodges.

The second item on page 8 of 27 February is a full page article **'Baths hotel for the sick - £20,000 Needed to Complete Our New Hospital - Administrative Block Need - Wanted: 2,000 people in Outside Area to give £10 each - Warm tributes to Bath press'.** It is the AGM of the RUH in the Guildhall. **The President of the RUH Aubrey Bateman "recognised the fine work of Mr FH Pine in the Friendly Societies' scheme and said that no-one regretted more than the Managing Board that he felt it necessary to resign. The record of his work, he said, would stand for all time as, but for his wonderful direction of that scheme and the income that had accrued from it, the hospital in its present form would no longer exist.** It was mentioned that the total sum collected by the scheme was £36,100.

The Archdeacon of Bath **moving the re-election of Mr Bateman as President said they all recognised (in the building of the new hospital) he had committed himself to a gigantic task and that he was pursuing it with immense courage and success. The motion was seconded by Mrs Forbes Fraser.** Mr Bateman noted that in 1931 8,000 Bathonians had been treated at the RUH and no fewer than 2,100 were in-patients. On a motion of Mr T Wills, seconded by Mr FH Pine the various elective members of the RUH Board were approved. **Mr Pine, in reply to a motion, said so long as he was of any use to the movement his services would always be available (applause). Touching upon his relinquishing the chairmanship of the scheme he said he understood that Mr Hamilton was going to become its chairman (applause).** A further £20,000 was needed to complete the new hospital - as the area covered by the hospital had a population of 200,000, if only 2,000 gave £10 that would do it. A number of complimentary remarks were made about the Bath press. Dr Fleming (a Bradford on Avon GP) as a former RUH medical student praised the RUH's liaison with the local cottage hospitals (as a virtual federation).

On to a new agenda at Combe Down with a report of **5 March 1932 'Combe Down Unemployed - No Love of Spadework- Futile Appeal'** relates to a meeting held in the Church Army Hut, Combe Down on the previous Wednesday to formulate a scheme to assist the unemployed in the parish which had proved a failure, owing to the apathy of the men concerned. The few unemployed who had attended the meeting - only 10 or 11 out of a total of 35 in the parish - made little or no advance to help the promoters in their kindly object. One man (Mr Butcher - returned from Canada due to ill health, and unable to claim unemployment benefit) addressed his fellow unemployed "You might as well put your backs behind a spade as do nothing" (referring to a suggestion to provide them with cheap allotments) - but there was no response from the others.

Mr FH Pine (chairman of the Parish Council) presided, supported by Major Clark, Mr RW Cornish (vice-chairman of the council) and Capt LS Goode (Church Army). Mr Pine said the meeting had been called as a result of a circular that Capt Goode sent out from the Social Centre. At a little meeting in his house - when the vicar, Major Clark, Mr Rivington and Capt Goode were present - it was agreed to extend the original proposals, as a neighbourly gesture to assist the Down's unemployed in accordance with the appeal of the Prince of Wales. He suggested the formation of a committee of 9 – comprising 3 unemployed, 3 parish councillors and 3 ratepayers out of which an executive of 5 would be chosen. Two adjudicators would be appointed to settle any difference in opinion. The first half years rent of an allotment was to be waived for an unemployed person.

"Mr Cornish said he wanted to find out what was in the minds of the unemployed. It seemed to him that a scheme such as the Chairman had outlined was preferable to seeing men drift into organisations which simply exercised a disruptive influence. They wanted to keep men fit for the more prosperous times that were coming". A Mr Tiley suggested poultry keeping as an alternative to allotments. Mr Butcher who had had the management of poultry in Canada said that it was a big question. It would have to be gone into thoroughly; it required skilled management and a certain outlay. The meeting ended inconclusively. *It is well worth reading this report in its entirety.*

The Chronicle and Herald of **12 March 1932** had an article **'Combe Down Housing - Claim for More Dwellings laid before RDC - Difficulties'** The Monkton Combe Parish Council meeting on the Tuesday had addressed the housing needs for the Combe Down and Monkton Combe area. Mr RW Cornish said that the 3 appointed representatives of the Parish Council had met the Housing Committee of the RDC in Green Park. It appeared to them that one or two gentlemen on the RDC were not particularly anxious to proceed. The RDC seemed to be using the uncertainty of Bath boundary changes as excuse for not proceeding.

The Parish Council representatives argued that they could proceed outside the boundary question to satisfy the requirements of Combe Down. The RDC officials thereupon promised them that the matter should receive fresh consideration immediately. That would be settled by April 1st, and a great deal of preliminary arrangements might be made by officials without consulting the Rural District Council as to expense. The Parish Council were asked for help in the consideration of sites.

The Chairman FH Pine thanked the representatives for their report - Messrs Daniels and Cleaves were then elected to a sub-committee to identify sites for housing to assist the RDC. FH Pine as council representative on the school managers voiced concern about the Chairman of the Board acting without approval of Board. The question of the unemployed was mentioned and the fact that they were not favourable to allotments - they were more inclined to window cleaning and other odd jobs. The matter was receiving the attention of Capt Goode of the Church Army. Messrs Cornish, Millett and Daniels were elected to an unemployed sub-committee that would also comprise 3 unemployed and 3 ratepayers.

The unemployment issue was further reported on in the paper on **26 March 1932** page 18 **'Allotment Scheme - Effort for Combe Down Unemployed'** This was a further meeting convened by Capt Goode of the Church Army at their Social Centre which established a *committee of R Daniels, CG Milett, R W Cornish (parish council reps), GT Rivingon, Major SH Clark, & Mr Rendle (rep Ratepayers), & Messers AJ Cleaves, Butcher and E Ball (Unemployed) with Capt Goode Secretary (with whom all unemployed were invited to register)*. The aim of a proposed programme of weekly meetings was to obtain a register of the unemployed, their capabilities and circumstances and to make an appeal to parishioners for work and financial assistance.

In same issue of **26 March 1932** Page 9 we are back to **'Combe Down Housing - Parish Council Want Something Better'**. Mr Cornish presided in the absence through illness of Frank Pine. A report on the accounts was presented by the Clerk (Mrs Page). Mr Cornish said something needed to be done about housing for people whose housing was not up to the 1932 standard. It was noted that the cost of building Council houses would fall to the council and a penny rate, and that the government granted a larger subsidy to rural areas than to a borough. There was a concern that the RDC lopping of trees in The Firs was excessive.

The main article on this page is also interesting - **'Chippenham Leaves Bath Friendly Societies' Scheme - Local Hospital to Go On Its Own - Decided at Request of Medical Staff - Doctors Remunertion - "More must be paid for Patients Sent to Bath"'** Chippenham Cottage Hospital planned to organise a contributory scheme of its own and this was proposed at an annual meeting of subscribers to the hospital. The rule allowing box holders 2 members on the committee would be deleted. It was hoped box holders of the Bath scheme would join the Chippenham scheme. As to the question of treatment at Bath under a Chippenham Scheme it was hoped they would treat the Bath hospital better than the Bath Friendly Societies had treated Chippenham Hospital having paid them the mean sum of 15s a week.

Now back to the unemployed and the allotments with firstly an article on **23 April 1932 'Aiding the Workless - New Committee at Combe Down'.** This deals with the annual meeting of Monkton Combe Parish Council where Mr Cornish reported on the new committee to aid the unemployed – a jumble sale had been held and a whist drive was contemplated. Mr Cleaves said that since the committee's first meeting work had been found for several of the unemployed in the parish. **Mr Pine was unanimously re-elected as Chairman with Mr Cornish Vice-Chairman.** It was decided to issue summonses over unpaid allotment rents, although only 23s was outstanding. Warning notices were to be posted in Firs Field – no ball games for over 14s and only soft balls.

'Allotment Thefts Monkton Combe Parish Council Take Action' is the theme of an article on **14 May 1932** (it cropped up again in 1933!). With *FH Pine presiding (with RW Cornish, R Daniels, CJ Millett, FJ Brown, SL Plummer and FR Munday)* great concern was expressed in the council about thefts from allotments – one person had lost 30 broccolis. Allotments were already hard to let and there was a risk tenants would give up. The council resolved to take all steps to tackle this issue.

On the **4 June 1932** we have another big 4 column spread on **'£44,000 Raised for Hospitals in 8 years - Magnificent Record of Bath Friendly Societies' Scheme - £5,099 Collected Last Year - Appeal to Districts to Play Their Part'.** In the past 8 years £36,100 had gone to the RUH and £4,700 to other hospitals. At a meeting on the Tuesday at the RUH of the Societies' Council and local chairmen, the vice-chairman FH Pine expressed satisfaction that in such difficult times they had achieved such a record (owing to a bereavement the Chairman F G Hamilton was unable to be present for the Friendly Societies' annual report).

The Annual Report is noted under **'Resignation of Chairman'** where it is reported "There had been considerable changes in the Executive in the past quarter, the most notable of which was the **resignation of its chairman, Mr Frank H Pine**. It was with great regret that the Executive accepted this, but there was no alternative as the activities of Mr Pine in other directions rendered it impossible for him to devote the necessary time to the work. **He had held the position since 1924, and its success was largely due to his efforts.** It was gratifying to note that he still continued to take an interest in the scheme and had **consented to act as vice-chairman**. The Executive was fortunate in being able to obtain the services of MR FG Hamilton, chairman of the

Management Board of the Royal United Hospital, as a successor to Mr Pine, whilst Mr Rawlinson has kindly consented to continue to act as hon. treasurer. Messrs Amesbury, Bishop and White have joined the executive, and to them a hearty welcome was extended."

The report noted that the Committee of Chippenham Cottage Hospital had given notice that they wished to discontinue the scheme in Chippenham and District that had been in place since 1927 and to establish a contributory scheme of their own. Steps would be taken to ensure Box holders in the area would not be disadvantaged. Despite arrangements with Frome Cottage Hospital receipts from the Frome area were disappointing. It was noted that the RUH had treated 10,000 patients in 1931. Details of contributions by county and area are fully listed. Of the £5,099 collected £2,226 came from Bath, £800 came from Somerset and £2,012 from Wiltshire, and £4,000 was paid to the RUH.

As foreshadowed in the previous article there is a report on **11 June 1932** on **'Peasdown Aids Bath RUH'** to the effect that at Peasdown Parish Room 'on Friday week' a quarterly cheque for £1,000 was handed to Hon Mrs Shaw Mellor as vice-chairman of RUH Management Board. A Musical Concert followed. Mr FH Pine (Vice-chairman of Friendly Societies' Council) attended and spoke after Mrs Shaw Mellor about the wonderful results achieved by the scheme.

So on to two successive monthly parish council meetings. Next to an article about Sir Alan Cobham and a flying pageant at Lansdown we see on 11 Jun 1932: **'Pilfering from Allotments - Reward for Detection of Thieves at Combe Down'.** It is once again Monkton Combe Parish Council with *FH Pine presiding (with R Daniels, EA Ansell, CG Millett, S Plummer and RW Cornish).* Frank Pine proposed putting up a notice offering a reward for information leading to a conviction for stealing from the allotments. A reward of £2 was agreed. Mr Cornish suggested that the corner of the Firs Field be barred off for children of school age, and swings and other amusement accessories be installed. Frank Pine objected to a sand pit as health authorities saw them as very unhealthy. He suggested a seesaw instead. The Firs Field committee was to look into the cost. It was reported that the Rural District Council was to consider housing at its next meeting. The Parish Council would ask the RDC for work to be proceeded with as soon as possible.

So we pick up on that last point in the report of **16 July 1932** with **'More Dwellings Needed - Combe Down and the Bath Rural Council - Parish Clerkship'.** The Monkton Combe Parish Council *with FHP presiding (with RW Cornish , FR Munday, EA Russell, R Daniels, CG Millett)* had a long meeting with much to discuss. The RDC had written asking for more information about extra houses being erected. Frank Pine read his reply stating that the erection of suitable houses was urgent and that every possible effort was desirable to carry into effect the requirements of the parish for reasons of health, decency and the moral influence of the young.

The question of the Clerkship was raised by Mr Munday proposing that the post should be advertised – he asked "Was the Council in order in appointing Mrs Page without giving others a chance of applying". Mr Cornish said "I know of nothing that compels us to advertise the post. We appointed her temporarily ...but Mrs Page had, in fact, acted in the capacity of clerk for several years." The Chairman appealed to the council to let matters rest as they were until March, when they would know if Mrs Page was going to continue on the Down. Mr and Mrs Page had served the parish for nearly 40 years. Everything was being done efficiently and what was more important, honestly. "It is" said Mr Pine "a great relief to me personally to know that Mrs Page is doing it" Swings and Seesaws were proposed for the Firs Field in time for the summer holidays.

And so to another funeral with a report on **23 July 1932** on **'The Late Mr Tom Wills'** and the funeral at Bath Abbey of the former solicitor **Mr Thomas Wills who had been Organising Secretary of the Hospital Box Scheme**. Workers in Hospitals, Friendly Societies and National Insurance activities gathered for a plain service. Mourners included T, G, D, W and C Wills, Messrs L Cann, EJ Dillon, FH Pine, GS Hodges, W Rawlinson, H Lavington, G & F Horstmann and EA Shellard. Those present at Abbey service included the Mayor Cllr Herbert Chivers, the Town Clerk (J Basil Ogden), Spa Director (J Hatton), Medical Oficer of Health (Dr JF Blackett), representatives (listed) of the Hospital Board, Nurses RUH, Bath Health Insurance Committee, The Law Society, the National Association of Clerks to Insurance Committees, the Bath Panel Committee, The Bath Friendly Societies Hospital Scheme etc.

On **3 September 1932** is a two column report **'Over £1,000 again for Bath RUH - Quarters Yield from Box Collections - The Late Mr Wills'.** The quarterly report notes with sorrow the death of Mr Wills Organising Secretary of the scheme since its inauguration; his son Mr Geoffrey G Wills was appointed to carry on for the rest of year. The quarterly cheque presentation on 21 September was to be conducted in Calne by its Mayor, Mr Gale. The report was signed by FG Hamilton (chairman), FH Pine (vice-chairman), W Rawlinson (treasurer) and Geoffrey G Wills (Acting Organising Secretary). A detailed list of collections is given.

So we move to **10 September 1932** and **'New Bath Hospitals First Visitor - Mayor Greeted at Combe Park - Tribute to Subscribers - Sir Harry Hatt Presents £2,750 Appeal Fund Cheque'.** Accompanied by a signed appeal letter from the Mayor the full page article has a picture of the new RUH 'nearing completion and probably in use in a few week's time'. Mayor Herbert Chivers was, on Thursday, the first official visitor and was welcomed by the President of the RUH Mr Aubrey Bateman. The first instalment of the Chronicle & Herald Appeal Fund of £2,750 was handed over by Alderman Sir Harry Hatt.

Among those assembled in the entrance hall were: The Archdeacon of Bath (Ven. SA Boyd), Lt-Col Egbert Lewis, Alderman Sir Harry Hatt, Ald SW Bush, Col the Hon HS Davey, Ald J Colmer, Mr Hugh Tow, Mrs Latter Parsons, Mr Douglas R Hatt, Mr JR Walker, Mr AJ Taylor, Mr FH Pine, Mr Edward Taylor, Mr CH Terry, Miss Vian (Matron), and Mr J Lawrence Mears (Secretary RUH).

Mr Bateman said he hoped the hospital would open free of debt and £91,000 had been so far raised of the original appeal. The old hospital had 140 beds, the new one 212 beds. "When we are able to put them all into occupation I hope that grim menace of the waiting list, with all the mental tortures it involves, will be removed" he declared. It was hoped Mr Stanley Wills (for his £20,000 donation) would agree to have a ward named after him. Tribute was given to Mr FG Hamilton the Hospital's Chairman (owing to business outside city he was unable to be present). Most of those present had been at the laying of the foundation stone 23 October 1930. Mayor Chivers regretted that the previous Mayor Chivers could not have been there. *The article is continued on the next page!*

On **17 September 1932** we have **'Children Beyond Control - Strong Remarks at Monkton Combe Council'**. One member said 'children are beyond control', another said 'When you try to reprimand children, you get abuse'. Horseplay had resulted in damage to the seesaw, said Mr Daniels. Messrs Daniels and Millett were to lock the swings and seesaw until repaired. Cell-worm was stated by representative of Somerset County Council as having caused the failure of the potato crop on the allotments. FH Pine was absent due to illness and *Mr RW Cornish presided with EA Russell, R Daniels, FJ Brown, CG Millett and Mrs Page (Clerk).*

Once again we find two items in the same paper of **24 September 1932**. Firstly on page 5 under **'Bath & County Notes'** (and the penultimate article in column 4 - before a report about the King donating Hampton Court grapes to the Mineral Water Hospital!) we have "Whilst Mr FH Pine, vice-chairman of the Bath Friendly Societies' Scheme was pleading the cause of the Royal United Hospital at Calne on Wednesdy evening, his thoughts were in a ward at the hospital, where his 22-years-old daughter, **Miss Edna Pine**, is a patient. Miss Pine entered the hospital on Monday for observation purposes." *(actually Edna was almost 24.)*

In the same issue of **24 September** covering 2 columns is **'Work Must Go On - Hospitals Need as Great As Ever - £900 Cheque'**. The article notes that the RUH had benefitted to the extent of £38,000 from the Friendly Societies' scheme. The Mayor of Calne (Mr FJ Gale) handed over a £900 quarterly cheque to Mr Hamilton (Chairman of the Hospital Management Board). Calne had contributed £2,667 in 7 years, but compared with the costs of treating Calne patients in 1931 there was a £59 deficit. *Supporting the Mayor were Mrs FJ Gale, Mr FG Hamilton (Bath RUH Chairman), Mr FH Pine (vice-chairman of the scheme), Mr W Rawlinson (Treasurer), Mr JW Wills (who had succeeded his father, the late Tom Wills, as organising secretary) Messrs GS Hodges, A Salter and W Amesbury (committee) Mr WS Griffin (Calne Secretary) and Capt C Herbert-Smith etc.*

The Mayor paid tribute to Tom Wills the late Organising Secretary. Mr FG Hamilton compared the new hospital with the existing building in the noisy heart of the city. Capt C Herbert-Smith proposed a vote of thanks to Mr Gale for his support for the scheme in Calne. Mr FH Pine seconded saying that Mr Gale's quiet and earnest manner and kindly way in which he put the case to people was telling and got home. Speaking of Tom Wills, he said Mr Wills very much admired the earnest and truly Christian manner in which Mr Gale had supported the scheme from the beginning.

Now for 3 items in the **15 October 1932** issue we begin on page 21 with **'Honoured Bath citizen - Vicars Tribute to Former Churchwarden - Mr H H Sprouting'** which was concerned with the funeral of Mr HH Sprouting (73). He was a churchwarden of St James's, trustee of the RUH, member of Management Board of Rivers St Nursing Home, Hon Secretary of the old Bath Orpheus Glee Society, and was for half a century with Stothert and Pitt Ltd. In attendance at the funeral were members of the Church, Stothert and Pitt Ltd., Cllr Aubrey Bateman President of RUH.....FH Pine (Friendly Societies Hospital Scheme) etc. A letter from FC Hamilton Chairman of RUH Board mentioned "His service to this Hospital, both as a trustee and a member of the Board, extending over a period of 31 years".

Elsewhere in these newspaper extracts I have read of men from Bath travelling to Jersey to pick potatoes but somehow I do not think that is linked to the next two items. The first item is on page 11 of the **15 October** paper and is headed **'Jersey Work Extended - Why Parish Councillor Resigned - Combe Down Affairs'**. It reports that the resignation of Mr AG Cleaves was accepted by Monkton Combe Parish Council because his work in Jersey had been extended for at least 12 months. To the chairman (Mr FH Pine) he expressed his thanks for the consideration they had shown him. Mr Pine voiced the council's regret at losing such an enthusiastic member as Mr Cleaves, but he added that they were glad to know that he had got work for so long ahead. Mr Cornish associated himself with Mr Pine's remarks. Mr H Robinson being next on the list, it was agreed to inquire if he would be willing to fill the vacancy. *Mr FH Pine presided at this meeting with the support of W Cornish, AG Millett, EA Russell, SI Plummer, R Daniels* and Mrs EM Page (Clerk). **Mr Cleaves remained in Jersey until just before the German occupation.**

And so on page 5 of the same issue of **15 October** we find under **'Bath & County Notes'** an item on **Potatoes** (third column, third untitled paragraph after Chairmanship changes): 'Mr FH Pine referred in gratifying terms at Monkton Combe Parish Council meeting on Tuesday to a courteous communication which had been received from the Somerset County Council on the question of trouble with the potatoes on the allotments. "It is very rarely that you get an official letter so kindly phrased and so painstaking in detail" he remarked'.

Next we move to another 3 item issue - that of **12 November 1932**. The first item on page 6 is beneath two austere portraits of the new Mayor Mr Rhodes Cook and his wife. It's headed **'For Benefit of Workless - Combe Down Effort to be Good Neighbours'**. Mr Cornish reported to Monkton Combe Council that a committee to aid the workless had been augmented and reorganised with Mr H Robinson in chair (with Messrs Cornish, Pine and Millett as members). Mr Cornish said it was a pleasure to serve on a committee that had such an efficient chairman as Mr Robinson.

Mr FH Pine endorsed Mr Cornish's remarks and stated that they were greatly indebted to him because he took up the hard task of trying to lick into shape the position as they knew it on Combe Down. Although Mr Cornish and the committee might not realise it they had done better than they had expected, they had obtained a lot of information that might not have been secured (hear, hear). Mr Pine said he was sure Combe Down should be extremely grateful to the unemployment committee which had been sitting for the past nine months. As to the future Mr Robinson had taken up a most difficult task, and he hoped very sincerely that everyone would throw their ideas into the common pot for the common good. He trusted that whatever the ideas they be expressed openly and then perhaps something would be achieved. If the parishioners of Combe Down recognised their obligations, he could see something beneficial resulting (hear, hear).

So, on page 16(?) of the **12 November** we return to the issue to the ongoing matter of **'Combe Down Housing - Parish's Appeal to Rural District Council'.** The Chairman Mr FH Pine disclosed that in reply to his request for information the RDC had said they were in communication with the owner of land on Combe Down but had not yet come to terms with him. Mr Cornish said that, in terms of finding employment and much needed housing, the matter should be expedited. Mr H Robinson had agreed to fill the council vacancy following Mr Cleaves resignation and was co-opted. He was welcomed by the Chairman, who expressed pleasure at seeing him a member of the Council again. They had been together for a number of years and he hoped his experience would be as valuable as in the past (hear, hear). *Mr FH Pine presided with W Cornish, AG Millett, EA Russell, SI Plummer, R Daniels, FR Munday and H Robinson.*

Finally in the **12 November** paper we have a 2 column spread on page 26 **'Another £1,000 cheque for RUH - £39,100 raised since scheme's inception'.** This foreshadowed another cheque presentation meeting in the New Hall, Odd Down the next Monday. *Those present at this quarterly meeting on the accounts were FG Hamilton, The Hon Mrs Shaw Mellor, Mrs EB Fisher, Mrs Newman, Mrs WM Hendon, Miss L Nash, Messrs FH Pine, A Salter, AS Gunstone, W Rawlinson, RJ Dyer (Box),etc.* Receipts and payments are listed including those to hospitals other than the RUH. Some reorganisation of the scheme was envisaged and the scheme's executive had submitted proposals to the Friendly Societies Council. Mr Dyer referred to the Chippenham and Freshford Hospitals going over to the Hospital Savings Association Scheme.

On page 26 in the following **19 November 1932** issue is the report of the presentation of **'£1,000 for Bath Hospital - Friendly Societies' total £43,568'.** The presentation at the New Hall, Odd Down was to Mrs Herbert Chivers (the ex-Mayoress, on behalf of the hospital as Aubrey Bateman the Hospital President was away). *Mr FH Pine (vice-chairman of the hospital scheme presided, supported by Messrs FG Hamilton (chairman of the hospital and chairman of the hospital propaganda scheme), W Rawlinson (hon. treasurer of the scheme), ET Billet (Odd Down District Chairman), A Salter, S Gunstone, FJ Amery, Mrs Gordon Smith, Messrs J Lawrence Mears (secretary and superintendent of the hospital), and Geoffrey G Wills (secretary of the scheme).* Mr Pine called for volunteers to help develop the Odd Down district and 5 ladies and 2 gentlemen volunteered.

A second item in the same issue of **19 November** under **'Armchair Musings'** on page 7 (end of column 1) is under the sub-headings **'Making up the Muckle'** and **'More might be done'.** The columnist reflects that "in the coffers of the RUH is another thousand pounds, the yield of 3 month's contributions by those who continue the excellent box-collection scheme inaugurated some years ago by the Bath and District Friendly Societies...." He concludes that more needs to be done and that if anyone needed to know who was in his local committee for a collecting box, he could apply to Mr Pine at 17 The Firs.

On **3 December 1932**, bottom of column 2, there is a box advert: **'Organising Secretary Sought - for Royal United Hospital (Bath) Box Collecting Scheme'** with applications to the Chairman of the Hospital by 14 December,

Lastly for this year, on **17 December 1932** we have **'Fulfilment of Bath Hospitals dream - RUH moves house'.** This recounts that "in a few hours on the Sunday Morning the

RUH moved from Beau Street to Combe Park". Actually the first patient, a baby, moved in on the Saturday. Four St John ambulances ferried the 35 patients with 60 or 70 St Johns' Ambulance Men and the Red Cross Corps. The services of the Bath Fire Brigade Ambulances had not to be called upon. Mr A Bateman, President of the RUH and Mr FH Pine (Vice-President of the Friendly Societies Scheme) were present to welcome the patients. In the past 3 weeks admissions had been limited to emergency patients. *(The views on the world's ills of the Chief Whip Mr Kennedy of the previous Labour Government in the adjoining article are interesting).*

THE OLD RUH AT BEAU STREET 1910

THE NEW RUH AT COMBE PARK 1932

THE NEWSPAPER RECORD 1933-1934

1933-1934: Last 2 years with the Parish Council - FHP joins Hospital Board (40 articles)

There appears to be a slackening in the number of articles on Frank Pine, the Hospital Scheme and the parish council in these two years, as compared with the previous two years. Of course the daily newspaper record may well tell a different story.

1933:The Box Scheme Develops - Housing a Key Parish Council Concern

The Bath and Wilts Chronicle and Herald of **7 January** begins the new year with **'Bath Hospital Box Scheme - Whole Time Organiser Appointed'** which reports that to enlarge the usefulness of the RUH Box Scheme the Friendly Societies' Council had amended the scheme to include out-patients. **Mr Wilfred J Jenkins** had been appointed as a full-time organiser at its new offices of Shepherds Hall, Princes St., Queen Square.

On **14 January 1933** is a piece headed **'Combe Down Affairs - Meeting of the Parish Council'**. *Mr FH Pine presided at this meeting, with W Cornish, AG Millett, EA Russell, R Daniels, FJ Brown and H Robinson.* It was decided that the swings in the Firs Field were to be taken down until better weather. Mr EA Hancock was to be paid the reward of £2 for information leading to a conviction of those pilfering produce from the allotments.

On **25 February 1933** we find the quarterly report on the hospital box scheme with, among the usual headlines, **'Another £1,000 for Hospital - Many Increased Benefits'**. The Mayor of Bath (Cllr Rhodes G Cook) presented a cheque to Mrs F Maddox, member of Hospital Board of Management at the Guildhall on the Wednesday. The sum that had been raised since 1923 was £41,000. There was an urgent need for more collecting boxes to be taken up for the scheme - that now offered extra benefits, including free outpatient and dental treatment. The new organising secretary of the scheme from January 1, 1933 was Mr Wilfred J Jenkins.

"Mr Frank H Pine, in an interesting manner, gave the history of the Box Scheme, commencing with a letter being written to the Press, in March 1923, by Bro. Lavington, of the Shepherds, and he (Mr Pine) replying, taking up the challenge. He then remembered asking Col. Lewis, then Chairman of the Hospital, if he would accept help for the Hospital to the amount of £4,000 or £5,000 a year, and Col Lewis accepted it very, very quickly (laughter). From that time they had never looked back (applause). What, Mr Pine said, they were anxious to get were some young men to come into the scheme and say 'When you are gone we will carry on'. There were on the Executive one over 80 years and others over 70 years and it was time young men came forward to train for the work. Where would the hospital be but for the £40,000 contributed by the scheme, and where would it be in the future if they did not carry on and maintain and improve the position they had already won?"

The chairman of the scheme, Mr Hamilton, spoke of the need to improve benefits of the scheme given that there were competing schemes. Attendance at the event included, from the Executive Committee: *FG Hamilton (Chairman), FH Pine (Vice-Chairman), Mr W Rawlinson (hon Treasurer), Mr A Salter, Mr HC Lavington, Mr AG Gunstone, Mr G Hodges, Mr H Bishop, Mr WF Amesbury and Mr W White.*

On **4 March 1933** on page 8 there was a 3 column spread entitled **'No Sweepstakes for new hospital - £145,000 already expended on new buildings - But £17,000 still required'**. This is a report of Cllr Aubrey Bateman presiding at the annual meeting of the RUH where he spoke strongly against suggestions that sweepstakes should be organised to help the institution. It would, he said, destroy the whole spirit of giving and inevitably result in the withdrawal of the regular and sustained supporter of the hospital, and injure its moral prestige. Cllr Bateman praised the voluntary hospital movement and said it would cost the city at least a shilling rate if they had to undertake the work of the RUH. The voluntary hospitals, in their great function of the advancement of teaching and research, could not be replaced by state institutions functioning under the control of municipalities, or of Government Departments. He praised Col Egbert Lewis for organising the move of the hospital on the day.

Aubrey Bateman was re-elected President of the RUH - on the motion of Major CE Daley, seconded by Mr FH Pine - the following were elected as the elective members of the Board of Management for the ensuing year: *Mr HJ Heston, Mr W King, Mr W Rawlinson, Mr FD Wardle, Mr E Ireland, Mr F Lace FRCS, Mr W Smith, Mr AL Fuller FRCS and Mr Douglas Hatt. The Mayor (Cllr Rhodes G Cook) sent his apologies.*

On **4 March 1933** we have also a small item in column 4 on page 19 **'RUH Box Scheme – Kingsmead and Twerton East Contributions'**. At a meeting of Box Scheme workers of the Kingsmead and Twerton East No1 District. Mr Wilfred J Jenkins (Organising Secretary) presided and a discussion led by FH Pine took place on the amended scheme and opportunities for its development.

On **11 March 1933** is a small item **'Wireless Collection - Hospital Scheme'**. At public meeting in Colerne, the Rector of Colerne (local chairman) said listeners to broadcast services should put donations in a hospital box *(in addition to paying the wireless license fee of 10/- the government had introduced in 1922!)*. FH Pine gave an address on voluntary hospitals and explained the amended hospital box scheme.

So, a week later, we find a two column report on **18 March 1933 'Disgrace to Parish - The Firs Field at Combe Down Criticised - Hard Courts Suggested'.** We are back at a monthly meeting of Monkton Combe Parish Council, with FH Pine in the Chair. Mr Cornish raised the point that 3 letters on housing issues had been put to Bath RDC without reply - Capt Daubeny was to be approached on the matter. It was proposed by Mr Robinson that Mrs Page was to continue as Clerk and this was seconded by Mr R Daniels - the Chairman noting that the question of her remaining on Combe Down had been resolved. With regard to the Firs Field, the need for concrete platforms under the swings, new signs and new tennis courts was proposed. Mr Robinson said the Firs Field needed improving; it was a disgrace to the Parish. The Chairman doubted that tennis courts would be a paying proposition. There were no parishioners for the parish meeting that followed *(not for the first time – see the report of 28 September 1929!)*. With a deficit on the allotments account there was concern that people were not taking up allotments. *In addition to the chairman FH Pine there was present Messrs RW Cornish, R Daniels, FJ Brown, Harry Robinson, CG Millett and the clerk, Mrs Page.*

On **1 April 1933 'Steady Progress - RUH workers at Odd Down'** is a report on further increase in receipts for the Box Scheme from Odd Down. At a meeting at St Philip's Institute, FH Pine explained the additional costs and benefits of the amended scheme (3d a week covering all dependant members of a family but with an additional 1d a week for children aged 16-21).

We are back at the annual general meeting of the parish council on **15 April 1933 with 'Monkton Combe Housing - Criticism of District Council Delay - Absent Councillors'.** After Mr Frank H Pine was re-elected chairman of Parish Council he acknowledged the loyal support he had received from the members in the past year, and he said he would be glad if those who could not attend meetings would let him know why they were not there. It was utterly impossible to conduct any business to finality when a portion of the council afterwards said 'I should have done this ...or that...or some other course altogether. Of the 9 members of the council there were present Messrs RW Cornish, R Daniels, EA Russell and FJ Brown with the clerk Mrs EM Page. *(So the absentees would seem to be Messrs H Robinson, CG Millett, SI Plummer and FR Munday.)*

Three letters written to Bath Rural District Council on housing had received a reply "Owing to the principle adopted by the Ministry of declining to sanction loans to local authorities for the erection of houses unless it can be proved to the satisfaction of the Ministry that such houses would not be built by private enterprise, my Council have been delayed in their proposed scheme for the erection of houses at Combe Down. You will appreciate the difficulty of proving that private builders will not undertake the erection of houses required if financed by building societies or other bodies. This

Council is to be abolished on April 1st next, and a new council formed, and the matter will in due course be taken up by the new Council."

The meeting noted that the RDC had easily erected houses elsewhere, as had the City of Bath. There was a concern that the monthly refuse collection was inadequate – especially in summer.

Oh well its back to the hospital for some good news, with 3 columns of page 8 on **13 May 1933** headed 'Hospital Box Scheme Forging Ahead - Splendid Start under Amended Plan - Quarterly Collections Increase - Effects of Chippenham's Succession Explained - £3,900 for RUH Last Year'. This was a report on the annual meeting of the Bath RUH Box Scheme. The Chairman Mr FG Hamilton noted the impact of the succession of Chippenham Cottage Hospital and adjoining villages to the Hospital Savings association. Having a new Organising Secretary, Mr Wilfred Jenkins, would help to keep in touch with all the wards of the scheme. A letter of sympathy was to go to Mr FH Pine who had not attended due to illness. The total receipts of £5,069 came from Bath (£2,292) Wiltshire (£1,790) and Somerset (£957). *Despite the bullish headlines this is, in many respects, a bit of a low point - for 3 or 4 years the scheme had fallen short of its objective of getting £5,000 a year for the RUH. The challenge of supporting a voluntary hospital by charitable and friendly society funding is clear.*

So is there any good news in the same issue of **13 May 1933**? Well, not really, as on the previous page 8 we have **'Petty Pilfering - Allotment Marauders at Combe Down'**. Petty pilfering had still been going on at the allotments and drastic steps would be needed if there was a recurrence. *Mr FH Pine was in the Chair of the Monkton Combe Parish Council (supported by Messrs RW Cornish, FG Brown, FR Munday, EEA Russell, CG Millett, R Daniels and Mrs EM Page (Clerk).* The housing question arose and the chairman proposed a meeting of applicants to stress the necessity for the number of houses to be built and to support the Parish Council; Capt Daubeny of the RDC was to be invited to attend the meeting. Swings could be in operation in the Firs Field again – subject to new footings being put in place. Mr R Daniels was left to arrange for the disposal of grass from the cutting of the Firs Field.

Another quarter passes and on **6 June 1933** it's **'£900 for Hospital - Mrs Douglas Hatt receives Cheque from Box Scheme'**. The cheque for £900 for the RUH handed was over by **Mr FG Hamilton (Chairman of the Scheme and until recently Chair now vice-Chair of the Hospital)** to Mrs Hatt (representing Mr Hatt, a Member of the Hospital Board) in the Baptist School Hall, Oldfield Park, on the Wednesday. *Also present were **Mr Frank H Pine** (vice-chairman of the scheme), Mrs Newman (Management Board), Messrs HC Lavington, A Gunstone, H Bishop, W White (executive committee), Miss Roman (secretary Prior Park ward), the Rev H J White, **Mrs Frank H Pine** and Mr Wifred J*

Jenkins (Organising Secretary). The chairman said we have built a beautiful hospital — now must extend the area of contributors and fill it.

Now you cannot say the local press doesn't try for an eye-catching headline, such as the one on **1 July 1933** which reads **'A Cigarette for the Hospital - How You can Make the Empty Wards Function - Big Threepennyworth'.** How to save 3d a week for the hospital - give up a cigarette every other day said the organising secretary Mr Wilfred Jenkins to an enquirer *(an interesting proposition given that Mr Wills of the tobacco company was a substantial contributor to the building of the new RUH).* It is reported that the amended scheme had had an enthusiastic response by offering, besides free hospital treatment, additional benefits comprising assistance towards dental treatment and dentures, convalescent homes, surgical appliances, glasses and ambulance and had led to 800 new contributors to the Box Scheme. Meetings of workers addressed by Mr FG Hamilton (Chairman) and Mr FH Pine (Vice Chairman) had been held throughout Bath and district. New areas had been recruited. At present the Box Scheme comprised 700 voluntary workers. There had been a wide distribution of leaflets through publications, libraries etc.

On **15 July 1933** we return to **'Combe Down Housing - More Accommodation Needed - Call on the Rates'** and an Issue that had been before Monkton Combe Parish Council for 2 years. The RDC letter responding to the parish council said that they proposed applying to the Ministry to sanction a loan to build 10 or 12 houses on the site the Rural District Council were acquiring. With the cost of houses 12s 6d a week and rent not exceeding 8s 6d the balance of 4s would fall on ratepayers. The Chairman said a reply had been sent to the RDC saying that the applicants were ready and willing to pay 8s 6d (even though it exceeded the rate paid on present poor accommodation).

On the point of reducing costs by building more houses the advice was that the Ministry would not allow more than 12 houses on the one acre plot of land the council were acquiring. The RDC was to be asked about a subsidy for the proposed development given that at the start of the 2 years the RDC had taken to consider the issue subsidies had been available. The Chairman emphasised that in the list circulated there were 15 very bad cases in existing houses, one of which was condemned 5 years ago. *Mr FH Pine presided at this meeting with Messrs RW Cornish, R Daniels, EA Russell, FJ Brown, H Robinson, C Millett and Mrs Page (clerk).*

The Chronicle on **5 August 1933** had a 2 column article **'Another £1,000 for Bath Hospital'** comprising another report on a quarterly meeting of Box Scheme. In total £1,280 had been raised in the quarter. The chairman of the Box Scheme, Mr Hamilton, indicated that local secretaries should not readily issue vouchers for treatment where contributions fell below 3d per week. Apologies for absence were sent from FH Pine Vice-Chairman.

So on **19 August 1933** we have **'Bradford does its bit'** and a report on the now routine piece of local theatre whereby a £1,000 cheque was handed over by Cllr JF Goodall (vice-chairman of Bradford on Avon UDC) to Mr W Rawlinson (Chairman of the RUH) at the Church Hall. The RUH Flag Day in Bath on 30 October was hoped to be extended to Bradford on Avon. In thanking the Chairman (Cllr Edwards) for presiding Mr FH Pine appealed to all to maintain hospitals on a voluntary basis which, he said, was preferable to State control.

Next we find two parish council reports. Firstly on page 1 of the issue of **23 September** is **'Combe Downs "Great Need" - County MoH on Housing Problem'** This reported that the Combe Down housing problem had been further considered by the Plans and Housing Committee of the Bathavon RDC. Dr. Savage (Medical Officer to the Somerset County Council) has visited Combe Down and whilst agreeing that there were no houses sufficiently bad as to call for demolition orders, had intimated to the Medical Officer for the district (Dr JM Harper) that there was a great need for further houses to abate overcrowding. The committee have been given instances of certain cases where conditions were particularly bad. Dr Harper was to give a complete report on all houses in the district by end of month.

Secondly on **30 September 1933** page 26 we have an article **'Combe Down Lighting'**. FH Pine, as chairman, asked the Parish Council to vote the usual sum of £120 for lighting. At the request of a parishioner the Bath Electric Light Committee were to be asked to extend lighting times for the last tram. *Members present: Messers FH Pine (chairman), RW Cornish, R Daniels, CG Millett, EA Russell, FR Munday and Mrs Page (Clerk).*

On **7 October 1933** we have virtually a whole page for **'Bath's Tribute to Col Egbert Lewis - Farewell to an Honoured Public Servant - Old Volunteers at Graveside of Their Former Chief'**. The report mentions that "In the parish church of St Mary the Virgin, Bathwick, where he had worshiped for over forty years a large congregation representing the many interests with which he had been associated through a long life of public service paid their last tribute on Monday to the memory of Col Egbert Lewis...and the great assembly of brother freemasons lined the nave."

At The Church many activities were represented in the crowded congregation: Councillors (the Mayor Cllr Rhodes Cook had to attend a family bereavement but the Deputy Mayor Cllr Herbert Chivers was present), JPs, 4th Somerset LI, and many Freemasons.

Hospital Representatives were Mr Aubrey Bateman (President), Mr W Rawlinson (Chairman), Mr FG Hamilton (ex-chairman), Mrs Latter Parsons, Col. HS Davey (hon. treasurer), Mr Lawrence Mears (secretary and superintendent), Mr W Jenkins (secretary contributory scheme), Mr Frederick Lace FRCS, **Mr F H Pine (vice-chairman***, Contributory Scheme), Mr WH Smith, Mr E Ireland, Mrs Maddox, Dr Mitchell, Mr A Salter, Mr J Milburn, Dr A Waterhouse, Mr HC Lavington, Mr AL Fuller, Miss S Vian (Matron) and Sister Blanchard. Forbes Fraser Hospital representatives were Col Dalrymple-Hay, Miss Bathard (Matron), Mr HJ Fricker (Secretary) and Mr WG Webb. Bath and Wessex Orthopaedic Hospital was represented by Mrs Francis Malett.*

Col Lewis had been the Chairman of the RUH Board before and after the Great War (and at the inception of the Box Scheme in 1923). He had been the proprietor of the former Bath Herald. Wessex Associated News, publishers of the Bath and Wilts Chronicle and Herald, were represented by Sir Harry Hatt (Chairman of the Directors), Mr Douglas Hatt (vice-chairman), Mr JH Walker (managing editor) ..... a long list includes in the middle **Mr Fred Cook** *(who appeared in a street photo with FHP sometime in the 1930s.)*

It's good news on **11 November 1933** with a 3 column report on **'Another £1,400 for The Hospital - All Round Increase in Box Collections in the September Quarter - Commendation for Scheme's Organising Secretary'.** With 'Gratifying Progress in All Quarters' a quarterly cheque was to be handed to Aubrey Bateman at St John's School Lower Weston on Wednesday 15th. The quarterly meeting of the Executive Committee and collectors took place at (the scheme's offices) Shepherds Hall, Princes Street.

The chair was taken by Mr FG Hamilton, in the absence of Mr W Rawlinson, and he was supported by Mr FH Pine and Mr Wilfred Jenkins Secretary of the Scheme. A tribute on the **death of Col Egbert Lewis** noted his original help in the construction of the scheme and his remaining a valuable member of the Executive throughout. The quarterly report was moved by Mr FH Pine who paid tribute to the energy and work of Mr Jenkins. Mr Jenkins said that in place of the old typed report in future there would be a **quarterly magazine** for circulation to all stewards of which 5,000 copies would be produced.

We end the year on **2 December 1933** with **'Whist at Combe Down'.** At the Church Rooms we find Frank H Pine was the MC at an event in aid of the Combe Down School Sports Fund - there were 16 tables with the prizes distributed by Miss M E Tanner.

1934: Housing and unemployed, Horace Beckingsale dies, scheme expands, FHP joins RUH Board

Our first item for 1934 is for **10 February 'A Good Cause - Concert at Combe Down for the Unemployed'**. It reports "Organised and arranged by an unemployed man (Mr Billings) a concert in aid of the fund for the unemployed raised in connection with the Social Service Committee (of which Mr H Robinson, of Bank House, is Chairman) was held on Wednesday evening in the Church Army Social Centre, Combe Down. The Hall was packed to capacity by an audience extremely appreciative of an unusually high class programme. Mr FH Pine acted as announcer and during the interval Mr Robonson expressed the thanks of the committee" - amongst several performers, Mr N Daniels gave a violin solo.

On **17 February 1934** it's **'Chief Trouble at Combe Down - Parish Council Discuss Housing'**. At Monkton Combe Parish Council on the Tuesday Mr FH Pine, in the chair, said "Our chief trouble is that the housing schemes for Combe Down have not got a move on. During the last two years we have been agitating to get more houses on Combe Down, and as yet nothing has materialised." He did not think the RDC had put as much 'punch' into it as they might have done.

Replying, Mr Macdonald (a member of the County Council, present at the meeting) remarked that he thought he could promise the meeting that houses would shortly be built in Combe Down and Monkton Combe. The Town Planning Act had made a start in that area about two months before. He said "I am working so that the beauty of the Limpley Stoke valley shall not be spoiled. There are some areas of Claverton where houses can be built without encroaching on the Limpley Stoke valley." The Chairman remarked that the ground upon which to build twelve houses had been purchased at Combe Down.

Mr Cornish said that the County Council officials had agreed there was a need for houses. He said "We have discussed it until we are sick of it, I should like to see something done. I should like the County Council to co-operate with the Rural Council, so that something can be done, then at last the parishioners will feel that we, as a Council, have done our duty." Concern was expressed about the refuse dumps on Combe Down - although there was no complaint about the weekly collections. Mr Robinson made a suggestion to have tennis courts on the Firs Field. *Mr FH Pine presided at this meeting supported by Messrs RW Cornish, R Daniels, FJ Brown, H Robinson, GG Millett and Mrs Page (clerk).*

Now for a family event, in the issue of **3 March 1934** we have **'Death of Horace Beckingsale - Former Secretary of Bath Friendly Societies Council'.** It reports "Many Bathonians will regret to learn of the death of Mr Horace Beckingsale, at Tooting, London SW at the age of 61. He was buried at Streatham on Tuesday. Mr Beckingsale was secretary of the Bath Friendly Societies Council in its early days, and a member of the Hearts of Oak. Mrs Beckingsale and 2 daughters survive. Mrs Frank H Pine of Combe Down is a sister." *(See also page 258 below for a London press report.)*

On **10 March 1934** it's an **'Eleventh Hour Surprise - Labour oppose Capt Daubeny at Combe Down - Bathavon Council'.** The report records that Labour were to oppose Capt Daubeny at Combe Down with Mr Bray a retired engine driver nominated by Mr Cornish and Mr Millett. There were to be contests in 6 wards in the Bathavon RDC elections. In Combe Hay, Kelston and Northstoke there were no nominations - so retiring members would be automatically re-elected without a poll.

For the last meeting on the parish council for Frank Pine and Robert Daniels we are back on **17 March 1934** to the issue of **'Unemployed at Combe Down - Parish Council Discuss Relief Work - Funds Offered'.** This was the last meeting of the outgoing Monkton Combe Parish Council prior to the recently elected council taking office. *Mr Frank H Pine was in the Chair, with Messrs RW Cornish (vice chairman), R Daniels, CG Millett, FJ Brown, SL Plummer, FR Munday, and Mrs Page (Clerk).*

Several allotment applications were considered. R Daniels was to put up the swings in the Firs Field for Easter. Mr Robinson said that the Unemployment Committee had voted £10 for the labour cost to repair the Church Army Hut in the Firs Field. A parish meeting followed with a handful of parishioners joining the councillors.

We next find 3 relevant articles in consecutive pages of the Chronicle and Herald of **24 March 1934**. We begin on page 10 with almost a full page spread on **'Funeral of Sir Harry Hatt'.** There is a report on the service at the Abbey. Sir Harry Hatt was vice-chairman of Wessex Asociated News. Following the procession there were, with many representatives from the family, people from Bath City Council (Including the Mayor Col. the hon. HS Davey CMG) and the Chronicle & Herald *(with reference to a photo of him with FHP that I have reproduced below - Mr Fred Cook was listed amongst the commercial rather than editorial staff).*

There were also many representatives at the funeral from Bath Conservatives, Bath Corporation Electrical Department, the Bath Gas Company, the Bath Chambers of Commerce, the Rotarians and very many other organisations. Under 'In the Congregation' Mr FH Pine is listed in the third paragraph sixth line.

Next, on **24 March 1934** on page 11 we have **'£44,000 from Box Scheme - £4,000 paid to RUH last year - Collections Increase'.** The 1933 Report of the Box Scheme on behalf of Executive Committee was signed by Mr FG Hamilton (Chairman), Mr FH Pine (Vice-Chairman), Mr W Rawlinson (hon Treasurer) and Mr Wilfred J Jenkins (Organising Secretary). A list of receipts and payments is given - total receipts were £5,636 (with £3,143 from Bath, £1,148 from Somerset and £1,344 from Wiltshire). The piece concludes that the preceding information was given in the first issue of "Our Hospital" the magazine of the Hospital Box Scheme.

Lastly on page 12 from **14 March 1934** we have Frank Pine joining the Hospital Board in the major two-column article **'Hospital benefits for those earning £6 a week - Bath RUH Scheme Broadened - Free Ambulance up to £1 max - Wilts Towns Friendly Rivalry'.** Hospital benefits were to be extended to those earning £6 a week (a fair bit above the average wage then) if they had children under 16.

Tribute was paid to Lt-Col Egbert Lewis who had died and to the hard work of Mr Wilfred Jenkins (Organising secretary). Mr Rawlinson was resigning from the Executive, he had been associated with the scheme from the start. A great increase in receipts for the scheme had happened, despite the loss of Chippenham and district from the scheme. *To represent the scheme on the Board of Management of the RUH the following were elected:* **Mr H Lavington and Mr FH Pine (Bath),** *Mr J Milburn and Mrs Newman (Somerset), and Mr Gale and the Hon Mrs Shaw Mellor (Wiltshire).*

"Mr FH Pine briefly referred to the inception of the scheme following a letter in the local press from Mr Lavington suggesting that something should be done to help the hospital out of its difficulties. Mr Pine told how the Friendly Societies' Council developed the scheme on the principle of people paying two pence a week as a thank offering for good health. Then eventually they grew into a contributory scheme, but they still had the advantages of that early work of the friendly societies. Now they had a full time organiser in Mr Jenkins. He felt the scheme was on the threshold of still greater success, but was anxious that the old friendly society feeling should be associated with it. It was the principle of the human touch and bond of fellowship with others that would succeed where others would fail. He appealed to all supporters to try and get one other supporter during the year. People more than ever realised the existence of the Hospital and the work it was doing. He was glad the outlying areas realised their responsibilities to the Hospital and he felt they were only too anxious to meet their obligation."

Now from the sublime to a report of **21 April 1934** on **'For good Cause - Whist Drive at Batheaston'** and a whist drive at Batheaston Rifle Club in aid of the RUH Box Scheme. In the interval Mr FH Pine thanked the company for their support.

For the last time in this narrative we return to the parish council to see Mr Cornish now presiding (a role he continued in for at least 9 of his remaining years on the council until retiring from the council in 1948 – in 1937 he became a JP). It is worth noting that Mrs Page carried on as clerk until 1949. The report of **12 May 1934** is headed **'Firs Field Wall'**.The Firs Field wall needed repairing and the Unemployment Committee was to help carry out repairs. *This Monkton Combe Parish Council meeting was attended by Messrs RW Cornish (Chairman), CG Millett, WJ Bray, LG Jordan, WF Williams, FG Prescott, SL Plummer and Mrs Page (clerk). Messrs Cornish, Williams and Bray were to represent the Parish Council on the Unemployed Committee.*

At last we begin to see some upswing in box collections above the original targets with a quarterly report of **19 May 1934** headed **'Still More money for RUH - Extra £100 from Box Scheme - All Round Increase in Contributions - £1,664 total in quarter'** raised. A cheque for £1,100 would be going to the RUH. Collections had amounted to £975 (in Bath), £330 (in Somerset) and £358 (in Wiltshire). The Scheme now had new headquarters in Broad St (in place of Shepherds Hall). Mr RR Glynn-Jones OBE was to replace W Rawlinson as treasurer.

Proposing that the report be adopted Mr FH Pine commented that the good results were due to the loyalty of the collectors and the goodwill of the box holders. He saw hope of realising an even higher sum in the future. People realised more fully the benefits of the scheme and their obligation to the hospital and, in addition, there were better times ahead. Mr Jenkins (organising secretary) spoke of the need for a uniform contributory scheme in the city in place of the four or five schemes now operating. A list of receipts and payments is contained in the article.

So we continue to the report column 3 page 20 in the issue of **9 June 1934 'Centenary of the Forresters'** and the Abbey service to commemorate the centenary of the Ancient Order of Foresters. Its Bath United District was founded in 1846 and Members wore their regalia. Canon Foster Pegg talked about the self help role of the Friendly Societies movement. Bros AS Gunstone, 'Rationals', and FH Pine, 'Hearts of Oak', were to conduct a deputation to the RUH on Sunday afternoon and regretted their inability to attend.

A report of **16 June 1934** is headed **'Mayor Receives Surprise'** and concerns a Gipsy Fair at Ralph Allen's Park. At this event Mr Frank H Pine presented the Mayor (Col the hon HS Davey) with a cheque towards the Mayor's New RUH appeal fund. The cheque for £65 was from over 330 Combe Down subscriptions. Mr Pine had organised a local committee when the Mayor launched his appeal and the cheque was the result. The Mayor said "I had no idea I was going to be the recipient of this cheque. £65 is a great deal of money and Combe Down is not a big place; all the more credit and honour to Combe Down that it should be able to do such a great thing for the hospital." The

Mayor spoke favourably of the Box Scheme and noted that a third of the income of the RUH came from the Box Scheme.

On **28 July 1934** we have a three column spread: **'Another £1,100 cheque for RUH - Over £400 more than in same quarter last year'**. Contributions in the quarter were £1,700. *Mr Hamilton, vice-chairman of the RUH presided supported by Mr WM Huntley (President of Bath Chamber of Commerce), Mr FH Pine, Mr W Rawlinson, Mr RR Wyn-Jones (box scheme treasurer), Mr Wilfred Jenkins (organising secretary) and Mr AS Gunstone.*

Following applications from persons above the income limit for the Box Scheme a plan was in hand for a new, and entirely separate, Paying Patients Scheme for treatment at Forbes Fraser for such people. The new scheme had been endorsed by the RUH Board and applications would be accepted from 1 September 1934. The list of collections includes a list of 18 firms making employees contributions. **Mr Frank H Pine spoke on the work of the former Treasurer Mr Rawlinson and read an address to him, signed by the founders of the scheme - Henry Lavington, Frank Pine, Arthur Gunstone and George Hodges.** Noting that Mesrs Lavington and Hodges were aged 79 and 84, Frank Pine remarked on the need for younger ones to take on some of the work – his speech noted that there was still a long way to go.

In the Bath Chronicle and Herald of **1 September 1934** the details are set out of what is now described as the Forbes Fraser Scheme. Firstly the paper's lead article on page 3 (after the adverts and photographs pages) is **'Hospital Boon for Middle Classes - Guinea a year for Forbes Fraser Hospital Treatment - Covers whole family - No Income Limit'** The key elements of the scheme, designed by Mr Wilfred J Jenkins (organising secretary of the Box Scheme but to be run by him independently of the Box Scheme) were:

> <u>Contributions:</u> £1 1s a year paid in advance, yearly or half yearly, extra 7s 6d for junior 16-21.
> <u>Benefits:</u> 3 guineas (£3 3s) a week nursing and maintenance at Forbes Fraser for 4 weeks in any 12 months or at any other approved hospital. A payment of up to £1 for an ambulance would be made in any 12 months.
> <u>Income Limit:</u> None.
> <u>Qualifications:</u> Benefits after 6 months membership. No payment for doctors. There was an age limit of 60 for joining scheme. No assistance for maternity or mental illness, accident cases covered by compensation, contagious or infectious diseases.
> <u>Offices:</u> Paying Patients Scheme, Broad Street Chambers, Broad Street, Bath

On page 9 of the same paper of **1 September** is **'Forbes Fraser Scheme - Acclaimed as a real boon - "Why I am Joining"'** says "The scheme by which treatment at the Forbes Fraser hospital, or elsewhere, can be obtained for four weeks in a year by the payment of a guinea a year has had an excellent reception in Bath .... Acclaimed as a real boon to the middle classes ...."

"Mr Frank H Pine expressed his warm approval for the scheme when approached by a Chronicle and Herald representative. He is particularly interested by reason of the fact that he was one of the founders of the Bath Hospital Box Scheme, was chairman for nine years and is now vice-chairman "The individual appears to be fading away; now it is all cooperation" Mr Pine remarked "The man who comes into this scheme is providing for the time of emergency, whether for himself or for his family, and he is making provision for a time when he less able to meet additional expense." Asked what he thought would be the effect on Bath private nursing homes, Mr Pine said they would be unaffected, they would certainly not be adversely affected. "The scheme" he remarked "does not mean that necessarily one benefitting under it will go to the Forbes Fraser Hospital, but may go to a nursing home of his or her choice and equally benefit by the new arrangement.""

The main hospital box scheme also now seems to be moving ahead, as indicated by a report of **3 November 1934** which is entitled **'Record Box Collection for RUH - £1,775 Collected in the quarter - Largest Amount in Any Three Months Since Scheme Began - £1,100 cheque to RUH'**. This concerns the Council of Bath Friendly Societies Hospital Scheme Quarterly Meeting at the RUH. *We have Mr FG Hamilton presiding with Messrs FH Pine, Gwynne Jones (treasurer) and Mr Wilfred Jenkins (organising secretary).* Receipts for the quarter were £1,013 (Bath - compared with £573 per quarter in 1932), £380 (Somerset), £380 (Wilts). Mr FH Pine moved the adoption of the report and pointed out that it was 11 years ago that the first meeting of the Friendly Societies was held to consider a scheme to help the hospital. Little did they expect it to reach the magnitude that it had. Mr Gunstone said the appointment of the energetic Mr Jenkins as full time organising secretary 2 years before had paid off.

On **24 November 1934** we see 4 columns on **'Bath Pays Tribute to Loved Physician - City mourns passing of Dr Vincent Coates - Representative Congregation at the Abbey'**. The church was filled to its doors with a crowd outside the Abbey. There is a long list of 'Medical Colleagues'. Under the next heading 'Representatives' we have in the first paragraph a list of those representing the Royal United Hospital: Mr F G Hamilton (Chairman), Mr W H Smith, Mr FH Pine, Mr A Salter, Dr Rankin (representing the resident medical staff), Mr LH Mears (secretary superintendent), Miss Vian (Matron) and three sisters. After a further long list of representatives we have a list of 'Prominent Citizens' - Also present were the Mayor (Mr Anthony Bateman) ..... A Mr H Rothery *(probably no relation to FHP's Canadian friend)* is listed in the fourth paragraph of the third column. The Archdeacon paid tribute to a man of great experience and success in the treatment of rheumatism and the allied diseases...at the Mineral Water Hospital.

Finally we end the year on **15 December 1934** with an item under **'Town & County notes - Box Pioneers'**: "A good deal has been written about the origin of Bath's wonderful hospital box collecting scheme. Behind it was Mr HC Lavington. A letter in our own columns contained the germ of the idea. Others played a great part in its inception. There were Mr Frank H Pine (Chairman of the Friendly Societies' Council) and Mr Walter Rawlinson. Nor must we forget the late Mr Tom Wills, the first secretary. But one who helped considerably always remained in the background. I refer to the late Col Egbert Lewis, who was Chairman of the hospital at the time. He and Mr Lavington really hammered out the original scheme. Col. Lewis knew all there was to know about hospital control and finance and his advice was invaluable." ***Now I wonder what inspired that?***

FRANK PINE - THE LATER YEARS

c.1935

c.1936 with Fred Cook of Chronicle

1937 Sandown Isle of Wight

c.1937

1938

THE NEWSPAPER RECORD 1935-1938
1935-1938 The Glory Years for the Box Scheme (29 Articles)

1935: Scheme raises £5,300 in last year; Ald. Spear's devotion

We start our press cuttings for 1935 in a buoyant mood with a four column spread in the **9 February 1935** issue which is headed **'Splendid work of Box Collection Scheme - £5,300 raised for RUH in last year - How Somerset and Wilts helped'**. The report on the box scheme for 1934 showed that the total raised in 1934 was £7,000 - £3,983 in Bath, £1,478 in Somerset and £1,538 in Wiltshire. A sum of £5,300 was paid to the RUH, payments of £580 were made to other hospitals and £133 for other benefits. The balance at the bank was £788. Administration costs of the scheme were less than 9%. A good start had been made with the Paying Patients scheme. Detailed lists of contributions show 25 employers making employees contributions in Bath and Wiltshire.

The AGM of the Box Scheme took place in the RUH Lecture Hall, with the Chairman Mr FG Hamilton supported by Mr Aubrey Bateman (President of the Hospital and Mayor of Bath), the Mayoress, Mr Frank H Pine (vice-chairman) Mr RR Glynnne-Jones (treasurer), Ald FW Spear and Mr J Lawrence Mears (secretary and superintendent). Mr Wilfred Jenkins (organising secretary) was absent due to influenza. The chairman, who read the report, remarked that the figures in the accounts included a cheque for £2,000 (compared with £1,100 for each of the previous quarters) that was to be presented that night. He said how much they were indebted to their organising secretary (Mr Wilfred J Jenkins) for this result. Mr Frank Pine in seconding the adoption of the report said he regarded what had been accomplished was only a foretaste of what might yet be accomplished.

The President spoke of the vindication of the 1930 decision to build a new hospital. He conceded that the box scheme had presented its largest ever cheque but he would not rest until all 4 lateral wards of the hospital were filled with beds. In the last year the RUH had cost £25,000 of which the Box Scheme had supplied over £5,000. Alderman Spear moved a vote of thanks to the President, Mr Bateman. In reply Mr Bateman praised Mr Spear's devotion to good causes. *The following were elected to the Hospital Management Board: Mrs Newman, Captain Smith, Mr FJ Gale, Mr FH Pine, Mr HS Lavington and Mr F Webb. Of the 9 nominations for 7 seats on the Executive Committee the following were elected: Messrs H Bishop, WH Burgess, ET Billet, FJ Gale, Capt Smith, F Webb and W White.*

Interesting to see Frank Pine in close proximity to Ald. Spear for whose company he had been in paid employment.

On **6 April 1935** the Silver Jubilee of King George V was approaching and we have a newspaper report headed **'Jubilee Plans at Combe Down - Proposal to Levy a Penny Rate Rejected - Committee Formed'.** A public meeting had been convened by Monkton Combe Parish Council to discuss arrangements on Combe Down for the Silver Jubilee. Mr RW Cornish (Chairman of the Council) presided, supported by the Vicar (Rev. F Last Bedwell), Mr RG Tucker (pastor of the Union Chapel), Mr H Noad and a majority of members of the council, together with Mrs EM Page (Clerk).

The Chairman remarked that the Parish Council had no desire to foist on the people celebrations of a character they might not desire, nor to finance them out of rates unless the parish was definite that that was more desirable than a public subscription. The aim of the meeting was: (1) to decide whether any celebrations should be undertaken (2) to voice suggestions for such celebrations (3) to decide on the method of financing them and (4) to elect a committee to carry out the wishes of the meeting. He advised them not to elect too large a committee that night, but to give the committee the power to co-opt those whose co-operation they might need.

The suggestions made included a non-denominational service, tea and sports, souvenir mugs for the children and for a subscription list to be opened. Mr Robinson resolved that a committee be appointed and Mr Bezer seconded the proposal. The committee elected comprised: Mr H Robinson, the Vicar, Mr Tucker, Mr & Mrs Noad, Mr Brown (schoolmaster), Capt Booth (Church Army), Mr. Cornish, Mr. Hancock, Miss Pullen, Mrs. Hobbs, Mr WJ Bray, Mr WF Williams, **Mr FH Pine** and Mrs Page (to act as Secretary). Capt Daubeny (RDC representative) was unable to be present but suggested that a penny rate could raise £40. The proposal to levy a rate was vetoed on the proposition of Mr Robinson seconded by Miss Ponting. The Chairman proposed a house to house canvass of funds to support whatever the committee proposed.

And so to the Silver Jubilee with the report on the celebration in Bath on **11 May 1935** with a full page report **'Splendid Finale to Bath's Jubilee Day - Great Throng on Recreation Ground - A Bath Cavalcade - Cebrations Conclude in Blaze of Torchlights and Fireworks'.** There were between 15,000 and 20,000 people on the Bath Recreation Ground – the football area was packed. There were music and gymnastic displays and a cavalcade on a giant screen, a torchlight tattoo and a firework display. The king's speech was relayed by loudspeakers. From the Pavilion came an 8 deep column of the City of Bath Girls School gymnasts in white blouses and black shorts. The City of Bath Boys School also gave a gymnastic display. Under the subheading **'Through City's Streets - Representatives in Bath Civic Procession'** we see that this included, for the RUH Box Scheme, **FH Pine** and HC Lavington (final column 13th item).

1935 Silver Jubiliee of George V in Bath

And on the Firs Field Combe Down

Most of page 17 of the paper published **25 May 1935** reported on the **'Funeral of Col Hon HS Davey - Citizens Tribute to a Life of Public Service'**. Mayor Aubrey Bateman led the procession with enrobed aldermen and councillors. At the top of the third column of the report it states that the RUH was represented by FG Hamilton (chairman), J Lawrence Mears (secretary superintendent), Miss Vian (Matron), Mr A Salter, the hon. Mrs Shaw Mellor, Mrs F Maddox, **Mr F H Pine**, Mrs Latter Parsons, Mr W H Smith, Mr W G Dyke, Mr R H Whittington, Mrs Gordon Smith, Mrs Newman, Mr Walter Rawlinson and Mr H C Lavington. Col. Davey was a former city councillor, mayor and hon. treasurer of the RUH. His wife's death had been reported on 2 January 1932,

On **21 September 1935** there is a report **'Our Hospital Workers'**. Appreciation of the work of Westmoreland Ward in promoting the box scheme was shown by Alderman and Mrs Jenkin hosting a social evening for workers in the ward at the Red House. Mayor Aubrey Bateman as Presdent of the RUH was present - so were Messrs FG Hamilton (RUH Chairman), **FH Pine** (vice-chairman of the Box Scheme), J Lawrence Mears (secretary superintendent), Mrs Mears and Mr Wilfred J Jenkins (organising secretary of Box Scheme. Mr Hamilton spoke of the value of the Box Scheme. Ald. Jenkins addressed the need for everyone without a box to have one. The Mayor said the Management Board was to open 2 more wards. He made a plea for a proper nurses' home: the temperature of the wooden huts for nurses had been 90 degrees in summer.

On **12 October 1935** we find an article about a former employee of Norton Dairies with the **'Funeral of Mrs Henley - Former Coleagues Last Tribute'**. it reads: "Several members of the staff of the old Bath and Somerset Dairy Company attended the funeral at Locksbrook Cemetery of Mrs. Henley (nee Miss Taylor), who until her last illness about three weeks ago, was in charge of the dairy at 20, Catherine Place. Mrs Henley was retained by the Norton St Philip Dairy when they acquired the business of the old company. The former members of the staff who attended the ceremony to give expression of their respect for a loyal and unselfish colleague were **Mr Frank H Pine** (assistant manager), Mr H G Collett (foreman), Mr W C Gazzard (cashier), Miss Fudge (Clerk), Mrs C Collett (butterwoman) and Messrs Dyer, Jones, Selway, Smith and Weeks (roundsmen)."

On **2 November 1935** there is an item **'Forbes Fraser Hospital - New Maternity Department - Opened by Lord Bath'**. A new maternity unit was opened by Lord Bath - and Mr AL Fuller Chairman of the hospital presided. The company included Mr FG Hamilton (Chair RUH), Major GD Lock, Mr W Rawlinson, Rev JC Church, Rev W Gregory Harris, Dr & Mrs CA Marsh, Mrs Forbes Fraser, **Mr FH Pine**, Mr A Salter etc....Mr HJ Fricker (Secretary of the hospital).....

1936: Lots of funerals including the King's

Entering the department of interesting names, we start the year with a report of **18 January 1936.** This gives us the heading **'Funeral of Mr James Riddle - Esteemed Combe Down Resident'.** Aged 84 Mr Riddle was the people's warden at Combe Down Parish Church. In the long list of those present at the church funeral there were: Mr GS Rivington and Major TH Clark (churchwardens), Mr WJ Bray and Mrs Page (representatives of the parish council), Mrs R Brewer and Mr AC Pavey (representing staff of Combe Down School), Capt CW Daubeny ....Mr WR Ings ....Miss M Ponting, Mrs Burridge....Mr F Pearce....Mr FC Appleby.... Mr H Robinson.... and **Mr and Mrs FH Pine.** As with most Combe Down funerals, the arrangements were by Mr CG Mannings.

Another funeral reported on **18 January 1936** has **'Mayoress as Mourner - Funeral of Mr JW Nicholls at Lansdown'.** Aged 45, for last 14 years he had been cashier at the Milsom Branch of National Provincial Bank. The Mayoress of Bath (Mrs JS Carpenter) was amongst the mourners and in the first of 3 paragraphs listing mourners is **Mr FH Pine.**

Lastly on **1 February 1936** **'Baths Homage of Sorrow'** (continued from page 3) there is a list of those who attended Bath Abbey on the death of King George V - **FHP** is listed in the first paragraph.

After 3 funerals we have (on page 7 at the end of column 2) on **22 February 1936** **'Whist for Hospital - Drive Final at Pump Room, Bath'.** This was the final of a competition organised by Mrs Shaw Mellor (Deputy Chairman of the RUH) in aid of the RUH. Mr Frank Pine was MC, Mrs Wesley Whimster organised the refreshments and Mr FG Hamilton (Chairman of the Hospital Board of Management) gave out the prizes.

So we come to the issue of **4 April 1936** and **'Bath & County Notes',** and in column 2 the item **'Accurate Arithmetic'.** "Amusement was caused at the RUH annual meeting by the President (Mr Aubrey Bateman) remarking that the £5,800 raised by the Box Collecting Scheme last year represented 1,392,000 pennies. Mr FH Pine, at a later stage, assured the President that his arithmetic was absolutely accurate! All stood in tribute to the memory of King George V before business was proceeded with." Medals were presented to 2 nurses for good service.

Next we have two more funerals. On **18 April 1936** it's **'Bath Citizens Tribute - Funeral of Alderman HC Smith - Manvers Street Service - Mayor and Corporation Attend'.** In over 2 columns it is recounted that the Mayor and Corporation attended a funeral of Alderman HC Smith (69) who had clearly a strong interest in Bath's parks. There was a

Guard of Honour from Bath Parks Dept. In a paragraph beginning 'The Congregation included' a long list follows which includes, at the end, **Mr FH Pine**.

On **2 May 1936** is a report concerning the **'Death of Mrs L M Linsley - Mother of Mrs FW Spear of Bath'**. Mrs Linsley was aged 83 and the mother of the widow of Alderman FW Spear. The funeral was at Trim Street Chapel, and in the second column of the report, under 'In the Congregation' (at the end of the second paragraph), is **Mr FH Pine**.

The Chronicle of **29 August 1936** had a front news page article (actually page 3 – page 1 was advertising!) on **'Hospital Box Scheme - Some Examples of Its Good Work'**. The article reports that Miss Rita Mauger, the former almoner of the RUH, contributed to the September issue of the magazine of the Box Scheme an article explanatory of its helpfulness. To the same issue **Mr FH Pine**, the vice-chairman of the Box Scheme, contributed a resume of the history of the Red Cross movement.

I would note also, as matter of passing interest, an adjoining article on the will of Mr Paul Jolly Chairman of Jolly & Sons of Bath, Bristol and Cardiff. Jollys are now part of the House of Fraser but retain their identity. The other major Bath department stores were Evans and Owens and Colmers (with shops in Bath, Bristol, Weston-super-Mare and Bridgewater) and the Co-op - all sadly no more.

On **14 November 1936** column 6 we have **'Mr SG Hodges Bereaved - Death of Friendly Society Workers Wife'**. It is reported that Mr GS Hodges' wife passed away at age of 84. Mr Hodges was one of the founders of the box scheme with Messrs AS Gunstone, FC Lavington, FH Pine and A Salter. Mr Hodges was for 34 years secretary of the Oldfield Park branch of the United Patriots' Friendly Society.

I would also note a preceding article on Monkton Combe Parish Council - Responding to a request for a better peak service, the officials of the tram company considered a 15 minute service to Combe Down adequate. Other issues considered were: more polling stations, an extra phone kiosk, and the council's Armistice Sunday wreath which Mrs Page (clerk) was to lay. *Mr Cornish presided with Messrs FR Munday, WJ Bray, LG Jordan, FG Prescott and WF Williams with Mrs EM Page (clerk).*

<u>1937: Scheme raises record £9,000 in last year, quarterly cheque for £1,700 to RUH</u>

We start the new year with the Bath and District Hospital Box Scheme going from strength to strength. The 4 column report of **27 February 1937** is headed **'Largest Quarterly Cheque for RUH - £2,500 From Bath Box Scheme - Additional Benefits - Record Collections of over £9,000 Last Year'**. The record collections of £9,358 in 1936 (£5,306 from Bath, £1,787 from Somerset and £2,264 from Wiltshire) represented an increase of £1,628 over 1935. Sums amounting to £7,000 were paid to the RUH, an increase of £1,200 over the preceding year, and over £3,100 greater than in 1932. Some £1,360 was paid to other hospitals and for additional benefits. On Wednesday a cheque had been presented at the Guildhall to RUH for £2,500. A refund of fees for those treated at the Forbes Fraser Hospital would be 30/- a week rather than 15/-.

The meeting was presided over by Mr FG Hamilton, supported by Ald. C Jenkin, Mr CE Kindersley, **Mr FH Pine**, Col. RR Glynne-Jones (hon. treasurer), and Mr Wilfred Jenkins (organising secretary). In seconding the adoption of the report **Mr Pine** said that the whole of the huge work had been done at an administrative cost of under 8%. The amount given to the hospital in the last year had been one quarter of its total income for the year; it had kept the hospital running for three months out of the 12. As representatives from the scheme on the **RUH Board of Management** the following were re-elected: Mr HC Lavington, **Mr Pine** and Mr Webb for Bath, Mrs Newman for Somerset, and Mr Gale and Capt Smith for Wiltshire. The Annual Report of the Box Scheme was reproduced with regard to its detailed receipts and payments.

On **1 May 1937** we have the headings **'£1,700 Cheque for RUH - £2,474 collected in the last quarter'.** On the Wednesday Mr RJ Dyer chairman of the Box District of the Bath RUH Contributory Scheme had presented a cheque for £1,700 to Mr A Norman Wills, the RUH's new Treasurer. *Mr FG Hamilton (chairman of the scheme) presided at the meeting, supported by* **Mr FH Pine** *(vice-chairman), Mr Wills, and Mr Wilfred Jenkins (organising secretary).* The sum collected in the quarter ending March was £2,474 (£1,429 from Bath, £454 from Somerset and £591 from Wiltshire) - an increase of £261 over the similar quarter in 1936.

I would also note the next item following the above report – 'Fancy Dress Parade - At Combe Down Labour Party's Last Dance of the Season' held at the Rockery Tea Gardens. Mr Cornish superintended the voting.

On **3 July 1937** in 'Bath & County Notes' (col3 item10) and **'Bath Hospital Stalwart'** it is reported: "Mr F H Pine tells me that Mr Frederick Wilton, whose death was announced on Wednesday, was the first secretary of a ward in the Hospital Box Scheme which was established in Twerton. Although at the time that he accepted this responsibility, Mr Wilton was 74 years of age, he did a great deal in setting an example to others by his energy and enthusiasm. Mr Pine is curtailing his holiday in the Isle of Wight in order to attend the funeral." (I have reproduced pictures of Frank and Lilian on holiday on the Isle of Wight – probably their only proper holiday together.)

So the next week in the issue of **10 July 1937** we have (end of col 1) **'Buglers at Funeral'** and the funeral of Mr Frederick Wilton aged 88. He served in campaigns in India and for more than 2 years in the Great War. Mr Wilton's widow was unable to attend the funeral as she was indisposed in Barnstaple. Mr Wilton was borne to his last resting place by the RSM and the Colour Sergeant of the Somerset LI Buglers sounded the last post. The Mourners were fully listed – mainly family. The final paragraph reads: "Mr FH Pine was also amongst those at the graveside in company with representatives of the British Legion and the Royal United Hospital."

Meanwhile life had been continuing as normal on the Monkton Combe Parish Council but an interesting item about its chairman appeared in the paper on **31 July 1937** headed **'Combe Down Labour JP'** the article states:

> **"Mr RW Cornish of Combe Down has been appointed a Justice of the Peace for the County of Somerset, and after taking the oath, he will sit on the Weston (Bath) Bench.** Mr Cornish is a native of Warminster, and a compositor by profession. He served his apprenticeship with the 'Warminster Journal' and or the past 25 years has been a member of staff of Wessex Associated News, Ltd., owners of the 'Bath Chronicle and Herald', the 'Wiltshire News', and the 'Somerset Guardian'. He is well known in connection with his political activities, being a keen supporter of the Labour Party.

> "Before going to live at Combe Down Mr Cornish was a vice-president of the Bath Labour Party for a number of years, and he unsuccessfully contested three municipal elections, firstly against Councillor H Cleaver, secondly against Councillor George Long, and thirdly against the late Councillor W H Crossman. He is a past-president of the Bath branch of the Typographical Association, and is now serving his third term of office as a member of Monkton Combe (Combe Down) Parish Council. For the first three years he was vice-chairman of the Council, and the second three chairman. During the war he served for 12 months in the RAMC."

On **30 October 1937** we have the headlines **'Backbone of the Hospital - Mayor's Praise for RUH Box Scheme - £1,700 Record Cheque'**. "If by nothing else the friendly societies of Bath have justified themselves by starting this scheme" said Mayor Cllr W F Long when he accepted a cheque for £1,700. He was presiding at the quarterly meeting at RUH with Mr FG Hamilton (chairman of the scheme), **Mr FH Pine** (vice-chairman), Col RR Glynne-Jones (hon. treasurer) and Mr Wilfred Jenkins (organising secretary), with the treasurer of the hospital Mr Norman Wills, amongst the audience. The scheme collected £2,638 in quarter (£1,509 from Bath, £491 from Somerset and £638 from Wiltshire) with increases from all areas, from household boxes and from employers' contributions. Payments of over £320 were made to over 25 hospitals besides the RUH, and £112 was paid in additional benefits, in the quarter.

Mr F H Pine said they had originally had an ambition to raise £5,000 a year for the hospital. By that evening's cheque they would have paid to the RUH £5,100 in nine months that year, so he thought they had achieved their objective very well (applause). Major Daley paid tribute to work of Mr Wilfred Jenkins, organising secretary, a former journalist, who had plans to stand as a parliamentary candidate, and to the support of the local press for scheme. In the next year there would be an appeal for a new nurses home (pre-empted in the current year by the Royal National Hospital for Rheumatic Diseases appeal). The Mayor commended the 600 volunteer workers for scheme. He suggested building the nurses home at the Forbes Fraser and that there should be paying beds at the RUH.

We end the extracts from this year with **6 November 1937** and the headlines **'Passing of Bath Councillor - Mr Edward White's Long Service'**. Edward White was a Bath Councillor from 1921 and, as a dairyman, was President of Bath Dairyman's Association 1928-1936. He served on the Markets, Parks, Surveying and Watch Committees. He was a Conservative. There was a civic procession before his funeral at Holy Trinity Church that included the Mayor Mr WF Long. At the Church Representatives of Public Bodies included "Bath RUH Box Scheme: Mr. FH Pine (Vice-Chairman), Mr WJ Jenkins (Secretary)".

1938: Scheme raises £10,500 with £7,800 to RUH in last year - First £2,000 cheque - Connie Pine's Wedding

Our extracts from 1938 begin with a high on **5 March 1938** and the headlines **'Box Scheme Breaks All Records - Collections for 1937 Amounted to Nearly £10,500 - £7,800 paid to Hospital in last year'**. The annual meeting of the Box Scheme had been held at the Guildhall on the Wednesday Evening. *The Annual Report was signed on behalf of the executive by FG Hamilton (Chairman), FH Pine (Vice-Chairman), Mr RR Glynne-Jones (hon. treasurer) and Wilfred J Jenkins (organising secretary).*

Collections showed an increase of £1,130 over 1936 and the payment to the hospital was £800 in excess of 1936. Scheme Income had practically doubled since 1923. Area totals collected were: Bath £6,044, Somerset £1,921, Wiltshire £2,523. There had been increases of £689 from household boxes and £440 from workplace deductions from wages. More workplace groups had been formed and had come into the flat rate scheme. There is an impressive list of 70 firms signed up for employees contributions - but half a dozen major firms in Bath had still not signed up.

Mr Frank H Pine, seconding the report, reminded his hearers that it was only as recently as 1923 that they started with the aim of raising £5,000 a year... The public loved the voluntary hospital system, and wanted to maintain it; they did not want state aided hospitals. The voluntary system had faithfully served the people of this country for a long period, and long might it remain so.

There were seven nominations for six representatives from the Box Scheme Council to the RUH Board of Management, and the following were elected by ballot: Messrs WH Burgess (Bradford on Avon); RJ Dyer (Box); HD Lavington (Executive); Mrs C Newman (Upper Weston); **Mr FH Pine** (Executive) and Mr F Webb (Bath). There were 16,000 subscribers to the Box Scheme said the Mayor, in accepting the cheque, but it was not enough.

When I was at school in Bath I remember selling programmes for the Rotary Club's Bath Carnival in aid of the Cheshire Homes in Keynsham (and visiting the house of Mr Horace Bachelor of the 'Infradraw' method of football pools prediction). Anyway, on **23 July 1938** we see the report **'£2,040 Carnival Cheque for RUH - Bath Rotary's Object Achieved'**. A £2,040 carnival cheque was accepted by Mrs Shaw Mellor on Tuesday on behalf of the Hospital Management Board at the Old Red House Restaurant following a luncheon. With this cheque the Rotarians and Soroptimists had now raised £6,000 towards a new RUH Children's Ward to be named the Bath Rotary Club Ward.

After luncheon those present viewed a colour film of the carnival. At end of column 3 is a report of the unveiling ceremony for the new ward at which friends of the RUH, in addition to members of the Rotary Club, were present. *The company included Mr Aubrey Bateman (President of the Hospital), Messrs FG Hamilton and W Rawlinson (Deputy Chairmen), Mr J Lawrence Mears (secretary superintendent),* **Mr FH Pine**, *Miss Maud Wood (President of the Soroptimist Club), Mrs Scott White (President-elect) and many members of the medical profession.*

On **30 July 1938** we read of **'Hospital Schemes Rapid Advance - Quarterly Cheque for £1,900 - Increased scope necessitates change of name'**. The chairman FG Hamilton announced that the Freshford area, formerly in association with the Hospital Savings Association had now become part of the Box Scheme. Some 9 other areas were also coming into association with the Box Scheme. These included districts in Wiltshire, Gloucester and Devon. The schemes were formerly linked with the Hospital Savings Association but this was now withdrawing to its London districts and Bath had been invited to be 'parent' of the schemes in question. So it had been decided to change the name to 'Bath Region Hospital Contributory Scheme'.

The association with the other schemes would be called 'The Hospital Service Scheme' and would be administered from the office of the Bath Scheme, with Mr Jenkins as the organising secretary of the Association. Mr Terry (hon surgeon RUH) accepted the cheque and referred to the opening of a new hospital at Melksham that afternoon. **Mr**

FH Pine (Vice-Chairman) made special mention of their admiration of the Rotary Club for undertaking the carnival and carrying it through so successfully.

Detailed figures of receipts and payments are listed in the report. In the quarter £2,943 had been collected, £358 more than in the same quarter of the previous year with £1,715 from Bath (a £245 increase), £510 from Somerset (a £30 increase) and £717 from Wiltshire (a £83 increase).

So now we go to family event, for which I have several photographs. This time the article is a long-preserved copy of the daily paper of **1 August 1938** (rather artistically dated, perhaps by FHP) and it concerns the wedding of Connie Pine and Albert Taylor. Headed **'Wedding of Miss C Pine - Interesting ceremony at Combe Down'** it reads:

> "Great interest was taken in the wedding at Holy Trinity Church, Combe Down, on Monday, of Miss Constance Evelyn Pine, second daughter of Mr and Mrs Frank H Pine, The Firs, Combe Down, and Mr Albert John William Taylor, Tranmere, Birkenhead, second son of Mr and Mrs John Taylor of Birkenhead. The bride's father has long been known in connection with his work on behalf of the Royal United Hospital and the bride has been active in the life of the parish in which she has resided. She has been a member of the tennis club, of the GFS, the church choir when the choir was augmented by ladies, the Old Scholars' Association and of the Dramatic Club, she having taken part in every play produced since the club's foundation.

> "The vicar (the Rev. E Roberts MA) officiated. Given in marriage by her father, the bride wore ivory cloque, with veil (kindly lent by Mrs H Taylor) and carried a sheaf of Harrisii lilies. She was attended by her sisters - the Misses Phyllis, Edna and Lena Pine - whose dresses were of floral crepe. Their brooches were the gift of the bridegroom. Mr Alex Kilpatrick of Birkenhead was the best man and Messrs F Maggs and H Taylor were the groomsmen.

> "**The Service**. Miss C Long, a friend of the bride, was at the organ. As the congregation assembled she played 'Melody' (Powell), 'In a Monastery Garden' (Kettleby), 'Serenade' (Schubert), and a waltz in A Flat by Brahms. The bridal party were met at the west door by the Vicar and proceeded to the chancel during the playing of the wedding march from 'Lohengrin'. The hymn 'Oh Perfect Love' was sung, and Medelssohn's Wedding March was played as the bride and bridegroom left at the close of the service.

"A reception took place at the Avenue Hall, the catering being by the Old Red House. Minehead was chosen for the honeymoon. The bride's travelling costume was a two-piece tan Angora, with silver fox fur, the latter the gift of the bridegroom. All the flowers for the ladies and gentlemen were the gifts of Mr A J Caudle, Bath."

On **15 October 1938** is a Chronicle article on the re-vamped Assembly Rooms **'Bath Re-opening Souvenir Booklet'.**

It is one of several front page articles covering 4 columns about the Royal visit to re-open the Assembly Rooms (*to which FHP was invited – I have his invite reproduced here*).

Other aspects of the celebrations mentioned include a proposed Ball and other entertainments, and the souvenir booklet on the re-opening *(I have FHPs copy). Sadly the renovated Assembly Rooms were gutted in the Bath Blitz a day or so after FHP died.*

On **29 October 1938** we have a further record of the booming success of the Box Scheme in the latter part of the 1930s when the original targets were being exceeded by a factor of two - the headlines state **'Another record for RUH Box Scheme - First £2,000 cheque in September Quarter - Substantial Improvements in Each Section - Mrs Shaw Mellor's Tribute'.** "Bath Regional Contributory Scheme, better known as the Bath RUH Box Collecting Scheme, which now includes contributions from groups of employees as well as collections by means of household boxes, achieved another record total last quarter, a cheque for £2,000 being received on Wednesday evening at the institution by the chairman (the hon. Mrs Shaw Mellor) from the hands of Mrs Frederick Newman, secretary of the Weston branch." This contrasted with the sum of £1,700 handed over in the same quarter of the previous year. The total sum collected in the quarter was £3,168, an increase of £530 over the same quarter of the preceding year (with Bath contributing £1,822, Somerset £559, and Wiltshire £786).

Amongst those at the head of the room with the hon. Mrs Shaw Mellor were Mr FG Hamilton (chairman of the scheme), **Mr FH Pine** (vice-chairman of the scheme), Col RR Glynne-Jones (hon. treasurer), Mr Wilfred Jenkins (organising secretary), and Mrs Frederick Newman. Mrs Newman expressed her pleasure at being asked to serve on the

Board. Mrs Shaw Mellor remarked on the achievements of the past 14 years when the first of the Friendly Societies' payments had prevented the hospital doors from closing. The £2,000 did not include the receipts from the 2,000 workers from Corsham, who had come into the scheme, or the 1,400 from Melksham who had come into the scheme due to the work of the organising secretary, Mr Jenkins.

A separate adjoining article under the heading of **'Bath Paying Patients - Scheme has Another Good Year'** reports that, according to its 4th Annual Report, this scheme - run in conjunction with the Bath Regional Hospital Contributory Scheme - had had a satisfactory year with £717 in contributions. It was proposed that a no claims bonus would be included in the scheme. The scheme's Chairman is recorded as Mr FG Hamilton with **Mr FH Pine** (Vice-Chairman) and Col RR Glynne-Jones (hon. treasurer).

THE NEWSPAPER RECORD 1939-1949

1939-1949 The last lap and Postscript (23 Articles)

1939: Scheme raises £12,807 with £8,800 to RUH in last year

I begin with a reference to Frank Pine's oldest daughter, my Aunt Phyllis (although I have recorded her involvement with the Old Scholars amateur dramatics elsewhere). On **25 February 1939** we see a report on the Friday Circle of the Bath branch of the British Empire Shakespeare Society and its reading of 'Anthony and Cleopatra' in which Phyllis Pine participated (she was to be 34 on March 2).

Whilst storm clouds might have been gathering internationally the Box Scheme was still going from strength to strength - on **4 March 1939** the headlines were: **'Mayor Praises Provident Organisations - Collections for Bath Hospital Scheme Up - Biggest Yet Quarter Cheque'** the article reads "During 1938 a sum of £12,807 11s 1d was collected under the auspices of the Bath Regional Hospital Contributory Scheme. This was £2,318 7s 1d more than in 1937."

According to the annual report, the area totals were £7,085 for Bath (an increase of £1,041), £2,149 for Somerset (an increase of £228) and £3,572 for Wiltshire (an increase of £1,048). There had been an increase of £1,253 in the amounts collected from collecting boxes and of £1,065 in the amounts received from groups of workers in deductions from wages. A total of 87 companies are listed with employees' contributions amounting to £3,126. The sums paid to the RUH were £8,800 (£1,000 more than in 1937) with £1,978 paid to other hospitals and with £894 paid in other benefits. Administration costs were £766 in 1937 and £969 in 1938 (7%).

At the annual meeting of the scheme at the Guildhall the Mayor was presented with a record Quarterly Cheque for the RUH of £3,100. *At the meeting Mr FG Hamilton (chairman) was supported by the Mayor (Capt Adrian Hopkins MC), Mr Wilfred Jenkins (organising secretary), Mr FH Pine (vice-chairman) and Cllr SH Rawlings.* The area covered by the scheme had been enlarged by the transfer of Melksham and Freshford from the Hospital Savings Association. Mr Hamilton referred to the Hospital Service Scheme and said the alliance of the group of contributors under that scheme had taken effect from October 1st. It was being administered separately from main scheme, with separate acounts.

The Mayor noted that against a contribution of 13s. per year the charge per day at the hospital was 9s. 5d. and he expressed pleasure that Corsham was now in the scheme. The following were elected as representatives to the RUH Board of Management: Mrs

Newman, Mr Webb, Mr HC Lavington, Mr Dyer, **Mr Pine** and Mr Burgess. The amounts that had been raised from collections and from the contributory scheme for employees were listed in detail in this article on the annual report.

It had remained, since the opening of the new RUH, that the nurses accommodation had left much to be desired and the Chronicle and Herald of **22 April 1939** headlined **'£50,000 Appeal for New RUH Nurses Home - Inadequate Army Huts To Be Replaced - Urgent Need forms 'local crisis' says Alderman Bateman - Means to Reducing Hours of Work'.** An appeal was launched at the annual meeting of the Royal United Hospital at the Guildhall on Tuesday by President Aubrey Bateman who described the nurses need as a local crisis. The Hon. Mrs Shaw Mellor, Chairman of the Board, who was to be the driving force behind the appeal, noted that it had been postponed 2 years before so as not to clash with the new undertaking for the Royal National Hospital for Rheumatic Diseases. If nurses had a modern home with indoor recreative facilities it would enable their working hours to be reduced to a 96 hour fortnight.

Ald. Bateman reminded those present that some 10 years before, at the same venue, he had presided at his first meeting of the RUH. In 1932 when they had moved to the new hospital, the number of patients had been 2,759; in the last year the number had been 3,854. In 1929 the hospital had a deficit. In the last year there had been a deficit of £3,261 – but rather than reducing the number of patients it could be dealt with by increasing subscribers. He referred to a Parliamentary Bill to exempt hospitals from local rates - he hoped it would go through. When they built the new hospital their funds did not extend to replacing the army huts of 1915 and build a proper nurses home. *(Unfortunately the war was to curtail the plans for that nurses home.)*

The resignation of the Matron Miss Vian to do other work after 8 years service was noted. The Mayor (Capt Adrian Hopkins MC) moved the re-election of Aubrey Batman as President, and **Mr FH Pine**, seconding, said Ald Bateman was no figurehead. He had worked with him and knew his value.

On **18 November 1939** in the final column of page 4 are the headlines **'Bath Hospital Box Scheme Forges Ahead - Another £2,000 cheque for Royal United'.** "The Bath Hospital Regional Scheme goes from strength to strength. An increase of no less than £925 was shown in the receipts for the September quarter as compared with the relative quarter of last year. Towards this advance Wiltshire made a splendid contribution of £928 extra, largely through the medium of group employees' subscriptions (Bath was down by £48). In view of the difficulties of war the executive has decided that it would be inadvisable to hold the customary quarterly meeting of the Hospital Scheme Council, associated with the usual presentation of a cheque to the Royal United Hospital." A cheque for £2,000 had been sent - collections in the quarter were £4,094 (Bath £1,773, Somerset £574, Wiltshire £1,745). Payments to other hospitals amounted to £1,176.

"The Executive, of which Mr FG Hamilton is Chairman, Mr FH Pine Vice-Chairman, Col RR Glynne-Jones TD, hon Treasurer, and Mr Wilfrid J Jenkins, Organising Secretary, express its special thanks to all the voluntary workers in the scheme...this assistance has in many cases been necessarily associated with difficult conditions."

In the same issue of **18 November 1939** there is (on page 15 final column) an item on the **'Bath Hospital Box Scheme - List of Bath and County Collections'** which, apart from giving a breakdown of the figures from the Bath Region Hospital Box Contributory Scheme Quarterly report, also notes the challenges for collectors working in the black-out.

1940: Funeral of Hubert Beckingsale - £4,148 raised in a quarter - voluntary/municipal distinctions ended

On 16 February 1940 Hubert Beckingsale wrote to his niece, my mother Lena Pine, on Garlick & Sons notepaper in red pencil to wish her

well on her birthday (a red letter day). Recovering from flu, he did not seem well in the letter and said he would not be visiting Combe Down on the Sunday – and probably not until Easter. Clearly things did not happen that way because in the paper of **13 April 1940** there was an item entitled **'Loved Monkton Combe - Funeral of Mr Hubert Beckingsale'**. On page 17, at the end of the third column we read:

"In the peaceful and old world charm of Monkton Combe, which he loved, Mr Hubert Beckingsale, who died at the residence of his sister, Mrs F H Pine, Come Down, Bath, was laid to rest today. *(i.e. from 17 The Firs – he shares the same grave as his parents, sister Lillian Pine and Frank, Phyllis and Edna Pine at Monkton Combe Churchyard – see 'Epilogue' section.)*

"Mr Hubert Beckingsale was the younger brother of the late Mr Horace Beckingsale, who was well known in Bath in connection with the Friendly Society Council and the Hearts of Oak Society. During the Great War he served in Mesopotamia, joining up the day after his experience of a raid on Hull. For the past few years he was employed by

Garlick's Ltd., men's outfitters, Castle Street, Bristol ..... those present included Mrs E Fullman (sister), London, Mr F H Pine (brother-in-law), The Misses P and E Pine (nieces)......Mrs FH Pine and Miss Lena Pine were unable to attend.

"Floral tributes included those from Edie and Fred *(Fullman, My mother's Aunt Edie and husband Fred);* Lil and Frank, Phyllis, Edna and Lena; Connie and Albert; Kathie, Pauline, Doreen and Alec and May (all nephews and nieces at Glasgow); Mr and Mrs and May Pinhorn; Gertie *(Rivers?)* at Aldershot; the directors and fellow workers at Garlick & Sons..." *(More biographical details of Horace are in the section on the Beckingsales below - I would note also in this newspaper a following item about the death of Combe Down butcher Fred Pearce)*

On **8 June 1940** in the Somerset County Herald we have another funeral notice that is probably quite irrelevant to our narrative - probably involving another Pine family. It is the **'Late Mr CJ Goodland Bridgewater - Former Member of Town Council - Large Gathering at Funeral'.** Mr CJ Goodland (73) was a former member of Bridgewater Town Council. The mourners included Mrs Norah Waters and Mrs Frank Pine (nieces).

On **7 September 1940** with Britain standing alone against the Fascist powers the spirit of 'keep calm and carry on' was alive in Bath with the headings **'Bath Hospitals cheque for £2,200 - Increase of over £46 during last quarter - Contributors' Splendid Wartime Effort'.** Out of £4,148 collected in quarter a cheque of £2,200 for the RUH was accepted by Frenchwoman Mrs HH Butcher who said: "It is this sort of thing all over the country that confirms one's faith in ultimate victory. Hitler or no Hitler the hospital will carry on and fulfil its obligations." Also present were Mr FG Hamilton (chairman), Mr JA Coles (secretary of Walcot South) who presented the cheque, **Mr Frank H Pine** (vice-chairman) and Mr Wilfred J Jenkins (organising secretary).

The quarter ending June had produced contributions of £4,148 comprised of £1,839 from Bath, £578 from Somerset and £1,730 from Wiltshire. Payments to other institutions were £1,021 with £370 in other benefits. Wives of servicemen could automatically take over the boxes. Discounts were to be given to those paying up front rather than by a quarterly box (i.e. £12 rather than 3s 3d a quarter. More beds were available than in peacetime. *(There is also an interesting article on the page in the next column about schoolteacher conscientious objectors, involving a CBBS teacher).*

On **6 October 1940** is the report **'Hospital in Wartime - Back-breaking work cheerfully carried on - Patients from Bombed Areas'.** Ald Aubrey Bateman presiding at annual meeting of the RUH at its lecture theatre related how staff were co-operating with the Ministry of Health in dealing with air raid casualties from other parts of the country and mothers and children from bombed areas. He spoke of co-operation with St. Martin's

Hospital in overcoming certain war-time difficulties and suggested that this was a happy augury for the future of hospital work in the city and districts.

Warm thanks were extended to the Bath Region Hospital Scheme for its £9,000 contribution to the maintenance of the hospital during the year, being £200 more than in the previous year. When war broke out arrangements were made to increase the number of beds. In this connection St Martin's Hospital co-operated and he wished to pay a sincere tribute to the Health Committee of the City Council. This, he thought, was a happy augury for the future. No one could foreshadow what the future position of municipal and voluntary hospitals would be when the war was over, but the happy relationship between the RUH and St Martin's was symptomatic of days to come, they had every reason to look forward to the future with confidence in that respect.

He expressed disappointment at abandonment of the nurses home appeal due to the war with only £3,676 collected. He was concerned about the impact of war on the number of subscribers, although the decrease in subscriptions for the year was only £86. He hoped that by the next annual meeting in 1941 peace would have come. Proposing Mr Bateman as President, Mr HC Lavington congratulated him on his selection as Mayor of Bath for 1940-41. As seconder, Mr FG Hamilton noted that, although he had turned 90 Mr Lavington was still active as a member of the Hospitals Management Board. The meeting ended with a cordial vote of thanks to the President by **Mr FH Pine**, seconded by Mrs Shaw-Mellor.

On **26 October 1940** we are told of **'Combe Down Resident - Funeral of Miss Ruth Norman'** No information on the lady is given but the chief mourners were: Miss K Edwards (cousin), Mrs W Kellaway, Miss Wren, Miss Stickley, Mrs Norrish, **Mr Pine and Miss Pine**. Friends at the Union Chapel Combe Down included........Mrs Burridge, Miss Ponting .... Floral tributes were received from ......**Mr & Mrs FH Pine and family**.

1941: St Martin's and RUH are equal choices - Lavington resumé of scheme

It's 1941 and the British Empire will still be alone against the Nazis until 22 June (when Russia was invaded) and 7 December (the attack on Pearl Harbor) but there are still many semblances of normality in the local press.

However on **1 March 1941** we see, in the 4th column of page 17, that the dividing line between voluntary and municipal hospitals was narrowing - with the item **'Bath Hospital Box Scheme - Organiser Replies to Bathavon Critics'.** The Organising Secretary Mr Jenkins was reported as saying that an allegation made at the Bathavon RDC that the Box Scheme was not fulfilling its obligations to its members by sending them to public institutions was misleading. Members were admitted to the RUH when doctors decided they should. The RUH was at full capacity due to the war.

> "It must be remembered that the Minister of Health considers that the hospital accommodation of the country, whether voluntary or municipal, may be regarded as one service for the treatment, not only of civilians, but also of service men and women. The line of demarcation between the voluntary or municipal hospital has therefore largely been given up. It is questionable whether it will ever come back again in its old form because a new hospital system for the whole country is being planned and it will include both municipal and voluntary hospitals.

> "Regarding the position of the Bath Hospital Scheme in these new conditions, it should be remembered that changes have been made in the rules to meet the circumstances of the times and to safeguard the interests of the contributors. Before the war the scheme made no payment for treatment in a municipal hospital but in September 1939, it was decided to include such treatment in its benefits. If therefore there is no accommodation available at the Royal United Hospital for a particular patient and he is sent to St. Martins Hospital, a payment is made by the scheme and he receives free treatment for at least a 10 week period and frequently longer....... Present conditions call for a united hospital service and not for an attempt to draw a line between the voluntary and municipal hospitals, which are each doing their best for the health of the community."

This is an interesting point at which to recap on the achievements of the Box Scheme with an article in the Chronicle of **17 May 1941 'Saved Bath Hospital - Story of Box Collecting Scheme'.** The article reads:

"An interesting resume of the inception, development and establishment of the Bath and District Friendly Societies' Box Collecting Scheme to help the funds of the Royal United Hospital has been written by Mr Henry C Lavington of 22 St Mark's Road, Bath. He recalls that, following the annual meeting of the Hospital in February 1923, when there was an overdraft at the bank of £11,288 5s, the Board sent out an SOS, in which a possible closing of the doors of the institution was ominously predicted.

"Box Scheme Established

The scheme was 'born' at a meeting of the Shepherds' Home Lodge No 955 and the late Lieut-Col Egbert Lewis, then chairman of the hospital, interviewed Mr Lavington. As the outcome of this conference a meeting of the Friendly Societies' Council was held at which the scheme was placed on a business footing and officials were appointed. Mr Lavington tells of the difficulties experienced by the 'disciples' in getting to remote villages in Wiltshire and Somerset to address meetings advocating the box scheme. By the end of December 1924, 13,300 boxes had been delivered to the homes of people and £4,900 was handed over to the hospital.

"Widespread Benificence

It is interesting to record that three of the original members of the executive who were responsible for setting up the scheme - Messrs AS Gunstone, HC Lavington and **FH Pine** are still associated with its executive. In 17 years £135,700 6s 8d has been collected, of which £96,900 has been handed over to the RUH and £20,426 18s 7d to other hospitals and institutions with the balance devoted to convalescent homes and the supply of optical and surgical appliances." *Mr HC Lavington, the initiator of the Bath Hospital Scheme died 23 November 1943.*

And a Chronicle article of **8 November 1941** (column 2 of page 8) on **'Bath Paying Patients Scheme - Extension of Benefits Foreshadowed'** offered a very satisfactory report on the year's activities. A significant extension of benefits was being worked on. In the 12 months ended 31 August £1,060 was received from subscriptions, an increase of £123 over the previous year. A sum of £500 had been transferred to reserves making the sum on deposit £1,566. Signing the report on behalf of the executive were: Mr FG Hamilton (Chairman), **Mr FH Pine** (Vice-chairman), Col RR Glyne-Jones (hon Treasurer) and Mr Wlfred J Jenkins (organising secretary).

It is interesting to note the preceding Article: **'Bath RUH Part in Future - No Loss of Tradition'**. Here reference was made to the hope of inaugurating a co-ordinated hospital service in the surrounding counties that had been expressed by the President (The Mayor Mr Aubrey Bateman) at the annual meeting of the RUH on the Friday. He stated that, when the Association of Municipal Corporations had agreed upon the framework of conferences (which had for their purpose the co-ordination and reconstruction of the hospital services in any particular area), a further meeting would be held. In any....scheme for the reorganisation of the vast hospital service in the country, present institutions - like the RUH - which had proved their worth, their value, their indispensability, would no doubt be brought into the wider movement without losing any of their traditions and their innumerable virtues.

Mr Bateman noted that the cost of hospital supplies had increased 33%. "Subscriptions had not correspondingly increased. The increase in taxation, the national saving effort and the like, had all left their marks on the voluntary subscriptions and donations usually given to the hospital." The RUH had a deficit for the year of £1,928 but the Forbes Fraser had an annual surplus of income over expenditure of £3,391 said the Treasurer (Mr A Norman Wills). The average cost of a patient per day had risen from 9s 2d to 12s 4d. The cost of services to voluntary schemes and municipal authorities would have to reflect a general one third increase in costs. All legacies since 1933 to the end of 1940 bequeathed to the hospital (£73,893) had not been used for maintenance purposes but applied to capital.

1942: Death of Frank Harold Pine

Not until the end of 1942 was there any sign in North Africa, Eastern Europe or the Pacific that the advance of the Axis Forces could be stemmed. In the face of RAF bombing attacks on key German cities the Nazis unleashed their Baedeker raids on historical British cities like Coventry, Exeter ... and Bath. In the meantime the local press carried as best it could.

On **31 January 1942** the Chronicle contained a report that FH Pine was seriously Ill. The gossip column **'Bath and County Notes'** contains in its second column the subheading **'Other Invalids'**: "I am sorry to hear two other Bathonians – one prominent as a hospital worker, the other as a business man - are seriously ill in their homes. They are Mr F H Pine, of 17 The Firs, Combe Down and Mr FJ Oram, of Dorchester Street, harness manufacturer, who lives at 34 Longfellow Avenue. A member of the Management Board of the Bath Royal United Hospital, Mr Pine is also one of the pioneers of the Box Collecting Scheme, connected with the institution, and is its present vice-chaiman. He was for a number of years, chairman of Monkton Combe Parish Council."

So we sadly come to **25 April 1942**, and (on page 4 column 3) there is a key biographical article, with a photograph, headlined **'Bath Hospital Scheme Pioneer - Death of Mr Frank Pine'**. It reads: "A pioneer of the Bath Region Hospital Contributory Scheme, and a well-known figure in the business life of the city, Mr Frank Harold Pine passed away at his home, 17 The Firs on Friday. His death, which will be deplored by a wide circle of friends, follows a lengthy illness.

"Mr Pine was one of a small band of enthusiasts who, 20 years ago, under Friendly Society auspices, launched the Hospital "Box Scheme" of which he later became the chairman. He resigned this position in 1932, since when he has been vice-chairman. He was also a member of the Management Board of the Bath Royal United Hospital.

"Among Mr Pine's other public work was membership of Monkton Combe (Combe Down) Parish Council, of which he was chairman for two or three years. In the days of the old Bath and Somerset Dairies he was Assistant Manager under Mr Baylis Tucker and for a time manager of the Norton Dairies. Subsequently he joined the administrative staff of Spear Bros. and Clark Ltd. at Bath.

"He was an amateur artist of considerable talent and an enthusiastic photographer. He is survived by a widow and four daughters."

I think there are some errors in this report. He was chairman of the Bath Council Friendly Societies from 1923 (not mentioned in this report) when the Box Scheme was started. Also he was chairman of Monkton Combe Parish Council from 1922 until 1934 with just a gap of a year or so.

In the same issue of 25 April 1942 we also find FHP's death announcement under **'Births, Marriages and Deaths':** **Pine** - Frank Harold, beloved husband of Lillian Pine, passed away at 17 The Firs, Combe Down, APRIL 24TH 1942, aged 65 No mourning.

He died on the Friday and the above newspaper extracts were published the following day - but that Saturday Night the Bath Blitz began (lasting Saturday 25 April – Monday 27 April). I have not so far tracked down any press report of FHP's funeral. Of course there were many to be buried after the blitz (there was even a mass grave). What did he die of? Well from the fact that I have few photos without him holding a cigarette - lung cancer would have been a fair bet! However he was certified as dying from coronary thrombosis.

<u>1943: FHP Lives!</u>

Frank Pine's renown remained alive after his death, as the following entries show,

Firstly on **17 July 1943**, bottom of column 3, there is a record of Phyllis Olive Pine passing her optical exam - headed **'Optical Examination'** it reads: "Miss PO Pine, daughter of the late Mr Frank Pine, a former chairman of the Monkton Combe Parish Council and one of the pioneers of the Bath Hospital Box scheme, has passed the Women's Optical Assistants' Examination, She has been a member of the staff of Messrs Tovey, the Ophthalmic opticians of New Bond Street, Bath for 25 years - all her business life."

Secondly on **18 December 1943** we learn that Edna Pine had become the new Secretary for Combe Down for the Box Scheme. In the 3rd Column under **'Round the Town'** we read (beneath 'School Holidays') that "Edna Pine, daughter of one of the founders of the Bath Hospital Box Scheme, has been appointed the new secretary of the scheme for the Combe Down district in succession to Mr JL Hancock who, after 10 years splendid service, is retiring owing to ill-health and advancing years."

1944: F I Tovey

On **21 October 1944** is the report on the **'Death of Mr FI Tovey - Well Known Bath Optician'** The report notes that the death occurred on Monday of one of Bath's oldest opticians, Mr Frank Ivor Tovey of 12 New Bond Street aged 84. From a family of watchmakers in Honiton, Devon he set up as a watchmaker in Westgate Street in the 1880s. Removing to New Bond Street about 10 years later he took up the study of optics. He leaves 3 daughters.....Miss Irene Tovey (who is also a sight-testing specialist).The staff at Tovey's were represented by Mr S *(Stanley)* H England ...Miss T *(PO!)* Pine.

I believe Irene Tovey ran the company until her retirement at 65 in 1959 – shortly before which Phyllis Pine was appointed to the Board of Directors of FI Tovey and Stanley England became Managing Director. In an undated press cutting from the Bath Chronicle and Herald in 1959, I have an article on Irene Tovey's retirement that noted that she was one of the first women to qualify as an ophthalmic optician at the age of 17 in 1913. Her main leisure interest was the Argyle String Orchestra, of which she had been Treasurer for 37 years. Her path would have often crossed with Norman Daniels, a leading light of the Combe Down Old Scholars, who was also a keen member of the Argyle String Orchestrain the late 1930s (at least until his marriage in 1941).

Stanley England had also been a stalwart of the Combe Down Old Scholars (in close association with Norman Daniels, Phyllis, Lena and Connie Pine) – and he clearly maintained his thespian interests. The press article records that he had been with FI Tovey since 1914 – four years before Phyllis Pine joined the company - and was (in 1959) well known as the secretary of the Bath Operatic and Dramatic Society.

The article records that Miss PO Pine, a past President of the Bath Business and Professional Women's Club, had spent the whole of her business life in optical dispensing.

A 1930s Tovey's brochure: 4 extracts

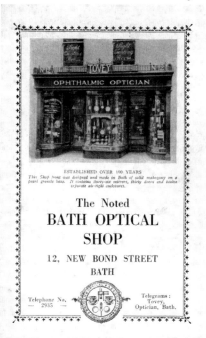

ESTABLISHED OVER 190 YEARS

This Shop front was designed and made in Bath of solid mahogany on a pearl granite base. It contains thirty-six mirrors, thirty doors and twelve separate air-tight enclosures.

The Noted
BATH OPTICAL
SHOP
12, NEW BOND STREET
BATH

Telephone No.
2935

Telegrams :
Tovey,
Optician, Bath.

F. I. TOVEY, B.O.A.

F. I. TOVEY is not a medical man and does not treat eye diseases; when these are discovered in testing the case is referred to an oculist.

THIRTY-FIVE years unbroken practice as an Ophthalmic Optician should be a good qualification for the work on the ground of experience.

F. I. Tovey was one of the first to test the sight in a scientific manner before supplying Glasses. He was also one of the earliest members of the British Optical Association, which has done so much to protect public interests by establishing higher education for Opticians.

Mr. Tovey's training was gained under a distinguished tutor, viz. :—Mr. J. H. Sutcliffe, the inventor of the " Uni-Bifocal " Lens, the "Keratometer," and other optical instruments.

1

Miss IRENE TOVEY.
F.B.O.A. (HONS.), F.S.M.C.

MISS IRENE TOVEY has passed the highest examination of the British Optical Association held at the London University, and is thereby entitled to the letters F.B.O.A. (Hons.) after her name. She is also Freeman of the City of London and Spectacle Makers' Co., F.S.M.C. She has passed every possible British Optical Examination at the earliest possible time.

These Examinations are conducted by some of the most eminent Doctors of this country. She has now tested over thirty-three thousand cases, examining by the subjective and objective method and testing also for heterophoria. These different methods are separate confirmations of results. Miss I. Tovey's unique successes are a world's record and have aroused great interest. The *Daily Mirror* and many other papers have published her photograph and drawn attention to her opening up a new semi-professional career for ladies.

2

No other firm in England has a more highly qualified sight-testing staff practising in one business.

Our Staff
At 12 New Bond St., Bath

THE Members of the sight-testing staff have passed all the possible London optical examinations which include the recognition of eye diseases and have had extensive experience in London and elsewhere. They have the distinct advantage of being able to consult one another on any case presenting any peculiar difficulty. Thus, our Patrons are assured of obtaining the services of assistants of real ability, who have been chosen for their respective departments and trained to the highest efficiency.

4

Phyllis O Pine middle right

1945: Marriage of Lena Pine and Herbert Daniels - Japan Capitulates!

Firstly the press cutting that began my quest - from the daily edition of the Chronicle and Herald of **Tuesday 14 August 1945** - the wedding of Herbert Daniels & Lena Pine with a photo on the front page the day Japan Capitulated headed **'HOSPITAL BOX PIONEERS DAUGHTER'** it reads "Miss Lena Pine, youngest daughter of the late Mr FH Pine of Combe Down Bath, whose ardent pioneering work did so much to ensure the success of the Bath RUH Box Scheme was married on Saturday to Mr HF Daniels. Here they are leaving Holy Trinity Combe Down."

The following Saturday, on **18 August 1945** we get the full report on the wedding under **'Local Weddings'** and the subheading **'Mr Herbert Daniels and Miss Lena Pine'** we read: "Prior to joining the WAAF three and a half years ago, Miss Lena F Pine was Secretary of the Combe Down Old Scholars Association, a member of their Dramatic Club, and a member of the Girls' Friendly Society. She was the daughter of the late Mr Frank Pine and Mrs Pine, of Combe Down, Bath, whose ardent advocacy and work did so much to ensure the success of the Royal United Hospital Box Scheme after its inception.

"On Saturday Miss Pine was marred at Holy Trinity church to Mr Herbert Daniels of West Bridgford, Nottingham, third son of Mr and Mrs W Daniels of Littleton Drew, Chippenham, Mr Daniels was, for some time, working at the Bath Orthopaedic Hospital, until he went to Nottingham, where he is engaged in work for the Cripples' Guild. The vicar of Combe Down, the Rev. E Roberts, officiated and Mrs Shute, a friend of the bride, was at the organ.

"The bride, given in marriage by Mr A J Caudle (a friend of the bride's late father) was attired in shagreen two-piece suit, with toning accessories, and carried a bouquet of red roses. Accompanying her was Miss Edna F Pine, a sister. Mr William Spooner, of Maperley, Nottingham, a friend of the bridegroom, was best man. After a reception at the Rockery Cafe, the couple left for a honeymoon in London. Their future home will be at West Bridgford, Nottingham."

I have no record of who attended the Rockery wedding reception – just a single wedding group photo taken on what looks like a sunny day. The Rockery was a series of tiered rock gardens, with a tea house in its midst, which was set in a disused stone quarry. It was a great place on a sunny day but rather dismal mid-winter (as it was for Edna Pine's wake in December 2001). Sadly it is no more – just a small housing estate.

As befitted its times (of rationing) the reception may have been a modest affair. However I do have my mother's wedding present list which also reflects its times. No vacuum cleaner, electric kettle or toaster (that might have featured on a pre-war list). They were unlikely to have been made in the UK in war-time and the shipping, trade and payments position in 1945 prohibited their importation. There was a lot of cash and cheques and clearly some Pyrex was available. Even so it

LENA FLORENCE PINE.

With
Mr. & Mrs. Herbert Daniels'
Compliments.

12 Chestnut Grove,
West Bridgford,
Nottingham.

August 11th, 1945.

provides interesting reading – not least for bringing together some of the people in this narrative.

Names	Gift
FAMILY	
Mrs L Pine	Walnut table, chiffonier, other furniture, small table & bed
Phyllis Pine (LFPs Sister)	Cheque (all Kitchen Utensils etc.)
Edna Pine (LFPs Sister)	Electric Iron & Tea Knives
Connie & Albert Taylor (LFPs Sister & husband)	Cheque £5/5/0
Flo & Will Wiltshire (Stapleton-Cousins of A Beckingsale?)	Cash
May & Doreen Beckingsale (& Warden)	1 doz Teaspoons, 2 Aprons
Aunt Edie & Kath & families Fullman (& Drummond)	Dining Cloth - Damask
Reg & Gertie Filer (Grandchild of Ellen Beckingsale?)	Embroidered Table Cloth
Mr & Mrs W Daniels (Parents to HFD)	Cheque
Mr and Mrs Tom Daniels (HFDs Brother & Wife)	Cheque
Mrs Gale & Mr D Daniels (Aunt Minnie & Uncle David)	Cash
Mr Robert & Miss Vi Daniels & Mabel Symons (8 The Firs)	Cash & Box of Groceries
Aunt Emmie (Emily) Dudley (nee Daniels - lived in Bath)	Kitchen Cloths
FRIENDS & NEIGHBOURS	
Mr and Mrs Caudle (FHPs Friend - gave bride away)	Electric Table Lamp & Shade
Capt & Mrs Booth (Church Army Combe Down)	2 Linen Pilowslips
Rev John & Mrs Crees (Catholic Priest & Mother)	
Rev & Mrs Roberts (Vicar Holy Trinity Combe Down)	Ash Tray in Oak Stand
Mr Bill Spooner (Best Man from Nottingham)	Irish Linen Tablecloth Lace Bordered - matching
Mrs Spooner	2 Table Runners - matching
Miss C Spooner	Setee Set - matching
Miss (I) Tovey (Optician)	Bread Board and Saw
Mrs Elliott (Neighbour - 18 The Firs)	Cheque (Pouffe and Kilner preseving outfit)
Mrs Fisher (Neighbour - 16 The Firs)	Glass Cruet Set
Mrs Maggs (Active in Socials - Combe Down Resident)	Cheque (Bedspread)
Mr and Mrs McNamara (Combe Down Residents)	Cheque £5
John & David McNamara (Combe Down Residents)	Cake Stand
Miss Barnes (& Nora)	Bread and Joint Carvers
Eileen Beer (Combe Down Resident)	Letter Holder & Butter Knife
Mrs & Miss Bird	Silver Spoon
Miss Blake	Bed Jacket
Min & Clive Castle (they feature in photo albums)	Cash
Miss Chivers	2 Towels
Miss K Colmer	Toast Rack
Mr & Mrs Copsey	Cut Glass Fruit Bowl & Servers
Mr & Mrs Ted Davies	Framed Motto
Mr and Mrs Alec Dunning	Cheque
Miss Edwards	Cash
Mrs George (& Betty)	Triple Pyrex Oval & 2 Dozen Pegs
Mrs Greenman (& Margaret)	Cash
Mrs Gregory	Cash
Miss Hardyman (Neighbour – 4 The Firs)	Coffee Pot

Mrs Jesse Hawkins	Cash
Mr Hillier (Combe Down Resident)	Oak Tray & Brush & Crumb Tray
Mr & Mrs McNidder	6 Serviette Rings
Mrs Page (Clerk to Monkton Combe Council?)	2 Tray Cloths
Mr Arhur Pittard (A work colleague of HFD?)	Cash
Mrs L Polly	Cash
Miss Ponting (Teacher to LFP & John & Roger Daniels!)	Cut Glass Vase and Cake Doyleys
Gertie Rivers (Friend - I recollect her from 1950s)	Aluminium Saucepan, 2 Pilow Slips, Pastry Board & Roller
Miss V Saunders	Cash
Mrs Shakestry	Egg Cups in Stand
Mrs Shute (& Graham)	Glass Honey Jar
Ena Swift	Embroidered Pillow Cases
Miss Wherret (& Jean)	Pair of Pillow Cases Initialled
Mrs Williams	Tea Cosy
Mr & Mrs Ernie Williams	Kitchen Cloths
Miss Wratislaw	Deep China Bowl and Silver Spoon
Diana Wratislaw?	Bread and Joint Carvers
Cis and Bill	2 Towels & 4 Glass Cloths

This wedding present list is interesting in showing an extensive number of representatives of the Daniels and Beckingsale families. Representatives of 3 religious groups are there. Mrs Page, Clerk to Monkton Combe Council also appears as do many neighbours and friends – 73 pesons in all.

Miss Ponting, a young teacher at Combe Down School, when my mother was there, was also my teacher in my final year at Newbridge Junior School. Here she is – in 1926 at Combe Down School and about 30 years later - in her late fifties. Liz Pevitt (nee Baxter) took the second picture in the New Forest when we were on our way back from the School Leavers Outing - she can remember getting the train to Southampton, and then a coach took us back to Bath.

Two Combe Down Weddings

Connie Pine & Albert Taylor
Monday 1 August 1938

Lena Pine & Herbert Daniels
Saturday 11 August 1945

Mr Cornish was often mentioned by my mother and her sisters - although my brother and I cannot remember the context it was not to our recollection that he was mentioned in any unflattering way. Certainly, like Frank Pine, he stood the test of time as chairman of the parish council as in the paper of **12 April 1947** we read **'Eighth Year in Succession - Combe Down Council Re-elects its Chairman'.** "Mr RW Cornish was unanimously re-elected chairman at the annual meeting of the Monton Combe Parish Council on Wednesday, on the proposition of Mr Chittenden, seconded by Mr F Vallis. Mr Cornish has been a member of the council for 16 years and this is the eighth successive year he has been chairman. Previously he was chairman for a period of 3 years and vice-chairman for 3 years. During all this time he has never missed a council meeting or a parish meeting... It was reported that the cost of adding 16 names to the Combe Down War Memorial would be £51..."

> Mr Cornish would have been vice-chairman of the parish council 1931-34 and chairman 1934-37 and 1939-1948. Mr Vallis joined the parish council in November 1940.

In 1947 we get closure in two more events.

On **6 September 1947** we read in the Bath Weekly Chronicle and Herald **'Bath Hospital Scheme To End with June Quarter Next Year'.** The report says that the Bath Hospital Box Scheme was to end after the June quarter 1948 as the appointed day for start of the National Health Service was 8 July "Stating this in 'Our Hospital' the scheme magazine the Organising Secretary (**Coun.** Wilfred J Jenkins) advises secretaries and stewards that no contributions should be collected to cover any period after June 1948, as it is anticipated that the hospital benefits will then be discontinued."

"It is most encouraging to know that, in spite of all our difficulties at the present time, our collections continue to show a substantial increase, he says, The report of the Executive Committee records an increase for the March quarter of over £306 and it includes an increase in each area, with increases in the amounts received both from household boxes and groups of employees. The total amount collected in the quarter was £7,058." The totals were: Bath £3,395, Somerset £1,144, Wiltshire £2,519.

**It is interesting to compare this with the adjoining article** Royal United Hospital's Deficit of £52,401 _**(about £1.9m in current terms)**_ Last Year £35,000 Investments Sold – Grave Situation The article notes that £11,000 was paid over to the hospital by the contributory scheme in 1946 _**(about £424,000 in current terms)**. **In 1923 the aim of the box scheme was to raise £5,000 (c £254,000 in current terms) annually to meet a**_ *cumulative RUH deficit of £10,000 - and an annual deficit of £4,000. Now in 1947 the scheme had raised £7,048 in a quarter - or about £28,000 a year (which would amount to £1m in current terms) although not all of it would have gone directly to the RUH.*

I have probably the 2 last letters that my grandmother Lilian Pine wrote to my mother (we were then living in Nottingham). The first dated 7 September 1947 begins 'How are you all, especially John he is such a dear'. She mentions her aliments but had been into Bath on the Wednesday and on a taxi trip to Colerne on the Thursday and asks 'How did you like the photo of John and myself' (this is a picture I have reproduced below). In her second letter of 14 September she says 'my hands are dreadful now and my feet are peeling. I feel so disheartened; it's taking so much money. I don't have the Dr so often now.' She also says 'I shall be glad when Con has her baby ... if it is like John I shall have some lovely grandchildren'.

Sadly she did not live to hold John Taylor as we see from the newspaper report of **4 October 1947** - the death of Lillian Pine is reported on page 7, column 2, item 4: **'Widow of Council Chairman Dies'**. "The death occurred on Monday at 17, The Firs, Combe Down, Bath of Mrs Lilian Pine, widow of Mr FH Pine, known as one of the prominent honorary workers on behalf of the Royal United Hospital, and as Chairman of the Monkton Combe Parish Council. Mrs Pine had been a semi-invalid for many years, but had been able to go out in a wheelchair. She is survived by her four daughters, two of whom are married."

Lilian Pine died on 26 September at Combe Down, Bath. She was 70 and her occupation was given on her death certificate as 'widow of Frances Harold Pine accountant'. She was certified as dying from 'hemiplegia and aretino sclerosis', as certified by R Lane Walmeley. P O Pine, daughter, was the informant. *Might she (and her husband Frank and her brothers, Herbert and Hubert who died aged 61) have lived longer with better (i.e. free and comprehensive) health care? After all her mother and sister Edith lived well into their 80s.*

1948 – 1949 Loose Ends

I will continue for two more years so that we can pick up on two of the personalities who were a feature of the narrative in the 1930s - Mr Cornish and Mrs Page.

On **16 October 1948** is the heading **'To Double their Membership - Monkton Parish Council Want To Be Twelve'** under which we read "At a meeting of the Monkton Combe Parish Council, at the Church Rooms, Combe Down, on Tuesday night, it was suggested that an increase should be made in the membership of the council. After some discussion it was decided that, at the next election, the number should be increased from the present half dozen to twelve. Mr J Rosser, manager of the Combe Down branch of the National Provincial Bank was chosen to fill the vacancy on the Council caused by the resignation of Mr Richard Cornish JP, for many years its chairman. A query was raised by the chairman (Mr A Vallis) .....

Then on **13 November 1948** we see **'To Meet At Monkton - Change for Parish Council'**. "Of the nine members of Monkton Combe Parish Council only three are from Monkton Combe; the remainder represent Combe Down. In over half a century of existence the Council has met only once at Monkton Combe - until April, when Mr RW Cornish JP was succeeded by Mr F Vallis, it had never had a man from the village as chairman. Mr Vallis, formerly Bristol City goalkeeper for seven years, had lived in the village since he became cricket coach at Monkton Combe School, 20 years ago - and to mark the fact that at last a man from Monkton is chairman, the council decided on Tuesday evening to hold their next meeting in the village, at the schoolroom."

> *Wikipedia says that **Frank Vallis** was born on 5 May 1896, in Bristol, and that he died on September 1957, in Bath, Somerset. He was the Bristol City goalkeeper 1919-1926 with 219 appearances. In 1926-1927 he had two appearances with Merthyr Town before breaking his leg in a match with Bristol Rovers. After retiring Frank Vallis coached football and cricket at Monkton Combe School in Bath and served as chairman of the local parish council.*

Finally we come to the retirement of Mrs Page - on **16 April 1949** under **'Parish Council's New Clerk - Monkton Combe Man Appointed'** "It was decided at a meeting of the Monkton Combe Parish Council on Tuesday night to appoint Mr DA Turner of Tudor Cottage, Monkton Combe, as Clerk at a salary of £30 per annum. Mr Turner, who is 35, was educated at Bristol Cathedral School and the Merchant Venturers' College, Bristol. He is a member of the Bath Repertory Company and a member of Bath Abbey choir. He is employed by the Bristol Aeroplane Company. There were fifteen applications for the post, which was rendered vacant by the retirement of Mrs E M Page, who is leaving the district."

> *Mrs Page had given her husband a great deal of help with his work and was of assistance to the Council after his retirement and death in 1931 at the age of 76, even during the brief interregnum of Mr Little towards the end of that year. She was appointed clerk firstly on a temporary basis in January 1932 at an annual salary of £16, later on a permanent basis. So she continued until 1949! On her retirement the council presented her with a hand bag!*

COMBE DOWN OLD SCHOLARS

On **17 May 1927** the Chronicle had a report oddly titled (because at least half its members were female) **'Combe Down Old Boys – A Thriving School Association'** as it reports the first social of the newly formed Combe Down Old Scholars Association. At this event over 150 old scholars were present together with the Pesident of the Association (the Rev GE Watson), Col. Pilcher, Miss Harley-Smith, Messrs Easterfield, Clark, Rivington, Robinson, Pine, Stockall, Mr and Mrs Carter and Mr and Mrs H Collins. Capt. CW Daubeney and Mr EM Butler (both managers of the school and vice-presidents of the association) wrote to reget their inability to attend.

The evening opened with community singing and from 8pm until 11.30pm there were games, dances and songs. The school's headmaster Mr HH Collins (Chairman of the Association) expressed thanks for the spade work done by the joint secretaries, **Phyllis Pine** and Eileen Russell and Mr L Cheasley – also to the joint treasurers Miss M Tanner and Ethel Russell. "At the end of the evening **Mr F Pine** (as a parent of four old scholars of the school expressed his appreciation of the work done in the School, and his hope was that the spirit shown that evening would develop into a vital force for the benefit of Combe Down." My mother's photo album for the period has the following photograph of "The First OSA Social 1927 May 5th".

At the Combe Down School Annual Prize Distribution on 6 August 1927, Captain Daubeny (the RDC Councillor) expressed pleasure at the formation of the Combe Down Old Scholars Association.

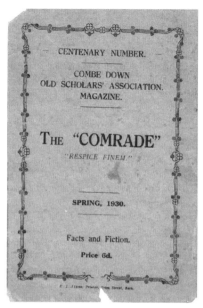

CENTENARY NUMBER.

COMBE DOWN
OLD SCHOLARS' ASSOCIATION.
MAGAZINE.

THE "COMRADE"
"RESPICE FINEM."

SPRING, 1930.

Facts and Fiction.

Price 6d.

It is clear from the sole copy of their magazine that I have ('The Comrade' of Spring 1930) that the scope of Association was quite ambitious.

It is the 'Centenary Number' to celebrate the founding of Combe Down Upper School in 1830 in connection with the Weymouth House School, as the Headmaster Herbert Collins pointed out in an article in which he invited the OSA to raise £50 a year for the school's building fund.

Two other articles make it clear that the magazine was not covering its costs – so there may not have been many further issues (although it was still going in 1932 – see below).

The scope of the OSA was clear:

- 3 socials a year (as had been held in the year ending June 1929),
- An annual concert (as had been held in December 1928 but not 1929),
- One or two stage productions (a play 'The Spooker' had been written and directed by Archie Burridge and Norman Daniels for which Mr Daniels had designed and built a proscenium and scenery with the help of Messrs Patch and Russell),
- Sporting activities such as the Old Scholars Tennis Club (when the Church Army premises were available),
- A branch library had been run by the OSA in the Church Rooms,

- Prizes for the school had been subscribed by OSA members,
- An outing to Bournemouth had been arranged and there were plans for further outings (perhaps like the cycling holiday reported on in the magazine),
- Monthly whist drives were planned to raise money for scenery.

From the above copy of 'The Comrade' it appears that the President of the Association was the vicar and the Vice-Presidents included a number of local worthies – Captain Daubeny (the RDC Councillor) and a number of parish councillors including Col. Pilcher, H Robinson – and Mr F H Pine (who had spoken eloquently at the school prize-giving in August 1924). Prominent in the officers of the society were all the Pine girls – and the family names of Daniels and Russell were also prominent.

In the section on Robert Daniels I have reproduced a poem by Norman Daniels on 'The Village Blacksmith' from this magazine. 'The Comrade' also contained adverts for GH Pratt (Grocer), A Russell (Coal Merchant and Haulier), G Mannings (Builders and Undertakers), EA Russell (Builder and Decorator), F Rhymes (Newsagent and Lending Library), EG Morgan (Grocer), Fred Russell (Builder and Decorator), and Fale and Ralph (Garage).

In this note I am focusing on the Combe Down Old Scholars Association's musical and dramatic productions - because they brought together members of my two families, the Pines (Phyllis, Connie and Lena Pine - my mother) and the Daniels (Norman Daniels and Mabel Symons).

I am sure there were many activities of the association that were not reported in the press articles I can access, but in the main text about Frank Pine I have referred to a Combe Down Old Scholars Whist Drive on Wednesday 3 February 1932, at which Frank Pine presented the prizes - as mentioned in the weekly Chronicle and Herald of 6 February 1932. In the newspaper report on my parent's wedding it is mentioned that my mother Lena Pine had been secretary of the Old Scholars Association - perhaps in succession to Mr Cheasley who is mentioned in that role below (in the May 1932 review of 'Yellow Sands' which he produced). So the following newspaper record is obviously incomplete.

Although I can find no press report of the first Combe Down Old Scholars concert, that was given jointly with the school, Norman Daniels' daughter Ruth Lafford has given me a copy of its programme. It was on 6 December 1928. Part one was given by 'Present Scholars of the school' and comprised songs by the school choir, country dancing by the Junior Scholars, scenes from Dickens by the Senior Scholars, and a Military Medly.

As noted above, the second half was performed by Members of the Old Scholars Association and comprised the play 'The Spooker' by Norman Daniels and Archer Burridge, songs by Miss Mabel Gerrish and a sketch 'The Crowd' concerning an incident during a coal strike. The cast for 'The Spooker' comprised Mrs A Pearce, Phyllis Appleby, L Cheasley, Philip Richards, Gilbert Thomas, Archer Burridge and Ted Gerrish. In 'The Crowd' sketch were G Richards, A Burridge, Violet Daniels (as 'Lady X' - the only time I have a record of her in these productions), Mabel Symons, Phyllis Appleby, Connie Pine, Olive Appleby, Albert Kellaway, L Cheasley, Edna Pine (as a 'flapper'! - this is also my only record of her in these shows), Marge Warren, Eileen Russell, Ron Brinkworth, and Phyllis Pine (but no Lena Pine).

On **1 March 1930** there is a newspaper report **'Combe Down Old Scholars - Excellent Programme at Second Annual Concert'** at the Church Rooms. It notes that "the artistic scenery and proscenium were the entire work of members of the OSA.**'Sunrise Land'** a Japanese play by the children of the school was the first item...... During the interval the Vicar (the Rev G E Watton) spoke about the school's centenary, and the headmaster (Mr H Collins) thanked the Misses Tanner, E Russell, A Candy and Messrs Cheesely and Richards, members of the staff, who had worked hard in connection with the play. A humorous sketch **'The Tax Collector'** by Miss C Pine and Mr E Gerrish was admirably presented, and character songs 'Poor John' and 'I like scented soap' by Miss M Gerrish was admirably presented. These were followed by a play **'Have You Anything to Declare'** a scene at the Customs by members of the OSA ... J Pothacary ... Miss O Appleby ... Mr A L Burridge ... the Misses M Warren, Eileen Russell, M Symons and Mr E Gerrish."

A similar joint concert with the school was held on 1 May 1930 according to a Chronicle Press Report published in the following week and reprinted on Saturday **10 May 1930** entitled **Combe Down Concert**. In the first half the school reprised **'Sunrise Land'**. Once again the children taking part were Kathleen Killaway, Kathleen Sweet, Myrtle Beazer, Doreen Miller, Joan Wilkinson, Charles Wherrett, George Pothecary, Leslie Robinson, Dennis Kendall, Marjorie Odie, Joyce Kendall, Jack Rose and Granville Davis, "the whole was a polished piece of acting."

"After an interval in which an efficient orchestra under the direction of Norman Daniels, gave musical selections, two one act plays were given by members of the Old Scholars Association, the first being **'Aunt Marie's Wireless'**". The cast comprised Albert Gerrish, Constance Pine, Jack Potecary, Lena Pine, Mabel Symons and Ada Lock. "The second playlet was a more ambitious venture namely the **'Playgoers'** by Arthur Pinero, but the capable presentation well justified the attempt. The part of the attractive young wife bent on giving her servants some pleasure was gracefully taken by Miss Constance Pine, and as her husband, Mr Lesley Cheasley also played well. The part of the parlourmaid with her refained accent was deliciously presented by Miss Ada lock, while the dignified deportment of the Complete Cook was well acted by Miss Lena Pine, who indeed gave a perfect presentation of the part. They were well supported by Miss Mabel Symons, Miss Nora Lock, Miss Vera Gray ...and Archer Burridge.

In a short speech the headmaster of the school (Mr Herbert H Collins) said that the proceeds of their February concert had not quite covered the cost of the fine proscenium, the work of one of the old scholars, Mr Norman Daniels, and it was hoped to make good that deficit and so swell the funds of the CDOSA that the centenary of the school (which was this year) might be marked by a handsome present to the school by its old scholars (laughter and applause)."

At present I have no record of any further Old Scholars concerts - perhaps the idea of a joint concert with the school faded as the idea of adult amateur dramatics took hold. It seems likely that the first full dramatic production was in May 1931, 'The Farmers Wife' in aid of the Managers' Senior School Building Fund. The report in May 1932 on 'Yellow Sands' suggests there was no intervening production. In 1933 The Old Scholars performed 'Lord Richard' in February and 'They Wanted Romance' later that year but I have no record of any production in 1934. There were productions in February 1935 and 1936 followed by productions in the May and December of 1936. I have no record of a production in 1937, but there were at least two in 1938 and one in 1939.

A year passes and the Chronicle and Herald of **9 May 1931** reports on **'Old Scholars Play - Eden Philpotts Comedy at Combe Down'.** It tells us "Eden Philpotts's glorious Devonshire comedy **'The Farmers Wife'** was presented with real flair by the Combe Down Old Scholars Association at the Combe Down Church Room on Thursday evening... in aid of the Managers' Senior School Building Fund."

The cast included Ada Lock, Archer Burridge, Constance Pine, LL Cheasely, Vera Gray, Philip Richards, Nora Lock, Gilbert Thomas, Ethel Russell, Mabel Symons, Chrissie Long, Kathleen Sweet, William Holley, Albert Kellaway, William Curtis, Jack Pothecary, Tom Williams, Lena Pine and Herbert Jordan

We have an interesting report on **16 January 1932** of **'New Year Social – Combe Down Old Scholars Association Event'** "A large company attended" at the Church Rooms with games, dancing and novelty items until 11.30pm. "Streamers, hats and masks added much to the gaiety, as did also a short vaudeville interlude arranged by the MC Mr Archer Burridge, and given by Miss M Gerrish, Miss C Long and Mr V Daniels. Music for dancing was provided by the Seoni Dance Orchestra. At 10 o'clock the usual custom – originated with the birth of the OSA – was observed, and every old scholar present joined in singing the School Song. During the interval, Mr Collins, the retiring headmaster made a short speech, in which he expressed his extreme regret at leaving Combe Down School where he had been for 21 years .... Mr Collins also spoke of the **Old Scholars Magazine** – the only one of its kind in Somerset – and hoped that every member would support it." *Interesting to see a reference to Mr V Daniels – was this a miss-print for Norman Daniels, or was his sister Violet Daniels also involved?*

So we pass to a report of **21 May 1932 'Combe Down Dramatics - Old Scholars' Production of "Yellow Sands"'**. We are informed that "The dramatic society connected with the Combe Down Old Scholars' Association gave performances on May 11th and 12th at the Church Rooms, Combe Down of that delightful comedy 'Yellow Sands' by Eden and Adelaide Phillpotts, to enthusiastic audiences.

"Following their great success with 'The Farmers Wife' it was decided to attempt the more difficult but subtle **'Yellow Sands'** which, like its predecessor, enjoyed a long and successful London run.... (the production) testified to the capable work of the secretary of the Association Mr LL Cheasley, who produced the play. **"Delightful Scenery**.... was designed and painted by Mr Norman Daniels, and the success of the production was enhanced by the artistic and colourful settings. Mr Daniels was also in charge of the orchestra." The cast (omitting part names) were: Archer Burridge, Vera Gray, Philip Richards, Gilbert Thomas, Jack Pothecary, Ada Lock, Lena Pine, Constance Pine, Mabel Symons, Ethel Russell, William Curtis.

Next on **25 February 1933** is the report on **'Lord Richard' - Old Scholars' Association Delight Combe Down Audience'** at the Church Rooms Combe Down on Wednesday evening. In the presentation of the play **'Lord Richard in the Pantry'** there is special praise for Mr Archer Buridge as Lord Sandridge, Miss Mabel Symons as Evelyn Lovejoy and Mr Jack Pothecary as Carter. Other performers (omitting their parts listed in the press item) were: Ethel Russell, Ada Lock, William Curtis, Monty Gilard, Constance Pine, Lena Pine, Phyllis Pine, Vera Gray and Gilbert Thomas. "The scenes were designed by Mr Norman Daniels."

On **19 December 1933** there is a report of the play **"They Wanted Romance"** a comedy in 3 acts put on at the Church Rooms by the OSA on 13 and 14 December 1933. It is their only play for which I have a printed rather than cyclostyled programme. The play was written and produced by OSA member LL Cheaseley because, as the programme noted, previous plays had involved the payment of nine guineas authors' fees in each case - leaving little money in hand - so a non-royalty play was needed. "If the proceeds are adequate it is hoped to plan future productions on a more ambitios scale than has been attempted before, and also to arrange a series of talks and playreadings which will assist in the work of the Dramatic Society." The press report was complimentary about the acting and said "The play is well balanced and reveals the authors undoubted talent as a playwright".

The action of the play took place in the Marlowe Arms, an old Inn dating back to the 17th century, in an isolated spot on the outskirts of the Hamlet of Little Bagworthy, between the hours of 10 p.m. and I p.m. on the followiag day. The cast comprised Ada Lock, Mabel Symons, Jack Pothecary, Albert Gerrish, George Pothecary, Lena Pine,

William Curtis, Montague Gillard, Constance Pine, Eileen Russell and Archer Burridge. The scenery was designed by Norman Daniels and made entirely by him with the assistance of T Patch.

So after a gap for 1934 (for which I can trace no records – press or otherwise) we find the report of **23 February 1935 'Tilly of Bloomsbury - Combe Down Players in Popular Comedy'.** It reads: "The Combe Down Old Scholars Association Dramatic Club have given two performances this week of the popular comedy **'Tilly of Bloomsbury'** at the Church Rooms, Combe Down. It is evident that the experience gained in the last six years the club has been in existence, together with a commendable team spirit, has resulted in a production of which the players may justly be very proud.

"A feature of the production was the fine stage settings and lighting. These were the work of Mr Norman Daniels, who is to be heartily congratulated on the effects he has achieved.... Ada Lock made a very appealing Tilly, and Edward King a gay and light-hearted Dicky. Lena Pine as Lady Marian, invested that character with all the necessary hauteur and snobbery, while Jack Pothecary, as Stillbottle, and George Pothecary, as Percy Welwyn, made the best of their opportunities for fun-making. Constance Pine and Ted Gerrish, as Mrs and Mr Welwyn, filled difficult parts with confidence. Admirable support was provided by Mabel Symons as Amelia, Ethel Russell as Connie, Phyllis Pine as Grandma Banks, Vera Gray as Sylvia, Monty Gillard as Abel Mainwaring, Gilbert Thomas as Milroy and Reg Lock as Pampherston. The part of Percy Welwyn was played at the second performance by Archer Burridge."

So far as the record goes, 1936 was a busy year, starting with the report of **8 February 'Lilies of the Field - Combe Down Old Scholars Production'** "The dramatic section of the Combe Down Old Scholars Association presented a comedy at the Church Rooms on Wednesday night, and will repeat the performance tonight at 8pm. In previous years their producer was Mr LS Cheasely, but he was unable to undertake the production this year, and the Association has been very fortunate in securing the valuable help of Mr H Humphries and Mr RG Knowles, who have had wide experience in play production." The programme states that the play was by John Hastings Turner.

The cast is as follows (omitting their parts as listed in the press item): Jack Pothecary, Constance Pine, Mabel Symons, Ethel Russell, Lena Pine, Monty Gillard, Joyce Johnson, Philip Richards, Robert Patch, Blanche Coombes, Phyllis Pine. "The scenery and lighting were once more in the capable hands of Mr Norman Daniels, while the incidental music was given by Miss C Long."

Unusually for a dramatic club a major production was preceded by a social - as the report of **26 April 1936** reveals. It is headed **'Combe Down Social'** and relates that "The

Combe Down Old Scholars Association held a jolly social at the Church Rooms on Thursday evening. The Association welcomed a new jazz band, who made their debut at this function under Mr Leslie Robinson. The players are all old scholars of Combe Down, very enthusiastic, and their programme was varied and popular. The arrangements for games, dancing and other items were handled by Mr A Burridge, this time with the help of Mr J Pothecary. A number of those present are presenting a play next Tuesday, Wednesday and Thursday 'The Passing of the Third Floor Back' and, owing to the heavy expenses in production, are anxious for a full house each night."

Now for a play that was a major event for my mother Lena Pine - it was the play she often spoke about and I have a cutting of the following review that she or Phyllis clipped from the paper. It is from the paper of **2 May 1936** and headed **'Third Floor Back - Performance by Combe Down Amateurs'** It comments " 'Ambitious' must have been the opinion of many Combe Down residents when they heard that the Dramatic Club of the Combe Down Old Scholars Association were poducing Jerome K Jerome's famous play **'The Passing of the Third Floor Back'**. Its production on Tuesday evening was, however, a great success.

"Among the characters, Mrs Sharpe, the landlady, whose fame has become almost immortal, was played by Miss Constance Pine, and was excellently portrayed. So too was Stasia (Miss Phyllis Pine). Miss Joyce Barter characterised the high falutin, sneaky Miss Kite very well indeed and Miss Mabel Symons was equally successful as Vivian. The part of the stranger, the most difficult of all, was admirably portrayed by the producer, Mr RG Knowles. The other players also did well. Mr RG Knowles produced the play most excellently, and the scenery and the lighting were in the efficient hands of Mr Norman Daniels. The music was by Miss C Long and others." The full cast list included Ethel Russell as Mrs Tompkins, Lena Pine as Mrs de Hooley, Robert Patch as Collector for Band, Monty Gillard as Major Tompkins, George Pothecary as Christopher Penny, J Siddall as Harry Larkcom, Philip Richards as Jape Samuel and Jack Pothecary as Joey Wright.

Finally for 1936, a new play by a local author with the item of **5 December 1936** on **'Combe Down Amateurs - Good Acting in Bath Author's Play'** It reports that "The first of a three-nights' performance of the play **'Mrs Char'** written by Mr WST Payne of Bath was presented by the Combe Down Old Scholars Association at Combe Down Church Rooms on Tuesday. Briefly the plot concerns the daughter of the mistress of the house, who becomes a servant for a period, to discover what it is really like.... All the cast combined in fine teamwork which reflects credit on the producer, Mr RG Knowles." The cast comprised: George Pothecary, Joyce Richards, Philip Richards, Lena Pine, Constance Pine, Miss M Simons, Ted Kelleway, Monty Gillard, Jack Pothecary. No indication of the quality of the play!

I have no record of any OSA productions in 1937 – perhaps they were struggling with the costs issue – certainly there is nothing in the press record for the Saturday Chronicle for 1937. However, we find in the paper of **5 February 1938 'Three Act Play - Presented by Combe Down Old Scholars Association'** *(on Wedneday 2nd and Thursday 3rd February as the programme, that Ruth Lafford has let me see, records)*. We are told "The dramatic section of the Combe Down Old Scholars Association this year chose Gertrude Jennings's three-act play **'Isobel, Edward and Anne'** for their annual production. The first performance of which was given on Wednesday Night in the Avenue Hall ..... *(the report next summarises the plot)...* George Pothecary and Winnie Poole gave a delightfully easy and natural performance as the two lovers. (The part of Anne will be played by Mabel Symons at the second performance.)

"As Edward Carew, the pompous husband, Leslie Robinson gave a very good study of a long and difficult part. Isabel, his wife, was played by Constance Pine in a most capable manner. Lena Pine as Stephen's mother sustained the 'below stairs' character throughout, while Phyllis Pine was effective as Lady Massingham, the society woman out for new 'affairs'. Well filled roles were those of Alice by Ethel Lewis and Jack Pothecary as Mathews. The whole production was well dressed, and ran very smoothly under the production of Mr Stanley England. All entrances and exits were well timed, and movements most natural and easy. The association are very fortunate in possessing an excellent carpenter and designer in Mr Norman Daniels, who again produced a very attractive set for the play. Incidental music was played by Miss C Long. The play was repeated on Thursday evening." *Stanley England was an optician at Toveys (and fellow director) with Phyllis in the 1950s and 1960s.* Following this successful production the OSA held a Valentines Day Dance at the Church Rooms, to raise funds, as reported in the Weekly Chronicle on **19 February 1938**.

We all remember Arnold Ridley as Private Godfrey in 'Dad's Army' and forget that he was a celebrated playwright in the 1930s - particularly with his 1923 play 'The Ghost Train' that was filmed several times and is still performed. On **22 October 1938** is a report of the Old Scholars performing another Ridley play. **'Combe Down Old Scholars - In Arnold Ridley Play at Avenue Hall'** reports: "The dramatic section of the Combe Down Old Scholars Association gave the first performance of their winter production on Wednesday evening at the Avenue Hall ...... The play chosen was Arnold Ridley's **'Recipe for Murder'**. This is quite a new style of play for these amateur players, and perhaps an ambitious one. The evenness of the performance for the first night, however, showed that the parts had been well studied and rehearsed, and that an excellent team spirit is enjoyed by this young company. To portray the character of Fluffy, the old, loyal, trusted servant, who brings the only comedy into the play, without losing the tense dramatic atmosphere, requires some skill, and this was sincerely done by Mabel Symons.

"The devoted son of the house, John Summers, who risked murder to protect his mother and sister, was played by George Pothecary, who gave a sterling performance of a long and difficult role. As the foil to this character Victor Newman, playing Henry Willett, the well meaning author friend of John Summers, brought lightness into the play. Throughout the story Jack Pothecary, as Dr Naylor, played with sympathy the role of the family friend of Mrs Summers. The latter character, Phylis Pine made an appealing and lovable mother whom all wished to save from worry. Leslie Robinson, as Richard Cheriton blackmailer, made one feel he had only his desserts when he met his death, and Winnie Poole and Montague Gillard made a charming pair of lovers, for whom everything comes right at last. Without the hard work and clever designing of Norman Daniels the Dramatic Club could not stage such attractive scenes and praise is also due to Stanley England for the efficient and smooth way in which the whole play was presented. Incidental music was played by Mrs Brewer and Miss C Long."

My last press report is from **6 May 1939 'A Successful Comedy - "Capt X" at Combe Down'** which tells us that "The Combe Down Old Scholars Dramatic Society, following their recent success with Arnold Ridley's 'Recipe for Murder', on two evenings last week presented a three act comedy **'Captain X'** by Herbert Swears in the Church Room. This comedy, which was in direct contrast to the previous performance, was well presented to two enthusiastic audiences. The action of the play takes place at Kings Folgate, a country mansion, and the society was greatly assisted in their production with two excellent sets deigned and made by Norman Daniels." The commended cast comprised Philip Richards, Jack Pothecary, Victor Newman, Mabel Symons, Lena Pine, Winifred Poole, Marjorie Jordan, John Davis, Leslie Robinson, Monty Gillard, Ronald Gillard, Leslie Fale. The producer was Mr SH England and Mr Bob Patch was stage manager. Incidental music was played by Mrs Brewer and Miss Verrier.

The OSA may have effectively disbanded during the war – yet I have a photo from about 1943 of my mother Lena Pine in WAAF uniform and Phyllis in a peasant girl's stage costume (reproduced after my Epilogue Section). I do know that in the 1970s my mother had charge of a residue of OSA funds and that she visited Combe Down School to donate them at a special school assembly. As noted above she had been OSA Secretary before joining the WAAF.

"THIRD FLOOR BACK"
Performance by Combe Down
Amateurs

" Ambitious " must have been the opinion of many Combe Down residents, when they heard that the Dramatic Club of the Combe Down Old Scholars' Association were producing Jerome K. Jerome's famous play, " The Passing of the Third Floor Back." Its production in the Parish Hall on Tuesday evening, was, however, a great success. Among the characters, Mrs. Sharpe, the landlady, whose fame has become almost immortal, was played by Miss Constance Pine, and was excellently portrayed. So, too, was Stasia (Miss Phyllis Pine). Miss Joyce Barter characterised the high falutin, sneaky Miss Kite very well, indeed, and Miss Mabel Symons was equally successful as Vivian. The part of the Stranger, the most difficult of all, was admirably portrayed by the producer, Mr. R. G. Knowles. The other players also did well. Mr. R. G. Knowles produced the play most excellently, and the scenery and the lighting were in the efficient hands of Mr. Norman Daniels. The music was by Miss C. Long and others.

The Cast.

Mrs. Sharpe	Constance Pine
Stasia	Phyllis Pine
Miss Kite	Joyce Barter
Mrs. Tompkins	Ethel Russell
Collector for Band	Lena Pine
Major Tompkins	Robert Patch
Vivian	Mont. Gillard
Christopher Penny	Mabel Symons
Harry Larkcom	George Pothecary
Jape Samuels	J. Siddall
Joey Wright	Philip Richards
The Third Floor Back	Jack Pothecary
	R. G. Knowles

COMBE DOWN AMATEURS—A scene from "The Passing of the Third Floor Back," to be produced by members of Combe Down Old Scholars' Association at the Church Room to-night.

The above picture is from a weekday edition of the Bath Chronicle and Herald and shows, left to right, Phyllis Pine, Connie Pine and Mabel Symons with two of the gentlemen. Also from the Saturday edition is a copy of the press review. On the next page I have a selection of photographs of OSA productions.

COMBE DOWN OLD SCHOLARS—A SELECTION OF SHOWS

1930 A Japanese Operetta

1931 The Farmers Wife

1932 Yellow Sands

1933 Lord Richard in the Pantry

1935 Tilley of Bloomsbury

1936 The Passing of the Third Floor Back

1936 Mrs Char

1939 Captain X

THE COMRADE.

SPRING   1930

COMBE DOWN
OLD SCHOLARS' ASSOCIATION.

President,
Rev. G. E. Watton.

Vice=Presidents,
Mr. E. M. Butler, Mr. and Mrs. Carter, Mr. T. H. Clarke,
Mrs. Collins, Captain Daubeny, Mr. E. Easterfield,
Miss C. Harley Smith, Mr. A. A. Milsom, Col. Pilcher,
Mr. F. H. Pine, Mr. H. Robinson, Mr. G. Rivington,
Mr. E. J. Shelford, Mr. A. H. Stockall.

Chairman,
Mr. H. H. Collins.

Hon. Secretaries,	Hon. Treasurers,
Mr. L. Cheasley.	Miss Tanner.
Miss L. E. Russell.	Miss Ethel Russell.

Press Secretary,
Mr. R. Richards.

General Committee,
Mrs. Pearce, Misses Warren, Wherrett, I. Morgan, Clifford,
Boseley, N. Lock, Stennard, C. Pine, and E. Pine.
Messrs. Patch, V. Williams, Burridge, Brinkworth,
Daniels, Thomas, Gerrish, Atkins, Robinson, and Gillard.

Entertainments Committee,

Misses Gerrish, Daniels, Lock, Pratt, Long, Warren,
Appleby, Messrs. Burrage, Daniels, Thomas, Gerrish and
Pothecary.

Catering Committee,

Mrs. Pearce, Mrs. F. Russell, Mrs. A. Russell.

Magazine Committee,

EDITOR—Mr. G. Thomas,   EDITRESS—Miss C. Pine,
Misses A. Lock, and L. E. Russell.
Messrs. Patch, A. Burridge, and Atkins.

ROBERT DANIELS AND FAMILY

Robert and his parents and siblings

From Sue Daniels' work on the Daniels family tree it appears that **Robert Daniels** was baptised on 5 July 1868, presumably soon after his birth. He was the **second child** of Thomas Aliffe Daniels (1825-1893) and Emma Chappell (1842- 1911); they were married in 1864. **Their first child Amy Grace** was born in 1866, but she died in 1887 at the age of 21. I will say more about Robert, the second child, below.

The third child was David born in 1870 (died 1949). In 1891 at the age of 20 he was living in Police Quarters at Bethnal Green 458 Police Station as a 'Vectis Police Constable'. On 29 June 1893 at the age of 22 he married Edith Mary Mason at St Anne's Church, Tottenham – his father Thomas was listed as a General Dealer. Although her age was given as 22 she may have been born in 1866 in Newington/Islington – her father was a schoolmaster. In 1901 they had moved from South Newington to 39 Selkirk Road, Tooting in South London. Still a Police Constable his age was given as 30 and hers as 32. By then they had a family – daughters Edith (7), and Amy (4) and sons Thomas (3), and Robert (1).

By 1911 the family had moved into a property of 6 rooms at 43 Selkirk Road, Lower Tooting. The eldest daughter Edith may have moved away as she was not listed in the census for this address. However, in addition to Amy Grace, Thomas George and Roberts Redvers there were 3 more children – Herbert Edward (8), Elsie May (2) and Doris Mabel (0). Also living with them is a nephew Frank Daniels (6) – perhaps the son of Daniel Herbert Daniels or even his sister, Fanny – and a border, a married woman called Maryan Newman.

It would appear that, perhaps worn down by such a large household (or struck down by the influenza epidemic), David's wife Edith M Daniels died in December 1920 at the age of 52. I believe that, at the time of his death in 1949, David was living with his sister Minnie at Brook Cottage, Castle Combe. His daughter Amy, who was born 22 Aug 1896 in Littleton Drew, died on 29 April 1946, in Wandsworth. On 18 October 1916, at Holy Trinity Church, Upper Tooting, London, she married James John Bartlett (born 9 Nov 1892 in Battersea), who died 6 Jun 1960 in Newport, Isle of Wight. There were two children to the marriage; John David Bartlett (4 Oct 1920 - 9 Feb 1995), who married Eleanor Joan Howard on 24 August 1941, and Eleanor who was born 23 Sep 1922 in Winchester, Wiltshire and who died 12 July 1989 in Scotland.

The fourth child was Fanny Elizabeth, born in 1873. In 1881 the census showed her living (aged 8) with her parents Thomas and Emma, and the rest of her family, in

Littleton Drew. In 1891 she was a Servant with Samuel Spill (Widower) and his children at 12 Keyford Street, Frome. I cannot trace her in the 1901 census. However I believe she may have been living with her brother Robert on Combe Down – she was certainly present at his wedding to Annie Poole in 1891 (see the picture in the section on Robert below).

In 1911 she was at the same address as her brother Robert - at 1 St Kilda Villa's, Combe Down. She is on a separate sheet as she is a Companion and Amanuensis to 71 year old Rose Rich. Rose Rich is listed as a lodger so Robert Daniels is Head of Household. I have a photograph (which I have reproduced below) of Robert Daniels and his family at St Kilda'sa Villas from which his son Norman is absent – but on the back Norman has noted that one of the people is his Aunt Fanny.

> Rose Rich was a lady of independent means. According to a notice in the London Gazette of 3 March 1916, Rose Emma Rich (formerly of 1 St Kilda Villa's, Combe Down) died on 26 November 1915. Her will was proved in probate registry on 29 December 1915 and Bull and Bull of 3 Stone Buildings, Lincolns Inn WC solicitors to the executors of her estate (Henry Walter Rich, retired railway superintendant and Edgar William Austin, accountant) gave notice for claims aginst her estate to be made by 3 April 1916. Her effects were £2,682. It is worth noting that in 1891 Rose Emma Rich (born in Chelsea) was, at the age of 51, living with her widowed aunt Julia Sotheby at Prior Park Road, Lyncombe Rise, Bath (both living on their own means) with a servant Annie Poole (22) who became Robert Daniels' wife. I am not sure if any of her money came to Annie or Fanny!

Fanny married at the age of 44 to a Thomas William Jones aged 30 and a gardener on 29 October 1918 (Q4 Bath 5c 1170 - Bath Register Office: I have the wedding certificate). Her sister Emily Dudley was a witness at the wedding in the Late Countess of Huntingdon's Chapel, Vinyards, Bath. At the time of the marriage her residence was 1 St Kilda's Villas, Combe Down (where her brother Robert and family were living).

Sadly she died on 2 October 1926 at Frome Road House Bath at the age of 53 (Q4 Bath 5c 580: I have the death certificate). After an inquest the coroner's verdict was that she had died of a ruptured aneurism of the aorta. At the time her address was 4 Rose Cottage, Batheaston, Bath and she was the wife of William Thomas Jones, labourer. It is unlikely that there were children of this marriage.

The fifth child was Daniel Herbert (1875 – 1934). In the 1881 census at the age of 5 he was listed as Herbert Daniels living at home with his parents Thomas and Emma in Littleton Drew. He was still at home in 1891 when he was working as an agricultural labourer. However in 1893 he left home to join the navy – in which he served for 25 years until 1918. The first ship he served on was Vivid II and his last ship was the Challenger. In the 1911 census he was serving in China and the East Indies and was married. His service in the Royal Navy may well have been an inspiration to his nephew (my Uncle) Gilbert. The modern ships of the Royal Navy needed lots of people below decks and he rose from Stoker to Stoker Petty Oficer in 1911 and then to Assistant Chief Stoker and Chief Stoker.

I have a rather poor picture of him from about 1903 (reproduced here – he is on the right in uniform) with Robert Daniels and his family and Worthy Daniels.

He married on 13 July 1910, to Beatrice Hull born 1888 in Plymouth, Devon and who died 1965 in Bristol. I have their marriage certificate that shows that they married at the Parish Church, East Stonehouse, Devon. Daniel Herbert's address was listed as HMS Royal Oak.

His Naval Service might be the reason I have only found one possible birth to the marriage, Jean Daniels born 6 Aug 1921 in Plymouth. However it is possible that nephew Frank Daniels (6) who was living with David Daniels in 1911 was his son. Daniel Herbert died 13 September 1934 at the age of 59 at Steps Cottage, Littleton Drew. Administration of his will was grated to his widow Beatrice Bessie Daniels for the effects of £247 1s 1d.

The **sixth child** was my grandfather **Worthy** (baptised 6 January 1878 and died 24 May 1949 aged 72) who, on 22 February 1904, married Lucy Mortimer (baptised 22 August 1880 who died 20 August 1959 aged 79). They are buried in Littleton Drew Churchyard. I have more to say about them and my immediate family in the next section on 'A Voyage Around My Father'.

There were two more children: **Minnie (1880-1950) and Emily (1884-1956). Minnie's birth** was registered in Chippenham in the third quarter of 1880 and she was baptised in Littleton Drew on 27th June 1880. She was recorded in the censuses as living with her parents in Littleton Drew in 1881 (11 months) and 1891 (10). In 1901 (20) she was single and a Ward Maid at Grove Hospital, Tooting Graveney, London (listed as an Officer in the column headed 'Relation to Head of Family or Position in the Institution'). In 1911 (30 and single) she was living in Littleton Drew (almost certainly in Steps Cottage) with her mother Emma, widow, who was 68, and Minnie was listed as House Keeper. My great grandmother Emma (who had previously been living with Robert on Combe Down) died there on 29 September 1911.

Minnie married a William James Wheller Gale in 1924 in Chippenham. Unfortunately their marriage did not last very long as he died on 27th July 1926 at the age of only 53. William Gale was a Relieving Officer and Registrar of Births and Deaths in the 1911 census and in fact was the one who registered my father's birth in 1913 and Sue Daniels father's birth in 1921. They lived in a house in Castle Combe called Brook Cottage where she probably lived until she died June 1950, aged 69. Her grave is in Castle Combe Churchyard.

In her will she left money to my father Herbert, his brother Tom, her nephew Ken Daniels (I have seen a picture of Ken in the late 1940s at Brook Cottage with his head bandaged), niece Maureen and 'niece' Mabel Symons. Here, for the record, I am pictured in August 1949 at Brook Cottage with Aunt Min, Uncle Dave, Grannie Daniels and my parents (two months before the birth of my brother Roger).

Emily Daniels was Minnie's younger sister, and was born and baptised in 1884. In 1908 she married a Frederick John Dudley in the Register Office in Bath - he was a cabinet maker (perhaps with Bath Cabinet Makers). In the 1911 census they were living on Combe Down at 2 De Montalt Cottages – not far from where her brother Robert Daniels and his family lived, with her sister Fanny Elizabeth, at 1 St Hilda Villas. They were still living there more than 20 years later (according to the Post Office Directory for 1932) and had a daughter, Joan Elizabeth (born 1909), who in 1938 married Sidney Mann in Bath. Emily died in Bath aged 72 in 1956 and her husband Frederick John Dudley died in 1975. So my father had 2 aunts and an uncle living on Combe Down (*I am indebted to Sue Daniels for some of the preceding information on Minnie and Emily*).

Robert's Life and family

The census of 1871 shows Robert Daniels aged 2 living with his parents, Thomas (agricultural labourer aged 44) and Emma (28), with sister Amy G (5) and brother David (7 months) in Littleton Drew. The 1881 census shows the same family with the addition of Fanny, Herbert, Worthy and Minnie - Amy, now 15, was listed as a servant. In the census of 1891 Robert Daniels no longer appears in the list for the family home – indeed he had moved to Combe Down, Bath.

From 1883 we have a record from the Wiltshire and Swindon Record Office that I believe my Uncle Cyril persuaded Norman Daniels to deposit there in 1980, according to correspondence copied to me by Ruth (nee Daniels) Lafford. This apprenticeship indenture record (catalogue ref 1658) shows that Robert Daniels of Littleton Drew was indentured in 1883 as an apprentice to William Bushell of Burton, blacksmith in the parish of Nettleton. Clearly he was following in the footsteps of his grandfather David Chappell (1779-1858), father of his mother Emma, who had been the village blacksmith at Littleton Drew. So in the census of 1891 we find Robert Daniels, blacksmith, at the age of 22 living as one of 3 lodgers with Anne Sumsion (and her grand-daughter Ellen) at 3 Raby Place, Combe Down, Bath.

He married Anne Poole in 1891 and his children were born in 1895 (Violet), 1897 (Norah) and 1900 (Norman). I am grateful to Ruth and Janet Lafford for supplying the adjoining wedding photograph (and the one above of Daniel Herbert Daniels). In this wedding photograph of Robert and Anne are 'Uncle Tim' best man, an unknown man, and Fanny Daniels.

In the 1901 census Robert Daniels (Shoeing and General Smith) is living at 1 Edwards Cottages, Blacksmiths shop, with his wife Anne (they are both 32) along with daughters Violet G (6) and Norah V (3) and son Norman R (9 months). Also living with them is his widowed mother Emma (58 - Monthly Nurse, born Wilts, Littleton Drew). I believe the blacksmith's shop was behind the Horseshoe pub, which is sadly no longer a pub.

Special Constables, Combe Down

APPLEBY, FREDERICK	...	WEST POINT.
DANIELS, ROBERT	...	1, ST. KILDA VILLAS.
FISHER, FREDERICK	...	THE AVENUE.
FRANKLING, FREDERICK	...	4, ISABEL PLACE.
HANCOCK, WALTER	...	6, ROCK COTTAGES.
JONES, WILLIAM	...	9, DE MONTALT PLACE.
MALLETT, FRANCIS	...	LONGWOOD.
MILES, WILLIAM	...	4, RABY PLACE.
MILSOM, ALGERNON C.	...	DE MONTALT.
MORRIS, THOMAS	...	2, PRIORY PLACE.
PEACE, OSWALD	...	2, ST. KILDA VILLAS.
WHITAKER CLARENCE	...	10, RICHARDSON AVENUE.
YORK JOHN	...	3, PROSPECT PLACE.

It is, I guess, around the middle years of the first decade of the 20th century that Robert Daniels was a Special Constable on Combe Down. I have an undated list of Special Constables for Combe Down supplied to me by Ruth Lafford. We are unsuare of its date or source.

I am not sure how soon after 1901, nor how long before 1911, Robert and his family moved to 1, St Kilda Villas but I have found out that Algernon Milsom had moved away from Bath by 1911. Looking at the ages of Robert and some of the others on this list I would say that 1905 give or take a couple of years is a fair date for this list.

As noted above, the 1911 census had the family living at 1 St Hilda Villas, Combe Down - my great grandmother Emma had gone back to Littleton Drew to live with Minnie. Violet, now 16, was listed as a dressmaker. They must still have been there in 1918 when Fanny Daniels got married.

One extra person who resided with Robert Daniels when they moved to 8 Richardson Avenue (later known as The Firs), Combe Down, was his niece Mabel Symons. She was a close friend of my mother, Lena Pine (and much involved with her and Norman Daniels in the Old Scholars productions). Her parents James Symons and Mary Poole had married in 1894 and Mabel was the youngest of their 6 children.

In the 1911 census for 46 Holloway, Bath we find Mr James Symons (Building Worker aged 44) living with his wife Mary (43) with their children Ernest (14), Sidney (10), Richard (9), Harold (7) and Mabel Evelyn (1). So Mabel's Siblings were Ernest Anthony James (born 1896), Sydney Roland (1900), Richard (1901) Harold (1903) and Dora Gertrude (1905) who is not listed in the census because she died in 1906 having lived less than 12months (Q3 Bath 5c 307).

Mary Poole was the sister of Robert's wife Annie (as the newspaper report below confirms, Poole was her maiden name). It seems likely that Mabel (born in 1909) was taken into the care of Robert and Anne after her mother Mary died in 1918 aged 51 (Q2 Bath 5c 585). In her later years she worked at the Admiralty, Combe Down. Mabel Eveline Symons, of 8 The Firs Combe Down, died on 11 December 1968 (Q4 Bath 7c 242) following signs of premature dementia, she was 59. The probate records for Bristol record her estate as valued at £1,408. I do not know if she kept in touch with her birth family. Her eldest brother was Ernest Anthony James Symons and he married Elizabeth May Brint, on 19 Jun 1926, at St Marks Church, St Marks Road, Lyncombe, and lived until 1963 (he features in a Brint family photograph that Malcolm Conroy sent me).

The eldest of Robert Daniels' children was Violet Grace Daniels. She never married and lived most of her life at 8 The Firs until her death in 1979. The 1932 Post Office Directory lists her as retailing gowns, coats etc at 42 Bradford Road. In the 1950s she worked from home as an agent of Spirella corsets. I remember visiting her a few times – it must have been a lonely life after the death of Mabel, who also lived at 8 The Firs for most of her life and for the latter part of her working life worked in the Admiralty (Ministry of Defence) at the Foxhill Hutments.

Robert Daniels' wife Anne died in March 1941 and Robert Daniels himself died on 29 December 1949 (see the press reports below). Probate was granted on 19 May 1950 to Violet Grace Emma Daniels, Spinster and Norman Roberts Pretoria Daniels, Draughtsman, for the effects of £1,463 2s. 3d.

Norah and her family

The second of Robert Daniels' children, Norah Victoria E Daniels (born 1897) married a George Hooton in Bath (probably Combe Down Church) in 1921. They lived at Walnut Tree Farm, Milton Keynes. They had 3 sons John (1923-2010), Lawrence (born 1930), and Malcolm G (born 1932) who married Margaret Lindsay in 1957. Norah and George both died in 1987.

From 1979 onwards my brother Roger and his family lived near Milton Keynes when he joined the Planning Department of Milton Keynes Development Corporation. When, sometime after 1980, our parents visited him they went to visit George and Norah Hooton, and met Lawrence and John. Although Norah was our father's cousin, our mother seemed more interested in getting in touch and probably knew Norah better than our father did. Their then middle-aged single sons, Lawrence and John were running their farm (Walnut Tree Farm). In Milton Keynes you will still find business names registered for the farming business variously as G Hooton and as L & J Hooton.

Walnut Tree Farm was acquired by Milton Keynes Development Corporation and developed during the 1980s as the mainly residential area that is now known as Walnut

Tree (part of Walton parish). The Hootons continued to live at the residential buildings of Walnut Tree Farm and the brothers acquired land to the east, towards Newport Pagnell, to continue farming, although they were already in their 50s.

My brother found an obituary online for *'John Norman Hooton of Walnut Tree, Milton Keynes passed away peacefully on 6th April 2010 aged 86 years.'* A current online telephone directory lists David C Hooton of Walnut Tree, Milton Keynes. However at the time of writing his brothers Laurence and Malcolm are still very much with us and I was pleased to have had a couple of phone conversations with Laurence, who sent me some photographs.

Norman and his family

The third of Robert's children was named Norman Roberts Pretoria Daniels as he was born on 5 June 1900 a few days after Lord Roberts captured Pretoria in the Second Boer War (31 May 1900). From his youth he was keen on scouting – as a photograph of him in 1914 shows. A press cutting from 30 April 1932 shows Norman Daniels playing a full role in writing scout plays, making scenery for, and acting in, their productions. These were talents he also deployed in the same era for the Combe Down Old Scholars where his musical talents were also deployed. He also designed and painted some outstanding scenary for productions mounted by Combe Down School in the 1930s. He also wrote a play for the Combe Down Old Scholars concert in 1928.

In 1918 he joined the army at the tail end of the Great War and was a member of the army of occupation until 1921. According to a press cutting following his death, he studied art in his spare time in Germany. With regard to his musical talents I have two press cuttings from the Bath Chronicle and Herald for Saturday 26 November 1938 and Saturday 1 April 1939 that relate to concerts by the Argyle String Orchestra, under Algernon Salter LRAM at the Argyle Lecture Hall, to raise funds for the church. Mr N Daniels was listed amongst the second violins in the 22 piece orchestra that included Miss IM Tovey as one of the viola players and Miss EM Tovey as one of the cellists. Currently I can find no earlier or later press reports on this orchestra that lists Norman Daniels. However other press cuttings show that he was much in demand at concerts and socials for violin solos. His future wife Marjorie was also an accomplished singer as many press reports logged below attest. An article in a Bristol paper from about 1930 records Norman's fraustrated desire for a career in art.

As the press record below records, on 10 May 1941 Norman Daniels married Alice Marjorie Stockall at Holy Trinity Church Combe Down. She had been head teacher of Hinton Charterhouse School, and they were both around 41 years of age. The press report notes Norman as a member of the Argyle Orchestra, with a strong involvement in the scout movement on Combe Down.

I am indebted to Laurence Hooton for giving me the contact details of Norman Daniels' daughter Ruth who has greatly supplemented the material I have on Norman and his wife Marjorie and their offspring. Their daughter Ruth was born on 25 October 1942 at Freshford Cottage Hospital (where I was also born in 1947). Ruth has sent me a copy of a charming letter my mother wrote to Marjorie on 29 October 1942 (from LACW LF Pine 454589, WAAF Section (Pay Accounts) RAF Cosford, nr Wolverhampton). Their son Paul was born on 30 January 1944.

Ruth married Brian Lafford in 1969 and later the same year Paul married Caroline Cameron. Ruth and Brian have 2 daughters, 3 granddaughters and one great grand son - and live in Plymouth. Paul and Caroline have lived in New Zealand since 1972 and were visited by Norman and Marjorie in 1975 (shortly after which their first son died at 2 years old from complications after hole in the heart surgery). Their youngest unmarried son still lives in New Zealand – the 2 older sons live in Australia. Paul and Caroline have 3 grandchildren.

According to a press report following his death, Norman Daniels served in the army throughout the war. That is not strictly true – although he was in the Home Guard. Whilst the Blacksmith's business was registered on 29 January 1940 as Robert Daniels and Son, I believe Norman had no active part in the business after his marriage and trained as a draughtsman, working for Aldrige and Peacock at Peasedown St John and then for Welding Industries up to his retirement in 1965.

After they were married Norman and Marjorie initially lived with her aunt in Seymour Road, Bath, until it was blitzed (see adjoining photograph supplied by their daughter Ruth Lafford). They then had a little cottage at Peasedown St John. Their daughter Ruth was born in 1942. Soon after their son Paul's birth in 1944 they moved to Penn Lea Road, Bath: probably because Welding Industries (ex Aldrige and Peacock) had moved to Bristol. In 1952 they moved to Apple Blossom Cottage, Golden Valley, Bitton.

When the children were school age Marjorie returned to teaching, as a supply, before becoming head of Upton Cheyney School (taking over from the head teacher that had replaced her in 1941!). Ruth has said to me "I wish I had inherited Mum and Dad's talents! I used to love listening to their duets on piano and violin."

Norman and Marjorie moved to Bouverie Drive in Market Lavington in 1971 in order to be near their daughter Ruth, then living at Potterne. In 1975 they had visited Paul near Christchurch in New Zealand.

Marjorie died in January 1983 and Norman in October of the same year. A funeral service was held on 20 October at St Mary's Church Market Lavington, followed by a cremation at Bath. He was recorded in the press report as being a founder member of the Lavington Day Centre and a keen chess player with the Rev. Norman Miller and Lavington School pupils.

Ruth Lafford has sent me a copy of a letter my mother had written to her on the death of her father, Norman. My mother had read a newspaper report of his death later on the same day that she had written to Norman's sister Nora (Hooton). My mother's letter noted "As you know I had known both of them since my early schooldays and when we formed our Old Scholars association, your father was always ready and willing with his artistic abilities to do the scenery and help us all." My mother was referring to not only to him but also Marjorie (who had been a long-term friend of Violet Daniels according to Ruth).

The Press Record

We start our press cuttings on Robert Daniels and his family with Robert Daniels providing Monkton Combe Parish Council with an estimate to repair a fence - at the same meeting FH Pine's predecessor as chairman, Mr Stickland, was elected, as the Bath Chronicle of **28 September 1911** reports:

'**Monkton Combe Parish Council - Chairman's Resignation**' Mr H Bennett presided with Messrs WJ Patch, R Potts, FJ Brown, FR Munday, and W Miles. An estimate was received from Mr Robert Daniels in reference to a fence at Combe Down Quarry. The Clerk Mr EP Page was asked to set work in hand. The clerk read a letter of resignation from the council of the Chairman Mr Warren, having not been supported and indeed insulted at a parish meeting. Mr Stickland was elected to fill the council vacancy. Mr Miles, as one of the eldest members of the council, was elected Chairman.

As already noted, the Bath Chronicle of **2 March 1912** had an article '**Combe Down Unionists - Annual Supper and Smoking Concert**' at the Victoria Rooms, Hadley Arms, Combe Down. Amongst the local worthies with Robert Daniels was a Mr Pine.

On **12 May 1917** is a report in columns 7 and 8 on '**A Combe Down Smash**' about a court case concerning the liability for a collision between a tram-car and a laundry van at the Hadleigh Arms, Combe Down. Towards the end of this report we find Robert

Daniels was a crucial witness. The jury concluded that although the tram driver was diverted by chatting up the conductress, the van driver was at fault. The evidence that was crucial came from "Robert Daniels, blacksmith, who arrived on the spot just after the accident, said he traced the wheel marks of the laundry van from The Avenue to the tramlines, and saw that the driver had cut the corner instead of taking a sweep round the left on the proper side." It is interesting to see Robert using the forensic skills of a Special Constable!

Next on **3 July 1926** is a report that concerns both Robert & Norman Daniels headed **'Motorcyclists Collide - Head-on Impact at Combe Down'.** Why the accident occurred at 8am is not clear. "The cyclists were Mr Norman Daniels (26), the Firs, Combe Down, a single man, who works as a wheelwright and general smith with his father, Mr Robert Daniels and Herbert Smith, of Hinton Charterhouse, also a single man, and employed by Messrs Manning and Sons as a plasterer. They simultaneously reached Mr W Pearce's butchers shop, outside of which a cart was standing, and met in the middle of the road."Both were injured by being thrown. Daniels escaped the more lightly, getting off with face abrasions, Swifts chief injury being a broken collar bone. The latter was conveyed to the Royal United Hospital by Mr Ernest Bishop, of Come Down and Daniels was taken to the institution by his father,"

Details of Robert Daniels participation in the Monkton Combe Parish Council between 1928 and 1934 is extensively chronicled in relation to the press cuttings on Frank H Pine. Also I have recorded separately the musical and dramatic activities of the Combe Down Old Scholars Association so I will not dwell on the detail of those activities. However I will note that Norman Daniels was in charge of designing and creating the scenery and lighting for most of their productions and on the occasion that an orchestra was needed he took charge of it. On the performing side Mabel Symons, Connie, Phyllis and Lena Pine played many key roles.

I will now take a look at the press cuttings that have much to say about the talents of Norman Daniels and his wife to be, Marjorie Stockall. They also throw light on the social life of Combe Down in the period of the Old Scholar's Association – say 1927-1939.

I will start with **4 March 1927** when the Chronicle reported **'Soprano Soloist - At Combe Down Organ Recital'** as follows: "Miss Marjorie Stockall was the soloist at the vocal and organ recital held after evensong on Sunday at Holy Trinity Church Combe Down, and gave accomplished renderings of M Kennedy Fraser's charming composition 'The Christ Child's Lullaby' and 'The God of Love my Shepherd is' (Eric Thomas). Miss Stockall, who is the daughter of Mr and Mrs AH Stockall of Combe Down, and who teaches at Upton Cheyney (Bitton) School, has a pleasing soprano voice, and her enunciation was particularly good."

On **26 January 1929** the paper reported on **'Mid-Norton Brotherhood – Visit of Bath Concert Party'** that included Marjorie Stockall who sang 'Nursery Rhymes from London Life' and 'Home a Long'.

On **16 March 1929** a report headed **'Greatly Beloved – funeral of Mrs AH Stockall – Internment at Monkton Combe'** was concerned with the death at her home of 5 Westbury Avenue, Combe Down, of Marjorie's mother Kate (a supporter of the Workers Educational Association). On **27 April 1929** there is a report headed **'Combe Down Recital – Miss Marjorie Stockall the Vocalist'**. She sang 'My Heart Ever Faithfull' (Bach) and 'Guardian Angels' (Handel).

Amongst the wealth of material that Ruth Lafford has shown me are some undated newspaper cuttings which I have been able to date as they were reproduced (from the daily paper) in the Weekly Bath Chronicle - which is available on-line. However there is an Evening Times article that I can only guess comes from 1930 - or possibly 1931. The article's multiple headings read **"Blacksmith as West Playwright - Artist Before a Forge - 'Edgar Wallace' of Bath - Youth's Dreams - Hope to Find Outlet for Talent (Evening Times Exclusive) - Bath, Tuesday".**

"On Combe Down there is a forge where, for a generation, the name of Daniels has stood for good shoes. Twenty years ago a stream of horses came to the forge to be shoed, and Mr Robert Daniels served his custom well. His son now works beside his father, and all manner of ironwork is carried out for the residents. Few passers-by who see the young man swinging a hammer have any idea that he has dreams of literature and art. Fewer know that he is a playwright and has had his own 'thriller' played before a crowded hall in Combe Down.

"When tonight the Irish Players perform in the Avenue Hall, they will stand behind a beautiful floral proscenium which is the unaided work of the young blacksmith. Standing in his leather apron, he told of his dreams of an art career, writes an Evening Times reporter. The proscenium is an ambitious work measuring 27 feet by 22 feet, and is floral in design, surmounted by a conventional kingfisher. It is really a triumph of colour and after the style of Dulac, the French master.

"The play which Daniels wrote is called 'The Spooker'. He takes a great interest in the Combe down Old Scholars Association, and designed and executed the proscenium for their annual entertainment. He hopes some day to find an outlet for his talent and would willingly forsake the forge - if it were possible."

I suspect the Irish Players were not performing Norman's play that had been part of the Old Scholar's 1928 joint concert with the school. Norman's proscenium had been completed by 1930 (the two OSA concerts that year were, in part, to pay for its cost). Also I can only find 3 references in the on-line copies of the weekly Bath Chronicle to the Irish Players - all from 1930. Finally I assume the *Evening Times* was the Bristol *Times and Echo* which I believe ceased publication in 1931 in a deal between its publisher, Lord Camrose, and Lord Rothermere publisher of the *Bristol Evening World* to end competition between their papers in Bristol and Newcastle (leading to the creation of the *Bristol Evening Post* in 1932 by the Times and Echo's former readers).

On 18 **January 1930** a weekly chronicle item under a heading '**WEA Social'** says that a WEA social was held at Citizens House the previous Saturday. "An excellent musical programme was presented. It included songs by Miss Marjorie Stockall and Mr A Maurice..." Marjorie appears again in an article of **5 April 1930** under a heading '**Countryside Music – Lansdown School's Success at Gloucester Festival'**. This was a competition in which 56 villages in Gloucestershire were represented in 1,400 entries, and was adjudicated by HW Sumsion, organist of Gloucester Cathedral. "In the class for schools of under 70 scholars Upton Cheyney Council School, Lansdown, the winners of the shield in that class last year, were placed second, being just one mark behind the winners (Kingscourt Junior Council School): Miss A Marjorie Stockall, of Combe Down, headmistress, conducted the Upton Cheyney Choir. The items sung were 'Blackbirds and Thrushes' (Sharp) and 'The Coalman' (Sharman)."

Meantime Marjorie and Norman appear together in an **18 October 1930** report on '**Combe Down's Vicar – parting gift to Mr and Mrs Watson'** - a social gathering to say farewell and present gifts to the departing vicar who had preached over 1,000 sermons at Combe Down. 'Among the items of the evenings programme were: - Violin duet, Miss Rivington and **Mr Daniels**; piano solos, Miss R Pearce and Miss P Miller; songs, **Miss M Stockall;** recitations Miss Collard; song, Mr AW Francom." In showing off his gifts "the Vicar displayed a large picture showing the origin of the Church Rooms, designed by **Mr Norman Daniels.** It is a fine design, showing the dedication of the rooms (in which it is to be hung) and relating how the project was accomplished and the rooms handed over to the church."

On **20 December 1930** is an item headed '**Combe Down Social – Lord and Lady Weymouth attend it.'** The social at the Church Rooms was chaired by Captain Daubeny. "An excellent programme was given, 'The Spiral Staircase' (a mime) Miss Webb, Mr and Mrs England and Mr and Mrs Dutton; Mr Armitage at the piano; Miss Gerrish, comic songs; **Mr Norman Daniels** and Mr Chappell, violin duets and solos, Miss Christina Long was the accompanist and gave a pianoforte solo. Refreshments were served by the ladies committee – Mesdames Morris, Burridge, Ricketts and Pearce."

Marjorie and Norman appear on the same bill in an article dated **31 January 1931** entitled **'Combe Down Social – Large Attendance at Annual Parish Gathering'.** The programme consisted of a concert, arranged by the organist, Mr WA Bishop, and speeches by the vicar and churchwardens. "songs were given by the vicar, Mrs Webster and **Miss Marjorie Stockall**, recitations by Miss J Eldred, violin duets by Miss G Rivington and **Mr N Daniels** and Messrs **N Daniels** and W Chappell, dances by the Misses M Odey and B Patch (pupils of Miss Audrey Ford), and piano solos by Miss P Miller, Miss R Pearce and Mrs Webster …"

A report of **30 June 1931** is headed **'Combe Down 'Civic' Days – Mayor of Bath tells Some Reminiscences – At Parochial Fete'.** The Mayor opened the fete and at the end of the article a list of helpers includes "Local Orchestra, arranged by **Mr Norman Daniels."** On **15 August 1931** there is a report **'Sweet Pea Wedding'** in which the prevailing colour scheme was pink and blue, in delicate sweet pea tints. The wedding at Old Widcombe's picturesque church the previous Saturday afternoon and involved a Miss Phoebe Allin, daughter of the late Captain Allin of 'The Dell' Widcombe (a member of the Bath Ladies Rowing Club) and Mr Robert CM Richards a teacher at the Combe Down Senior School (his father was a member of the Chronicle and Herald's linotype department). The best man was Mr Norman Daniels.

Now for another item involving Marjorie and Stanley England (a stalwart of the Combe Down Old Scholars). It concerns The British Empire Shakespeare Society (of which my Aunt Phyllis Pine, and fellow Old Scholar and work colleague of Stanley, was latterly a member). Dated **14 November 1931** the piece is headed **'The Play's the Thing'** and refers to a sketch at a BESS concert involving Mr FH Hamilton, Mrs Doreen England, Mrs Ida Lakey, Miss Mavis Thorley, Mr Leslie Moore, Mr SH England and Mr R Lakey. **Miss Marjorie Stockall** and Mr H Dutton were involved in the musical items and Miss Kathleen Stockall was involved in the sketches. Miss Terry's Ladies' Orchestra also played.

On **5 March 1932** an article **'Headmistress Honoured'** reads "Past and present scholars, their parents and friends of Upton Cheyney Council School, near Bitton, joined with their teachers and all the managers in a farewell gift to Miss A Majorie Stockall, who has been headmistress of that school since 1926, and on Tuesday took up a new appointment at All Saints Senior School, Clifton, Shefford, Bedfordshire." She was presented with an inscribed 8 day clock in a leather case.

The article continues "Miss Stockall, who is an Old Sulian and a past member of Bristol Operatic Society and of Bristol University Madrigal Society, is well known as a talented vocalist. In her new post she will teach singing throughout the school as well as art and history. She is the second daughter of Mr AH and the late Mrs Stockall, of Westbury Avenue, Combe Down, and niece of Mr Alfred Hopkins, of the Bath Education Office."

On **30 April 1932** under **Scout Notes by Hiker** is a piece reprinted from earlier in the week entitled **'St Georges Day Service'** with a second sub-heading **'Combe Down Scouts'** under which it is reported that "The 10th Bath (Combe Down) Rover Crew presented their 2nd annual concert with great success at the Church Rooms. The programme consisted of 4 plays 'Sold', 'Fire', 'The Big Fight' and 'The Man of Mystery'...... The plays were written and the scenery painted by the Rover Leader Mr N Daniels and the play 'Sold' in one scene depicted the interior of the Pig and Weazle and the bottles and barrels of beer were painted so realistically that I am afraid more than one tongue in the audience was hanging out." Norman Daniels played the Man of Mystery.

A report of **10 February 1934** is headed **'A Good Cause'** and concerns a **'Concert at Combe Down for the Unemployed'** "Organised and arranged by an unemployed man (Mr Billings), Combe Down, a concert in aid of the fund for the unemployed raised by the Social Service Committee (of which Mr H Robinson of Bank House is chairman), was held on Wednesday evening in the Church Army Social Centre, Combe Down. The hall was packed to capacity by an audience exceedingly appreciative of an unusually high-class programme.

"**Mr FH Pine** acted as announcer, and during the interal Mr Robinson voiced the thanks of the committee to the organiser, and to the artistes for their interest and work." Amongst a list of performers, **Mr N Daniels** is recorded as having contributed a violin solo.

Meantime Marjorie Stockall was back in the area as a report of **21 July 1934** records **'Hemmington Senior Scholars to be transferred to Radstock'**. Somerset County Education Committee in Bridgwater had decided on the Wednesday that senior scholars of Hemmington Council School (of which Marjorie Stockall was headmistress) were to be transferred to Radstock Council School.

On **7 September 1935** a report headed **'Chuch's Valued Ally'** reports on the annual fete at the Church Army Social Centre, opened by the Ven SA Boyd (Archdeacon of Bath Abbey) – the Vicar F Last Bedwell presided – and the work at the Centre of Capt and Mrs Booth was praised in providing accommodation for the destitute. The article gives a list of stall holders and notes that the fete concluded with a social evening in which "Mr Cherret was the MC and Miss Gerrish was the pianist. Violin solos were played by **Mr Norman Daniels**."

Under **'A Credit to the School'** the weekly Chronicle records on **19 December 1936** (in an article republished from earlier that week – minus a photograph) that "The Church Rooms at Combe Down were crowded on two evenings last week on the occasion of the presentation by the scholars of the Senior School of the Japanese operetta 'Princess Ju Ju". The cast included Jean Harvey as the lead and George Sumsion as the Emperor. Other parts included Douglas Stennard, John Davis and Frank Ford (a full list is given). "Mr Wallace Brown (headmaster), who was responsible for the play, at the close of Fridays performance, thanked all those who had contributed to the success of both performances and particularly mentioned **Mr Norman Daniels** (an old boy), who had specially designed and executed the whole of the scenery."

The Chronicle of **4 November 1937** reported the **'Death of Mr AH Stockall - Member of Bath Engineering Firm'**. This was Marjorie's father – the report says: "The senior member of the firm of Stockall and Son, general engineers, of St James's Street, South, Bath, Mr Alfred Henry Stockall died at 6 Westbury Avenue, Combe Down, on Saturday, aged 67. Mr Stockall's father, who is in his 92nd year, founded the firm in 1886. He retired a number of years ago and was succeeded by Mr AH Stockall." The funeral was on the Wednesday at Combe Down. The immediate family mourners included "Mrs AH Stockall (Widow) Misses Kathleen, Marjorie and Francis Stockall (daughters)..." The mourners also included a Miss Daniels (presumably Marjorie's friend, Vi).

On **18 December 1937** the Chronicle reported on a **Combe Down Play – Presentation by Scholars** – "Scholars of Combe Down School presented during last week a play produced by the headmaster Mr Wallace Brown, which was extraordinarily well given, in elabourate settings not usually expected from school students. Those who assisted were Miss M Tanner, Miss E Webb, Mrs R Brewer and Miss M Odey. 'Zurika and the Captive Princess' is a 3 act period play in gypsy and 17th century settings .... the scenery was of an attractive nature, this, with the lighting was entrusted to **Mr Norman Daniels**....The play was presented on Wednesday, Thursday and Friday in the Church Rooms."

As already mentioned there are the two press reports recording Norman Daniels' membership of the **Argyle String Orchestra** of **26 November 1938** and **1 April 1939**. In a report of **7 October 1939** of **'Combe Downs Show Night'**, **Norman Daniels** was but a steward for the event.

So we move on to **29 March 1941** and the Bath Chronicle and Herald report **'Combe Down Resident - Funeral of Mrs R Daniels at Monkton Combe'**: "The funeral of Mrs R Daniels of 8 The Firs, Combe Down, Bath, who died at the age of 72, took place at Monkton Combe Church on Wednesday afternoon. A service was held at Monkton Combe Church at which the Rev E Roberts (vicar of Combe Down) officiated.

"The chief mourners were Miss VG Daniels and Mrs J Hooton (daughters), Mr Norman Daniels (son), Mr James Poole (brother), Miss Mabel Symons, Mrs Spratt and Miss E Osmond (nieces), Mr Herbert Daniels (nephew), Messrs David and Worthy Daniels and Mrs Gale (bothers and sister-in-law), Miss M Stockall, Mrs Preddy, Mrs Burridge, Mr Jay, Miss Tavener, Miss L Pine and Mrs Pearce.

"Floral tributes were as follows: To dearest Mum from her loving husband Bob, Vi, Norah, Norman, Mabs and George "Til we meet again", to dear grandma with love from John, Lawrence and Malcolm......in kind remembrance from Mr and Mrs Pine and family ..... in loving memory of dear Annie.... in loving memory of a kind neighbour, Mrs Pearce, Eric and Tony.... in loving memory from Worthy, Lucy and Bert; in loving memory from Dave and Minnie."

This confirms that Worthy's brother David (baptised 1870 and who died 1949) and sister Minnie (baptised 1880 and who died 1950) were probably living together in Castle Combe (see my earlier photograph of them with me). As noted above, Minnie's married name was Mrs Gale. It is interesting to note that Herbert Daniels and Lena Pine both attended the funeral - clearly my parents were well acquainted a year before FHP died.

Next, at the age of about 41 Norman Daniels marries - a report in the paper of **17 May 1941** (col 2) is as follows: **'School Head - Combe Down Wedding of Miss A Stockall'**

"The wedding of Mr Norman Daniels, only son of Mr Robert Daniels and the late Mrs Daniels of Combe Down with Miss A Marjorie Stockall, second daughter of the late Mr and Mrs Alfred H Stockall took place at Holy Trinity Church Combe Down on Saturday, the vicar (The Rev E Roberts) officiated. The bride is the late head teacher of Hinton Charterhouse School and the bridegroom, who is a member of the Argyle Orchestra, has for many years been interested in the scout movement on Combe Down.... The reception was given in the drawing room of the Pump Room...The honeymoon is to be spent in Devon. Among the many wedding gifts were those from the children and managers of Hinton Charterhouse junior school and the Argyle Orchestra."

Lastly in the issue of **31 December 1949** we read **'Was Prominent Resident of Combe Down - Death of Mr Robert Daniels'**. "The death has occurred at his home 8 The Firs, Combe Down, of Mr Robert Daniels a former Member of Monkton Combe, Parish Council and Treasurer of the Combe Down lodge of the Wiltshire Working Mens Benefit Society. He was 81. He was a prominent member of Monkton Combe Conservative association, almost from its inception, and always took part in any activity associated with Combe Down.

"He came to Combe Down from a village near Chippenham about sixty years ago and, after working as a journeyman blacksmith for some time, opened up a business which he carried on, with his son, until age forced his retirement. He had been in failing health for some years. His wife died some years ago and he is survived by his son, Norman, who lives in Weston, and two daughters - Violet, who lived with him, and a married daughter who resides in the Eastern Counties. His niece, Miss Mabel Symons, who lived with him from childhood, had been devoted in her attention to him during his long illness. The funeral will take place at Monkton Combe on Saturday after a service at Combe Down Church."

The Heritage of the Combe Down Blacksmith

Although I have no specific dates, as I have noted above Robert Daniels was, for a period of time, a part-time Special Constable on Combe Down (he was one of 13 Special Constables on Combe Down). Certainly his forensic skills of observation are clear in the above press report from 1917 about the Combe Down tram crash.

He was an active member of the Conservative Party and of the Wiltshire Working Men's Conservative Benefit Society. His grand-daughter Ruth has supplied me with a copy of a document dated 13 March 1928 (signed by Captain Daubeny as chairman of the parish meeting) that confirmed his election for a term of 3 years as a Parish Councillor.

Following an examination, he was registered as a Member of the Worshipful Company of Farriers in on 10 May 1898. In January 1940 his business was, as noted above, registered as Robert Daniels and Son through the auspices of the National Master Farriers and Blacksmiths Association. However he and Norman may have ceased to have had an active part in it much after that. His legacy - in terms of the gates to the Firs Field, Combe Down - survived into the late 20th century.

Norman worked with his father as a blacksmith but he also had many other talents – as a designer of scenery and stage fittings for the Combe Down Old Scholars theatrical productions. He also played a part in writing and directing shows and, as a member of the Argyle Orchestra, he was an accomplished musician; he would perform in and conduct an orchestra for the shows.

Robert and Norman Daniels had direct experience of how, in the twentirth century the traditional role of the Blacksmith was disappearing as cars replaced horses and the blacksmith took on something of the role that is now the preserve of bodyshops in modern garages. To sum up this section a poem is a good option.

Those familiar with the traditional role of the Village Blacksmith (as potrtrayed in Longfellow's famous poem) will appreciate the quality of the following pastiche by Norman Daniels that was published in the Spring 1930 edition of 'The Comrade', the Combe Down Old Scholars Magazine:

THE VILLAGE BLACKSMITH.
(Another version to date.)

Of course you've heard about the smith
Whose face was like the tan,
Who looked the whole world in the face
And owed not any man,
Which, even in the best of times,
Is more than many can.

The chestnut tree has been cut down
That feathered many a joke;
More room was wanted, so it fell
To the village woodman's stroke;
They sold the timber up in town,
As good old English oak!

The smith, of course, is older now,
And has a lighter touch,
And still he earns whate'er he can,
But doesn't sweat so much;
He knows the tricks of cars, and can
Manipulate a clutch.

His men shoe far less horses, but
They never feel a slump,
For even motor cars break down
When two together bump;
And many others stop to fill
With petrol at the pump.

The children coming home from school
Still gather as of yore,
They love to see a car in bits
Upon the smithy floor,
And talk about "Tin Lizzies" from
The shelter of the door.

The chara's and the buses stop
Because it is a stage;
His daughter sells out cups of tea,
(Commission plus her wage)
In summertime she takes a lot,
She's nippy for her age.

Yes, there's a moral for us all,
In these light-hearted rhymes;
In business, standing still's the worst
Or almost, of all crimes.
Cut out your "chestnut" policy,
And hustle with the times.

N. R. P. DANIELS

The following map of Combe Down from the early 20th century (before Richardson Avenue - The Firs was built) shows the location of the smithy.

Line of The Firs **Gates installed by Robert Daniels** **The Other Smithy** **Mr Robert Daniels Smithy behind the Horseshoe Pub**

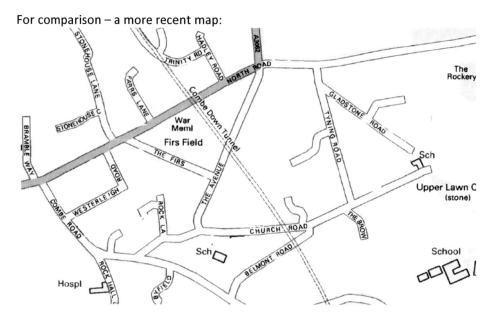

For comparison – a more recent map:

ROBERT DANIELS & FAMILY

1. Robert Daniels c1890   2. Robert c.1900 with Mr Jones   3. Robert c.1900
4. Robert and family 1900   5. Robert &Anne c.1910 with sister Fanny Daniels Norah and Vi
6. Robert and family with Teddy the dog in 1920.

ROBERT DANIELS & FAMILY: VIOLET, NORAH & MABEL

1. Mabel c.1938
2. Summer 1948 Vi, Robert and Mabel
3 1948 Robert Daniels with my father
Herbert, me and Mabel
4. Vi Daniels, Mabel and Vi's sister Norah
Hooton at Walnut Tree Farm c1955
5. Vi, Norah and George Hooton
18 February 1969 at Bitton Church
marriage of Ruth Daniels (Norman
Daniels' daughter).
6.Norah and George Hooton 31 March
1981 60 years wed.

NORMAN DANIELS

1. In c.1910   2. In 1914 as a scout
3-5. In the occupation army in 1921
 - and in civies
6. Wedding day 1941 with Marjorie
7. In 1957 at the wedding of
Malcolm Hooton with Marjorie,
Mabel and Vi

THE TALENTS OF NORMAN DANIELS

Art College Germany 1919 and Sets for the OSA and School (Princess Ju Ju)
In the Argyle Orchestra 1938 (rear fifth left) Irene Tovey (front third right)

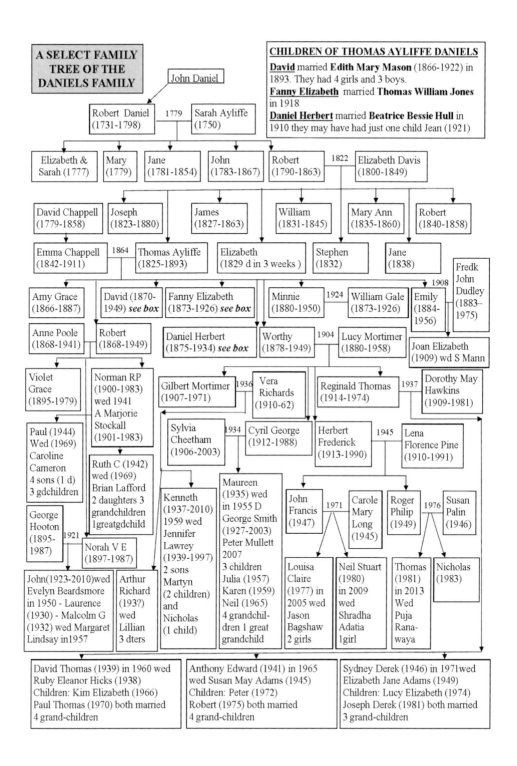

A SELECT FAMILY TREE OF THE DANIELS FAMILY

John Daniel

Robert Daniel (1731-1798) — 1779 — Sarah Ayliffe (1750)

CHILDREN OF THOMAS AYLIFFE DANIELS
David married **Edith Mary Mason** (1866-1922) in 1893. They had 4 girls and 3 boys.
Fanny Elizabeth married **Thomas William Jones** in 1918
Daniel Herbert married **Beatrice Bessie Hull** in 1910 they may have had just one child Jean (1921)

Elizabeth & Sarah (1777)
Mary (1779)
Jane (1781-1854)
John (1783-1867)
Robert (1790-1863) — 1822 — Elizabeth Davis (1800-1849)

David Chappell (1779-1858)
Joseph (1823-1880)
James (1827-1863)
William (1831-1845)
Mary Ann (1835-1860)
Robert (1840-1858)

Emma Chappell (1842-1911) — 1864 — Thomas Ayliffe (1825-1893)
Elizabeth (1829 d in 3 weeks)
Stephen (1832)
Jane (1838)
Fredk John Dudley (1883–1975)

Amy Grace (1866-1887)
David (1870-1949) *see box*
Fanny Elizabeth (1873-1926) *see box*
Minnie (1880-1950)
William Gale (1873-1926) — 1924
Emily (1884-1956) — 1908

Anne Poole (1868-1941)
Robert (1868-1949)
Daniel Herbert (1875-1934) *see box*
Worthy (1878-1949) — 1904 — Lucy Mortimer (1880-1958)
Joan Elizabeth (1909) wd S Mann

Violet Grace (1895-1979)
Norman RP (1900-1983) wed 1941 A Marjorie Stockall (1901-1983)
Gilbert Mortimer (1907-1971) — 1936 — Vera Richards (1910-62)
Reginald Thomas (1914-1974) — 1937 — Dorothy May Hawkins (1909-1981)

Paul (1944) Wed (1969) Caroline Cameron 4 sons (1 d) 3 gdchildren
Ruth C (1942) wed (1969) Brian Lafford 2 daughters 3 grandchildren 1greatgdchild
Sylvia Cheetham (1906-2003) — 1934 — Cyril George (1912-1988)
Herbert Frederick (1913-1990) — 1945 — Lena Florence Pine (1910-1991)

George Hooton (1895-1987) — 1921 — Norah V E (1897-1987)
Kenneth (1937-2010) 1959 wed Jennifer Lawrey (1939-1997) 2 sons Martyn (2 children) and Nicholas (1 child)
Maureen (1935) wed in 1955 D George Smith (1927-2003) Peter Mullett 2007 3 children Julia (1957) Karen (1959) Neil (1965) 4 grandchildren 1 great grandchild
John Francis (1947) — 1971 — Carole Mary Long (1945)
Roger Philip (1949) — 1976 — Susan Palin (1946)

John(1923-2010)wed Evelyn Beardsmore in 1950 - Laurence (1930) - Malcolm G (1932) wed Margaret Lindsay in1957
Arthur Richard (193?) wed Lillian 3 dters
Louisa Claire (1977) in 2005 wed Jason Bagshaw 2 girls
Neil Stuart (1980) in 2009 wed Shradha Adatia 1girl
Thomas (1981) in 2013 Wed Puja Ranawaya
Nicholas (1983)

David Thomas (1939) in 1960 wed Ruby Eleanor Hicks (1938) Children: Kim Elizabeth (1966) Paul Thomas (1970) both married 4 grand-children
Anthony Edward (1941) in 1965 wed Susan May Adams (1945) Children: Peter (1972) Robert (1975) both married 4 grand-children
Sydney Derek (1946) in 1971wed Elizabeth Jane Adams (1949) Children: Lucy Elizabeth (1974) Joseph Derek (1981) both married 3 grand-children

A VOYAGE AROUND MY FATHER

I have so far given my father a walk-on part in this saga - as it has hitherto focussed on my maternal grandfather, my mother and others of my family who lived on Combe Down. However I began this exercise addressing the issue of how my brother and I came to be. I began with wanting to know something about my grandfather Frank Pine and I feel I now know a great deal. Conversely, thanks to the work of my cousin's wife Susan Daniels, I felt comfortable about what I knew about the Daniels family. However a few words about my father's immediate family may be due.

Although I have a John Daniel heading the family tree, in a letter that my Uncle Cyril sent to Norman Daniels on 27 January 1980 he records:

> "The Daniels family were strong dissenters and so we are not often found in the parish records. Dissenters were numerous in this area *(of Wiltshire)* and were probably supported by the Lord of the Manor of Grittleton, Col. White, who was an officer in Cromwell's Army and Governor of Bristol Castle during the Civil War.

> "However a John Daniels is found in the Littleton Drew Register for 1676 when his daughter was baptised, and in 1795 Robert Daniels had his five children baptised. Their ages ranged from 11 to 4 years. In 1798 he died and his farm passed into other hands. The farm was enclosed and became part of Manor farm in 1847. Jack Daniels who, today farms at Burton, is descended from Robert Daniels' eldest son John - and Robert Daniels jnr who died in 1863 and was the father of Thomas Daniels – and was the youngest son *(of Robert Daniels: Thomas Daniels was the father of my grandfather Worthy Daniels – and therefore Cyril and Norman's grandfather)*.

> "The earliest Daniels I have found is Robert Daniell of Castle Combe recorded as a merchant and taxpayer in 1576. It seems possible the Littleton Drew family is a branch of that family."

Cyril Daniels began but never fuly completed a history of Littleton Drew from the very earliest times with reference to the field pattern and Roman remains. I helped him with some photographs of the village. I made some effort to get his amazing copperplate handwriting into type, since he had made me his literaray executor, but it is thanks to the diligence of his grand-daughter Julia Todd that its 3 volumes are available in PDF form. I feel that there is a great story to be told about the people of Littleton Drew in the nineteenth and twentieth century.

I never lived there, but I did experience from visits there from the early 1950s a living village – with its post office, pub and annual gypsy fair and gymkhana. Some of that experience is reflected in the following account.

My paternal grandfather Worthy Daniels married Lucy Mortimer (1880-1959) and they lived at Steps Cottage and latterly Ivy Cottage, Littleton Drew. Their children were Gilbert (1907-71), Cyril (1912-1988), Herbert (1913-1990), Thomas (1914-1974). Herbert married Lena Pine (1910-1991) and their children were me, John (1947), and my brother, Roger (1949). I married Carole Long (1945) in 1971 and our children were Louisa (1977) and Neil (1980). Louisa married Jason Bagshaw 29 July 2005 and on 24 June 2010 their daughter Florence was born to be followed by Genevieve on 21 November 2013. On 8 December 2009 Neil married Shradha Adatia in Mumbai and on 11 June 2015 their daughter Jane was born.

The Daniels' line can be traced with greater facility than some because the family mostly lived in Wiltshire, particularly two villages: Littleton Drew and Castle Combe. Until the 1960s the freeholds of the cottages in Castle Combe were owned by the Manor. In Littleton Drew the cottages were either owned by the Duke of Beaufort estate or by the church. The exceptions were 2 cottages owned by the Daniels family since the 17th century – Steps Cottage and Ivy Cottage (as pictured left and right below in 1986 before renovation).

The village website notes that Littleton Drew is a small linear isolated village north of the M4 and west of the Fossway. It dates from before the Norman Conquest, being known at that time simply as "Litle Tun" (little farm). From the 13th Century it became known as Littleton Dru, Walter Driwe Dreu having held the manor from about 1220. The axis of the village runs roughly North-South and is less than half a mile long. The building materials are described as being predominately local rubble stone. The village could perhaps be described as having two parts, pivoting around the church and the vicarage. The southern part consists of Townsend Farm, with some other barns and cottages. There has also been some modern 'infill' development between this part and the church, severing the links this area had with the rest of the village.

Although Castle Combe has often been noted as one of England's prettiest villages, Littleton Drew's claim to fame is that it may be one of England's thankful villages (where all the men went to the Great War and returned safely). Whether that is true or not – there is no war memorial in the village. Worthy Daniels was a village butcher and so served in the Catering Corps away from service in the front line; I believe that Lucy (bringing up 4 boys) then also worked as a District Nurse. Between the wars his sister Minnie was postmistress at Castle Combe. In her twenties his sister Emily was a domestic servant in Bath before getting married to a cabinet maker to live in Bath.

Lucy Mortimer grew up in Acton Turville, Wiltshire. Her father died in 1882 when she was 2 and she did not get on with her stepfather (since 1889), Job Brown. She left home quite young and became a nurse in the London area, notably Horton near Epsom. Her younger sister Annie Mortimer (1882-1975 - she died in a retirement home in Bristol) in 1913 married Frederick Weston, a machinist from Swindon, and they went to live in Tottenham. Carole and I remember visiting my Great Aunt Annie there in 1969. Annie and Fred had a daughter Nancy who died young leaving 2 boys (albino twins).

My father Herbert went to stay with Fred and Annie for extended periods, almost as an adopted son, and it was in a swimming pool in Tottenham that he contracted Polio in 1926 and was hospitalised at Bath. It was the nursing skills of his mother Lucy that got him back on his feet. In 1929, at the age of 17, he went to the Derwent College for disabled adults in Oswestry founded in 1928 by Dame Agnes Hunt (generally recognised as the first orthopaedic nurse) where he learned the trade of surgical appliance mechanic.

My father, Herbert (Lucy and Worthy's third son), first started school at the early age of 3 in June 1916 according to the Littleton Drew School log – his younger brother Tom also started at the age of 3 in September 1917. In both cases it was probably due to having a working mother. Littleton Drew School closed in July 1926 and the pupils transferred to Grittleton School.

The photograph on this page shows Littleton Drew School about 1918. Seated on the ground are Cyril Daniels (second from left), Gilbert Daniels (next to Cyril - third left), Tom Daniels (third from right) and Herbert Daniels (far right).

Below is a picture of the schoolroom and school house at Littleton Drew as it is today. The adjoining house is where Tom and Dorothy Daniels lived.

The development of local motor transport services after the First World War hastened the closure of local village 'dame' schools like Littleton Drew which merged with Grittleton. Jim Flint (who I remember running coach services from his depot at the bottom of the village lane on the Burton Road) would put straw in his lorry, that might otherwise carry livestock to market, in order to ferry the children to school in the 1920s.

I well remember one of Jim Flint's Bedford coaches groaning up the village early in the morning in the 1950s when I went with my father at the weekend to stay at Ivy Cottage with my grandmother. I might then have awoken in the second bedroom of Ivy Cottage to gaze from the window at a carpet of bluebells in Old Lands Wood. I also remember the Beaufort hunt coming through the village and the hounds rampaging through the cottage gardens opposite. Later in the year I might have gone to see threshing outside Harry Salter's barn. According to the website of the Bristol Vintage Bus Group - in 1990 Flints Coaches were operating routes 74 Badminton - Acton Turville - Castle Combe – Chippenham and 76 Malmesbury - Sherston - Luckington - Badminton - Acton Turville - Bath. Here is a picture of Flint's coach depot at the bottom of the village in 1986.

Grittleton school records show that Herbert Daniels left school to go to Bath hospital for his polio in 1926 but was readmitted in January 1929 to catch up with his schooling before leaving in December 1929 to go to Oswestry. He later worked at Bath Orthopaedic Hospital (with a short period in Nottingham in the late 1940s) in due course part of the Royal United Hospital Bath where he ran the surgical appliance workshop.

At Oswestry he made friends with Dorothy Dawes and Jack - or John - Morris (who was later in hospital management at the Royal Free Hospital Hampstead). I got to know him and his wife Winifred, and younger son Malcolm, when I was at college at UCL and lived in Hamsptead at a hostel that Jack found for me. I have kept in contact with Malcolm and his wife Inger and in 2015 Carole and I visited them at their amazing home in Suffolk, with its astounding collection of objets d'art. Here are two pictures from Derwent College – my father on the right in the first one and in the centre, with Jack Morris on the left, in the second. The third photograph is of Miss Dorthy M Dawes from the 1960s. She lived at 119 Derby Road Nottingham with a Miss Lewis.

Of my father's 3 brothers my grandmother managed to pay for the eldest, Gilbert, to go to Grammar School. The next eldest Cyril was the first from the village school to secure by examination a free place at Chippenham Grammar School (and he was the last - since it closed soon after, with pupils transferred to Grittleton School). According to Littleton Drew School records, on 27th June 1924 they had been notified that Cyril Daniels had passed the second part of an examination for a free place at Chippenham. On 12th September 1924 Cyril Daniels left Littleton Drew School in order to attend Chippenham Grammar School. He had strong political and intellectual interests and wrote the, as yet unpublished, history of Littleton Drew mentioned above.

I am not sure what Gilbert did after school – I guess he was not very academic and for a village lad to hold his own at a grammar school must have been very daunting. By 1930 he had joined the Royal Navy (perhaps inspired by the naval experiences of his Uncle Daniel Herbert). Granny (Lucy) Daniels had, in Ivy Cottage, several souvenirs he had brought back from abroad – hollowed out coconuts, brazil nuts and blue pictures made from butterflies wings. Gilbert rose in the navy to Petty Officer - but acts of recklessness led to demotions too. He was torpedoed and shipwrecked twice in the war and only just survived. After the war he became a railway ganger – in charge of a track repair team. Here is a picture of Gilbert in the 1960s.

I am not sure when Gilbert's first son Richard (aka Arthur) was born. I understand that Gilbert and Vera were married after his birth. I think Richard stayed with his mother during the war, but his brother Ken was effectively evacuated to Littleton Drew for the war – I think Worthy and Lucy did not know about their first grandchild Richard until very late in the 1940s. Both Richard and Ken did well in the Plymouth Dockyard exams after leaving school. Richard worked at the Bristol College of Advanced Technology and then (as it became) Bath University, retiring as a Senior Lecturer – Cyril, who had worked at Westinghouse before and during the war, was also a senior lab technician at both establishments but he and Richard tended to avoid crossing paths. Richard married Lillian and they had 3 daughters.

Gilbert's second son Ken Daniels was born 21 August 1937 and he was enrolled at Grittleton School, Wiltshire, in September 1942 (according to school records). He left on 23 July 1948 for Chippenham Grammar School. So he spent a large part of his formative years living with his grandparents, Worthy and Lucy, at Ivy Cottage. Ken also visited his Great Aunt Minnie at Brook Cottage in Castle Combe. I recollect a photo of Ken with his head bandaged, after an escapade, in the garden of Brook Cottage – the last cottage on the west to the south of the village before the bridge. By all accounts his mother Vera was made a nervous wreck by the wartime bombings of Plymouth. I remember her in the late 1950s as a chain smoker.

In the 1960s after Vera's death Gilbert married Doris, the widow of a close friend. Ken married Jenny and he was a policeman in Plymouth for several years before going to South Africa to join the South African police (not to the taste of his communist and anti-apartheid Uncle Cyril). Ken and Jenny returned to the UK in the mid 1990s when Jenny became ill. After she died in 1997 Ken eventually returned to South Africa where his two sons were living. Ken died in South Africa in 2010 having recently married Eunice. I am pleased to say my Daniels cousins and I have kept in touch with his son Martyn and wife Karen since then and they joined us for a family gathering in 2013.

The Weddings of Cyril and Sylvia, Tom and Dorothy

Cyril Daniels married Sylvia Cheetham in 1934 and their daughter Maureen was born in 1935. In later years they moved from Chipenham to Fishponds, Bristol. Thomas Daniels married Dorothy Hawkins in 1937 and their sons were David (1939), Tony (1941) and Derek (1946). They lived at The School House, Littleton Drew (with the large adjoining redundant school room sometimes used for village socials). Tom was a baker by trade (though latterly a long distance lorry driver). Both were great cooks and teas there were particularly memorable (especially on Coronation Day when we were picked up by Tom and his Royal Enfield motorbike and sidecar to see the Coronation on a small TV screen). Dorothy kept fowl and grew vegetables in a largish kitchen garden between the Rectory and the Plough Inn (where Dorothy's laconic brother Frank had a regular place).

The Plough Inn is now sadly closed – it's just a house (see my adjoining picture of it in its heyday) and with that change of use a photograph that was in the bar may well have disappeared – it was from 1900 when they sold Duck Ales and I believe a great-great uncle Frank Porter was pictured as the landlord. Certainly my great-great grandmother Grace Chappell (maternal grandmother to my grandfather Worthy Daniels) was listed in the censuses of 1861, 1871 and 1881 as landlady of The Plough. Her daughter Hannah Chappell married Frank Porter, a butcher, in 1885 and she was landlady of The Plough in the 1901 and 1911 censuses.

As fully recounted elsewhere, my parents married in 1945 and initially lived at 12 Chestnut Grove, West Bridgford. I was born at Freshford Nursing Home near Bath in 1947, at the time my parents were living in Nottingham at 25 Portland Road and my father was working for the Cripples Guild. My brother was born in Nottingham in 1949 and in May 1950 my parents moved to Bath, and my father returned to work on surgical appliances at the Orthopaedic Hospital.

In the 1950s I started school at Weston St John's School – my boomer generation so increased the school intake that my friend Philip Russell and I began school in huts in Victoria Park, Bath (on the lower common where the swings and apparatus are now). We then moved to the Victorian structure opposite Turveys Stone Masons on the Lower Bristol Road.

Junior School was the brilliantly modern Newbridge Junior School. There we had many good teachers, including the 'kindertransport' refugee, Dietrich Hanff, who kept beehives on the school's orchard and who was a very creative teacher. His brief and incomplete biography published in 1995, 3 years after his death at the age of 72, was entitled 'Out of Nazi Germany'. In my last year year Miss Ponting (who taught my mother at Combe Down) was our form teacher (see the note above following my parents wedding in 1945). She was somewhat given to dozing off and Elizabeth Baxter (married name Previtt) often had to collect fish for her cat at lunctimes, from a shop at the top of Chelsea Road.

In the late 50s and early 60s I and my brother went to the grammar school (The City of Bath Boys School) and in mid-late 60s I studied for a degree in International Relations at University College London, under John Wear Burton, followed by a career in the civil service (the Departments of Trade, Industry, Transport and Communities and local Government covering trade issues, exports of mining machinery, imports of textiles, the India and Japan desks, aviation security, bus regulation, toll roads and policy on privately rented housing amongst other things). My brother studied PPE at New College Oxford and did a Masters in Town Planning at University College London, followed by a career in town planning in local government and private consultancy.

My father retired from the Orthopaedic Hospital workshop, of which he had been in charge, in December 1973. At the time his Aunt Annie was living with them. He died in 1990 and my mother in 1991 – they had lived to enjoy having 4 lovely grandchildren.

A SELECTION OF DANIELS FAMILY PICTURES

1898 Emma Daniels, mother   c1917 Cyril, Gilbert, Tom   c.1934 Cyril Daniels &
of Worthy, Minnie & Emily   (front) & Herbert (right)   parents Lucy & Worthy

John Roger &   Cyril Daniels 1960s   1971: Thomas, Herbert and Gilbert Daniels
Granny D 1951

Nancy, Lucy Worthy, Annie   Daniels Cousins gathering 2007
Bert & Ken (bandaged)

Weddings: 1971 John & Carole Long
1976 Roger & Sue Palin
2005 Louisa & Jason Bagshaw
2009 Neil & Shradha Adatia in Mumbai
2013 Roger's son Tom and Puja Ranawaya in Italy

<u>Also:</u> 2015 John & Carole's grand-daughters
Genevieve, Florence & Jane 2015 Carole & John

THE BECKINGSALES

The Family History

If Britain has been a nation of shopkeepers then the Beckingsale family of Cheltenham certainly played their part in that heritage with 5 or 6 shops under the family name at various times – had they pooled their resources they could have had a decent department store that might have rivalled Cavendish House! There is evidence that even those who emigrated to the antipodes opened shops there.

I have a press cutting from a Cheltenham paper of 1985 with a picture taken in 1935 of the Cheltenham men's outfitter's shop of A Beckingsale 111 High Street Cheltenham – one of the two hand-made shirt-makers in pre-war Cheltenham (for those who could afford it). They had a factory in Trinity Lane and the business was founded in 1864. It is clear that Thomas Beckingsale had established himself as a grocer by the 1830s in Cheltenham High Street as a **Gloucestershire Chronicle** report of Saturday 5 March 1836 relates to some meat stolen from Mr Thomas Beckingsale. The **Cheltenham Chronicle of** Thursday 2 April 1846 has a report of Mr John Beckingsale who was a grocer at 187 High Street. The **Cheltenham Chronicle** of Thursday 27 December 1849 has a report about butter stolen from Mr Thomas Beckingsale at 187 High Street by an elderly lady who had been a customer of some 20 years. For some reason the name used varies from Thomas to John and back again.

It is interesting to note that **The Cheltenham Annuaire for 1865** lists:
A Beckingsale Hosier 111 High Street
F Beckingsale Grocer 187 High Street
T Beckingsale Grocer 426 High Street
W Beckingsale Drapers 429 High Street *(but he is missing from the next entry)*

Four years later **The Cheltenham Annuaire for 1869** has on page 222:
A Beckingsale Hosier 111 High Street
F Beckingsale Grocer 187 High Street
T Beckingsale Grocer 426 High Street
Beckingsale & Taylor Drapers 368 High Street *(could this have been the same business as that of W Beckinsale in the previous entry?)*

From page iii of the 1869 Annuaire, it is clear that F Beckingsale was also one of the North Ward Commissioners under the Cheltenham Improvement of Health Act 1852 (for better paving, lighting etc.). On page vi he was also on the street and cemetery committees. **The Cheltenham Annuaire for 1873** has F Beckingsale as additionally on the Finance Committee.

Although the Beckingsales may have disappeared from Cheltenham High Street by the 1950s it is clear (from a BBC Gloucester history website article about Bishops Cleeve, Cheltenham in the 1940s by David Wilson) that Bishops Cleve had a grocers shop under the name of AR Beckingsale (there is a picture). David Wilson described it as the more upmarket of the two grocery shops in the village. Another website of historic Bishops Cleeve photographs shows that, trading as EM Beckingsale, the shop was still there in 1985.

The Beckingsales may not have left much of an indelible mark on Cheltenham High Street. However between the London Road and the lower High Street between St Paul's Street South and King Street is a passage called Normal Terrace. The street name **Normal Terrace** came into use sometime around 1874, but the lane was originally called *Beckingsale's Passage*. The old name lingered for a long time even after the new one was introduced. The southern entrance is through a shop which has for many years been Harding's electrical shop. On the other side there is still, in 2015, the remains of an old Beckingsale shop front (see the picture at the end of this section).

I remember seeing a family tree of the Beckingsale family that was once in my Aunt's Phyllis and Edna's possession but it does not seem that my brother and I had it passed on to us, so I have had to go to some lengths (many on-line searches) to recreate what is of interest to me. Initially I was not sure how our branch of the Beckingsales linked in to the owners of the various owners of shops and the shirt factory.

I began by noting that in the 1841 census there was listed a John Beckingsale (40) as a grocer with a wife Ruth (35) and a family of 4 children, namely Mary (15), Elizabeth (10), Richard (7), William (5) and Frederick (18 months). As suggested above in relation to the press reports I feel that John and Thomas Beckingsale may well have been the same person. The names and ages of the children accord with advice I have been given by genealogist Kate Beckingsale, with whom I have corresponded. The only child missing in this census is son Thomas (aged 8) – and there could be good reasons for this. This information is confirmed by another genealogist Ken Powis - the younger Thomas Beckingsale (1833-1869) was married to Elizabeth Comely (1830-1883) his Great, Great Aunt on his mother's side of the family. I am most obliged to those two genealogists for filling me in on the senior Thomas (John) Beckingsale (1800-1850) and his parents and siblings. Thomas senior presumably started the grocery business at 426, High Street Cheltenham, before handing it on to Thomas Junior.

Thomas Beckingsale Senior married 3 times. His first wife was Sarah Gibbs (1801-1829) and they had two children Mary (1825-1891) and Sarah who may well have perished in 1929 following her mother's death in child birth. Thomas Beckingsale Senior then married Rizpah Truby (1803-1835) – his sister Mary had married a John Truby. They had

4 children Elizabeth (1831-?), the aforementioned Thomas (1833-1869), followed by Richard (1834-?) and my ancestor William (1835-86) who in 1865 was (as noted above) a Drapers at 429 High St, Cheltenham.

Thomas Beckingsale Senior finally married Rizpah Truby's sister, Ruth (1805-1873). They had 5 more children: Edward, Frederick (1839-1917 who, as noted above, was in the 1860s a Grocer at 187 High Street, Cheltenham), Lucy, Albert (1842-1917) and Edwin (1846-1929). As noted above, Albert was in the 1860s a Hosier at 111 High Street, Cheltenham. He was also the father of the missionary Jennie Beckingsale (1872-1911) who died in China and whose two books ('Pomegranate – The Story of a Chinese Schoolgirl' and 'Children of Cathay; A Story of the China of To-Day') have surprisingly come back into print (print on demand).

In 1851 William Beckingsale (15), my ancestor, appears to have been an apprentice living in a draper's household at 135 High Street, Cheltenham as a drapers assistant. In 1861 aged 25 William was married to Ellen (33) and they were living at 430 High Street Cheltenham, with a family of 3 children: William Wood (3), Alice Jane (2) and Sidney (18 days). He was working as a draper with 2 assistants in Cheltenham; there appear to have beeen 2 servants living in the same house - Anne Stark (23) and Sarah Stark (20).

It is possible that his business in Cheltenham failed because, as noted above he was listed in the Cheltenham Annuaire for 1965 but not in the one of 1869. However in 1871 William Beckingsale (35) was re-married to Anne Dash (33) with his original family, now comprising 4 children. It is possible that the birth of the fourth child Ellen in 1862 had something to do with the death of his first wife Ellen around this time.

William, Anne and family were now living in Westgate Street, Gloucester but his occupation was still listed as Draper. It is interesting that the Gloucester Citizen of 26 September 1878 had an advert for a grocer Richard Beckingsale of 30 Westgate Street.

It is worth noting here that the young Ellen married Owen John Filer in 1884 (whose family allegedly had a paper doilies factory in Scotland). My mother often mentioned the Filers. In 1891 Owen and Ellen and their children Willaim (5), Ellen (3) and Owen R

(1) were living in Derby. Owen John Filer died in 1900 in Buton on Trent. So by the 1901 census Ellen Filer was a widow and living in Bristol at Park Place, Eastville with children William G (15 – born in Manchester), Ellen G (13 – born in Derbyshire), Owen L (11 – born in Derbyshire), Leonard Beckingsale Filer (7 – born in Burton on Trent) and Ewart L (2 – born in Burton on Trent). In 1911 the family were at 50 Raymond Road, Victoria Park, Bedminster Bristol. The family had certainly been on the move!

Leonard, born in 1893 married Jeanetts MW Hancock in 1919 and the family were living in Grimsby, Lincolnshire when in 1920 Kitty was born, followed by Ronald in 1922. I have a rather attractive family picture from about 1934, but I have not established the names of the younger children. In 1939 in Cleethorpes Lincolnshire, Kitty married George F Couzens and in 1946, also in Cleethorpes, Ronald married Margaret Hughson. It seems likely that he died in Surrey in 2001.

In the 1881 census William Beckingsale and Anne were living in Shaftesbury but now they had an entirely new young family of 4 children. They were Horace Beckingsale (8) born in Evesham, (Worcestershire), Edith Beckingsale (5), Lillian Beckingsale (4 - my grand-mother) born in Stratford on Avon (Worcestershire) and Hubert Beckingsale (2) born in Bath Somerset. His family also had been on the move!

In Loving Memory of

WILLIAM BECKINGSALE,

32, WEST STREET, BRISTOL,

(LATE OF CHELTENHAM,)

Who Died March the 26th, 1886,

AGED 50 YEARS.

Interred at Greenbank Cemetery, Bristol.

On 26 March 1886 William Beckingsale of 32 West Street, Bristol died at the age of 50 – perhaps worn out by a large family and frustrated ambitions! He was interred at the Greenbank Cemetary, Bristol. In the 1891 census Anne Beckingsale (53) was described as Wife (not widow) and as the head of household living on her own means. Horace Beckingsale (18) was at work (not clear what) and Edith Beckingsale (15) was a Draper. Lilian Beckingsale (14) is described as a Milliner and Hubert Beckingsale (12) was still at school.

They were living in Clifton, Bristol at what looks like Argyle House (there is an Argyle Place on this page of the census which exists in BS8 Clifton today). It is interesting that, at this time, Frank Pine (aged 14) and his family were living at 1 Gordon Terrace – I cannot trace a Gordon Terrace today but it is possible that, just as there is a Primrose Terrace in part of Gordon Road BS8 today, some of the houses in that road may have been named Gordon Terrace in 1891. Clearly Frank Pine and Lillian Beckingsale were living fairly near to each other in their teens and early twenties.

The story now moves on to 1901 when Frank and Lillian were married and living at 2 Pulteney Grove, Bath in the same house as their subsequent life-long friends, the Pinhorns (John and Marian and 11 month old daughter May Edith). At the same time we find that Horace Beckingsale (28) had also moved to Bath, to 42 Powlett Road, Bathwick – and Horace was described as an Ironmongers Assistant. He had been married since 1897 to a Paulina Winterhalder – born in Falmouth Cornwall). So in 1901 he was living with his wife Pauline (32) and a daughter Doreen (1) born in Bath. Annie Beckingsale (64) his Mother was living with them.

In 1911, at 42 Powlett Road, Bath, Horace Beckingsale (38 - described as 'Commercial Traveller Ironmongery') was living with his wife Pauline (42) and 2 daughters: Doreen (11) Daughter and Kathleen May Beckingsale (7) - born in Bath. Anne Beckingsale (73), his mother, was living with them.

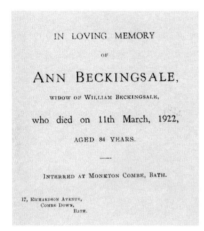

IN LOVING MEMORY

OF

ANN BECKINGSALE,

WIDOW OF WILLIAM BECKINGSALE,

who died on 11th March, 1922,

AGED 84 YEARS.

——

INTERRED AT MONKTON COMBE, BATH.

17, RICHARDSON AVENUE,
COMBE DOWN,
BATH.

Anne Beckingsale was living at 17 The Firs Combe Down when she died at the age of 84 in 1922 (according to a newspaper report). "The mourners were Mr Horace Beckingsale (son), Mr Hubert Beckingsale (son), Mrs F Fullman (daughter – i.e. Edith), Mr & Mrs FH Pine (son in law and daughter) Mr S Beckingsale (stepson – i.e. Sidney), Mr G Wiltshire, Frome (cousin), Mr Frank Wiltshire (cousin). Those unable to attend through illness were Mr E (Edwin?) Beckingsale, Cheltenham (brother-in-law), Mr WR Armstrong, Wootton Bassett (cousin), and Mr A Humphries, Wootton Bassett (cousin).

Floral tributes were sent from Mr & Mrs Horace Beckingsale (London), Mr and Mrs F Fullman (London), Mrs Filer and family (Bristol), grandchildren, Mr and Mrs F Wiltshire, Mr and Mrs EH Wherrett, Mr & Mrs FH Pine, Mr Hubert Beckingsale and Mr S Beckingsale."

Hubert Beckingsale was born 17 October 1878 in Bath. It does not appear that he ever married. At his death on 3 April 1940 he appears to have been living at 17 The Firs. He was 61 and Dr Hagenbach certified his death as due to cerebral thrombosis. His death certificate gave as the informant his brother in law Frank Pine and his occupation was given as an outfitters assistant. The newspaper report reproduced above recorded that Mr Hubert Beckingsale was the younger brother of the late Mr Horace Beckingsale, who was well known in Bath in connection with the Friendly Society Council and the Hearts of Oak Society. During the Great War he served in Mesopotamia, joining up the day after his experience of a raid on Hull (my brother has his First World War medals). For his last few years he was employed by Garlick's Ltd., men's outfitters, Castle Street, Bristol. I have two or three photographs of him from after the First War and in the 1930s.

I have also been pleased to have traced something of the life of my mother's Aunt Edith – Lilian's and Hubert's sister Edith A Beckingsale. She was born in 1875 in Stratford on Avon. In 1911 she was in the household of a Draper Henry Smith at 103 - 107 Mitcham Road Tooting, south-west London. She put her age down as 32 (not 36) and was one of 14 in that household who were the draper's assistants (living above the shop – as in the HG Wells' novel 'Kipps'). One of the others was a Frederick Fullman (33) whom she married that year. Here is a photo of Edith and Fred in about 1935.

Also I have reproduced below a photograph from the late 1930s that shows Hubert with Frank and Lilian and, I am sure, Edith, Fred and their daughter (who was called Kath). The newspaper report of 13 April 1940 on the death of Hubert notes that Edith and Fred sent floral tributes. Edith may also have attended Frank Pines funeral as I recollect an anecdote of my mother about being in Bath with her Aunt Edie when a German plane machine gunned the street (if there is any truth in that it would have occurred during the Bath blitz – say on the Monday).

In 1942, having regard to a letter from Lilian Pine about the Martha Castle estate (see the section below about the sad life of Anne Beckingsale), it appears that Edith and Fred were living In Mitcham Surrey at 182 Tamworth Lane, Tamworth Park. In 1941 Kathleen Jane Fullman (1913-1991) married Donald Drummond (1912-1989) and their son Colin was born in 1944, and was my Aunt Edna Pine's god-child. In 1966 he married Irene Barr and had children, but they subsequently separated. Edith appears to have died in 1957 and Fred in 1958. They lived south of London.

I am not entirely sure how life progressed for Horace Beckingsale prior to his death in Tooting in 1934. I suspect that Horace and Frank Pine were quite close – he witnessed the wedding of Frank and Lillian. From the Bath Chronicle of Thursday 22 February 1903 they were both present at the Hearts of Oak Benefit Society Second Annual Dinner. FH Pine and H Beckingsale were listed as members of the local committee and H Beckingsale proposed a toast. In 1911 for the Bath Branch Annual Dinner of the Hearts of Oak Friendly Society at Fortt's Restaurant Mr Beckingsale sent a telegram regretting his absence. At a Hearts of Oak outing in 1913 Frank Pine and H Beckingsale are listed in the party. My impression is that, with Edith and Fred already there, Horace and his wife naturally gravitated to the Tooting area of South London.

The Bath Chronicle and Herald of 3 March 1934 had an article headed **'Death of Horace Beckingsale - Former Secretary of Bath Friendly Societies Council'** It reported that "Many Bathonians will regret to learn of the death of Mr Horace Beckingsale, at Tooting, London SW at the age of 61. He was buried at Streatham on Tuesday. Mr Beckingsale was secretary of the Bath Friendly Societies Council in its early days, and a member of the Hearts of Oak. The extract from the local newspaper for Tooting reproduced here suggests that his death was sudden – following a church meeting. The newspaper report says that he was manager of Smith Brothers furnishing department in the Mitcham Road and that he had been with the company for 17 years (i.e. since about 1917).

Here is a picture of Horace and his wife Paulene (c.1932) with son in law Alec Warden (whose wife Doreen may have taken the picture) and daughter May Beckingsakle (far right). My brother and I got to know Horace's daughters Doreen (who married Alec Warden in 1929 and had a son John) and May.

They all lived in adjacent Edwardian maisonettes in a terrace in Tooting Bec. Doreen and Alec lived at 109 Mantilla Road - where Alec had a whole room of books - and May lived at 113 Mantilla Road. Doreen and May both died in 1986 and Alec passed on a year later.

Doreen and Alec's son John Warden (born 1934) married Winifred Glasscock (born 1934) in 1958 at Holy Trinity Church Tooting (which his grandfather had attended). Sadly John and his wife Winifred were not long-lived. She died in 2005 aged 70 and he died in 2009 aged 75. They were survived by their children David (born 1969) and Margaret (born 1972).

May Beckingsale (who had in the past had worked at Freeman Hardy and Wilis the shoe shop in Tooting) visited us at 25 Penshurst Way a couple of times and gave our son Neil a knitted toy Lamby that he treasured. They were my last links with my Beckingsale line.

I am grateful to my wife's cousin Gordon (David) Williams for the following photograph from October 2015 of what remains of a Beckingsale shop front at Normal Passage (formerly Beckingsale Passage) at 331 Cheltenham High Street (a different location from the Beckingsale High Street shops mentioned above).

The Census Data

1841 Census
Cheltenham St Mary's
John Beckingsale (40) Grocer – I am fairly convinced that he also went under the name of Thomas
Rula (Ruth?) Beckingsale (35) Wife
Mary Beckingsale (15)
Elizabeth Beckingsale (10)
Richard Beckingsale (7)
William Beckingsale (5)
Frederick Beckingsale (18 months)

1851 Census
Cheltenham - 135 High Street
William Beckingsale (15) – the census takers writing is difficult to decipher but he appears to be an apprentice living in a drapers household.

1861 Census
In the Civil Parish of Cheltenham, South Ward, Ecclesiastical parish of St Mary, House 430
William Beckingsale (25) Head - Draper with 2 assistants born Cheltenham Glos
Ellen Beckingsale (33) Wife - born Wooton Bassett, Wilts
William Wood Beckingsale (3) Son - born Cheltenham Glos
Alice Jane Beckingsale (2) Daughter - born Cheltenham Glos
Sidney Beckingsale (18 days) Son - born Cheltenham Glos
Anne Stark (23) Assistants Domestic - born Wooton Bassett
Sarah Stark (20) Assistants Domestic - Naunton

1871 Census
In the Civil Parish of Holy Trinity, City of Gloucester, Municipal West Ward, 24 Westgate Street
William Beckingsale (35) Head - Draper born Cheltenham Glos
Anne Beckingsale (33) Wife - born Wooton Bassett, Wilts
William W Beckingsale (13) Son - born Cheltenham Glos
Alice Jane Beckingsale (12) Daughter - born Cheltenham Glos
Sidney Beckingsale (10) Son - born Cheltenham Glos
Ellen Beckingsale (8) Daughter - born Cheltenham Glos
William H Corbett (19) - Drapers Assistant - born Worcester
Mary A Sterry (16) - Domestic Servant - born Longhope Glos

1881 Census
In the Civil Parish of St Peter, Municipal Borough of Shaftsbury, Angel Square
William Beckingsale (45) Head - Drapers Assistant born Cheltenham Glos
Anne Beckingsale (43) Wife - born Wooton Bassett, Wilts
Horace Beckingsale (8) Son - born Evesham, Worcestershire
Edith Beckingsale (5) Daughter - born Stratford on Avon, Worcestershire
Lillian Beckingsale (4) Daughter - born Stratford on Avon, Worcestershire (from 1900 she was Lilian, one middle l)
Hubert Beckingsale (2) Son - born Bath Somerset

1891 Census
Clifton, Bristol - Argyle (?) House
Anne Beckingsale (53) Wife Head of household living on own means - born Wooton Bassett, Wilts
Horace Beckingsale (18) Son (job indecipherable) - born Evesham, Worcestershire
Edith Beckingsale (15) Daughter Draper - born Stratford on Avon, Worcestershire
Lillian Beckingsale (14) Daughter Milliner - born Stratford on Avon, Worcestershire
Hubert Beckingsale (12) Son scholar - born Bath Somerset

1901 Census
Bath, Ward of Bathwick - 42 Powlett Road
Horace Beckingsale (28) Head Ironmongers Assistant - born Evesham, Worcestershire
Pauline Beckingsale (32) Wife - born Falmouth Cornwall
Doreen Beckingsale (1) Daughter - born Bath, Somerset
Annie Beckingsale (64) Mother - born Evesham, Worcestershire

1911 Census
Bath, Ward of Bathwick - 42 Powlett Road
Horace Beckingsale (38) Commercial Traveller Ironmongery - born Evesham, Worcestershire
Pauline Beckingsale (42) Wife - born Falmouth Cornwall
Doreen Beckingsale (11) Daughter - born Bath, Somerset
Kathleen May Beckingsale (7) Daughter - born Bath, Somerset
Annie Beckingsale (73) Mother - born Evesham, Worcestershire

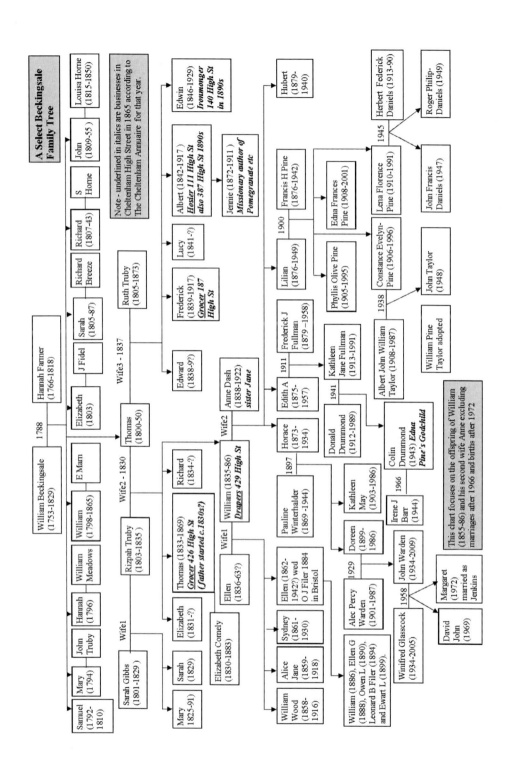

A Select Beckingsale Family Tree

Note - underlined in italics are businesses in Cheltenham High Street in 1865 according to The Cheltenham Annuaire for that year.

This chart focuses on the offspring of William (1855-86) and his second wife Anne excluding marriages after 1966 and births after 1972

William Beckingsale (1753-1829) — Hannah Farmer (1766-1818) — 1788

Samuel (1792-1810)
Mary (1794)
John Truby (1796)
Hannah (1796)
William Meadows
William (1798-1865)
E Mann
Elizabeth (1803)
J Fidel
Sarah (1805-87)
Richard Breeze
Richard (1807-43)
S Horne
John (1809-55)
Louisa Horne (1815-1850)

Thomas (1800-50)
Wife3 - 1837
Ruth Truby (1805-1873)
Wife2 - 1830
Rizpah Truby (1803-1835)
Wife1
Sarah Gibbs (1801-1829)

Mary (1825-91)
Sarah (1829)
Elizabeth (1831-?)
Thomas (1833-1869) *Grocer 426 High St (father started c.1830s?)*
Richard (1834-?)
Edward (1838-9?)
Frederick (1839-1917) *Grocer 187 High St*
Lucy (1841-?)
Albert (1842-1917) *Hosier 111 High St also 387 High St 1890s*
Edwin (1846-1929) *Ironmonger 140 High St in 1890s*
Jennie (1872-1911) *Missionary author of Pomegranate etc*
Hubert (1879-1940)

Elizabeth Cornely (1830-1883)
Ellen (1836-63?)
William (1835-86) *Drapers 429 High St*
Wife2
Anne Dash (1838-1922) *sister Jane*

William Wood (1858-1916)
Alice Jane (1859-1918)
Sydney (1861-1930)
Ellen (1862-1942?) wed O J Filer 1884 in Bristol
Pauline Winterhalder (1869-1944)
Horace (1873-1934)
Edith A (1875-1957)
Frederick J Fullman (1879 –1958)
Lilian (1876-1949)
Francis H Pine (1876-1942)

William (1886), Ellen G (1888), Owen L (1890), Leonard B Filer (1894) and Ewart L (1899).

1897
Kathleen May (1903-1986)
Doreen (1899-1986)
1929
Alec Percy Warden (1901-1987)
1911
Kathleen Jane Fullman (1913-1991)
Donald Drummond (1912-1989)
1941
Albert John William Taylor (1908-1987)
1938
Constance Evelyn-Pine (1906-1996)
1900
Phyllis Olive Pine (1905-1995)
Edna Frances Pine (1908-2001)
Lena Florence Pine (1910-1991)
1945
Herbert Federick Daniels (1913-90)

Winifred Glasscock (1934-2005)
John Warden (1934-2009)
1958
Colin Drummond (1943) *Edna Pine's Godchild*
Irene J Barr (1944)
1966
William Pine Taylor adopted
John Taylor (1948)
John Francis Daniels (1947)
Roger Philip-Daniels (1949)

Margaret (1972) married as Jenkins
David John (1969)

262

THE BECKINGSALES –FIRST TO LAST

<u>Left</u> c.1900 Anne Beckingsale (nee Dash) Hubert Beckingsale
c.1914 and mid 1920s (with Frank & Lilian Pine)
<u>Below</u> Late 1930s Hubert with Edna, Frank, Lena, Lilian & the
Fullman family: Fred & Edith (nee Beckingsale) & daughter Kath
In 1948 Phyllis, Edna, Doreen (nee Beckingsale) & Alec Warden
In 1978 Doreen Warden (nee Beckingsale), Lena Daniels,
Alec Warden, Louisa and Carole Daniels, May Beckingsale,
Herbert Daniels.

SHOPPING WITH THE BECKINGSALES IN CHELTENHAM

T. BECKINGSALE,

WHOLESALE AND RETAIL

Tea Dealer, Grocer,

BACON CURER AND CHEESE FACTOR,

426, HIGH STREET,

CHELTENHAM.

A. BECKINGSALE.

111, HIGH STREET,	387, HIGH STREET,
Opposite the Plough Hotel.	Plough Hotel Buildings.
INDIAN OUTFITS.	CAPS ... ... 1/- to 4/6
DRESS SHIRTS ... ... 3/6 to 6/6	BAGS and RUGS.
DRESS GLOVES ... ... 1/- to 2/6	DRESSING GOWNS 17/11 to 63/-
DRESS TIES ... ... 6½ to 5/6 doz.	DRESS & FANCY WAISTCOATS
DRESS COLLARS ... 6½ to 9/- doz.	
WINTER HOSIERY, &c.	HATS.

5 per cent. Discount for Cash.

F. BECKINGSALE & SON

Family Grocers, . .
Purveyors of High-class Provisions.

Established over 70 years.   Telephone No. 164

Manufacturers of the celebrated Royal Cheltenham Sausages.

Noted for Finest Quality York Hams.
Finest Smoked Wiltshire Bacon.

140, High St., CHELTENHAM.

ESTABLISHED 1864

A. BECKINGSALE,

—— SHIRT ——
MANUFACTURER,

HOSIER AND GLOVER.

OUTFITS FOR INDIA, THE COLONIES,
COLLEGES AND SCHOOLS.

" "

Cash Discount 5 per cent.   National Telephone, 406.

" "

III, HIGH ST., CHELTENHAM.
Opposite THE PLOUGH HOTEL.

METHYLATED SPIRIT.

E. BECKINGSALE,

140, HIGH STREET,
CHELTENHAM,

Ironmonger, Cutler,

OILMAN, TINMAN,
LOCKSMITH, BELLHANGER,
GAS FITTER,

&c.

PURE
DEVONSHIRE
CREAM
FROM
BECKINGSALE
140 HIGH STREET
CHELTENHAM

<u>A selection of Beckingsale Adverts</u> T Beckingsale (1859) at 426 High Street
F Beckingsale (1907) at 140 High Street, E Beckingsale (1890s) Ironmomger
A Beckingsale (1890s and 1907) the shirt-maker at 111 & 387 High Street.
Also EM Beckingsale (c1985) grocers at Bishops Cleeve.

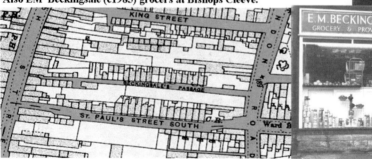

E.M.BECKINGSALE
GROCERY & PROVISIONS

A Map from the 1920s Showing what is now Normal Passage as Beckingsale Passage

ANNE BECKINGSALE (NEE DASH) – A SAD CASE STUDY OF DEPRIVED CHILDHOODS

There is much in the accounts of my mother's family, the Pines, to suggest that the middle class Victorian ideal of a close knit family that could offer their children a happy childhood was far from the norm for most people. Children could be deprived of one or both of their parents from an early age. They could be farmed out to grandparents, uncles and aunts (where there was support from an extended family) or even farmed out to strangers (as in the case of Frank Pine).

The life of my great grandmother Anne Beckingsale (nee Dash) is tinged with sadness in terms of her own childhood and the childhood she was able to afford her children. Conceivably her daughter Lilian had as difficult a background and upbringing as her husband Frank Pine.

Anne Dash was born in 1838. The next year her mother died - probably in childbirth of Edward who also died that year. In the same year her father died – he may have pre-deaceased her mother. Anne was 2, her bother Samuel was 6 and her sister Jane was 4. My cousin's wife Jill Taylor found the following record in the National Probate Index (original punctuation):

28 February 1866 Letters of Administration (with the Will annexed) of the personal estate and effects of Edward Dash late of Wootton Bassett in the county of Wiltshire Baker deceased who died 31 May 1839 at Wootton Bassett aforesaid left unadministered by Elizabeth Dash Widow the relict sole executrix and residuary legatee named in the said Will were granted at the Principal Registry to Samuel Dash of Brinkworth in the county aforesaid Tailor the administrator of the personal estate and effects of the said Eizabeth Dash he having been first sworn. Former Grant Prerogative Court of Canterbury August 1839. (Effects under £100)

So Edward and Anne died within a few months of each other in the same year and their son didn't secure his very modest inheritance until 1866.

In 1841, after her parents had died (following the death of baby Edward), Samuel, Jane and Anne lived with their grandmother Ann Dash in lodgings until she died in 1846. In 1851 Anne was living with her Aunt Anne Wiltshire's family, along with her aunt Mary

Aland. Where were Jane and Samuel? Well Samuel at 16 was living in Cricklade with a tailors' family, the Hopkins, as an apprentice. Jane may have been at boarding school at the time.

Anne Dash married William Beckingsale in 1865 (as his second wife) but he died in 1886 leaving a young family of Horace (13), Edith (11), Lilian (10), my grandmother, and Hubert (7).

I was drawn to looking into the linked fortunes of the Aland, Dash and Wiltshire families after seeing papers of Lilian Pine's concerning a solicitors' correspondence. This sought to trace the beneficiaries of the estate of a Martha Castle who died in 1937 – particularly the heirs of Samuel Dash who had died in America, presumably before 1900. The only other heirs were the Wiltshires, Lilian Pine and the daughters of Horace Beckingsale. The modest sums involved were not settled until 1946. Curiously I do have here a photo of Mary and Martha Castle (I suspect that William Castle also died prematurely).

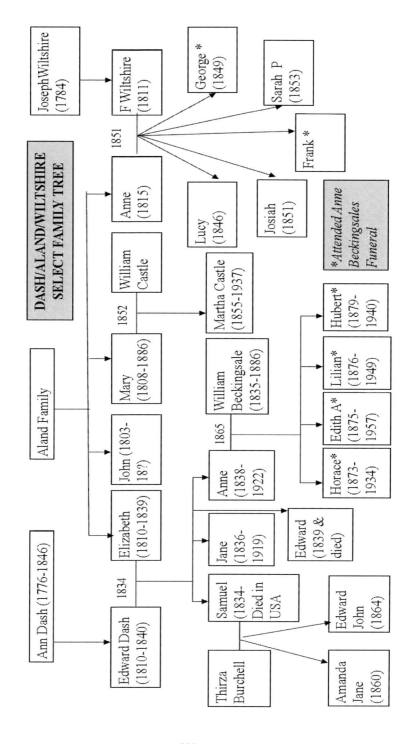

DASH/ALAND/WILTSHIRE SELECT FAMILY TREE

JosephWiltshire (1784)

F Wiltshire (1811)

1851

George * (1849)

Sarah P (1853)

Frank *

Anne (1815)

Lucy (1846)

Josiah (1851)

Attended Anne Beckingsales Funeral

William Castle

Martha Castle (1855-1937)

Aland Family

1852

Mary (1808-1886)

John (1803-18?)

William Beckingsale (1835-1886)

1865

Hubert* (1879-1940)

Lilian* (1876-1949)

Edith A * (1875-1957)

Horace* (1873-1934)

Anne (1838-1922)

Elizabeth (1810-1839)

Jane (1836-1919)

Edward (1839 & died)

Ann Dash (1776-1846)

Edward Dash (1810-1840)

1834

Samuel (1834-Died in USA)

Thirza Burchell

Edward John (1864)

Amanda Jane (1860)

267

EPILOGUE

As I pay a final tribute to my grandfather I have to say 'thank you Frank Pine for all that I have learned in my search for you'. I feel that I have got to know you rather well, even though you never lived long enough for us to be personally acquainted. You were quite a talented fellow and left behind a remarkable record – in terms of your leadership of a dairy, as an accountant, and as chairman of local authority, friendly society and hospital committees. You also left behind a far too small collection of your photographs and paintings. You were a leading light in the local horticultural society and many social activities. You also valued your military service in which you rapidly rose to Corporal – I remember seeing your army sword.

Through you I have discovered the significance of the development of the friendly and fraternal societies in the nineteenth century. They provided the basis for the modern trades' union movement and for schemes of insurance against ill health and unemployment, and for death benefits. State involvement went from legislation banning combinations of people pledged by secret oaths (but encouraging the insurance element) to the 1908 Pension Act and the 1911 National Insurance Act (which provided a role for the friendly societies), but with the reformed Poor Law proving a safety net of sorts.

I can see how Frank Pine and his Brothers in the Hearts of Oak, and in other friendly societies enjoyed regular sociable gatherings before and during the First World War. However in the 1920s they moved into wider activities through the Bath Council of Friendly Societies and the Bath Hospital Box Scheme. The same names keep popping up.

I have learned about the nature of the voluntary hospitals as charitable foundations for the treatment of ordinary people and the financial challenges they faced in the first half of the twentieth century. I have also seen how the Poor Law workhouses evolved into the municipal hospitals that achieved a sort of parity with the voluntary hospitals at the outset of the Second World War.

I am all too aware that, whilst Frank Pine played a key role in ensuring the financial survival of the RUH and its transfer to Combe Park, his success was in recruiting a great number of fingers for a dyke that was eventually burst by the pressures of the war. Also I have to say that I think he was wrong to think that the staff ethos of a self-less patient-centred care regime of the voluntary hospitals would not transfer into a state scheme.

In that regard my recent personal experience of elective knee surgery at the specialist Epsom Hospital unit was exemplary, not least in the care and skills of the staff. A night nurse spoke to me of her passionate belief in the NHS and mentioned the Danny Boyle tableau in the 2012 Olympics Opening Ceremony. Clearly for many of us pride in the NHS is part of our pride to be British. That it provides a service better than and cheaper than almost all other countries endorses the need for our politicians to support and fund its special ethos.

I can appreciate how new technologies and the rise of socialism impacted on the life of people in the twentieth century and posed new issues for those involved in local government. The Second World War so impacted on the lives of people in this country and ushered in such an era of social change that the achievements of the inter-war years, that pre-figured and laid the foundations for those changes, are too easily forgotten.

I have learned how geneaology is not just about following the numerous patriarchal branches of a family of a single name - inevitably one is drawn into looking at the equally numerous roots involving maternal roots and other family names. I am not just a Daniels, I am also a Mortimer or Chappell on my father's side. Maternally I am not just a Pine but a Beckingsale, a Dash or an Aland. Genetically I am even probably a Hampshire!

It is also interesting to reflect how in the mid to late nineteenth century the development of the railways led to the increasing mobility of working class people who travelled distances, unheard of in the previous century, in search of work. Whilst the Pine family spread from Ilfracombe in Devon to Clifton, Bristol and the Bromley area of East London, some of the Beckingsales were much more travelled.

If the places of the birth of their children is anything to go by, the census returns show William and Anne Beckingsale going from Cheltenham to Gloucester to Bath to Stratford on Avon, to Evesham, to Shaftsbury and finally, perhaps after his death, to Clifton, Bristol. William is commemorated in the churchyard at Monkton Combe, Bath. This probably occurred 56 years later when Anne was buried there – she had been living on Combe Down.

I have found out a great deal about the impact in the nineteenth century that poverty, ill-health (the early death of a parent or spouse) and labour mobility (through the growth of the railways) had in terms of family relocation and also dislocation – with very young children being farmed out to grandparents, other relatives or to complete strangers. I can also see how people aspired to a better life with better living conditions and more leisure activities in the first half of the twentieth century.

I have seen how those changes in the twentieth century were exemplified in the lives of my mother and her sisters. In particular I have discovered the full extent of the commitment of my mother and her sisters to amdram. I can identify with her decade or so with the Combe Down Old Scholars that was founded about 1927. For over 40 years I have been a member of Banstead and Nork Amateur Operatic Society that was also founded around this time. In the 1920s and 1930s many people had a little more leisure time than before to pursue a growing range of extra-curricular activities.

In studying the casts of Old Scholars' productions, and in reviewing the names of Frank Pine's fellow councillors on Monkton Combe (Combe Down) Parish Council, names that were often on the lips of my mother and her sisters have somewhat come to life. I have also learned much about my Great Uncle Robert Daniels and his family and the part he and his family played in the life of Combe Down - and above all the links between the Pines and the Daniels.

I conclude with a picture of the Beckingsale family grave at Monkton Combe Church. It commemorates William Beckingsale (died 26 March 1866 aged 50), and contains the remins of his wife Anne (died 11 March 1922 aged 84), Hubert Beckingsale (died 8 April 1940 aged 61). Lilian Pine (born 5.12.1876 died 29.9.1947) and Francis Harold Pine (died 24 April 1942 aged 65). Also there is Phyllis Olive Pine (born 3 March 1905, died 4 May 1995 aged 90) and Edna Pine (born 22 October 1908, died 10 December 2001 aged 93).

RIP FHP

The Pine Sisters c.1913   c.1921   c.1943 Lena as WAAF - Phyllis as?

Lillian Pine & John Daniels 1947 & c1952 Edna, Phyllis, May Pinhorn, Connie, Bert & Lena
Front Row: John Daniels, Bill Taylor, Roger Daniels and John Taylor

Edna & Phyllis- Cardiff Business
& Professional Women's event 1967

Bert & Lena Daniels, Connie & Albert Taylor
c.1971

271

APPENDIX 1 - FRIENDLY SOCIETIES AND HEALTH FACILITIES AND IN BATH - KEY PLAYERS 1900-1939

I had originally intended to do a list of names with their various roles - but it is not possible to provide anything like full biographical information from the highly selective press reports currently accessible. In the period covered only a limited number of the AGMs and elections of the organisations listed below are given in the press reports, and reporting on particular meetings does not often give an indication of committee members, or officers not present. So I have produced chronological material (extracted from the main text) under a few headings.

Further research into the minutes of the RUH Board (held at Bath Guildhall) would be interesting - not least of all to see the diminishing role of 'subscribers' (wealthy donors who could distribute largesse in terms of entitlements to treatment) who had a strong role in 1911, and the growing role of Friendly Societies in electing their nominees. For example in 1934 six people were elected by the Friendly Societies and nominated to represent them on the Board alongside the otherwise 'elected members'. These included Mr FH Pine (Bath), and the Hon Mrs Shaw Mellor (Wiltshire). I am not sure whether she later became an 'elected member' but by the end of the 1930s she was Chairman of the Board.

Although I have distinguished between the Executive Committee of the Friendly Societies' Scheme and the Mayor's Propaganda Committee, the two were intertwined. Indeed from the start the support of Mayor Chivers was crucial in galvanising support for the scheme in the various wards and districts. His successor was Aubrey Bateman (who described Chivers as 'Baths greatest Citizen within living memory') and his focus was increasingly on his Appeal Fund for the building of the new RUH at Combe Park. Both mayors were, in turn, Presidents of the scheme as well as Presidents of the hospital - indeed Bateman remained as RUH President from 1932 well into the 1940s.

It is interesting to see certain names carrying through from roles in individual Friendly Societies through to the Bath Council of Friendly Societies to the Executive Committee of the Box Scheme to the RUH Board: such as FH Pine, HC Lavington, AC Wills, HF Fiddes, Arthur S Gunstone, AH Lavington, G Haverfield and WA King.

Hearts Of Oak

22 February 1903
Members include FH Pine, H Beckingsale, HC Lavington, AC Wills and HF Fiddes

23 February 1911 and 2 March 1912
FH Pine is listed as one of the hon. auditors and HF Fiddes is assistant hon. secretary

18 July 1912
Outing includes FH Pine. H F Fiddes, W J Scudamore (Senior & Junior), AC Burrell

22 March 1917
Officers elected were: President, Mr W J Scudamore; Vice President, Mr F H Pine; Treasurer, Mr A W Wills; Secretaries, Messrs F Hamblin and H F Fiddes; Auditors, Messrs F H Pine and G Haverfield; Friendly Societies Council, Messrs F H Pine, G Haverfield, G Morris, W Davey, F Hamblin and H Fiddes etc.

26 February 1926
Bath Branch of the Hearts of Oak Benefit Society, Mr FH Pine presiding. Others present included Mr HF Fiddes (delegate), Messrs JB Jones, FG Owens, H Pickett, J Morris, H Bees, GL Wetmore, G Cambridge, F England, G Haverfield, and JT Franks. **FH Pine was elected chairman and delegate to the Friendly Societies Council, along with Messrs Fiddes, Jones, Haverfield and Wetmore.**

Bath Council of Friendly Societies

27 October 1923
The first Meeting of the Council of Friendly Societies following the launch of the scheme. FHP was in the chair, with FH Wayne (hon. secretary), Thomas Wills (Organising Secretary), Mr Walter Rawlinson (hon. treasurer) with 17 representatives of friendly societies (Shepherds, Hearts of Oak, Rationals, United Patriots and Foresters) including Brothers Arthur S Gunstone, AH Lavington and HF Fiddes.

16 February 1929
Frank Pine was re-elected as Chair of Bath Friendly Societies Council. Vice Chairman (Bro WA King), Treasurer (Bro HF Fiddes) and Secretary (Bro WH Chorley) were re-elected. Bro HC Lavington was re-elected as the council's representative on the RUH Board.

22 March 1930
FH Pine was re-elected as chairman of Bath Friendly Societies Council. Also re-elected were Mr WA King (Vice-chairman), Mr W Chorley (secretary), and Mr FD Fiddes (treasurer) - tributes were paid to Bro Gunstone (Rationals) for his dedication to the hospital scheme.

4 July 1931
FH Pine (Chairman) with Messrs Knight, Gunstone, King, Chorley, Fiddes, Coles, Horwood, Haverfield and Amesbury

19 October 1931
Visit to Mineral Water Hospital led by Frank Pine with Ancient Order of Foresters, Bros WF Amesbury and W Chorley, Hearts of Oak, Bros FH Pine and HF Fiddes, Rational Friendly Society, Bros. W Horwood and I Pollard, Ancient Shepherds, Bros. I Coles, I Orchard and WR Perkins.

Bath and District Friendly Societies' Scheme: Executive Committee

6 October 1923
The Executive Committee consisted of the Chairman of the Friendly Societies' Council (i.e. F H Pine), Chairman of the Hospital Management Board (i.e. Col Egbert Lewis), the Hon Secretary, the Hon Treasurer and Messrs AS Gunstone, GS Hodges, WA King and HC Lavington.

9 May 1925
The quarterly meeting of the scheme - the President (the Mayor) was unable to be present, and **Mr Frank H Pine (the Chairman of the Council)** presided. Others present included Messers Walter Rawlinson, (hon. treasurer), T Wills (organising secretary), GS Hodges, WA King and HC Lavington (members of the Executive Committee), JB Jones, W and H Chorley, G Wetmore, W Horwood, F Orchard, C Crewe, J Pollard, Councillor B Knight, Perkins, T Ricks, Ponfield, F Harding (members of the Friendly Societies Council)."

30 August 1930
At Corsham with Lord Methuen, Mayor of Bath (Aubrey Bateman), the Hon Mrs Shaw Mellor, Mr FG Hamilton (Chair RUH Board), **Mr FH Pine (Chair of the Box Scheme)**, Mr W Rawlinson (Treasurer of the Box Scheme)

15 August 1931
Peasdown: **FH Pine (Chairman of the Friendly Societies' Council)** and Mr FG Hamilton (Chairman of the RUH Management Board). Also present AS Gunstone, J Lawrence Mears (Sec & Superintendent RUH) Tom Wills (Secretary Box Scheme).

5 September 1931
FH Pine (Chair), HC Lavington, FG Hamilton, W Rawlinson, A Salter (Executive Committee)

4 June 1932
Mr FG Hamilton, chairman of the Management Board of the Royal United Hospital, to succeed Mr Pine as Scheme Chairman, Mr Rawlinson to continue to act as hon. treasurer. Messrs Amesbury, Bishop and White were to join the executive.

24 September 1932
Chairman of Scheme: Mr FG Hamilton (Bath RUH Chairman), Mr FH Pine (vice-chairman of the scheme), Mr W Rawlinson (Treasurer), Mr JW Wills (who had succeeded his father, the late Tom Wills, as organising secretary) Messrs GS Hodges, A Salter and W Amesbury (committee).

25 February 1933
FG Hamilton (Chairman), **FH Pine (Vice-Chairman)**, Mr W Rawlinson (hon. treasurer), Mr A Salter, Mr HC Lavington, Mr AG Gunstone, Mr G Hodges, Mr H Bishop, Mr WF Amesbury, Mr W White.

6 June 1933
Mr FG Hamilton (Chairman of the Scheme and until recently Chair now vice-Chair of the Hospital) Also present **Mr Frank H Pine** (vice-chairman of the scheme), Messrs HC Lavington, A Gunstone, H Bishop, W White (executive committee).

11 November 1933
The chair was taken by Mr FG Hamilton in absence of Mr W Rawlinson, supported by **Mr FH Pine** and Mr Wilfred Jenkins secretary of the scheme.

24 March 1934
Mr FG Hamilton (Chairman), **Mr FH Pine (Vice-Chairman)**, Mr W Rawlinson (hon. Treasurer) and Mr Wilfred J Jenkins (Organising Secretary).

19 May 1934
Mr RR Glynn-Jones OBE was to replace W Rawlinson as treasurer.

9 February 1935
AGM of Box Scheme: Of the 9 nominations for 7 seats on the Executive Committee the following were elected: Messrs H Bishop, WH Burgess, ET Billet, FJ Gale, Capt Smith, F Webb and W White.

1 May 1937
Mr FG Hamilton (chairman of the scheme) presided at the meeting, supported by **Mr FH Pine** (vice-chairman), Mr Wills, and Mr Wilfred Jenkins (organising secretary).

30 October 1937
Quarterly meeting at RUH with Mr FG Hamilton (chairman of the scheme), with **Mr FH Pine** (vice-chairman), Col RR Glynne-Jones (hon. treasurer), and Mr Wilfred Jenkins (organising secretary),

5 March 1938
Annual meeting - report signed on behalf of the executive by FG Hamilton (Chairman), FH Pine (Vice-Chairman), Mr RR Glynne-Jones (hon treasurer) and Wilfred J Jenkins (organising secretary).

29 October 1938
Mr FG Hamilton (chairman of the scheme), **Mr FH Pine** (vice-chairman of the scheme), Col RR Glynne-Jones (hon. treasurer), Mr Wilfred Jenkins (organising secretary),

Bath and District Friendly Societies' scheme: Mayor's Propaganda Committee

6 October 1923
Mayor of Bath Cedric Chivers (chairman). The other officers were Chairman of the Council, Mr FH Pine; hon. secretary, Mr FH Wayne; organising secretary Mr T Wills; hon. treasurer, Mr Walter Rawlinson, (Manager, National Provincial and Union Bank of England).....

3 November 1923
A packed mass meeting at the Guildhall, Banqueting Hall was presided over by Mayor Chivers, President of the Propaganda Committee, and a long list of those supporting him included the Mayoress (Madame Sarah Grand), Major H G James (Chairman of the Kent and Canterbury Hospital Propaganda Scheme), Canon TG Gardiner, Lt-Col Egbert Lewis (Chairman of the Hospital Management Committee), Messrs Forbes Fraser, C Curd, WP Edwards, WH Smith, WA King, A Salter, HH Sprouting, B John, FG Wardle (Hospital Committee), Sir Harry Hatt, Messrs **FH Pine (Chairman of Council)**, W Rawlinson (hon treasurer), AS Gunstone, GS Hodges and HC Lavington (executive committee), Thomas Wills (organising secretary) .....(plus another 30 names).

16 May 1925

The Mayor (Cedric Chivers) presided and with him on the special platform were the ex-Mayor Sir Percy Stothert (Chairman of the Hospital Board of Management) and Lady Stothert, **Mr FH Pine (Chairman of the Executive Committee of the propaganda scheme)**, Mr Walter Rawlinson (treasurer), Mr WA King (executive committee), and Mr T Wills (organising secretary). Others present included the ex-Mayoress (Miss Foxcroft), Lieut-Col Egbert Lewis (ex chairman), and other members of the Royal United Hospital Board of Management.

15 June 1929

Annual meeting of chairmen of all districts in the Guildhall the Mayor (Cllr Aubrey Bateman, ex-officio President of the RUH) presided over a very good attendance which included Lt-Col Egbert Lewis (Vice-Chairman of the Hospital Board), **Mr Frank H Pine (Chairman of the Friendly Societies Scheme)** and Mr Walter Rawlinson (hon. Treasurer and vice-chairman) with apologies from Mr B John (Chairman of the Hospital).

30 August 1930

At RUH, **FH Pine as chairman of the Executive**, presided. Also present were Mr HJ Hamilton (Chairman of the RUH Board), Lt-Col Lewis, Mr L Mears (Secretary of the RUH).

RUH Board

1923

Col Egbert Lewis was Chairman of the hospital - as he was in 1911.

4 March 1933

Aubrey Bateman was re-elected President of the RUH and - on the motion of Major CE Daley, seconded by Mr FH Pine - the following were elected as the elective members of the Board of Management for the ensuing year: Mr HJ Heston, Mr W King, Mr W Rawlinson, Mr FD Wardle, Mr E Ireland, Mr F Lace FRCS, Mr W Smith, Mr AL Fuller FRCS and Mr Douglas Hatt.

14 March 1934

To represent the scheme on the Board of Management of the RUH the following were elected: Mr H Lavington and **Mr FH Pine (Bath)**, Mr J Milburn and Mrs Newman (Somerset), and Mr Gale and the Hon Mrs Shaw Mellor (Wiltshire).

9 February 1935

AGM of Box Scheme: Mr Aubrey Bateman (President of the Hospital and Mayor of Bath), Mr RR Glynnne-Jones (treasurer), and Mr J Lawrence Mears (secretary and superintendent). The following were elected to the Hospital Management Board: Mrs Newman, Captain Smith, Mr FJ Gale, **Mr FH Pine**, Mr HS Lavington and Mr F Webb.

27 February 1937

As representatives from the scheme to the **RUH Board of Management** the following were re-elected: Mr HC Lavington, **Mr Pine** and Mr Webb for Bath; Mrs Newman for Somerset, and Mr Gale and Capt Smith for Wiltshire.

1 May 1937

Mr A Norman Wills, RUH's new Treasurer.

5 March 1938

AGM Box Scheme - There were seven nominations for six representatives from the Box Scheme Council to the RUH Board of management, and the following were elected by ballot: Messrs WH Burgess (Bradford on Avon); RJ Dyer (Box); HD Lavington (Executive); Mrs C Newman (Upper Weston); **Mr FH Pine** (Executive) and Mr F Webb (Bath).

29 October 1938

Reference to RUH chairman (the Hon. Mrs Shaw Mellor)

22 April 1939

Reference to RUH Board chairman (the Hon. Mrs Shaw Mellor)
President Aubrey Bateman re-elected (president since 1932)

APPENDIX 2 - EXTRACTS FROM BATH POST OFFICE DIRECTORY 1932

The following extracts are reproduced because of their relevance to the main text. Apart from listing the residents of The Firs, Combe Down, it illustrates the significance of the different hospitals and Friendly Societies in Bath in 1932. It also shows that FHP still had chairmanship roles in the Council of Friendly Societies and the Hearts of Oak.

<u>**OCCUPANTS OF THE FIRS, COMBE DOWN**</u>

1. England Capt. John Russell
2. Grist Miss Ada
3. Long Miss Lucy E.
4. Hardyman Miss M. N.
5. Kettlety F. W.
6. Eldred Miss Julia
7. Pearce Mrs.
8. Daniels Robert
9. Butcher George
10. Tinklin P. E.
11. Macfarlane James
12. Smith I.
13. Bird William, M.B.
14. Ball Mrs. A.
15. Clark Mrs. G.
16. Linscott William E.
17. Pine Frank Harold
18. Elliot Guy
19.
20. Martin Miss
21. Dolman James, Patch Miss, dressmaker
21a Pearce W. R., hairdresser

BATH HOSPITALS (part extract)

ROYAL MINERAL WATER HOSPITAL
Upper Borough Walls
Founded 1737   Incorporated 1739

President—Godfrey Lipscomb
Treasurers—Brig.-Gen. Molesworth, H. G. Sheldon and Col. Maule

For extending to the poor of the United Kingdom the benefits which the hot springs of the city afford in such cases as rheumatism. palsy, gout, arthritis, diseases of the skin etc. Accommodation is afforded for 156 patients (87 males and 69 females).

Application for admission, with name, age, occupation, and parish of the applicant, a brief history of the disease (comprising its origin, date and present symptoms, and mentioning the parts principally affected), particularly stating whether any other disorder exists, must be sent to the Registrar of the Hospital, who will supply the necessary forms.

BATH ROYAL UNITED HOSPITAL
Beau   Street

President—Aubrey C. Bateman, J.P
Chairman—F. G. Hamilton
Deputy Chairmen—W. Rawlinson and F. D. Wardle, J.P

Matron—Miss Sylvia Vian
Visiting Medical Officer—J. R. Bennett, M.B., Ch.B.
Chaplain—The Venerable the Archdeacon of Bath
Secretary Superintendent—J. Lawrence Mears
Bankers—National Provincial Bank (Ld.) (Old Bank Branch)
Auditors—Ham, Jackson & Brown

For the relief of the poor of the city and neighbourhood, and for giving immediate assistance in all accidents. It contains 140 beds, and includes a special ward for children. The hospital is entirely free, and no letter of recommendation is required, but patients are invited to contribute towards the cost of their maintenance. All patients seeking relief must attend at half-past ten in the morning, with the exception of casualties and urgent cases, which are admitted at any hour of the day or night.

Out-patients unable to attend the Hospital, and residing within the limits of the district delineated on a map kept at the Hospital, will be attended at home by the out-patients' medical officer upon forwarding a letter to the Secretary. No patient whose case may admit of equal relief as an out-patient will be admitted as an in-patient.

FORBES FRASER HOSPITAL
Evelyn Road, Newbridge Hill, Bath

Chairman—Lieut.-Col. Egbert Lewis, V.D., J.P.
Secretary—Harold J. Fricker
Matron—Miss S. A. Bathard

A private paying hospital in connection with the Royal United Hospital for patients of limited means. There are 72 beds (24 private rooms and 4 wards of 12 beds each). An inclusive charge is made for nursing, board residence, etc., but patients pay their own surgeons and medical attendants. Applications for admission to be sent to the Secretary, from whom further particulars as to fees, etc., can be obtained.

BATH & WESSEX CHILDREN'S ORTHOPAEDIC HOSPITAL
Combe Park, Bath

Chairman—Mrs. Francis Mallett
Secretary—Harold J. Fricker
Matron—Miss B. J. D. Reid

An open-air Hospital of 90 beds for the treatment of children under the age of 16 years, suffering from tubercular disease of bones or joints, deformity or paralysis.

BATH HOMEOPATHIC HOSPITAL
4, Green Park

Medical Officer—F. Wells Seville, L.R.C.P., M.R.C.S
Hon. Dental Surgeon—D. Y. Hylton, L.D.S.R.C.S
Chemist—A. R. Neave, 33, Gay Street
Bankers—Westminster Bank (Ld.)

Established to afford relief to the sick poor of the city. Admission by payment. Out-patients are treated on payment of one shilling a fortnight. Urgent and necessitous cases free. Attendance Tuesdays, Thursdays, and Saturdays, at 9 a.m.

LANSDOWN HOSPITAL AND NURSING HOME
Lansdown Grove

Physician—F. Wells Beville, L.R.C.P., M.R.C.S.
Chaplain—Rev. G. L. Fitzmaurice, M.A.
Lady Supt.—Miss E. M. Humpherys.

Founded under the Jennings trust to provide skilled nursing and accommodation for all classes
It is entirely self-supporting, but contributions are accepted to its Benevolent Fund, which is applied to the service of poor patients seeking admission, thus aiding the charitable work of the Hospital.
Application for admission should be addressed to the Lady Superintendent. Cases of mental or infectious disease are not admitted.

BATH EAR, NOSE AND THROAT HOSPITAL.
Marlborough Buildings Established 1837

President—Rev. F. E. Murphy', M.A
Vice-President—Admiral Sir Richard Pierse, K.C.B., K.B.E., M.V.O
Hon. Surgeon—H. Norman Barnett, F.R.C.S. Hon
Radiographer—J. Forgan Grant, O.B.E., M.B., Ch.B., D.M.R.E
Hon. Anaesthetist—T. J. Cotter Craig, M.B., Ch.B. Hon
Pathologist—Alister Sutherland, M.B., Ch.B. (Edin.)
Hon. Registrar—William Love, M.B., Ch.B
Hon. Dental Surgeon—C. Murray-Shirreff, L.D.S.R.C.S. (Eng.)
Hon. Advisory General Physician—T. Wilson-Smith, M.D., M.R.C.P
Hon. Chaplain—Rev. Preb. F. E Murphy, M.A. Hon.
Treasurer—Arthur Francis, 37, Bathwick Hill
Hon. Secretary—F. M. Millard, 19, Camden Crescent
Matron—Miss Magill. Bankers—Midland Bank Limited (Metropolitan Branch), Old Bond street

The Hospital contains 52 beds. There is a paying department consisting of 20 beds in private and special public wards. Patients who occupy the free beds are expected to contribute towards the expense of their maintenance, unless they are unable to do so.

BENEFIT SOCIETIES (mainly extracts)

REGISTERED FRIENDLY SOCIETIES' COUNCIL.
President—F. H. Pine, Hearts of Oak.
Vice-President—W. A. King, Foresters
Treasurer—H. Fiddes, Hearts of Oak
Secretary—Wm. Chorley, 25, South View Road

ANCIENT ORDER OF FORESTERS.
Bath district
Established 1846 ; 18 Courts ; 2,016 Members

INDEPENDENT ORDER OF FORESTERS.
Founded 1874. Incorporated by Special Act of Parliament (Canada), 54, Vic. Chap., 104, Amended 59 Vic. Chap. 158.
Court Prince Bladud of Bath, 2,066.

UNITED PATRIOT'S NATIONAL BENEFIT SOCIETY
With Profit Sharing and National Health Insurance Sections

INDEPENDENT ORDER OF ODDFELLOWS
Manchester Unity.
10 Lodges comprising the Bath and Wells District. Established 1829
Gross Number of Members 3,252

LOYAL ORDER OF ANCIENT SHEPHERDS.
Ashton Unity
Established 1826
Secretary J. Coles, 13, Prospect place, Camden Road

HEARTS OF OAK BENEFIT SOCIETY
National Federation.

Bath Branch.
President—F. H. Pine.
Vice-President—J. E. Lanham.
Local Delegate—H. F. Fiddes
Treasurer—J. Haverfield
Hon. Secretary—J. S. Lang
Local Agent—H. F. Fiddes (junr.)

RATIONAL FRIENDLY SOCIETY ASSOCIATION.
(Approved under the National Insurance Act 1911 No. 138)

NATIONAL DEPOSIT FRIENDLY SOCIETY (APPROVED)
Established 1868
Bath District

PIONEER SICK BENEFIT AND PROVIDENT SOCIETY.
Bath Branch Secretary—W. A. Bishop, 11, Clarence Street

WILTSHIRE WORKING MEN'S CONSERVATIVE BENEFIT SOCIETY

WILTSHIRE FRIENDLY SOCIETY
Bath Branch Branch Steward—E. E. Pink, Cravenhurst, Prior Park Road

AFFILIATED SOCIETIES.

Ancient Order of Foresters.

Hearts of Oak Benefit Society.

Independent Order of Odd Fellows, Manchester Unity.

United Patriots' National Benefit Society.

Loyal Order of Ancient Shepherds.

Rational Association Friendly Society.

International Order of Good Templars.

Independent Order of Rechabites.

Bristol, West of England and South Wales Operatives' Trade & Provident Society.

West of England Temperance Friendly Society.

The Bath & District Friendly Societies' Propaganda Scheme to Assist the Funds of The Bath Royal United Hospital.

Tel. 377.

Central Offices:
9, KINGSTON BUILDINGS,
BATH
MR THOMAS WILLS,
Organizing Secretary.

The Bath & District Friendly Societies'
Propaganda Scheme to assist the Funds of
The Bath Royal United Hospital.

MOTTO

The Hospital is now in Urgent Need of Funds. It Requires your Help to keep its Doors Open.
1. The scheme aims at collecting annually for the Hospital, the sum of Five Thousand Pounds.
2. The scheme, to accomplish its objects, asks Twelve Thousand of the Inhabitants within the Hospital Area to contribute Twopence per week which would amount to Five Thousand, Two Hundred Pounds.

GENERAL

3. The Machinery for working the Scheme, shall be set up and put in motion in conjunction with, and approval of the Managing Board of the Hospital.
4. The scheme shall be under the control of the Bath and District Friendly Societies' Council (hereinafter referred to as the Council.)
5. All general work in connection with working the machinery shall be voluntary.

6. It shall be called the Bath and District Friendly Societies' Hospital Propaganda Scheme.
7. The Augmenting machine shall be known as The Bath and District Friendly Societies' Household Collecting Box Scheme.
8. The Council shall set up and work the scheme independently of the Hospital Managing Board, having its own Offices and Administration.

THE COUNCIL

9. The Council shall be the Central body to receive reports, to consider and resolve on all matters connected with the scheme and for this purpose may co-opt one representative to be nominated by each District Committee.
10. The Council shall appoint a Central Executive and delegate to them powers to co-opt other bodies, and transact such other business as may be remitted to them for the successful working of the scheme.
11. The Council may at a subsequent period (if found necessary for the successful development of the scheme) appoint a paid organizing and Clerical Staff.
12. No paid staff appointment shall be made, or duties commenced without first having been considered by the Council's Executive and approved for recommendation to the Council for adoption.
13. The Council shall at least once every quarter submit to the Hospital Managing Board a report of the results of the collections and general working of the scheme.

THE EXECUTIVE

14. A Central Executive shall be set up, and consist of five members appointed by the Council, together with the Hon. Treasurer, the Hon. Secretary, and the Chairman of the Hospital Managing Board.
15. They shall act on behalf of the Council in calling Public Meetings at the centre or in Districts to explain the Scheme.
16. They shall set up and organize the General working of the scheme under the directions and approval of the Council.
17. They may divide up the City and Villages within the Hospital area into sections and set up District Committees, and co-operate with them in working the scheme within the several areas.
18. They shall transact and put into operation any business that may be remitted to them by the Council.
19. They shall submit to the Council a quarterly report on the results of the collections, and the general working of the scheme.

BATH & DISTRICT COMMITTEES

20. District Committees when set up, shall act in conjunction with the Central Executive in operating the Scheme within their Area.
21. They may set up their own administration with delegated powers and appoint their own Chairman, Secretary and Stewards.
22. They shall co-operate with the Central Executive in organizing the District within their Area.
23. If the District Committee at a subsequent period find it necessary and advantageous to the working of the district, they may sub divide the District and organize on the same lines as their own district.

STEWARDS

24. The District Stewards will be allotted a certain number of houses within their district, and be responsible for the registration of the boxes and the collection of the money quarterly at the householder's residence.
25. The Method is, the Steward or Stewardess will first call on each householder within his Area with a circular letter which will explain the scheme.
26. That following the letter the Steward or Stewardess will make a personal call and canvass the householder to take a box.
27. To Solicit the Householder, and obtain a promise to place the Box on the Breakfast Table each Sunday morning and to contribute therein not less than Twopence a week.
28. During the first weeks of the months of March, June, September and December, to call on the householder and in his or her presence (or that of his or her representative) open the Box, count the contents, enter the amount, and sign the form on Box.
29. The Stewards will be provided with a book, in which all monies are to be entered.
30. The Steward will take the money collected to the District Secretary who will transmit it to the Treasurer.

HOSPITAL

31. The Secretary of the Hospital Board shall send a weekly list of patients treated at the Hospital within the Hospital Area to the Organizing Secretary.
32. The Organizing Secretary in turn shall send a list to the Secretaries of the Districts of the names of Patients treated within their Area.
33. If it is found that the Patient or Patients are not Box Holders the District Secretary shall inform the Stewards within his Area, who will call on the Patient and solicit him or her to take a Box.

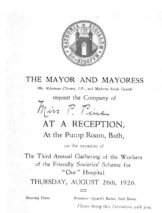

NOTES ON THE SCHEME BOOKLET

The booklet setting out the rules of the box scheme (the contents of which are reproduced above) was undoubtedly published at the scheme's inception in the second half of 1923. In principle voluntary hospitals were charitable undertakings, free at point of use. In practice, before the Great War, major donors could issue tickets of entitlement to treatment. The box scheme effectively evolved into an insurance-type scheme offering an increasing range of benefits or entitlements. This can be seen in the newspaper reports of 23 February and 6 June 1933 when the range of benefits was increased on the basis of a 3d weekly contribution. On 1 September 1934 the newspaper reported on the new Forbes Fraser Scheme that provided for full private hospital treatment with no £6 income limit but with the payment of 1 Guinea a year.

NOTES ON THE 1926 RECEPTION

The reception invitation reproduced above shows that the old friendly society ways of mixing business with pleasure continued. The Mayor, Cedric Chivers, was a strong supporter of the scheme from its inception until his death. Lord Methuen, who spoke at the above reception on 26 August 1926, was clearly much involved in the early promotion of the box scheme. Newspaper reports of 9 June 1928 and 30 August 1930 show him taking a lead in 2 meetings in his home base of Corsham.

APPENDIX 4 - EXTRACTS FROM PUBLISHED ACCOUNTS OF THE BOX SCHEME

Values in £ sterling

Year	RUH Deficit		SCHEME RECEIPTS - CUMULATIVE			SCHEME RECEIPTS FOR THE YEAR					
	Year	Cum	Total Collections	To RUH	Cottage Hosp	Year Total	To RUH in Year	To Cot Hosp	Year in Bath	Year in Somerset	Year in Wilts
1911	1,948	3,649									
1922	4,000	10,383									
1924						4,900					
1925											
1926						5,985					
1927			21,670	19,900	1,770	6,563	4,800	1,031			
1928						5,821	4,300	979	2,345	709	2,731
1929											
1930			33,999	32,100	3,958	5,028	4,000		2,213	682	2,132
1931			44,000	36,100	4,700	5,099	4,000		2,226	800	2,012
1932						5,069	3,900		2,292	957	1,790
1933				44,000		5,636	4,000	624	3,143	1,148	1,344
1934						7,000	5,300	713	3,983	1,478	1,538
1935											
1936						9,000	7,000	1,360	5,306	1,787	2,264
1937						10,489	7,800		6,044	1,921	2,523
1938						12,807	8,800	2,872	7,085	2,149	3,572
1939											
1940	1,928		135,700	96,900							
1941											
1942											
1943											
1944											
1945											
1946	52,401					11,000					

The figures for 1940 are from Mr Lavington's publication on the Box Scheme as reported in the press. The figure for 1946 shows the RUH facing a very large deficit to hand on to the NHS. The steady growth in income of the box scheme 1924-28 ended with the recession - but economic recovery 1934-39 showed a huge growth in its income.

APPENDIX 5 - HOSPITALS IN BATH – A SHORT HISTORY

Early Hospitals

Hospitals were originally based on religious communities. After the dissolution of the monasteries in 1540 by King Henry VIII the church abruptly ceased to be the supporter of hospitals, and only by direct petition from the citizens of London, were the hospitals St Bartholomew's, St Thomas's and St Mary of Bethlehem's (Bedlam) endowed directly by the crown; this was the first instance of secular support being provided for medical institutions.

Although some voluntary hospitals, like London's St Bartholomew's ('Barts'), could claim a medieval origin, it was in the mid-eighteenth century that the major foundations began. Early examples from the 1710s to 1730s include Guys and the Westminster in London, the Edinburgh Royal Infirmary in Scotland, and in the provincial cities Cambridge's Addenbrookes and the Bristol Royal Infirmary.

Early hospitals in Bath (St John's dating from the twelfth century, St Catherine's founded in 1522 and Bellot's Hospital founded in 1609) provided some medical and nursing care but were essentially almshouses for the elderly and impoverished. Before the growth of Bath (through wealthy visitors from the mid eighteenth century) the population of about 2,000 was too small to support a hospital.

The Royal Mineral Water Hospital

In 1597 an Act of Parliament received the Royal Assent. It gave a right to the free use of the baths of Bath to the "diseased and impotent poor of England". This caused the city to be inundated with beggars and, in 1714, the Act was repealed - but the beggarly stream still continued to flow. In order to control this problem but still offer support to those genuinely in need, the establishment of a Hospital for their reception was mooted. A public subscription was opened in 1723 and King George II was one of the first subscribers, giving £200 (worth £30,000 in 2015 values).

In 1738, John Wood produced completed designs for a General Hospital to be erected on the site of a theatre. Beau Nash was requested to take them to London for the inspection of the King and the Royal Family. Ralph Allen offered a free supply of Bath stone to build the Hospital. The inventor of the Bath Oliver Biscuit that is still sold in Waitrose - Dr William Oliver - was one of the founding physicians at the hospital. The Bath General Infirmary founded in 1737 and incorporated in 1739 was also known as **The Mineral Water Hospital**. Queen Victoria conferred the 'Royal' title in 1888.

In 1978, the hospital was the third from last of the English hydropathic hospitals to cease offering hydropathy. In 1993, it became an NHS Foundation Trust, specialising in Rheumatic Disease and Rehabilitation. It was announced in January 2015 that the Royal National Hospital for Rheumatic Diseases NHS Foundation Trust would be taken over by Royal United Hospital Bath NHS Foundation Trust, after financial debts had built up towards £2 million.

The Royal United Hospital

For much of this annex I have referred to Kate Clarke's excellent book, 'The Royal United Hospital – A Social history 1747-1947'. She records that Bath's first general hospital, the Bath General Infirmary or Royal Mineral Water Hospital (now the Royal National Hospital for Rheumatic Diseases) was originally only open to visitors from outside the city. So in 1747 the Bath Pauper Trust was founded to raise money for people needing medical advice and assistance. They based their services in a 'Dispensary' in Wood Street which later moved to Lower Borough Walls and became known as the Bath City Infirmary and Dispensary. By the end of the 18th Century the Infirmary was treating around 1,500 out-patients and 120 in-patients a year.

The scale of Bath's building boom created a heavy demand for an accident and emergency service, and in 1788 a new casualty hospital opened in Kingsmead Street, creating healthy competition between itself and the Infirmary. However, these two small hospitals were deemed inefficient and costly and plans were made for a merger. This new combined institution, sited between Lower Borough Walls and what is now Beau Street, was named the Bath United Hospital and opened in 1826. With growing demand for its services the building of an additional wing commenced in 1864. It was named the Albert Wing - after the recently deceased Prince Consort. This prompted Queen Victoria to bestow the title 'Royal' upon the hospital, and for the first time it became known as the Royal United Hospital.

Other Bath Hospitals

In 1880 the Municipal Fever Hospital opened on Claverton. In 1916 the Bath War Hospital was established at Combe Park Bath. It closed in 1929 but many of its huts were used for nurses' accommodation in the 1930s. In 1920 the RUH bought adjoining land at Combe Park with a view to re-locating part of the hospital there, as the premises at Beau Street were becoming cramped. In 1924 RUH Services were expanded with the opening of the Forbes Fraser RUH Private Hospital and the Bath and Wessex Orthopaedic Hospital for Children. By 1925 it was clear that the whole hospital needed to relocate. In 1931 the Beau Street premises were sold to Bath Corporation for use by the technical college and in 1932 the RUH moved to Combe Park.

During the 1920s and 1930s the former Bath Work House on Combe Down (built in 1836-8 by the Bath Poor Law Union) - St Martin's Hospital - evolved into a municipal hospital. In the Second World War it became an Emergency Medical Services Hospital and became a fully fledged hospital under the NHS. It was where the singer Eddie Cochran died in 1960. Between 1942 and 1945 there was an American military hospital on part of the RUH site – this later became the Manor Hospital. In 1947 all voluntary and municipal hospitals transferred to the NHS.

One other hospital in Bath, mentioned in the Bath Post Office Directory of 1932 and that is now part of the Royal United Hospital Bath NHS Foundation Trust, is the Bath Ear, Nose and Throat Hospital that was established in 1837. In 1959 the Ear Nose and Throat Hospital in Marlborough Buildings closed and transferred to the RUH. The Bath Eye Infirmary in Lansdown (that was established in 1811) followed suit in 1973.

Financing the RUH

Throughout its history the RUH had been dependent on charity and fund raising activities. In its early years most of the money for maintaining the RUH came from wealthy residents of the city whose annual subscriptions entitled them to vote in public elections for the doctors who worked at the hospital. Every year these subscribers were also allocated 'tickets of relief' according to how much they had contributed, and they would in turn hand these out to those they considered most in need of treatment. This ticket system lasted until 1905 when it was decided that admission should be authorised by doctors instead.

This alienated some subscribers who felt that they were losing the privilege of bestowing their charity (and their power) on poorer people. So it was decided that, though patients would be admitted in future at the discretion of hospital authorities, subscribers of five shillings upwards could still send letters of recommendation if they really wanted to.

However, at this point the type of subscriber had changed. In the first part of the 1800s there had been large donations from churches, from collecting boxes in all the fashionable meeting places, and also from many titled people, but income tax and the introduction of death duties reduced the number of wealthy residents and the amounts of cash given. By 1900 a large proportion of the funding came instead from pubs, from various local businesses, and from working men's associations.

During the Edwardian period there was regular concern about the annual deficits incurred by the RUH and by the mid 1920s something had to be done – which is where the Bath Council of Friendly Societies stepped in. Even with the box scheme the right to treatment – especially for those too poor to contribute to it – was still a muddy issue. In principle (as the Bath Post Office Guide of 1932 stated) the RUH existed "For the relief of the poor of the city and neighbourhood and for giving immediate assistance in all accidents". In principle the hospital was entirely free, and no letter of recommendation was required, but patients were invited to contribute towards the cost of their maintenance.

Many people in the 1930s thought that patients who made contributions received favourable treatment – and clearly that was the expectation of those who contributed to the hospital box scheme. The voluntary hospital system was effectively brought to its knees by the war – with its influx of patients from other areas (evacuees and military personnel) and the casualties of bombing. Government policy was that voluntary and municipal hospitals should be regarded as being on equal footing – so, despite complaints, box scheme members could be sent to St Martins for treatment. The box scheme held up well during the war but with other donantions drying up, and the cost of pharmaceuticals and other medical equipment escalating, the RUH ended up in 1947 with a huge debt – despite wartime appeals by Aubrey Bateman to the government for more funds (that were not always met).

APPENDIX 6 - COMBE DOWN - A SHORT HISTORY

Combe Down is a village (something of a dormitory) suburb of Bath with a population of 5,500 (having grown from about 2,400 in 1901) and is part of the Bath and North East Somerset unitary authority. Combe Down sits on a ridge above Bath approximately 1.5 miles to the south of the city centre, south of woodland overlooking the city. In Old English "Combe" is a word meaning a steep-sided valley and Down comes from the Old English meaning 'off the hill'.

Combe Down owes its existence to its proximity to Bath and in particular to the oolitic limestone (Bath Stone) that has been quarried there since Roman times. The Romans built their baths and temples in Acqua Sulis, as they called Bath, from this stone. After the Romans left Britain in 410 AD the stone was little used until the eighteenth century. The stone was then quarried by the room and pillar method (leaving pillars of stone to support the roof).

Combe Down village sits above an area of redundant 18th and 19th century stone quarries developed by Ralph Allen in the 1720s when Bath was beginning to be established as a resort. The village was founded by Ralph Allen in 1729 when De Montfort Place was built to house some of his quarry workers. Other quarry workers lived in a unique area of Willamstowe and its network of drungs (narrow pedestrian alleys enclosed by stone walls). Ralph Allen built a gravity powered cable railway down what is now Ralph Allens Drive to bring the stone down into the city from the mines. Just off Ralph Allens Drive is the National Trust managed Prior Park, the home that he built from 1738 to show off Bath Stone.

Unfortunately Bath Stone does not weather well when exposed to air and water (especially with strong winds - as experienced with the Combe Down War Memorial inscriptions in the 1920s – see my main narrative). Almost all the mines were closed in the nineteenth century when more accessible stone came from the Box area. However, building continued above ground, with some roads and houses eventually resting on only a thin crust - in places between only one and two metres deep - above large underground cavities with inadequate support.

Towards the end of the twentieth century there was an effort to map the old mines and to remedy the risks of erosion to the supporting pillars from air and water (there was a large pillar under 17 The Firs). Consequently the quarries were fully in-filled and stabilised during a central government-funded project which took place between 2005 and 2010.

From 1940 to 2011 the Admiralty (later part of the Ministry of Defence) had a 46 acre site at Foxhill on the Bradford Road. In 2013 site was sold to develop 700 new homes, open spaces and community facilities to be called Mulberry Park. A large former council estate also exists in this area.

A large public open space (The Firs Field) is the location for the village war memorial, a scout hut and a children's play area. Three parcels of land make up the Firs Field open space, two of which are under the control of the local Council. The deeds state that the Firs Field is intended for the recreation of the residents of Combe Down in perpetuity. The Firs Field was restored to meadowland status following the successful completion of the stabilisation works in 2010. A residents' group (The Friends of Firs Field) exists to ensure the appropriate representation of local residents' interests with regard to the management of the field.

Holy Trinity Church Combe Down was designed by Henry Edmund Goodridge (1797-1864) who designed Beckfords Tower on Lansdown Bath. The church was consecrated in 1835 but it was only in 1854 that Combe Down became a separate parish from Monkton Combe.

The Local Government Act 1894 provided for the establishment of elected civil parish councils in rural areas. Combe Down became part of the Parish of Monkton Combe. The Act also created a system of urban and rural districts with elected councils. These, along with the town councils of municipal boroughs created earlier in the century, formed a second tier of local government below the existing county councils. So the intermediate tier between the Monkton Combe Parish Council and the Somerset Couty Council was the Bath (or Bathavon) Rural District Council. A key focus of the Act was sanitation.

After attempts by Bath to take over Combe Down in 1911 (when sanitation was a key issue) and in 1931, Combe Down village was finally incorporated into the City of Bath in the 1950s. Bath and North East Somerset was created in 1996 by the Local Government Act 1992.

Sources: online - mainly Wikipedia

APPENDIX 7 - MONKTON COMBE COUNCIL MEMBERS (1900-1949)

This is an incomplete list of attendance by council meetings as it depends, in the hugely selective list of copies of the Bath Weekly Chronicle I have been able to download, on whether a particular newspaper report listed the councillors who attended the monthly meeting or (usually annual) parish meeting. In later years the practice of listing all the councillors generally ceased. I have also omitted from this list council meetings in the 1920s and 1930s (that I have downloaded and reported on in the main text) where the brief report omitted such a list.

In the following list the first column is the date of the press article (in reverse order 'yy/mm/dd') and the second column lists the Chairman. The third column also (but not exclusively) shows the Vice-Chairman.

Some interesting facts emerge. Firstly although the 1923 press article 'A Busy Combe Down Man' says Frank Pine had been a member of Monkton Combe Council for a few years I cannot find him attending as a member before 1920. Secondly there is a report that he succeeded Mr Stickland as Chairman but in fact Mr W Miles was Chairman for two years before FHP became chairman in 1922. Lastly his obituary in 1942 said he had been Chairman for two or three years. By my reckoning FHP was on the council almost continuously until 1934 and was Chairman from 1922-1934, with the exception of a year or so 1927-28 and a brief interregnum in 1931. So around 10 years at least as chairman.

Some of the longest-serving councillors were FR Munday (at least 1905 - to at least 1941) and W Miles (c.1902 - 1931 when he died in December), perhaps followed by FJ Brown (1910 - 1934) and EA Russell (c1919 - c1937). The Williams family also put in a good showing.

The following record reflects absences due to illness but also the fact that members were not always as assiduous as the chairman and vice-chairman in attending meetings. Another feature is the almost complete absence of women in this list - although the Clerk was Mrs Page for most of the 1930s and 1940s.

	1911-0202	1910-0512	19061129	19050420	1904-0825	1903-0423	1902-0904	1902-0424	1900-1011
CHAIRMAN	W Warren	W Warren	Mr EH Paine	Mr EH Paine	Mr EH Paine	Col. W Morrison	Col. W Morrison	Col. W Morrison	Col. W Morrison
	R Pott s	R Potts	W Davis	W Davis	W Davis		JW Soane	JW Soane	Hy Wolfe
	W Miles	W Miles	W Miles	W Miles	W Miles		W Miles	W Miles	
	F J Brown	F J Brown	WG Lane	WG Lane		J Stephenson	R Russell	M Coombe	J Stephenson
				C Plaister	C Plaister		TR Freeman	TR Freeman	H Morgan
		WJ Patch			H Russell	E H Paine	E H Paine	E H Paine	E H Paine
	W Williams	W Williams	W Williams		W Williams	W Williams	W Williams		W Williams
	H Bennet	H Bennet	H Bennet	H Bennet	H Bennet				
	FR Munday	FR Munday		H Willis	H Willis	W Davis	W Davis	W Davis	
	R Stennard	R Stennard							W Davis

297

	1914-0912	1914-0613	1913-0913	1913-0712	1913-0301	1913-0111	1912-0420	1911-1125	1911-0928
CHAIRMAN	HJ Stickland	HJ Stickland	HJ Stickland	HJ Stickland	W Miles	W Miles	W Miles	W Miles	H Bennett
	H Bennett	H Bennett	H Bennett	H Bennett	H Bennett	H Bennett	H Bennett	R Potts	R Potts
	W Miles	W Miles	W Miles						W Miles
	F J Brown	F J Brown	F J Brown	F J Brown		F J Brown	F J Brown	F J Brown	F J Brown
				E Dudley		H J Stickland	H J Stickland	H J Stickland	
	T Ellett	T Ellett	T Ellett	T Ellett			F J Patch		WJ Patch
							W Williams		
	W Williams	TC Morris		TC Morris	R Potts				
		FR Munday	FR Munday	FR Munday	FR Munday	FR Munday	FR Munday	FR Munday	FR Munday
						HH Stennard		HH Stennard	
	G Treasure	G Treasure							

	1915-0619	1915-0918	1916-0325	1916-0617	1916-0916	1917-0106	1917-0317	1919-0920	1920-0619
CHAIRMAN	W Miles	HJ Stickland	HJ Stickland	H Bennett	HJ Stickland	HJ Stickland	HJ Stickland	HJ Stickland	W Miles
					H Bennett	H Bennett	H Bennett	H Bennett	FH Pine
		W Miles			W Miles			W Miles	
	F J Brown	F J Brown		F J Brown			F J Brown	F J Brown	
	T Ellett		T Ellett					EA Russell	
	W Williams				W Williams	W Williams	W Williams	J Williams	W Williams
	TC Morris	TC Morris		TC Morris	TC Morris				
						FR Munday			
	G Treasure	G Treasure	G Treasure		G Treasure	G Treasure	G Treasure		F C Appleby

299

CHAIRMAN	1923-0512	1923-0421	1923-0217	1922-0819	1922-0513	1922-0422	1921-0827	1920-1120	1920-0828
	FH Pine	FH Pine	FH Pine	FH Pine	FH Pine	FH Pine	W Miles	W Miles	W Miles
	H Robinson		H Robinson		H Robinson	H Robinson	FH Pine	FH Pine	FH Pine
	W Miles		W Miles	W Miles		W Miles			
		FJ Brown	FJ Brown	FJ Brown	FJ Brown	FJ Brown			FJ Brown
		EA Russell	EA Russell		EA Russell		EA Russell	EA Russell	EA Russell
	J Williams			J Williams	J Williams	J Williams		W Williams	W Williams
	F Miller	F Miller	F Miller	F Miller	F Miller	F Miller		E Dudley	
	FR Munday	FR Munday	FR Munday	FR Munday					
	T Sansum	T Sansum	T Sansum	T Sansum	T Sansum	T Sansum			
								F C Appleby	F C Appleby

300

	1923-0714	1923-0915	1923-0922	1923-1013	1923-1222	1924-0329	1924-0419	1924-0705	1924-0816
CHAIRMAN	FH Pine	FH Pine	FH Pine	FH Pine	FH Pine	FH Pine		FH Pine	FH Pine
	H Robinson	H Robinson	H Robinson			H Robinson	H Robinson		
	W Miles	W Miles	W Miles	W Miles		W Miles	W Miles	W Miles	W Miles
		FJ Brown			FJ Brown	FJ Brown	FJ Brown		FJ Brown
		EA Russell	EA Russell		EA Russell	EA Russell	EA Russell	EA Russell	EA Russell
	J Williams		J Williams				J Williams	J Williams	J Williams
	F Miller	F Miller	F Miller	F Miller		F Miller	F Miller	F Miller	F Miller
	FR Munday	FR Munday							FR Munday
	T Sansum			T Sansum	T Sansum	T Sansum	T Sansum	T Sansum	T Sansum

	1927-1112	1927-0423	1927-0312	1926-0424	1926-0213	1925-0919	1925-0613	1924-1018	1924-0920
CHAIRMAN	H Robinson	FH Pine	FH Pine	FH Pine	FH Pine	FH Pine	FH Pine	FH Pine	FH Pine
	Lt-Col A J Pilcher	H Robinson	H Robinson	H Robinson	H Robinson	H Robinson	H Robinson	H Robinson	H Robinson
	FH Pine	O Hopkins	O Hopkins	O Hopkins			O Hopkins	W Miles	W Miles
		FJ Brown		FJ Brown	FJ Brown	FJ Brown		FJ Brown	
	EA Russell	EA Russell	EA Russell	EA Russell	EA Russell	EA Russell		EA Russell	EA Russell
		AC Milsom	AC Milsom			AC Milsom	AC Milsom	J Williams	J Williams
		Lt-Col A J Pilcher		Lt-Col A J Pilcher			Lt-Col A J Pilcher	F Miller	
								FR Munday	
		T Sansum		T Sansum	T Sansum	T Sansum	T Sansum		T Sansum

	1928-0421	1928-1117	1929-0615	1929-0914	1929-0928	1929-1214	1930-0215	1930-0322	1930-0412
CHAIRMAN	H Robinson	FH Pine	FH Pine	FH Pine	FH Pine	FH Pine	FH Pine	FH Pine	FH Pine
	FH Pine	FH Pine	H Robinson		H Robinson		H Robinson	H Robinson	Lt-Col A J Pilcher
	WD Longman	WD Longman							
	FJ Brown	FJ Brown	FJ Brown				FJ Brown		FJ Brown
	EA Russell		EA Russell	EA Russell			EA Russell	S Plummer	S Plummer
	R Daniels	R Daniels	R Daniels	R Daniels	R Daniels		R Daniels	R Daniels	R Daniels
	Lt-Col A J Pilcher	Lt-Col A J Pilcher		Lt-Col A J Pilcher					
		FR Munday		FR Munday	FR Munday		FR Munday	FR Munday	FR Munday
		JR England			JR England		JR England		

303

	1930-0712	1930-0913	1930-1004	1931-0214	1931-0314	1931-0418	1931-0516	1931-0815	1931-0912
CHAIRMAN	FH Pine	FH Pine	FH Pine	FH Pine	RW Cornish	FH Pine	FH Pine	FH Pine	FH Pine
	Lt-Col A J Pilcher		Lt-Col A J Pilcher	Lt-Col A J Pilcher	F Miller	RW Cornish	RW Cornish	RW Cornish	RW Cornish
				W Miles	AE Cleaves		AE Cleaves	AE Cleaves	AE Cleaves
		FJ Brown					FJ Brown	FJ Brown	FJ Brown
							S Plummer	S Plummer	
					EA Russell		EA Russell	EA Russell	
	R Daniels		R Daniels	R Daniels	R Daniels		R Daniels	R Daniels	
	H Robinson	H Robinson	H Robinson	H Robinson	CG Millet		CG Millet	CG Millet	CG Millet
		FR Munday	Mr Warren				FR Munday		
							F Miller	F Miller	

	19310912	1931-1224	1932-0213	1932-0514	1932-0611	1932-0716	1932-0917	1932-1015	1932-1112
CHAIRMAN	FH Pine	FH Pine	FH Pine	FH Pine	FH Pine	FH Pine		FH Pine	FH Pine
	RW Cornish	RW Cornish	RW Cornish	RW Cornish	RW Cornish	RW Cornish	RW Cornish	RW Cornish	RW Cornish
	AE Cleaves	AE Cleaves							H Robinson
	FJ Brown	FJ Brown		FJ Brown			FJ Brown		
	S Plummer			S Plummer	S Plummer			S Plummer	S Plummer
			EA Russell			EA Russell	EA Russell	EA Russell	EA Russell
			R Daniels	R Daniels	R Daniels	R Daniels	R Daniels	R Daniels	R Daniels
	CG Millet	CG Millet	CG Millet	CG Millet	CG Millet	CG Millet	CG Millet	CG Millet	CG Millet
	FR Munday			FR Munday		FR Munday			FR Munday
					EA Ansell				
	F Miller	F Miller							

305

	1933-0114	1933-0318	1933-0513	1933-0715	1933-0930	1934-0217	1934-0317	1934-0512	1935-0112
CHAIRMAN	FH Pine	FH Pine	FH Pine	FH Pine	FH Pine	FH Pine	FH Pine	RW Cornish	RW Cornish
	RW Cornish	RW Cornish	RW Cornish	RW Cornish	RW Cornish	RW Cornish	RW Cornish		
	H Robinson	H Robinson		H Robinson		H Robinson		WJ Bray	WJ Bray
	FJ Brown	FJ Brown	FJ Brown	FJ Brown		FJ Brown	FJ Brown	LG Jordan	LG Jordan
	EA Russell		EA Russell	EA Russell	EA Russell		S Plummer	S Plummer	
	R Daniels	R Daniels	R Daniels	R Daniels	R Daniels	R Daniels	R Daniels	WF Williams	
	CG Millet	CG Millet	CG Millet	CG Millet	CG Millet	CG Millet	CG Millet	CG Millet	GC Millett
			FR Munday				FR Munday		
								FG Prescott	

306

	1935-1109	1937-0213	1937-0717	1937-0731	1937-0814	1938-0312	1938-1217	1939-0218	1939-0617
CHAIRMAN	RW Cornish	RW Cornish	H Robinson		H Robinson	H Robinson	H Robinson	RW Cornish	RW Cornish
			RW Cornish		RW Cornish		RW Cornish		
		LG Jordan		WJ Bray	Mrs Crisp				
		WF Williams			W Dukett				
					EA Russell				
							FR Munday		

	1949-0528	1948-1016	1947-0412	1947-0118	1946-1221	1945-1117	1944-0115	1941-0614	1940-1116	1940-0309
	F Vallis	F Vallis	RW Cornish	RW Cornish	RW Cornish	RW Cornish	RW Cornish	RW Cornish	RW Cornish	RW Cornish
			F Vallis	F Vallis				HF Walters	HF Walters	
						WJ Bray				
								F Vallis		
						WF Williams		WF Williams		
								FR Munday		
								FG Prescott		

APPENDIX 8 - NOTABLE MAYORS OF BATH IN THE PERIOD 1900-1950

Or as otherwise mentioned in the text

1914-5 Frederick William Spear (Spear Bros & Clark)

1915-6 Harry Thomas Hatt (Chairman of the Bath Chronicle 1925)

1920-1 James Henry Colmer (Chairman of Colmers Department Stores)

1922-3 and 1924-9 Cedric Chivers (Chairman of the Bookbinders and a great supporter of the RUH - died in office)

1929-1930, 1934-5 and 1940-43 Aubrey Bateman (President of the RUH from the late 1920s until well into the 1940s)

1931-2 and 1945-6 Herbert Chivers (died in office)

1932-3 Rhodes G Cook

1935-6 and 1939-40 James Sidney Carpenter LLD

1937-9 Adrian Edmund Hopkins MC Capt.

Note on Frederick William Spear (Spear Bros & Clark)

When George Spear was in his 20s he began as a small wholesale provision dealer in Bristol in 1875. He was soon joined by his brothers Fred in 1876 and Edward in 1879. In 1898 they acquired the business of William Clarke and Sons and the company became Spear Bros and Clarke Ltd. They opened shops in Bath and Chippenham and their speciality was Bath chaps (boiled pigs cheek rolled in breadcrumbs). The brothers sold a whole range of pork products – pies, Bath sausages, black puddings, saveloys, polonies and faggots. They also supplied other businesses throughout the south-west. They made their deliveries in a fleet of distinctive green vans bearing the company logo.

In 1916 they acquired in Chippenham a factory that had been built by the Wiltshire Farmers' Co-operative Association but which had been closed for some years. In 1956 the number of pigs cured in the factory varied from 100 to 300 a week. When founder George died in 1914 he was succeeded by his brother Fred, who allegedly was known by all the staff as 'Mr Fred' and who became Mayor of Bath. When he died in 1935, Edward became chairman. The Post Office Directory of 1932 records Frederick William

Spear JP as living at Esher house Beechencliff and Edward A Spear as living at Ivy Bank, Entry Hill. The Spear family provided funding in the 1920s that enabled the privately owned Avenue Hall to be purchased and it reopened in 1926 as the Church Rooms as they are today.

The Bath Weekly Chronicle & Herald report of 26 October 1935 devoted 4 out 5 columns on page 23 to Fred's funeral. It was entitled "Bath's Last Tribute to a Beloved Citizen" and "Bath's Mr Great Heart". The Funeral was held at Manvers Street Baptist Church (because of family ties) rather than the Abbey. The Council were fully represented at the funeral and the newspaper report recounted his 29 years service as Councillor and Alderman, having been elected as Mayor in 1914. He was Chairman of the Council's Finance Committee for 17 years and was a member of the Education Committee during the whole period of his City Council service.

George's son, George Junior, became a director when his father died, and his son Richard eventually became chairman. The business moved to Broad Plain, off Old Market, Bristol in 1963. In 1973 Spears were taken over by Unigate who closed the shops and concentrated on wholesale distribution from factories in Bristol, Chippenham, Cornwall and Kent. At the time, the company employed 185 people. A few months later, Spear Bros merged with Bristol coffee company Carwardines in a £800,000 deal. A new factory was fitted out at Brislington and new sales depots created in Swindon and Cardiff. In 1975, the firm was sold to two ex-directors of Trowbridge meat company Scot Bowyers. That company, which specialised in pork pies, closed its doors in 2008.

Sources: Bristol Evening Post, Wikipedia, Bath Chronicle and Herald, Post Office Directory, Combe Down Heritage Society

Note on Cedric Chivers

Cedric Chivers was a great supporter of the Hospital Box Scheme and set in hand an appeal to raise funds to build a new hospital for the RUH in Combe Park - an exerise which his successor Aubrey Bateman carried forward with some vigour. Chivers set up his bookbinding firm in Bath in the 1870s and he was mayor of Bath six times. In its heyday, more than 300 people were employed at its base in Combe Park but the company went into liquidation in 2004. After his death in 1929 his successor Aubrey Bateman described Chivers as the greatest Bathonian in living memory.

Cedric Chivers patented hand oversewing in 1904. He opened operations in New York City, and by 1908 his American operation had served up to five hundred libraries in the

United States. However oversewn bindings are also often very tightly bound, so it is difficult for books' spines to open fully and lie flat. From a conservation standpoint, a primary concern about oversewing is that it is essentially irreversible. By 1986, most librarians and conservators had agreed that the threats of oversewn bindings outweighed their benefits. Now various types of adhesive bindings, especially double-fan adhesive, are favoured by library binders. Even Cedric Chivers admitted, in 1925, his methods were the best which at that time could be contrived, but allowed that there were complaints about the durability of some of his bindings as pages broke away from the sewing.

Trowbridge-based Cromwell Press bought the assets of bookbinders Cedric Chivers in 2004 after it went into liquidation. Cromwell set up Chivers Bookbinders to offer antique book restoration, paper conservation and journal binding, capitalising on the name of Cedric Chivers. Cromwell - which itself was saved from closure by Limpley Stoke businessman John Boden in January 2009 also went into liquidation in 2010 with the loss of 40 jobs. Before being bought by Cromwell, Chivers had been based at Pucklechurch near Bristol.

Source Bath Chronicle and Wikipaedia

Note on Sir Percy Stothert and Stothert and Pitt

Stothert & Pitt were a British engineering company founded in Bath in 1785 by George Stothert. Robert Pitt joined the company in 1844 and the firm became Stothert and Pitt.

Stothert and Pitt were a fairly paternalistic company. Even before the inception of the Box Scheme, Stothert & Pitt and a few other Bath employers had been arranging for workers contributions of 1d a week for a flat rate of 15s a week hospitalisation costs for the worker and his dependants. I am not sure when Sir Percy Stothert was Mayor of Bath (a newspaper article of 16 May 1925 refers to him as an ex-mayor - but I can only find a John Stothert Bartrum, serving in 1881 and 1889, in a list of Bath Mayors). However in May 1925 Sir Percy Stothert, as Chairman of the Royal United Hospital Board of Management, took a leading role in promoting the Box Scheme

Stothert and Pitt were the builders of a variety of engineering products ranging from dock cranes to construction plant and household cast iron items. Stothert and Pitt supplied their earliest electric powered crane to Southampton Dock Authority in 1892. Electric cranes were lighter than steam cranes and could straddle a rail line for loading from a ship alongside a quay. In 1912, Stothert & Pitt's design team, led by Claude Topliss, developed an improved design of level luffing gear, which greatly improved the speed and efficiency of cargo handling cranes fitted with it. In 1927, Stothert & Pitt produced the first bulk-handling crane.

By the late 1960s the firm had begun to lose its way as a result of foreign competition – not least in the former colonies. The firm was sold to Robert Maxwell's Hollis Group in 1986. Following the collapse of Maxwell's empire a management buy out was undertaken in 1988. But this failed and the company closed in 1989, resulting in all the works shutting down.

The demise of Stothert and Pitt was part of the de-industrialisation of the UK that started in the 1980s under the Thatcher government. Bath lost its status as an industrial city as firms ceased their productive activities in Bath. This included firms like Charles Bayers Corsets whose factory that adjoined one of Stothert and Pitts closed in 1982 (established in 1892 – it was the first factory in Bath with an integral electic light supply). Apart from Chivers Bookbinders there was Isaac Pitman the printers and publishers, bought out by rival Pearsons in 1982. Harbutts Plasticine established in 1897 by an art teacher closed its factory in Bathampton in 1983, with production relocated to Thailand).

Bath Cabinet Makers (BCM), where Emily Daniels' husband Robert Dudley probably worked, was established in 1892 as an art nouveau craft furniture maker. BCM ceased to be independent in 1959 and in the 1970s became part of the Herman Miller Group but still making quality furniture.

The Horstmann Gear Company was a major manufacturer in Bath, but in 1994 the Horstmann family sold out after 140 years, and in the year 2000 manufacturing moved to Bristol. My parents rented their home at 17 Foxcombe Road, Bath, from Ken Horstmann and I briefly worked at their Newbridge works making trip leavers as a vacation job, whilst I was at university.

Other Bath companies to wax and wane between the 1950s and the end of the century were Sparrows Crane Hire and CH Beazer the housebuilders. In my first job in the civil service dealing with import duties I had lunch with George Sparrow who was trying to import a Gottwald crane from Germany (perhaps the sort of thing Stothert and Pitt could once have thought of making?).

APPENDIX 9 - A SHORT BIBLIOGRAPHY

As this little personal and social history is focussed on the available newspaper record and conventional births, marriages, deaths and census data, I have not used many alternative sources. However, apart from on-line sources credited in the text, the following items are of interest:

The Royal United Hospital 1747-1947 by Kate Clarke (Mushroom Publishing, Bath, 2001)
Although only about 7 pages concern the period 1920-1939, and there is no direct reference to the Hospital Box Scheme, this is a fascinating book on the broad history of the hospital. It appears to be mainly based on the records available at Bath Record Office, in the Guildhall and in Bath Central Library, notably RUH minute books from 1820-1929 and the RUH Annual Reports (Year Books) for 1851-1927.

Discovering Friendly and Fraternal Societies by Victoria Solt Dennis (Shire 2005)
This has an interesting opening chapter on the History of the Friendly and Fraternal Societies, and their role in providing a measure of financial security against ill-health and unemployment - and also a milieu for social gatherings and entertainment.

The People - The Rise and Fall of the Working Class by Selina Todd (John Murray 2015)
Part 1 of this book paints an interesting picture of life 1910-1939 in which, even for the middle class in southern England in the steadily more affluent late 1930s, fear of unemployment and ill-health was ever present.

Working Class Wives – Their Health and Conditions by Margery Spring Rice (Penguin Books 1939)
This report, referred to in Selina Todd's book, shows how important the health of working class women was to the development of a prosperous country and its proposals offer key elements of the post-war welfare state.

Exploring Combe Down by Keith Dallimore (Millstream Books 1988)
This splendid book of drawings brings the history of Combe Down to life.

The Last Fighting Tommy by Harry Patch with Richard van Emden (Bloomsbury 2007)
This account of the life of Harry Patch the last surviving veteran of the trenches of WW1 has much to say about Combe Down and its people. He was a contemporary of many of my family and others of his family are mentioned in my records of the Monkton Combe Parish Council and the Combe Down Old Scholars.

Down Memory Lane (Millstream Books & Bath Chronicle 1997)
An interesting picture on page 102 was submitted by my Aunt Edna Pine of the Bath & Somerset Dairy at Bladud Buildings before the Great War.

Stothert and Pitt - The Rise and Fall of a Bath Company by John Payne (Millstream Books 1997)
This book offers some interesting insights into the social side of the company and its rather laid back working environment and reasonable union-management relations. But it is not a comprehensive history of the company in relation to its growth over 2 centuries and the development of its product lines in relation to world markets. Nor does it really explain how it came to fail from the late 1960s onwards.

The Bath Tranways by Colin Maggs (Oakwood Press 1992)
A complete study of the Bath Tram network

Pomegranate, The Story of a Chinese Schoolgirl by Jennie Beckingsale (Forgotten Books – Morgan & Scott 1910)
A condescending and naive evangelical tale that seeks to throw a Christian light on traditional Chinese practices (notably the binding of feet – that was finally banned under Mao).

The Bath Post Office Directory 1932

Friendly Societies History *(http://www.friendlysocieties.co.uk/history.htm)*

From welfare state to welfare society Barry Knight 27 December 2012
(http://www.fabians.org.uk/from-welfare-state-to-welfare-society/)

The voluntary hospitals in history
(http://www.hospitalsdatabase.lshtm.ac.uk/the-voluntary-hospitals-in-history.php)

Combe Down Heritage Society
(http://www.combedownheritage.org.uk/

Prior to Now, Over 250 Years on Combe Down
http://www.combedown.org/

Old-Age Pensions Act 1908
National Insurance Act 1911
Local Government Act 1929

Annex A NEWSPAPER ARTICLES ON FRANK HAROLD PINE

In researching this book I have looked at over 370 press articles. The following articles are mainly from the Bath <u>Weekly</u> Chronicle & Herald which is so far all that has been scanned and released by the British Library.

Out of all the issues in the period 1900-1950, the search engine at *http://www.britishnewspaperarchive.co.uk* has identified the following 299 entries (although I have included some copies from the *daily* Bath Chronicle & Herald, which was published 6 days a week). Out of over 1,000 copies for the period 1922-1942 there are over 250 entries.

When and if the daily Chronicle & Herald comes on-line there could be much more than double this number. Key records of the street photo of FHP in the mid-30s and the weddings of Connie Pine to Albert Taylor and Lena Pine to Herbert Daniels, of which we have separate copies, were only in the daily Chronicle & Herald – as doubtless were the births of Connie, Edna and Lena Pine.

Also (listed in Annexes B, C and D) I have 13 press cuttings of the Pine Sisters and the Old Scholars Shows in the 1930s, 7 relating to R Daniels and 47 reports relating to Monkton Combe Council before and after FHP's involvement with it. The dates of press extracts listed below follow a yy/mm/dd system so that 010725 is 25 July 1901.

1901-1925 (74 Articles)

010725 Presentation at the Dairy - end col 3
020206 JC Pinhorn Loyal Order of Ancient Shepherds
030222 Hearts of Oak Second annual Dinner - 5th col
040303 Hearts of Oak Dinner - 5th col
050209 Hearts of Oak Dinner - H Beckingsale Sec - FHP
050309 Birth: (first item) Phyllis
110209 Bathwick Sunday School - Connie
110223 Hearts of Oak Annual Dinner - FHP hon auditor
120302 Hearts of Oak Bath AGM - FHP elected auditor
120302 Combe Down Unionists FHP & R Daniels
120718 Hearts of Oak Outing - col 5 item 5
121214 B&S Dairy Presentation by FHP col7
130118 local Intelligence col6 Heartsof Oak - item15
130823 Heats of Oak Benefit Society trip
150313 Local Intelligence - Hearts of Oak FHP auditor - col 4
151120 Military Wedding at Claverton - Col 3 item 8

170322 Local News FHP Hearts of Oak Treasurer - Cpl 2 Item 5
200424 Wiltshire Farmers acquire B&S Dairy col3para4
200619 Combe Down Affairs - Letting of Firs Field
200626 Bailis Tucker retires from B&S Dairy col3para6
200828 Combe Down Affairs - Misuse of Rec Ground
201120 Combe Down Affairs - Housing & Firs Field
210523 Reason of the War
210827 Combe Down Affairs - Lighting
220318 The late Mrs W Beckingsale
220422 Monkton Combe Council -FHP presided
220513 Monkton Combe Council - transfer of Firs Field
220603 Funeral of Mr G Weaver - FHP represents dairy
220617 Wilts & Somerset Farmers Staff Outing
220819 Parish Council Meeting - Firs Field-War Mem
230217 Busy Combe Down Man
230217 Combe Down Water - Parish Council meeting
230421 Monkton Combe Council - Firs Fieild - FHP re-elected
230714 Combe Downs Darkness - Parish Council
230908 Aid for the Hospital - Friendly Socs Big Scheme
230915 Combe Down fire appliances
230915 Kings Royal Rifle Corps
230922 Combe Downs Gas supply - Parish Council
231006 Helping Bath Hospitals
231013 Supporting Hospital Combe Down - Col2 Item5
231013 Reduced Rates Combe Down
231027 The Hospitals Need
231103 Our Hospital - 2 columns
231201 Progress with Hospital scheme - Col3 Item3
231222 Late Mr Hobbs Funeral
231222 Monkton Combe Council - Hobbs tribute
240226 Hearts of Oak Benefit Society - FHP Chair
240329 Batheaston & The Hospital - Col2 Item3
240329 Combe Down Affairs - FHP to resign
240419 Monkton Combe PC-FHP to resume chair
240614 Hospital Aid Scheme Colerne – end col 2
240705 Combe Down War Memorial
240802 Combe Down School Prizegiving
240816 Combe Down Affairs - Electric Lighting
240920 Combe Down Affairs - Memorial Tablet
241018 Combe Down Affairs - Gas & War Memerial
241220 Milk Supply Norton Dairies acquired col2

241231 Todays Personality - FHP
250307 FHP severs dairy link - Bottom Col 3
250321 Parting gift to Mr FH Pine
250418 Silver Wedding - Bottom Col 4
250418 Silver Wedding announcement
250509 Keeping the doors open
250516 80 Patients Waiting
250604 Personal Ad FHP seeks job
250613 Combe Down's Needs - Rec Ground
250627 Employees Tribute - FHP Chair of CD Church Council
250801 Bath Hospital
250905 Royal United Hospital - Marshfield Supporters
250919 Combe Downs Troubles
250919 Perfect Pests - Young Motorcyclists
251107 Our Hospital
251107 Linking Old Comrades - the Rotherys
251212 Opening the Hospital boxes - FHP letter

1926-1930 (56 Articles)

260206 Scheme in Chippenham
260206 Whist Drive - new Church Rooms
260213 Bath Hospital Scheme - Chippenham
260213 Monkton Combe PC - Fire Fighting
260424 Monkton Combe PC-Clerks salary - FHP re-elected
261023 Bath & County Notes - Col 2 Item 4
261030 Linking Up Trowbridge to Box Scheme -end col 4
270312 Combe Downs Water
270423 A Parish Council Chairmanship
270423 Bath County Notes - Col 3 Item 3
270423 Combe Downs Lighting Electricity to be installed
270618 Combe Down's Kindness
270730 A Sunday visit to Hospital
270806 Combe Down School
270903 The Hospital - scheme explained
270917 Our Hospital Mayors Reception
271112 Combe Down Council - end coll
280421 Monkton Combe Affairs - R Daniels joins PC
280609 Over £21,000 Hospital Box Scheme
280922 Cheque for £1,000 - danger of state aided hospitals
281027 FHP 52

281110 This Week in Bath - end Col 2 - Hospital scheme
281117 Monkton Combe Council
281201 New Hospital Scheme Castle Combe
290216 No Swapping Horses - Bath Friendly Soc Council
290615 A Great Work - Friendly Socs aid to RUH
290615 Monkton Combe council - Firs Cricket
290622 Mayors Garden Party
290914 Bath Friendly Societies Council FHP presides
290914 Combe Down Affairs
290921 £1,100 for Hospital
290928 Where were they - PC meeting
291130 Bath Friendly Societies Whist Drive
291207 Mayors Appeal for Bath Hospital - 3 columns
291214 Monkton Combe Parish Council
300104 Somerset Floods
300111 Somerset Floods
300125 Hospital Box Scheme - col2
300201 Lord Moyniham & appeal for New Hospital
300208 Flood Fund - Combe Down Parish Council
300208 £10,000 Cheque The Mayor and his doubting critics
300215 Combe Down Affairs - Hockey on Firs
300301 Mr JMSheppard
300301 Our New hospital
300322 Combe Down Council - Flood Response
300322 Officers Appreciated - New Bath Hospital Scheme
300412 Lamps - damaged
300510 The New Bath Hospital
300531 The New Bath Hospital
300712 Combe Down Affairs
300830 Bath Friendly Societies Fine Work
300830 County Campaign for Bath Hospital
300913 Timber for Nothing - Council with R Daniels
300927 Declined with Thanks - Bath Friendly Societies Council
301004 Lighting
301026 Scheme in Trowbridge

1931 (37 Articles)

310103 Gifts from Christmas tree - children at RUH
310214 Monkton Combe Affairs - War Memorial upkeep
310314 Election of Parish Councillors - Labour invades

310411 Well Done Odd Down - col5
310418 Combe Down Affairs - FHP re-elected page 26
310418 Combe Down Affairs - FHP re-elected page 5
310425 Combe Down aids noble cause
310516 Combe Down Incident
310531 The New Bath Hospital
310606 Hospital Scheme £33,999 raised in 7 years - 4 cols
310613 Armchair Musings - Not 1 per cent
310613 Bath Hospital receives cheque for £1,000
310613 Combe Down Affatrs - Housing Problem
310627 Greater Bath Boundaries
310704 Bath Friendly Societies - FHP Chairs
310725 Not Fit for Pigs - slum houses
310815 Clerk who hates flattery - Page ill retires
310815 Hospital Box Scheme-co3l3
310829 Applications Invited - clerk advert
310905 Bath & District Collections for Hospitals
310912 Combe Down Council
310912 Friendly Socs give £1,000 to hospital
310912 Monkton Combe Housing
310912 TOC H at RUH
310919 Mineral Water Hospital Visit
310919 Monkton Combe appoints Little as Clerk
311003 Bath Butchers funeral coB-FHP reprsents Spears
311003 Combe Down Clings to Independence
311003 Parish Clerks Farewell (Mr Page)
311031 Hospital Box Scheme - no hitch
311121 Baths New Hospital to be debt free
311128 Death of Baths Clerk of the Peace - Col5 Para4
311128 Parish Clerks death - Mr Page
311205 Vicars Warden 25 years - Funeral
311212 Monkton Combe Council - morn Page -R Daniels unwell
311224 letters - FHP - Music for Hospital patients
311224 Monkton Combe PC - Little resigns

1932 (39 Articles)

320102 Death of Mr Miller Combe Down Councillor
320102 The late Hon Mrs Davey - end of friends list
320109 Combe Down Councillor
320116 Combe Down Losses

320206 Combe Down Old Scholars Whist
320206 Musings - Job Well Done
320206 Pioneer of Bath Hospital Scheme resigns Chair
320206 Workmates as bearers - Col3 (NB CBBS article)
320213 Bath Works Manager
320213 Combe Down Housing
320213 Hospital Box Scheme - Col5
320227 Baths hotel for the sick - tribute to FHP
320227 Mr W A King Bereaved
320305 Combe Down Unemployed - no love of spadework
320312 Combe Down Housing - FHP School Manager
320326 Allotment Scheme for Unemployed - R Daniels
320326 Combe Down Housing
320423 Aiding the Workless - FHP re-elected
320514 Allotment Thefts
320604 £44,000 raised in 8 years - 4 columns
320611 Peasdown Aids Bath RUH
320611 Pilfering from allotments
320716 More Dwellings Needed
320723 The late Mr Tom Wills
320903 Over £1,000 cash for RUH - the late Mr Wills
320910 New Bath Hospitals First Visitor
320917 Children Beyond Control
320924 Bath & County Notes - end Col 4 - Edna in hospital
320924 Work Must Go On - after Mr Wills
321015 Honoured Bath citizen
321015 Jersey Work Extended
321015 Potatoes
321112 Another £1,000 chequeforRUH
321112 Combe Down Housing
321112 For Benefit of Workless
321119 £1,000 for Bath hospital
321119 Armchair Musings-Making up Muckle-more might be...
321203 Advert for Organising Secretary of Box scheme
321217 Fulfilment of Bath Hospitals dream - RUH moves house

1933-1934 (40 Articles)

330107 Box Scheme - Full Time Organiser Appointed
330114 Combe Down Affairs
330225 Another £1,000 for Hospital

330304 RUH Box Scheme – col4

330304 No Sweepstakes for new hospital

330311 Wireless Collection - Hospital Scheme

330318 Disgrace to Parish - Firs Field

330401 Steady Progress - RUH workers at Odd Down

330415 Monkton Combe Housing

330513 Hospital Box Scheme Forging Ahead - *3* columns

330513 Petty Pilfering Combe Down Allotments

330602 £900 for Hospital

330701 A Cigarette for the Hospital

330715 Combe Down Housing

330805 Another £1,000 for Bath Hospital

330819 Bradford does its bit

330923 Combe Downs Great Need - Housing

330930 Combe Down Lighting

331007 Tribute to Col Lewis

331111 Another £1,400 for The hospital

331202 Whist at Combe down

340210 A Good Cause - concert for unemployed

340217 Chief Trouble at Combe Down - Housing - FHP Chairs

340303 Death of Horace Beckingsale - former Sec Bath Friendly Soc

340310 Eleventh Hour Surprise - Labour contest RDC

340317 Unemployed at Combe Down

340324 £44,000 from Box Scheme

340324 Funeral of Sir Harry Halt

340324 Hospital benefits for those earning £6 a week - FHP on RUH Board

340421 For good Cause - Rifle Club Whist Dnve

340512 firs Field wall Cornish now presiding

340519 Still More money for RUH

340609 Centenary of the Forresters- col3

340616 Mayor Receives Surprise

340728 Another £1,100 cheque for RUH - 3 columns

340901 Forbes Fraser Scheme in detail page 3

340901 Forbes Fraser Scheme page 9 FHP quotes

341103 Record Box Collection for RUH

341124 Tribute to Loved Physician

341215 Town & County notes - Box Pioneers

1935-1938 (31 Articles)

350209 Last Quarter Surprise

350406 Jubilee Plans at Combe Down
350511 Through Citys Streets - Jubilee Procession
350525 Funeral Col Hon HS Davey - FHP rep RUH
350921 Our Hospital Workers
351012 Funeral of Mrs Henley - Norton Dairies
351019 Death of Ald F Spear
351026 Ald F Spears Funeral
351102 Forbes Fraser Hosprtal maternity unit opened
360118 Funeral of Mr James Riddle
360118 Mayoress as Mourner - Mr JW Nicholls
360201 Baths Homage of Sorrow - in Abbey on death of King
360222 Whist Drive
360404 Bath & County notes - Accurate Arithmetic
360418 Bath Citizens Tribute - Aid Smith
360502 Death of MrsLM linsley mother of Mrs Spear
360829 Hospital Box Scheme - Col4
361114 Mr SG Hodges Bereaved - Col6
370227 Largest Quarterly Cheque for RUH - £2,500
370501 £1,700 Cheque for RUH
370703 Bath Hospital Stalwart - FHP curtails loW holiday - Col3 Item10
370710 Buglers at Funeral - Col1
370731 Combe Down Labour JP
371030 Backbone of the Hospital
371106 Passing of Bath Councillor Edward White
380305 Box Scheme Breaks All Records - FHP elected to Hospital Ctte
380723 Carnival Cheque for RUH
380730 Hospital Schemes Rapid Advance
380801 Connie & Albert's Wedding
381015 Bath Assembly Rooms Re-opening Booklet
381029 Bath Paying Patients

1939-1949 (27 Articles)

390225 Bath BESS - Phyllis Pine - Shakespeare
390304 Mayor Praises Provident Organisations
390422 £50,000 Appeal for RUH Nurses Home
391118 Box Scheme Colections in Blackout
391118 Box Scheme Forges Ahead
400413 Loved Monkton Combe - Hubert Beckingsale Funeral
400608 Goodland Funeral Bridgewater
400907 Bath Hospitals cheque for £2,200 - FHP vice-chair

401006 Hospital in Wartime - FHP at end col2
401026 Combe Down Resident - funeral Miss Ruth Norman
410301 Box Scheme critics - voluntary and municipal hospitals
410517 Saved Bath Hospital - story of Box Scheme
411108 Bath Paying Patients Scheme - col2
420131 FHP Seriously Ill - County Notes Other Invalids
420425 Bath Hospital Scheme Pioneer - death of FHP
420425 FHP Death Annoucement
430717 Phyllis optical exam
431218 Edna Pine new Secretary for Combe Down Box Scheme
441021 Death of Mr FI Tovey - PO Pine
450814 Wedding of Herbert Daniels & Lena Pine
450818 Wedding of Herbert Daniels & Lena Pine
470906 Box Scheme to end
470412 Eighth Year in Succession - Combe Down Council Re-elects Chairman
471004 Widow of Council Chairman Dies-Lillian Pine
481016 To Double their Membership - Monkton Parish Council To Be Twelve
481113 To Meet At Monkton - Change for Parish Council
490416 Parish Council's New Clerk - Monkton Combe Man Appointed

Annex B NEWSPAPER ARTICLES ON COMBE DOWN OLD SCHOLARS

Listed below are 17 articles, principally on the amateur dramatic activities.

270514 Combe Down Old Boys – First OSA Social
300301 Old Scholars Concert
300510 Combe Down Concert
310509 Philpotts Comedy
320116 Social – Vi Daniels
320521 Yellow Sands
330225 Lord Richards Play
350223 Tilly of Bloomsbury
360208 They Wanted Romance
360205 Combe Down Amateurs Play
360208 Lilies of the Field
360426 Social - Third Floor Back
360502 Third Floor Back
381205 Combe Down Amateurs Play
380205 3 Act Play – Israel Edward and Anne
381022 Ridley Play
390506 A successful comedy

Annex C NEWSPAPER ARTICLES ON ROBERT DANIELS AND FAMILY

Listed below are 31 press cuttings relating to Robert Daniels and family. However he, Norman and Mabel also appear in the lists at Annexes A, B and D

110928 Monkton Combe Parish Council estimate
170512 A Combe Down Smash - col2 para7
260703 Motorcyclists collide - Robert & Norman Daniels
270304 Soprano Soloist-Marjorie Stockall
290126 Mid-Norton Brotherhood - Marjorie Stockall
290316 Greatly Beloved - funeral of Mrs Stockall
290427 Combe Down Recital - Marjorie Stockall
300118 A Marjorie Stockall WEA Social col4
300405 A Marjorie Stockall Countryside Music col1
300913 Timber for Nothing Council with R Daniels
301018 Combe Down Vicar - N Daniels painting
301220 Combe Down Social - N Daniels
310131 Parish social
310620 Combe Down Civic Days Orch arr by N Daniels
310815 Sweet Pea Wedding - N Daniels Best Man
311114 A Marjorie Stockall - The Plays the thing col3
320305 A Marjorie Stockall Headmistress honoured col5
320430 St Georges Day - Combe Down Scouts - N Daniels
340210 A Good Cause Concert for Unemployed FHP & Norman Daniels
340721 A Marjorie Stockall Hemmington School col3
350907 Churches Value Ally - Norman
351116 Argyle Orchestra
361219 School Opretta Princess Ju Ju - Norman Daniels
370904 A Marjorie Stockall Death of H Stockall
371218 Combe Down Play - Zurika
381126 Argyle Orchestra
390401 Argyle Orchestra
391007 Concert N Daniels steward
410329 Combe Down Resident -Funeral Mrs R Daniels
410517 School Head weds Norman Daniels
491231 Was Prominent Resident -Death of Robert Daniels

Annex D NEWSPAPER ARTICLES ON MONKTON COMBE COUNCIL (NOT LISTED IN ANNEX A)

See also Appendix 3 – these are concerned with the periods before and after FHP's involvement in the council.

Before the 1920s	After 1934
001011	340512
020424	350112
020904	351109
030423	370213
040825	370717
050420	370731
061129	370814
100512	380312
110202	381217
110928	390218
111125	390617
120420	400309
130111	401116
130301	410614
130712	440115
130913	451117
140613	461221
140912	470118
150619	470412
150918	481016
160325	490528
160617	
160916	
170106	
170317	
190920	

INDEX

Combe Down – Key Persons

Combe Down – Key Persons (continued)

Combe Down Locations

Combe Down Vicars (mentioned in text)

Economic Political & Social Issues

Families

Leisure, Social & Charitable Activities